Climate Crisis and the Kleptocene

Climate Crisis and the Kleptocene

On the Commodification of Sentience

Wendy Lynne Lee

LEXINGTON BOOKS
Lanham • Boulder • New York • London

Published by Lexington Books
An imprint of The Rowman & Littlefield Publishing Group, Inc.
4501 Forbes Boulevard, Suite 200, Lanham, Maryland 20706
www.rowman.com

86-90 Paul Street, London EC2A 4NE

British Library Cataloguing in Publication Information Available

Library of Congress Cataloging-in-Publication Data

ISBN 978-1-7936-0796-6 (cloth alk. paper)
ISBN 978-1-7936-0797-3 (ebook)

∞™ The paper used in this publication meets the minimum requirements of American National Standard for Information Sciences—Permanence of Paper for Printed Library Materials, ANSI/NISO Z39.48-1992.

Contents

Preface vii

Introduction: "Watching as It All Goes Down the Drain" 1

Chapter 1: The Disarticulation of Value 17

Chapter 2: Normalizing the Disarticulation of Value Across Species: Response to David Wallace-Wells 49

Chapter 3: Commodification of Sentience in the Maintenance of Structural Inequality: More of David Wallace-Wells 79

Chapter 4: Paving the Road to the Kleptocene: The Salvation Capitalism of Michael Mann's *The New Climate War* 115

Chapter 5: How Animal Rights Ethics Sustains the Commodification of Sentience: Response to Gary Francione and Richard Epstein 161

Chapter 6: "Webs of Life" and Death in the Kleptocene: "As Food," the "Four Cheaps," and Jason Moore's (Unwitting) Invitation to the Geo-Logic of the "Black Anthropocene" 211

Conclusion 259

Bibliography 263

Index 277

About the Author 285

Preface

I am sometimes asked why the focus of so much of my work this last decade has been the climate crisis. I sometimes respond that it's not the crisis itself that drives me to scream "stop!" word after word, page after page. It's the poisonous concoction of arrogance, willful ignorance, and the fictions that blind us to the impacts of capital conquest. It's the idiotic fantasy that existential necessity somehow means "can never run out or be extinguished or be polluted beyond reclamation." It's the irreparable damage we've inflicted in the name of profit upon the only planet we have; it's that this "we" is grotesquely inadequate to capture the complex social and economic relationships that empower the very few at the expense of the very many. It's that it's neither alarmist nor naïve, as Andreas Malm puts it, to "dare to feel the panic" at the emergent reality of an Earth made uninhabitable by and for human beings—though perhaps a utopia for bacteria and viruses. It is the moral responsibility of the realist worn out by polite academic discourse to scream "stop!" Capitalism is not, at least in the first place, a system of economic exchange; it is an ideology of value that authorizes exchange value over all other—including that of sentient life and life itself. It is ontologically kleptocratic—the codified resource theft demanded by "grow or die." We can mourn the catastrophic consequences of capital's relentless plunder, but we have no excuse for feigning surprise. Still, I have other deeper reasons for screaming. I have a son, a daughter-in-law, a grandson who, as I write this, are being cheated—*like all sons, daughters, and children*—out of a future whose ecological and atmospheric stability has been sacrificed to hundreds of years of consumption, pollution, and waste; whose opportunities to experience beauty have been denuded and consigned to the past. I write to give hope to Lee, Courtney, and Jack. I write because I love them fiercely, and need them to be courageous. The virtually unchecked pursuit of profit casts a very dark shadow. It loiters over fire and flood; it beckons drought, disease, massive migration, and war. Perhaps what is required to make good on hope is thus neither love nor courage alone, but rather the humility to recognize that for all our bluster we humans own nothing. *The world is not property*: that is the revolutionary idea.

Wendy Lynne Lee
9.24.23

Introduction

"Watching as It All Goes Down the Drain"

"DARE TO FEEL THE PANIC"

In his introduction to *Profit: An Environmental History*, Mark Stoll provides a plausibly benign definition of capitalism—a definition he goes on to implode as woefully inadequate to the actual history of capital conquest:

> At its most fundamental level, capitalism is an economic system in which (usually) private owners of accumulated wealth or capital invest it for profit in enterprises of extraction and distribution of raw materials or of production and distribution of goods, where (ideally) unrestricted competition with other enterprises in a (more or less) regulated marketplace decides prices. *Note the qualifiers in parentheses.*[1]

What constitutes "accumulated wealth or capital" is left vague, but only for a moment before Stoll introduces us to the history of mining: "[t]he environmentally destructive mining that brings us the components of our cell phones is an ancient practice writ large."[2] And with this link of past to present, a seemingly benign definition of capitalism makes way for a long dirty trudge toward neoliberalism's globalized consumer capitalism.[3] With the mining of hydrocarbons as its lifeblood, extractivist capitalism stains the history of the planet and its species life in the dark hues of coal, and with it conquest, slavery, deforestation, disease, extinction, suffering, and unrestricted avarice in the pursuit of *profit*. "[T]hrough the stories of a series of individuals who represent either the opening of a significant new stage of capitalism or development of influential movements to control its environmental impacts,"[4] Stoll shines an unflinching light on the cost of "(ideally) unrestricted competition" to the planet, its atmosphere, ecologies, resources, and labor—human and nonhuman. He illuminates the extent to which our current perch on the brink of irrecoverable environmental calamity is the result of an economic system and its disciples whose quest for profit trumps all other values, including that of a future beyond the next novel technology. Stoll pulls no punches. The upshot of fossil fueled industrial capitalism is that "[a] global climate catastrophe is on its way,"[5] and it has deep historical roots. "Practices that evolved into war and slavery," in the interest of controlling resources, argues Stoll, "began at a very early date,"[6] evolved a *logic of commodification*, and gave rise to the essential components of capital: private property, exchange value, a profoundly distorted conception of planetary resources, and a fundamentally altered relationship with nonhuman nature.[7]

In short, it's not surprising that "[t]he ancient human activity of trade grew more capitalistic and drove ever greater exploitation of environmental resources."[8] Facilitated by mushrooming technological sophistication and wed, as Andreas Malm argues in *The Progress of this Storm*, to the fossil energy that changes everything "most dramatically when mobilized to propel machines and vehicles,"[9] the upshot of accounts like Stoll's is clear—though it's Malm who actually ventures to say it: we must "dare to feel the panic,"[10] provoked by the environmental crises to which we've contributed so mightily, especially anthropogenic climate change:[11]

> Any line on global warming that is not denialist must take cognizance of forces and causal powers oblivious to human predilections: one cannot abolish thermal expansion of the oceans by democratic decree. That is why one must have a line on global warming in the first place. That is also why it is a bad idea to dig up all the fossil fuels and set fire to them . . .[12]

Nonhuman nature doesn't give a tinker's damn about "human predilection." If digging up and burning all the fossil fuel, thereby altering the atmosphere and jeopardizing our existential condition, drives us to extinction—nonhuman nature won't care about that either. Yet, this objective reality is precisely why we ought to care about the "warming condition":[13] "[u]nderstanding the historical phenomenon [of global warming] appears to require realism about the past *and* about nature."[14] Indeed, according to Malm, the history of capital leaves us only two choices: "commit to the most militant and unwavering opposition to this system, or sit watching as it all goes down the drain."[15]

I'm with Malm, though, as we'll see, for somewhat different reasons that, insofar as we remain capable of moral outrage, should hasten our panic and galvanize opposition. I'll argue that, given its fundamental governing presuppositions, its *ontology*, capitalism is not merely irreconcilably incompatible with planetary and atmospheric limits, as Stoll and Malm would likely agree, it is inherently *kleptocratic and nihilistic* for reasons that reach beyond the arguments of both. Very briefly: first, following Malm's "epistemological climate realism," a significant number of the "we" know better than to continue patronizing fossil fuel extractivism, but we carry on as if we didn't.[16] This form of cognitive dissonance is, however, more than denial; it offers a particularly perverse opportunity for the capitalist exploitation of fear and anxiety. Second, the logic constitutive of the pursuit of profit precludes recognizing any value over exchange, including moral values associated with the *capacity for sentience*; and, third, because unlike earlier environmental crises, the climate crisis has no fix, but this cannot matter to kleptocratic capitalism because what the logic of commodification dictates is grow or die. The trouble is that the planet cannot sustain such an ultimatum. We can't grow fossils; one hundred year old trees take one hundred years to mature; the dilution of contaminated streams with toxic chemicals is not the solution to their repair; mountain tops cannot be put back; there's no Jurassic Park. An uninhabitable earth doesn't come with a coupon to swap it for a new one. To ignore these simple facts in the interest of our continuing consumption is effectively nihilistic—but more: the "warming condition" is a mirror of human chauvinism and hypocrisy like no other in that what it reflects is not only a planet, as Amitov Ghosh might put it, deranged by the pursuit of profit,[17] but a deeply inculcated disposition to believe a falsehood, namely, that the capitalism that got us into so much trouble can (somehow) get us out; that, confronted with the crises of its own making, capital will (somehow) undertake to reform its kleptocratic impulses. As we shall soon see, some of the most important environmental voices of our time espouse this delusion. It is the aim of this book to show why they're wrong—indeed, derelict.

THE VALUE OF SENTIENCE AS A THREAT TO CAPITAL

There is much to unpack going forward, but suffice this much for now: although Malm is dead-on when he argues that "[i]t is because all humans are material beings possessed with the property of agency that some of them can study the climate which some of them are changing,"[18] the agency that distinguishes most human beings from most species of nonhuman animal is, I'll argue, largely irrelevant to the capitalist's pursuit of profit except insofar as it can be harnessed and commodified toward production and consumption. That is, while agency certainly does matter with respect to the assignment of *culpability* for the climate crisis, this doesn't mean that calling out the responsible parties is likely to lead to militant opposition; agency is itself subject to the logic of commodification as is every other property of living and nonliving thing. Malm would likely agree, but *why* agency is so subject demands an excavation of the ontology of capital that probes its governing concepts even more deeply. Despite the fact that any hope for a livable future hangs on the agency of decent people, climate scientists, governments, and activist organizations, a defining trait of the Kleptocene—the globally enculturated normalization of resource theft or, as David Harvey puts it in *The New Imperialism*, "accumulation by dispossession"—is that nothing *can* have value outside the logic of commodification.[19] For as long as price is permitted to define value at the cost of all other values, agency is more likely to function as an instrument of capital than a weapon of resistance.

We don't, in fact, have to look further than some of the most celebrated voices among those who claim to be committed environmentalists to see that the agency associated with "some who study" is preemptively co-opted either by interests seeking to maximize profits before it "all goes down the drain," or by those seeking to mitigate the impacts of ecological destruction but yet preserve neoliberal capitalism. The first is illustrated by BP's CEO, Bernard Looney. In a recent interview Looney "labeled the oil and gas giant a 'greening company' which is carbon-intensive today, but planning for a net-zero [emissions] future."[20] BP advertises itself as a company that cares about its environmental "footprint." But this claim is a demonstrable lie. The oil behemoth's 2021 post-pandemic profits were "massive," and virtually all fossil-fueled.[21] Increasing its references to climate change in its annual reports from "22 to 329 mentions" between 2009–2020 didn't yield a reduction in BP's mining operations. In fact, the company's investment portfolio shows the opposite to be true.[22] The petro-giants, ExxonMobil, BP, Chevron, Shell run TV ads promising "net-zero" greenhouse gas emissions by some vague future date, but what such green-washing actually illustrates are the lengths to which the multinationals will go to conceal their destruction of the planet and its atmosphere so that they can pursue unimpeded their kleptocratic ventures.

The second set of "committed environmentalists," include a number of theorists, scientists, and self-styled eco-experts who advocate greenhouse gas mitigation strategies that promise we can have our ecological stability cake and our endless market growth too. I suggest, however, that these are the voices that pose an even greater danger to the planet than CEOs like Looney. Whether via a basic misunderstanding of capitalism's kleptocratic ontology or a whole-hearted embrace of capitalism as the natural state of humanity, these are the voices that effectively mollify our collective conscience right over the tipping point of no return. Consider, for example, self-described eco-modernist Michael Shellenberger, founder of *Environmental Progress* and the *Breakthrough Institute*.[23] Shellenberger argues for what he calls pro-growth market solutions to environmental crises. He claims that modern environmentalism is ill-equipped to address the climate crisis, and that climate change is not as serious an issue as it's made out to be. He has deep ties to organizations that lobby for the nuclear power industry, and he supports state house bills that protect coal plants.[24]

Unsurprisingly, a number of climate-scientists working in the mitigation trenches—as Shellenberger claims to be—have "disowned" him for playing "fast and loose with the facts."[25] Reckless representation of fact combined with a heedless embrace of neoliberalism *does* make for a toxic brew, locating Shellenberger's critics, it would seem, on Malm's side of militant opposition. But as we'll see, this is not only *not* the case, it matters greatly *that* it is not the case even if Shellenberger represents a particularly mercenary version of "have your cake and eat it too." The trouble is that while disowning Shellenberger locates his critics among the agents who study the climate as opposed to changing it, "study" is itself subject to the logic of commodification such that, as we'll see, the majority of its representative voices don't appear to be able to see beyond the reform of an economic system for which "reform" is just another form of greenwashing. Indeed, among the truly disheartening facts about human agency as it has been informed by the logic of commodification throughout the history of capital is that, whether or not it's a trait unique to homo Sapiens, it has been so fully co-opted as an instrument of capital that the very way its subjects think about environmental crises is from the perspective of maintaining the possibility of profit. Shellenberger may well play fast and loose with facts, but even his staunchest critics such as acclaimed climate scientist Michael Mann succumb to the delusion that market solutions can provide the road to climate salvation.

What creates the choice between militant opposition and watching it all go down the drain is not merely a human agency misdirected by greed or deluded by the idea that an economic system rooted in resource theft can be redirected toward ecological stability. As a matter of necessity, the logic of commodification precludes all other values as obstacles to exchange unless they can be exploited as a resource. That's why, as presumably Malm would agree, opposition must be militant—not reformist. Put differently: going down the drain is only *in the second place* the consequence of fetishizing fossil fuel; *in the first place*, it's the consequence of the *idea* that anything can be commodified, an idea that requires for its successful realization the subjugation of moral, civic, and aesthetic value to exchange value. It is this idea that defines the difference between what Jason Moore calls the *Capitalocene* and what I think is more accurately descriptive, the *Kleptocene*, and it's this difference that will come to distinguish revolutionaries like Malm from reformists like David Wallace-Wells, Michael Mann, Gary Francione, and though for somewhat different reasons, Moore.

At its ideological core, capitalism recognizes no morally relevant difference between living/nonliving, human/nonhuman, organic/inorganic, sentient/non-sentient, agent/non-agent, except insofar as the value we attach to such traits promises an avenue for exploitation or poses a potential obstacle that must be neutralized. As Christoph Hermann argues in *The Critique of*

Commodification, "[c]ommodification tends to promote more commodification—if not hindered by social forces and decommodifying policies."[26] The trouble with this framing is that there are no independent social forces short of militant opposition, and the concept of a decommodifying government policy seems virtually oxymoronic at this point in neoliberal history. Nevertheless, understanding the roles played by these sets of traits is crucial to understanding how we have arrived at the precipice of environmental calamity, and among the most important of these traits, I'll argue, is *sentience*—especially in its relation to suffering.

Unlike agency, the capacity for conscious experience—sentience—is a trait human beings share in common with countless other species. It thus poses a forceful obstacle to the logic of commodification precisely because we regard the prevention and/or avoidance of unnecessary suffering as morally significant—at least for human beings. Moreover, many species of nonhuman animals that may lack agency plainly do not lack sentience: my dog, Bohden, may not deliberate over his dinner entrée, but that in no way implies that he can't enjoy it. Capitalism cannot afford to acknowledge, much less acquiesce, to any such value for anyone or anything. To recognize the capacity for sentience as morally relevant creates a barrier to commodification not only because it singles out a potentially enormous range of creatures whose suffering is not unlike our own, but because it tacitly acknowledges the interdependencies of ecosystems and their inhabitants, including human-built ecosystems. As Malm might put it: strip mining operations destroy far more than digging giant holes in the ground; it destroys the existential conditions for a diverse array of species life—sentient and non-sentient. The same goes for logging in Old Growth Forest, building plastics factories, burning down the Amazon to graze cattle, or constructing strip malls and their parking lots. To whatever extent sentience can claim to be *morally considerable*, it demands militant opposition—and precludes reform. This isn't merely because some of the market solutions proposed for reducing greenhouse gas emissions are likely to fail, and thus accelerate the conditions for more fires, hurricanes, and the like, but because the moral considerability of human and nonhuman animal sentience, I'll argue, is fundamentally irreconcilable with the logic of commodification.

Put differently, if we're going to raise militant opposition to capitalism on the grounds that it destroys quality of life and the prospect of a sustainable future, it's not the appeal to the capacity for agency and the moral responsibility it entails that makes for our first line of defense; *it's avoiding the hypocrisy of our human chauvinism*. The capacity for agency makes us culpable, but it is the capacity for sentience and its potential to generate unnecessary suffering that produces the *substance* for which we are culpable. For what else would it be worth it to work up the courage to mount a militant opposition to capitalism save to prevent future instances of suffering? What sense would it make to reserve our militancy to the defense of human beings while at the same time undermining our efforts by conceding to the capitalist every other sentient entity? The Kleptocene can either be confronted or continued to cascading extinctions; militant opposition versus going down the drain. But given the many and complex interdependencies that characterize ecosystemic life on earth, there is no sense to be made of compassion for the suffering of one species of creature while we relegate every other to the logic of commodification, and there's no end to capitalism without the exposure and repudiation of its logic. Indeed, if our sense of righteous panic does not extend to the defense of nonhuman animals, we will doom ourselves to an agency whose militance and "unwavering opposition" will be muted at the fast-food drive-up window. *Militant opposition cannot brook hypocrisy.*

Grasping the role of sentience to the critique of the ontology of capitalism provides the critical link between the *Capitalocene* and what the history of capital reveals to have been an ideological "justification" for resource theft, as Stoll shows, from ancient times. While "Capitalocene" underscores specific features of contemporary neoliberalism, "*Kleptocene*" captures the key *conceptual* drivers, the basic assumptions about the planet, its atmosphere, its ecosystems and species life, that animate capital conquest. "Kleptocene" also intimates the moral, or rather, amoral disposition inherent to the logic of commodification, namely, its drive to sanctify theft as necessary to the production of endless profit. We suffer no shortage of critics of the Capitalocene, but we remain wanting with respect to understanding the kleptocratic ideology responsible for our environmental crises. Without that understanding, we find ourselves imprisoned by arguments that, like Stoll's, seem resigned to acquiescence, or more perilous, the reformist arguments of environmental theorists who seek to redeem its destructive impulses by harnessing it to (allegedly) less destructive technologies.

We'll thus consider the arguments of several influential contemporary environmental thinkers, particularly Wallace-Wells, Mann, Francione, and Moore each of whom "dare us to feel the panic" from different directions, in different ways. Or, as I'll show, they dare us—sort of; that is, until it comes to "militant opposition" against capitalism. And then they don't—for reasons I think it crucial to understand in order to appreciate the significance of Malm's two choices. Once again, suffice this much for now: while it's puzzling that, despite his compelling evidentiary justification for "militant opposition," Stoll seems resigned to going down the drain, he's still forthright about "life as we know it." While he values truth over preservation of the capitalist status quo, he doesn't seem to think there's a way out of our nihilistic dilemma:

> Household items, labor, energy, slaves, land, wealth, livestock, food, homes, and other structures, events, travel, taxes, books, education—what does not have its price? Today money rules all. Modern capitalism and, indeed, *life as we know it are unimaginable without it.*[27]

On the one hand, Stoll *is* right that money "rules all." Indeed, it's a bit ironic (and more than a bit troubling) that despite the title of Wallace-Wells's best seller, *The Uninhabitable Earth*, it's Stoll who speaks truth to power—that "life as we know it" is unimaginable save for a system of economy that has the capacity to obliterate that life. Wallace-Wells, on the other hand, appears to agree with Stoll that life outside of capitalism is unimaginable *and* that the climate is "endangered by it."[28] Yet, unlike Stoll, Wallace-Wells claims to be "optimistic" that technologies developed through the same unrestricted competition that brought us the climate crisis—carbon capture and geoengineering—"could bring the planet closer to a state we would today regard as merely grim, rather than apocalyptic."[29] In other words, for Wallace-Wells life sans capitalism is unimaginable, but this is acceptable (if grim) since technology can make the uninhabitable survivable (for a few). Given his optimism for what we might call *salvation capitalism*,[30] Wallace-Wells would presumably characterize Malm's two choices as "alarmist." But, as we'll also see in Mann, Francione, and (though more nuanced) in Moore, although Wallace-Wells claims that he is himself "alarmed,"[31] he not only can't see beyond capitalism as "life as we know it," he ends up committed to trying to save a system that, by his own admission, offers "grim" as a solution to "apocalyptic." But if "grim" is all that even the lucky few have to look forward to, perhaps it really is high time to sound the alarm.

"Grim" might also describe Stoll's view that "[a]t best we can work to ameliorate its [capitalism's] worst effects."[32] But why? Why should we settle for "grim"? Who is the "we" who'll be saddled with this "grim"? There are, after all, big winners like the petro-chemical behemoths, Big Agriculture and Big Animal Agriculture, and even bigger losers for whom "grim" would be a step up even now, for example, developing world and indigenous peoples for whom settling is really just another day of suffering. Fact is, the quest for profit has produced an ecologically, geopolitically, and socially degraded planet for all but (for now) a tiny fraction of the mostly white, male, wealthy, and lucky—as Stoll shows. Surely, coming to understand the motives and goals, the logic that has set us on the nihilistic path of destroying the finite and only planet we have should matter to us. And yet most of us, either out of denial, a sense of futility, or willful ignorance appear to be settled in, "watching as it all goes down the drain."

"LIFE AS SUCH"

One example of this drift toward unwitting concession despite otherwise excellent analysis is Nancy Fraser's *Cannibal Capitalism*. Fraser seeks to "counter the widely held view that capitalism propels the ever-increasing commodification of life as such."[33] She wants, in other words, to show that the values of "life as such" are beyond the reach of capital conquest, and that these values can offer an antidote to the malaise of life in capitalist society. She stipulates that "affective labor" includes "the work of birthing and socializing the young, building communities, producing and reproducing the shared meanings, affective dispositions, and horizons of value that underpin social cooperation."[34] She then argues that:

> In capitalist societies much, though not all, of this activity goes on *outside the market*, in households, neighborhoods, and a host of public institutions, including schools and childcare centers; and much of it, though not all, does not take the form of wage labor.[35]

While Fraser acknowledges that "social-reproductive activity is absolutely necessary to the existence of waged work," she nonetheless insists that the activities of reproducing "life as such" stand outside the logic of commodification. Such activity involves a version of the agency that Malm emphasizes in his discussion of who is culpable for the climate crisis, and yet for Fraser this "affective labor" is irreducible to the commodifying forces of capitalism.

But while we can certainly appreciate Fraser's valiant attempt to rescue "affective labor" from capitalist expropriation, her argument inevitably fails, and worse: it lends itself to a reformism incompatible with any hope for a survivable (if grim) future. There are at least two reasons for this: first, outside the wage does not mean outside the logic of commodification; far from it. What the history of institutions like "the slave plantation and the mechanized factory,"[36] show is that "life as such" neither is nor can be a barrier to the reduction of all value—moral, civic, and aesthetic—to the exchange value that forms the ontological bedrock of "unrestricted competition." Second, while capitalism does depend on the uncompensated reproductive labor supplied by women, the enslaved, and nonhuman animals, this does not and cannot imply that "living" can sustain any value beyond the reach of the exploitable and expendable. "Living" can no more constitute an obstacle to the logic of commodification than can the capacity for sentience. In fact, once suffering no longer poses a moral barrier, "living" is nothing more than a minor interruption. The factory "farmed" cow that's still alive after the stun gun is still gutted. The uncompensated labor performed by a working class woman after a long day working in a meat-packing plant won't save her from the Covid-19 infection that chokes her to death. As Stoll spells out, while the pursuit of profit "has transformed many times throughout its history," it does so in conformity to the objectives embodied in its *raison d'étre*: profit. "[W] hat does not have its price?"[37] Insofar as money does rule all, it entraps us in an existential paradox that has no outside: if "life as we know it" is "unimaginable" without capitalism,[38] life in the not too distant future is plainly unimaginable *with* capitalism—whether we *say* we value "living" or not.

Acknowledging, then, that however we conceive "life as such" with respect to the logic of commodification, capitalism involves the "structuring [of] social relations *as if* they were economic,"[39] what Stoll shows is that these relations have historically produced great wealth for some at the expense of life, limb, and existential condition for others. Consider, for example, plantation owners whose dependence on enslaved labor presages "the factories of industrial capitalism"[40]:

> capitalists invested in capital assets (processing facilities and enslaved "machines") and natural resources (soil and seed) and used energy (slave and animal muscle, fuel, and sometimes wind, water, or steam power) to produce a commodity for the market. The plantation as factory clashed with human will, as well as another force with a will of its own—nature itself.[41]

Or, consider the way Malm depicts the connection between human and nonhuman will when he argues that nonhuman nature is best characterized as "autonomy without agency":

> [f]rom the capitalist standpoint, however, the most disconcerting aspect might be the moment of uncontrollability as such, whether founded in a will or not . . . here, autonomy denotes not a moral capacity, but an ontological fact that capital has to wrestle with throughout its history. It is the fact that binds labour and nature together from the perspective of capital: as something that came before it, does not need it for existence, and might one day refuse to cooperate, whether as a crop failure or a mass resignation.[42]

That is, while we may think of resistance to commodification as the deliberate result of human decision-making, nonhuman nature is and will remain "intrinsically independent of capital."[43] Yet, while the "uncontrollability" of both nonhuman nature and labor precede capitalism, and thus do not depend on it for existence, this "ontological fact" does not preclude the fundamentally destructive ecological and social consequences of capital conquest. It's not that "living" and "nonliving" have no more effect upon exchange value *than* does sentience; it's that "living" and "nonliving" have no effect upon exchange value *because* sentience doesn't and can't matter to commodification—unless, of course, smiling happy cows sell hamburgers.

Whether as a "crop failure or a mass resignation," creeping desert or water war, firenado or viral pandemic, what Stoll and Fraser see, but Malm sees without recourse to reformist submission, is that without a resistance less "feeble" and more "ferocious" we are unlikely to "maximize the prospects for survival," for human or much of nonhuman life. Indeed, once we introduce the "warming condition," as Malm put it, that is, the *climate crisis* into the mix, we have no recourse but to include "life as such" including the affective labor that sustains it among the casualties of the commodifiable. But we'll not see *why* we must commit to "militant and unwavering opposition if we don't realize that "life as such" is precisely what is at stake. We won't "[d]are to feel the panic" unless we recognize that for the ontology of capitalism, nothing is sacred. As Malm makes the point:

> [w]e should conclude, first of all, that building a new coal-fired power plant, or continuing to operate an old one, or drilling for oil, or expanding an airport, or planning for a highway is now *irrational violence*, as it inflicts harm on other people and species.[44]

While "[c]apitalism's development," in other words, "was anything but predestined,"[45] the very idea that coal-fired power plants, oil drilling operations, airport expansions, etc. will continue to be built makes plain that capitalism is, as Fraser argues, "something larger than an economy."[46] This is understatement. Capitalism is *the* globally enculturated, "world system" without which life as we know it is *now* unimaginable despite the fact that the *only* future it can promise is one of irrational violence. Why is this? Why is there no sane prospect of a reformed capitalism, a technological mediation that can save us? Ashley Dawson offers a first clue:

> [c]apitalism is not necessarily more immoral than previous social systems with regard to cruelty to humans and the gratuitous destruction of nature. As a mode of production and a social system, however, capitalism requires people to be destructive of the environment.[47]

Dawson goes on to name "three destructive aspects of the capitalist system" he regards as particularly relevant to the current epoch, as Elizabeth Kolbert puts it, of the *Sixth Extinction*:[48] "(1) Capitalism tends to degrade the conditions of its own production; (2) it must expand ceaselessly in order to survive; (3) it generates a chaotic world system, which in turn intensifies the extinction crisis."[49] Like Stoll and Fraser, Dawson is certainly right, but also like his colleagues, Dawson's account doesn't go quite far enough. Indeed, what he doesn't quite capture is this: given that the survival of any capitalist enterprise depends on its uncompromising adherence to a logic of commodification, "degrades" must itself be understood to create new opportunities for profit; that is, "degraded" must be able to be invested with exchange value. "Degraded," is itself the commodity that makes transparent the logic of commodification because it shows the extent to which nothing, including life, is beyond the reach of becoming *disarticulated*—dismantled, reduced, denuded, discharged—as exchange value.

Dawson's certainly right that capitalism "generates a chaotic world system," at least from the point of view of its harms. But this system is more than merely frenzied, and while its impacts are often chaotic and unpredictable, the logic that produces them is not. On the one hand, such a system is thoroughly orderly and mechanistic: capitalism executes a logic for which everything—including living things, catastrophic events, wars, disease—is a potential commodity to be digested toward the objective of profit generation. On the other hand, such a system is inherently *nihilistic* because the logic by which it operates results not merely in degrading the conditions of its own reproduction, but in ignoring, concealing, and denying what it exhausts, pollutes, and cannot replace—creating chaos. Even as capitalism seeks to take advantage of the crises it creates to provide new opportunities and markets, it undermines its own capacity for commodification. As Malm forcefully argues "nature" is no mere idea: "conceptions of nature are culturally determined, but the referent is not thereby similarly constituted. Ten herders can draw very different portraits of the same goat, but that does not mean that the goat is a painting."[50] And it is precisely this objective fact that ignites the existential paradox with which we're now faced, namely, that "the biosphere itself might one day cease to be a suitable medium of existence because its fossil substrata have been made to serve industry."[51] Nature, autonomous if without agency, has ultimately nothing to fear, but we—especially the most vulnerable among us—do.

Although Fraser takes a similarly realist approach to her critique of capitalism, she paints a picture of a "societal order that empowers a profit-driven economy to prey on the *extra-economic supports* it needs to function—wealth expropriated from nature and subject peoples."[52] But a "profit driven economy" that's in a position to "prey on the extra-economic" has *already* expropriated nonhuman nature and subjugated particular peoples *as* "extra-economic." A people can be "subject" in many ways—politically, socially, economically. Yet when Fraser appeals to the image of the ouroboro that "eats its own tail" and then asks "Are we toast? Can we figure out how to dismantle the social system that is driving us into the jaws of obliteration?"[53] she leaves no room for an "economic" outside of capitalism. This runs contrary to her argument concerning the value of "life as such" and the "affective labor" she insists governs work outside of capitalism. Fraser can't have this both ways: if capitalism is the social system driving us to obliteration, the "we" sufficiently empowered to dismantle it can only come from the inside *because it is capitalism itself that defines "we."* Indeed, it is capitalism that defines "extra" as "uncompensated reproductive labor." To be clear, this is not to deny that there exist deeply rooted structural inequalities that advantage the capitalist by insuring a social system of reproductive labor that can be exploited as uncompensated and upon which wage labor is dependent. But this is not "extra-economic." From the point of view of the logic of commodification, it's simply "resource." Indeed, it is labor that's effectively *stolen*, and thus reinforces the kleptocratic character of capitalist ontology. This is also not to suggest that practices, traditions, and institutions are reducible to the solely economic; but "irreducible" does not mean "extra." Fraser asks, for example, whether capitalism is "necessarily racist?"[54] This is the wrong question. Capitalism is necessarily *mercenary*; the structural inequalities that maintain racism, sexism and speciesism provide resources from which the capitalist can extract cheap (or free) labor that help supply the imperative to "expand ceaselessly."

Capitalism is like the lizard who consumes its own tail, a monster whose voracious appetite and insatiable metabolism requires the entire planet, and more: grow or die. While its development may not have been preordained, and it has "no single place or time of origin," "some threads remain constant from the Age of Sharp Stones to the Age of Smartphones."[55] Such "threads," its logic of capital accumulation, do not, however, merely remain constant; they must be characterized as kleptocratic: rooted in irreparable, unsubstitutable, and technologically irreplaceable *theft of planetary resources, labor, and species life*. As Stoll argues:

> With each stage of economic development, people ratcheted up the efficiency of their exploitation of natural resources. Step by step, the process impoverished ecosystems and transformed landscapes. Today, consumer capitalism has magnified human environmental impact to a startling degree, exterminating species, deranging ecosystems, draining wetlands, redirecting and damming rivers, cutting down forests, and degrading soils . . . There's hardly a place or species on earth unaffected by human deeds and works—even to the bottom of the deepest ocean tranches, where high levels of toxic chemicals poison creatures and plastic bags float like pale ghosts.[56]

Yet, for all this Stoll ultimately concludes on something of a contradiction. The logic of capital insures that the planet's capacity to sustain *any form of life* will be eroded ever more irrecoverably, undermining not only its own conditions, but that of the planet's capacity to recuperate after anthropogenic catastrophe. This is not to say that there won't exist species of living things crawling, roaming, or buzzing about planet earth long after homo sapiens has either made its ignoble exit or somehow learned to live without wrecking the place. It's also not to say that, in making his focus extinction, Dawson misses other equally important environmental crises; he doesn't.

Rather, the point is to remind us that "extinction" intersects with capitalism in ways that exceed the loss of species, ways that expand and transform the meaning of "loss" in virtue of a logic of commodification that, more than chaotic, creates a "world system" destined not only for self-defeat, but predictable self-destruction. Defeat can be explained in terms of excess, but self-destruction demands a deeper interrogation into the conceptual origins and character of the logic itself. Indeed, what we'll discover is that "chaotic" is an exploitable appearance just as "crisis" is a potential market opportunity. That corporations like BP cash in on the climate crisis toward the pretense of "going green" is not really different from self-styled environmentalists like Michael Shellenberger who exploit the crisis to gain attention toward monetizing his support for the nuclear power industry. The logic of commodification doesn't produce a chaotic world system; it produces a nihilistic one for which the appearance (or experience) of chaos provides cover and opportunity, but whose driving mode of operation is as simple as it is psychopathological: profit at any cost, "life as such" be damned. And while there may be no ultimate morally compelling principle or idea that demands we care about living, much less suffering, even less the suffering of nonhuman sentient life—we *say* we do. If that is so, militant opposition to end the kleptocene is our only rational choice.

NOTES

1. Mark Stoll. *An Environmental History*. (Cambridge, UK: Polity Press, 2023), 5 (my emphasis).
2. Stoll, 12.
3. Stoll, 205–8.
4. Stoll, 4.
5. Stoll, 223.
6. Stoll, 6.
7. Stoll, 16.
8. Stoll, 19.
9. Andreas Malm. *The Progress of This Storm: Nature and Society in a Warming World*. (Brooklyn, NY: Verso, 2020), 170.
10. Malm, 226.
11. Malm, 152–3.
12. Malm, 152–3.
13. Malm, 11.
14. Malm, 25.

15. Malm, 226.
16. Malm, 127–32.
17. Amitov Ghosh. *The Great Derangement: Climate Change and the Unthinkable*. (Chicago: University of Chicago Press, 2017).
18. Malm, 130.
19. David Harvey. *The New Imperialism*. (Oxford: Oxford University Press, 2003), 67.
20. Anmar Frangoul. "BP CEO Says Oil and Gas Giant is a 'Greening Company,' Refutes Greenwashing Accusations." CNBC, 2.15.22. https://www.cnbc.com/2022/02/15/bp-ceo-says-oil-and-gas-giant-is-a-greening-company.html.
21. Frangoul. https://www.cnbc.com/2022/02/15/bp-ceo-says-oil-and-gas-giant-is-a-greening-company.html.
22. Damian Carrington. "Oil Firms' Climate Claims are Greenwashing, Study Concludes." *The Guardian*, 2.16.22. https://www.theguardian.com/environment/2022/feb/16/oil-firms-climate-claims-are-greenwashing-study-concludes).
23. The Breakthrough Institute. https://thebreakthrough.org.
24. DeSmog Blog. "Michael Shellenberger." https://www.desmog.com/michael-shellenberger/.
25. Sam Bliss, "The Stories Michael Shellenberger Tells." (Los Angelas Review of Books, 10.6.20). https://lareviewofbooks.org/article/the-stories-michael-shellenberger-tells/.
26. Christoph Hermann. *The Critique of Commodification*. (New York, NY: Oxford University Press, 2021), 92.
27. Stoll, 23 (my emphasis).
28. David Wallace-Wells. *The Uninhabitable Earth*. (New York, NY: Tim Duggan Books, 2019), 162.
29. Wallace-Wells, 31.
30. Wendy Lynne Lee. *Eco-Nihilism: The Philosophical Geopolitics of the Climate Change Apocalypse*. (Lanham, MD: Lexington Books), 2016), Ch. 6.
31. Wallace-Wells, 213.
32. Stoll, 9.
33. Nancy Fraser. *Cannibal Capitalism*. (Brooklyn, NY: Verso, 2022), 6.
34. Fraser, 9.
35. Fraser, 9 (my emphasis).
36. Stoll, 5.
37. Stoll, 23.
38. Stoll, 23.
39. Fraser, 17.
40. Stoll, 68.
41. Stoll, 68.
42. Malm, 199.
43. Malm, 198.
44. Malm, 18 (my emphasis).
45. Stoll, 5.
46. Fraser, 17.

47. Ashley Dawson. *Extinction: A Radical History.* (New York, NY: OR Books, 2016), 41.
48. Elizabeth Kolbert. *The Sixth Extinction.* (New York: Picador, Henry Holt and Company, 2014).
49. Dawson, 41.
50. Malm, 26.
51. Malm, 163.
52. Fraser, xvi (my emphasis).
53. Fraser, xvi.
54. Fraser, 30.
55. Stoll, 6.
56. Stoll, 6–7.

Chapter 1

The Disarticulation of Value

THE ONTOLOGY OF CAPITALISM AS THE DISARTICULATION OF VALUE

While there's little doubt that the history of extinction provides a vital barometer of capitalist resource theft, it doesn't explain in what the original sin, the prime *propellant* consists, the radicle (as it were) that anchors a logic of commodification so deeply woven into the ligature of human agency and institution that, despite its capacity for apocalyptic self-destruction, it feels as natural as breathing. Ashley Dawson argues that "capital remorselessly breaks down the complex natural world into impoverished but exchangeable forms," and that this becomes "particularly starkly evident when seen through the lens of extinction."[1] He offers a number of grisly examples from whaling to the American fur trade each of which illustrate the intimate relationship between the creation of steady demand for disarticulated animal body parts, the extinctions or near-extinctions that follow, and the decimating ecological as well as social impacts that, for example, the fur trade had on the indigenous peoples of the Americas.[2] But what Dawson insinuates yet doesn't fully interrogate, is the fateful *conceptual* judgment that propels capitalist expansionism to cross its Rubicon; the crucial *idea* that charts the course for a logic whose predictable outcome is irrecoverable ecological loss, human and nonhuman suffering for which extinction is just one barometer—but a vital one.

That crucial idea is *not,* at least in the first place, that inherent to capitalism is the necessity that everything, living or non-living, organic or inorganic, sentient or non-sentient, be potentially commodifiable, extractible, or disposable, though this is clearly true. It's not that "living" demands no special consideration from the capitalist before becoming subject to the logic of commodification; as we'll see, this is a consequence of capitalist ideology, but not an inherent feature. The crucial idea—the idea without which the pursuit of profit would be stifled in its quest to operate in sync with its elemental presuppositions, namely, that the planet is an inexhaustible repository of resources and that everything has the potential to be converted to exchange value—*is that the capacity for sentience can pose no obstacle or prohibition to commodification.* Or, to frame it as a moral proposition: insofar as the capacity for sentience poses no bar to commodification, its correlate, *suffering*, doesn't either. For, to state the obvious, sentience is a necessary condition for the experience of suffering; once the moral value of sentience is defused as a potential disruption to the logic of commodification, the value of experience *per se* is nullified other than as a potentially marketable commodity.

Indeed, to whatever extent sentience might be made to matter to the pursuit of profit, that is the extent to which an enterprise is prevented from maximizing its competitive advantage; no capitalist enterprise can afford such an exemption. "America's largest chicken company," Tyson, for example, advertises itself as "free range," and counts on consumers not to look, but just behind that advertising is a company whose first objective is maximizing its advantage:

> During their short stint on behalf of the Washington, DC-based animal rights group Animal Outlook, the investigator documented hours upon hours of the typical horrors found on chicken factory farms: tens of thousands of birds stuffed into dark warehouse-sized barns, many of them severely injured with gruesome lesions, injuries, and deformities. At more than one point, birds are deprived of feed or water, and there was also a rat infestation and footage of bugs crawling in the chickens' feed. Despite the horrific findings, they're not all that different from the conditions documented at other farms that raise chickens for Tyson and Tyson's competitors. But the investigation's most revealing finding had nothing to do with the conditions of the estimated 750,000 chickens raised annually at the Jetersville, Virginia, facility. Instead, it emerged from a surprisingly candid conversation the investigator secretly recorded between the farm manager and a Tyson Foods "broiler technician advisor," who worked with Tyson chicken farms in the area. In the video recording, the technician freely acknowledged that the chicken industry's "free-range" labels were essentially meaningless—a rare instance of an industry insider saying the quiet part out loud. The conditions are visibly at odds with Tyson's advertising claims that it treats animals humanely and raises "happy" and "healthy" chickens.[3]

The upshot's clear: if what "grow or die" requires is that market competition not be impeded by any value inconsistent with exchange, it's not surprising that the capacity for sentience must be precluded from the production calculus.

By the same token, however, that sentience is discounted as morally relevant, it is the same logic of commodification that paves the way for the commodification *of* sentient creatures—sometimes *as* sentient, for example, in zoos or rodeos; but far more often *as* the disarticulated bodies on our dinner plates, or *as* the laboring bodies of industrialized agriculture. In each case, the recognition of suffering as morally considerable is preemptively displaced by the pursuit of competitive advantage; it is this systemic excision of barriers that defines the kleptocratic, no holds barred, nature of capital conquest. This analysis, moreover, has important implications for what we mean by "Anthropocene," namely, that insofar as the logic of commodification forms an ontological and conceptual condition of what we mean by "capital," the Anthropocene must be located in its proper historical context as an episode of the Kleptocene, the world-as-market. While the Anthropocene is rightly identified with the emergence of neoliberal—mass industrialized, technologically facilitated—capitalism, its conceptual seeds are rooted in a suite of fictions that require the planet and its atmosphere to be what they cannot be, namely, inexhaustible. As we'll see, this governing set of myths convince us that we cannot steal what can never run out, can always be replaced, or has value only as exchange or consumption—like mass manufactured chickens. Of *course* the "free range" label is "essentially meaningless." It has to be; it always had to be.

Where sentience is no barrier to commodification, concepts like "living," "organic," and "endangered," can also be discounted. For while it's true (for now) that only living things can be things with the capacity to experience suffering, once sentience is vacated of its moral relevance, whether a thing is a living thing is unlikely to arise even as a point of inquiry. If the capacity for pain doesn't matter, why would its underlying condition matter *other* than to questions of its renewability as a resource or whether it poses an obstacle that needs to be neutralized? We engineer cows, pigs, and chickens, disarticulate them inside slaughter houses and meat-packing plants, and consume their depersonalized body parts largely, though willfully, oblivious of the facts about the misery of their short lives inside CAFOs: Concentrated Animal Feeding Operations (factory farms). But while maximizing supply to meet demand occupies the attention of meat industry CEOs, the incalculable suffering of animals whose dismemberment (such as debeaking) often begins long before their lives have ended plainly does not warrant concern, much less reconsideration of a business model.[4] In short, living is no bar to commodification *because* sentience isn't.

While Dawson's analysis of the relationship between capitalism and species extinction offers important insight into an ideology for which the natural world presents itself as a morally colorless assortment of "exchangeable forms," it ultimately fails to excavate the governing logic that facilitates such "remorseless" destruction. Dawson rightly characterizes the fur trade as ecologically damaging, but the foxes themselves receive little attention.

He understands the colossal devastation produced by whale hunting, but has relatively little to say about the whales; so too the decimation of the American Bison. It's as if the sentient animals themselves are, as Christophe Bonneuil and Jean-Baptiste Fressoz might put it, preemptively *dematerialized*—as fur, oil, hides.[5] The loss thus incurred through extinction is calculated as a loss of the exchange value previously available, a loss of, as some put it, "nature's services," but the animals themselves have already been absorbed into the logic of commodification merely as numbers. To be clear, this is not to suggest that Dawson doesn't care about nonhuman animal suffering; it's to suggest that the conceptual terrain upon which he articulates his critique of capitalism *is* the capitalist's insofar as it assumes without interrogation the "dematerialization" of nonhuman animals as instances of a species as opposed to sentient creatures. Dawson's is thus an example of an otherwise fine critique of capitalism coopted by a logic for which extinction presents a dilemma *only* because the dematerialization of nonhuman animals has not been addressed through their mass production.

Dawson is, however, not alone insofar as he overlooks the individual sentient animal for the merely individuated species. Bonneuil and Fressoz's discussion of capitalism's relation to "matter" in *The Shock of the Anthropocene* (2017) no more recognizes that materiality *embodied* in sentient creatures is radically different than that *enmattered* in non-sentient entities than does Dawson whose reference to species draws no distinction between the fox and the "natural world" it inhabits. Dawson's certainly right when he argues that the damage done to fox populations will redound to the indigenous communities dependent on them. He might respond that insofar as his focus is the impact on tribal communities already suffering the effects of colonialist subjugation, he can't fairly be accused of ignoring the importance of sentience. But, as we'll see moving forward, a critique of capitalism that privileges the capacity for sentience of one species of creature while ignoring that of another has already capitulated to the logic of commodification, and thus already acceded to the very subjugation it rightly condemns.

The long history of dehumanizing the "other" in order to enslave or otherwise subjugate them—nonhuman animals, the indigenous, the poor, women, and persons of color—testifies to what is not merely hypocrisy, but a "tenuous relationship with matter" whose value is determined by its capacity to be converted to exchange value. Matter takes many forms, but whether an instantiation of a particular form is a fox, a whale, a bison, a river, a human agent, or a stone has no more relevance to Dawson's otherwise trenchant critique of capitalism than it does for the pursuit of capital conquest itself—a blind spot that ultimately distorts his analysis. But the same holds largely true for Bonneuil and Fressoz. "Prevailing economic theory," they argue:

> Maintains a very tenuous relationship with matter. It envisages goods according to their psychological effects, as purveyors of utility, rather than according to their material characteristics. In the same way, capital is not conceived as a concrete set of productive equipment, rather as assets generating financial flows. This dematerialization has the effect of naturalizing the exponential growth of the economy during the Anthropocene by disconnecting it from any material substratum.[6]

Indeed; but, like Dawson, what Bonneuil and Fressoz miss is that this tenuous relationship itself presupposes that whatever constitutes an obstacle to it has already been nullified—in order to make the relationship *less* tenuous, so that goods can be experienced as desirable, without moral reservation, so that "financial flows" can be streamlined without interruption. This "dematerialization has the effect of naturalizing the exponential growth of the economy" precisely because it has preemptively exorcized any impediment whose suffering screams might inform us of our hypocrisy, that might remind us that events such as extinctions are clues about what's going down the drain.

Capitalism is thus not rightly described as nihilistic because what a successful enterprise disarticulates *first* is the animal, but because what it disarticulates *first* is the value of sentience itself; the dismemberment of bodies merely materializes consignment to exchange value. Whether the chicken, cow, or pig in being stunned and dismembered is alive, or conscious, terrified, or in pain has no calculable value at all; thus, there can be no judgment of a capitalism that is excessive. "Excess" presupposes limits that can be exceeded. But having vanquished the value of sentience, *the logic of commodification has no limits*. Its product is simply the materialization of what is inherent to its character: *kleptocracy*, that is, profit by any means necessary. We rightly call this theft, robbery *knowingly* perpetrated against the planet, its ecologies, and denizens, because the logic falsely *simulates* what the planet cannot sustain: endless resources and bottomless receptacles for pollutants and greenhouse gases. What we experience as extreme weather, drought, firenado, pandemic are, from the logic's point of view, simply the side-effects of value disarticulated, rearranged and repackaged as "product," "side-effects" that corporations like Tyson work fast and furiously to disassociate from themselves and their activities. Consider the chickens once more: "[c]hickens raised for meat have been bred to grow so large, so fast, that their spindly legs often buckle under the enormous weight of their bodies. The cruelty is built into their genetics, forcing them to live in chronic pain and struggle to stand."[7] The cruelty, in other words, is built into a logic blinded by design to the limits of its material conditions, the suffering of its "product," and the nihilism of its pursuits.

THE LOGIC OF COMMODIFICATION AND THE IDIOM OF EXTRACTION: DENY, BURY, LIE, STEAL, REPEAT

One way to understand Dawson's "chaotic world system" is that although it's responsible for "remorselessly breaking down the complex natural world," the logic that mechanizes this process is transparent and mercenary. In at least two ways the logic of commodification behaves like a virus: first, it's anthropogenic. While viruses are naturally occurring, human activities encourage zoonotic transmission, mutation, and increased virulence in a number of ways.[8] Similarly, the logic of commodification thrives on human consumption driven by "needs" created through "viral" advertising, social expectation, and the enculturated belief that capitalism is simply a mirror of human nature. For example, Tyson typically uses breeder birds in its advertising rather than "broilers" because the breeders are prettier, creating a more appetizing association between the consumer and the company.[9]

Second, the objective of capitalist enterprise, to replicate exchange value by whatever means necessary, is instantiated in the logic much like a virus replicates in the body of its host. Like its viral analogue, the logic of commodification is predictable with respect to its goal, and unpredictable with respect to precisely the course it will take to realize it. That it will "select" a course maximally efficient and least expensive—predictable; that its chief beneficiaries among the chaotic world's most fortunate are in a position to know what is that course or its possible consequences even for themselves—less so. That "maximally efficient and least expensive" could chart a course to self-destruction: ignored, elided, and denied precisely *because* it's predictable. Just as a virus can, and sometimes does, kill itself by killing its host, so too a capitalist enterprise can pollute or exhaust its resources beyond reclamation. What makes such an eventuality unpredictable is not that these limits go unrecognized. It's that what the logic of commodification requires in order to drive endless growth is denial, that is, the carefully coifed and maintained lie about endless abundance, sometimes during the very scramble to identify new resource sites.

Consider, for example, the story of ExxonMobil, and the lengths to which the company went to bury what it knew *forty years ago* about climate change:

> Exxon was aware of climate change, as early as 1977. . . . This knowledge did not prevent the company . . . from spending decades refusing to publicly acknowledge climate change and even promoting climate misinformation—an approach many have likened to the lies spread by the tobacco industry regarding the health risks of smoking . . . Experts, however, aren't terribly surprised. "It's never been remotely plausible that they did not understand the science," says Naomi Oreskes, a history of science professor at Harvard University. But

> as it turns out, Exxon didn't just understand the science, the company actively engaged with it. In the 1970s and 1980s it employed top scientists to look into the issue and launched its own ambitious research program that empirically sampled carbon dioxide and built rigorous climate models. Exxon even spent more than $1 million on a tanker project that would tackle how much CO_2 is absorbed by the oceans. It was one of the biggest scientific questions of the time, meaning that Exxon was truly conducting unprecedented research.[10]

Perhaps even less surprising than that a behemoth multinational would bury unfavorable facts, is that ExxonMobil utilized what it was learning about climate change to develop strategies for gaslighting a public confronted more and more frequently by its environmental impacts. ExxonMobil's interest was clearly not in acting to stem or at least mitigate against the effects of the coming crisis. What the company needed to know was what to make sure didn't see the light of day, at least while it sought contracts to extract the last possible hydrocarbons from fragile ecosystems like Alaska's Arctic Refuge (ANWR), home to a number of engendered species.[11]

The business plan that the company developed on the basis of its extensive climate modelling strives neither for chaos nor order, but profit by whatever route can achieve it for as long as possible. That ExxonMobil knew just how bad the predictable impacts of climate change might be can be derived from the lengths the company went to conceal its research, to plead ignorance when its complicity in the effort to bury the science began to leak, and the effort the company made to refurbish its image once it became clear that its climate change research was some of the best to date. There is, however, nothing surprising here. Forty years of compiling data, mapping trajectories, and hiding the results is a product of the same cost/benefit analysis that goes into determining any ExxonMobil venture. Wherever projected revenues are significant enough to be worth the risk of environmental destruction, species extinction, cultural ruin, and community displacement, the answer is yes. So long as the real costs of extraction, production, and transport can be externalized onto the planet, its atmosphere, and its inhabitants buried under layer upon layer of "free market" advertising, the answer's yes: the value of the planet can be disarticulated into parts per billion carbon emissions.

Malm captures what we might think of as the psyche of ExxonMobil in his discussion of Steve Coll's *Empire: ExxonMobil and American Power*, arguing that Rex Tillerson "whose career at ExxonMobil spans forty-one years," ten as CEO, is best depicted as "a paragon of banal evil":

> Under him [Tillerson] and his predecessor, ExxonMobil engaged in a series of imperialist ventures in places such as Aceh, Equatorial Guinea, Iraq, Nigeria, and Chad; it moved swiftly to benefit from the retreating Arctic ice and drill for more oil to burn. Coll explicates why imperialism is a necessary imperative of

> this corporation: 'the object of Exxon's business model lay buried beneath the earth. Exxon drilled holes in the ground and then operated its oil and gas wells for many years, and so its business imperatives were linked to the control of physical territories."[12]

Setting aside for the moment the colonialism built into this "imperative," what becomes clear in these two stories about drilling and denial is that ExxonMobil is certain that it can count on consumers to be too busy filling up our cars with cheap gas to think about where the gas came from, say, Nigeria, or whether the atmosphere can absorb without impact what spews from our exhaust pipes. The company itself is busy cashing in on the disastrously retreating Arctic ice its drilling activities have helped to generate. ExxonMobil bet it would take a calamite to get consumers to notice their slowly but surely vanishing coastlines, and that if these coastlines were somewhere other than where the wealthy build their beachside estates mostly Global North consumers would simply continue to look away from places like Chad, Guinea, or Iraq. Having buried their research a bit like an armadillo buries its feces, even images of rapidly calving icebergs, vanishing polar bear populations, disrupted Caribou migrations, displaced Inupiat villagers, families fleeing California wildfires, or the growing evidence of a link between the climate crisis and viral outbreak has yet to sway the company from deploying its army of lobbyists, political campaign donors, and elected representatives to curry favor in the direction of a permit to drill in the *Arctic National Wildlife Refuge*, ANWR.[13] Indeed, even as the Biden administration reintroduces the United States to the *Paris Climate Agreement*,[14] Texas Governor Greg Abbott ignores the potential for future climate change impacts like Hurricane Harvey,[15] threatens lawsuit to protect the state's oil revenue,[16] and appeals to the short-term benefits of job creation to sustain the state's lucrative relationship with ExxonMobil.[17]

ExxonMobil epitomizes what David Wallace-Wells in *The Uninhabitable Earth* calls "the rule of capital."[18] That is, the multinational company is no outlier with respect to the lengths it will go to insure continuing profitability, but rather models how the logic of commodification constitutes and sustains the circulatory system of every capitalist enterprise. Invoking the profit motive to oxygenate its "organs and tissues," its research, internal memos, and public-facing ad-campaigns, ExxonMobil pursues whatever means are necessary to sustain production, market products, avoid regulation, encourage consumption, and beat competitors. Despite, moreover, what would seem to pose the greatest challenge to the multinational's bottom line, namely, "Big Green" environmental organizations like the *World Wildlife Federation* (WWF) who've been sounding the climate crisis alarm for decades, nothing could actually be further from the truth. Looking mainly to blunt the consequences of what they see as corporate excess, the Big Greens tend to avoid any probing examination of the logic upon which they are themselves dependent as non-profits beholden to the generosity (or perhaps the guilt) of well-to-do donors, namely, the logic of commodification. But this avoidance effectively provides cover for some of the planet's worst polluters: Big Oil, Big Gas, Big Agriculture, and Big Animal Agriculture. Environmental organizations like WWF have raised awareness concerning, for example, species endangered by drilling in ANWR, especially polar bears, caribou, snowy owls, snow geese, and indigenous human cultures like the Inupiat. But insofar as their criticism of ExxonMobil constrains itself to the consequences of drilling for the atmosphere and for biodiversity—*carefully avoiding an interrogation of the logic that would compel its shareholders and donors to recognize the suffering of individual animals or the lives of particular villagers*—their warnings actually reinforce capitalism's basic premise that nothing lay beyond the limits of conversion to exchange value, and that the rule of capital is not bound by any moral principle or value. In short, where the focus remains the regulation of excess, the fundamental structure of capital conquest continues to go uninterrogated.[19]

The Big Green message to ExxonMobil may be implicit or unspoken—but it's loud and clear: "the rule of capital is not our target, and thus neither is its most basic activity: the disarticulation of all value and re-composition as exchange." A "green" corporation is one that ostensibly supports "sustainability," but this remains defined in terms of human interests, including the preservation of markets. What the message embodies, in other words, is a *marriage of convenience*: by recognizing climate change as a "risk," ExxonMobil legitimates the Big Greens who "demand" that the oil and gas industry support sustainability. But the Big Greens protect ExxonMobil's bottom line by tailoring their criticism to "excess," but not to the company's "right" to the profits of extraction, and certainly not to the morality of capitalism. It's hard to imagine a clearer example of this mutually reinforcing relationship than the company's sustainability statement: "ExxonMobil is committed to producing the energy and chemical products that are essential to modern life and economic development, in a way that protects people, the environment and the communities where we operate. This includes mitigating the risks of climate change,"[20] which, of course, is a lie.

Given this marriage, it's hardly surprising that the Big Greens have largely failed to blunt the environmental impacts of corporate excess that define their missions. Polar bear populations continue to dwindle. Indeed, "[a] dire new climate report projects polar bears could reach extinction within the next 80 years . . . the carnivores could be starved into extinction by 2100 as the Arctic sea ice continues to shrink at alarming rates, making it hard for the bears to hunt for food."[21] Greenhouse emissions continue to accelerate—even in the wake of Covid-19: "Greenhouse gas concentrations—which are already at their highest levels in three million years—have continued to rise . . . [W]hile many aspects of our lives have been disrupted in 2020, climate change has continued unabated."[22] So long as criticism of corporations like ExxonMobil fails to get at its root mechanism—mistaking the rule of capital for "excess" that can be made subject to reform or regulation—it's destined to remain party to the extinctions and environmental calamites the Big Greens claim to address. To be clear: this is not about a lack of courage or fortitude to take on multinational behemoths like ExxonMobil; the rule of capital preempts both. It's that even the best of intentions, for example, genuine concern for the fate of polar bears and the indigenous communities that depend on them, are rendered irrelevant from the outset by the fact that the logic of commodification goes uninterrogated. As Malm remarks of Rex Tillerson: "[t]his man will act as he intends, come rain or shine. This is the sort of intentionality that presently occupies the highest seats of state power. It burns in the heart of a collective super-agent. Its bearers aim to never cease to be victorious."[23] It's hard to imagine a more perspicacious image of the modern kleptocene or the agency responsible for it.

Consider once more the World Wildlife Federation. As its website references to "beef," but not to cows makes clear, WWF takes the rule of capital for granted, and thereby renders itself largely impotent with respect to having any impact on animal agriculture's massive greenhouse gas emissions. That is, while WWF is rightly critical, for example, of the massive greenhouse gas emissions emanating from factory farm waste lagoons, their criticism is likely to have little impact so long as the object of animal agricultural production receives as little attention as does oil drilling in Chad or Nigeria. The object of the factory farm, of course, is no more merely "beef" than cows are carrots. But insofar as Big Greens like WWF focus virtually exclusively on the impacts of greenhouse gas emissions on human populations, they miss the fact that the logic that governs the capitalist production adversely affecting human life and health is the logic that permits the commodification of the factory farmed nonhuman animal; the subjugation of human and nonhuman animals are, in fact, inextricably linked. Nancy Fraser flirts, without quite acknowledging, this connection when she observes that:

> Consider, first, the internal links between natural despoliation and racial/imperial expropriation. Claims of terra nullius to the contrary, the chunks of nature that capital appropriates are virtually always the life conditions of some human group: their habitat and meaning-laden place of social interaction; their means of livelihood and material basis of social reproduction. Moreover, the human groups in capital's crosshairs are virtually always those that have been stripped of the power to defend themselves . . .[24]

While Fraser certainly captures an aspect of the impact of capitalist expropriation on human communities in relation to the damages exacted against nature, the "chunks" she refers to preemptively exclude the "life conditions" of nonhuman animal species; in effect, nonhuman animal life is simply absorbed and thereby rendered invisible in her analysis as "chunks of nature." But this omission allies Fraser with the Big Greens who also take great pains to highlight the impacts of capitalist expropriation on vulnerable human populations, and thus effectively reduce nonhuman animal life to "chunks" that can't be stripped of the power to defend themselves because their value as sentient entities has already been stripped down to exchange value.

The upshot here is that arguments very much like Fraser's are often reflected in the ad campaigns of environmental organizations who claim to be acting on behalf of the planet and its inhabitants, but whose actions actually help reproduce the logic of commodification. One compelling example that nonhuman animals are reducible to "chunks of nature" is that animal welfare and/or suffering doesn't feature anywhere on the websites of Big Greens like WWF, or in their discussions of "Beef." As Carol Adams might put it, the cows whose factory farm lives are horrific regardless the sanitized images to which we're treated on the WWF website, actually function in the same way as a resource for the Big Greens as they do for Big Animal Agriculture: as an "*absent referent*": fully depersonalized, preemptively stripped of any recognition of the capacity for sentience, and converted into the exchange value "beef" commands in the global markets.[25] The value of the cow is *disarticulated*—both in the reference to "beef" and materially as an embodied creature. The issue for WWF members and donors isn't whether nonhuman animals should be objects of human consumption, but simply how to make sustainable the production of beef (pork, poultry) in a world caught between the competing interests of increasing demand for meat and the need to curb greenhouse gas emissions.[26] There is no such thing as sustainable animal agriculture but, figuring this out won't be due to some deeper interrogation concerning whether sentient creatures ought to be regarded as morally considerable—we have already crossed that Rubicon. Should the factory farm ever be abandoned, it will likely be because the potential for climate change calamite will make hamburgers too pricy.

THE COMMODIFICATION OF TRADITION AND THE "ETIQUETTE OF DENIAL"

Until fairly recently, few have considered in any sustained way the morality of wet markets, at least in light of their potential relation to habitat loss, deforestation, as disease vectors—or as a materialization of the commodification of sentience. Among other things, wet markets sell live animals, wild and domesticated, provide subsistence livelihoods to small farmers, and form part of cultural tradition in many countries, in this case—China. While animal rights defenders have sought on occasion to bring attention, for example, to the cruelty of the Chinese dog meat trade,[27] it's the advent of SARS-CoV-2 (Covid-19) and its impacts on human health that has incited the condemnation of wet markets despite accusations of cultural imperialism and hypocrisy. Yet, as Matthew Scully writes for *National Review*, when cultural tradition collides with market forces in the midst of global pandemic, the issues become far more complex:

> Already, in the Western media, chronologies of the pandemic have taken to passing over details of the live-animal markets, which have caused viral outbreaks before and would all warrant proper judgment in any case. News coverage picks up the story with the Chinese government's cover-up of early coronavirus cases and its silencing of the heroic Wuhan doctors and nurses who tried to warn us. To brush past the live markets in fear of seeming "xenophobic," "racist," or unduly judgmental of other people and other ways is, however, to lose sight of perhaps the most crucial fact of all. We don't know the endpoint of this catastrophe, but we are pretty certain that its precise point of origin was what Dr. Anthony Fauci politely calls "that unusual human–animal interface" of the live markets, which he says should all be shut down immediately—presumably including the markets quietly tolerated in our own country. In other words, the plague began with savage cruelty to animals.[28]

What has changed, in other words, is not merely the advent of Covid-19, and the prospect of its *zoonotic transmission* from nonhuman animals to human beings, but that whatever the issues concerning judgments of cultural imperialism, the threat posed by asymptomatic spread takes priority precisely because the "endpoint of the catastrophe" is existential.[29] As Scully might agree, "endpoint" is a relative term; after all, it can just as well describe "savage cruelty" to a single creature as it can the human body count from coronavirus. But as Scully also observes, although "the plague began with savage cruelty to animals," we only seem to become courageous enough to brave the criticism that condemning wet markets is racist or xenophobic when we can safely shift the focus from the savagery to nonhuman animals to the prospect of global pandemic sickening and sometimes killing human beings. In short, we exploit the moral imperative to protect human health as a shield against accusations of cultural imperialism.

Yet, while Scully is certainly right to point out the hypocrisy in condemning Chinese wet markets even as we ignore the misery that characterizes American factory farms, the conclusion he draws, that plagues "have a way of prompting us to take stock of our lives and remember what really matters" seems tepid, even resigned. Taking stock of our personal shortcomings is unlikely to pose any real threat to the capitalist forces and institutions that materialize animal cruelty in the name of profit—wet markets, factory farms, the dog meat trade, circuses, zoos. Indeed, as the evidence of the speedy post-pandemic return to wet markets and fast food shows, leaving it to individual consumers whose traditions are already corrupted by mass marketing is not likely to reduce the quotient of suffering for human or nonhuman beings. In short, my "wow, I should do better" won't liberate a single pangolin nor will it stave off the next pandemic.

Consider a different example, one that strikes a somewhat similar chord as Scully's, but is more directly critical of the capitalist forces at work in the zoonotic transmission of disease, yet fails to arrive at what is arguably Scully's most important insight, namely, that "the plague began with savage cruelty to animals." In *Cannibal Capitalism*, Nancy Fraser argues that:

> [t]o see why [the advent of Covid-19 "establishes beyond all doubt the need to abolish this social system one and for all"], *consider nature*. It was none other than capital's cannibalization of that vital support of its own existence (and ours!) that exposed humans to SARS-CoV-2. Long harbored by bats in remote caves, the coronavirus that causes Covid-19 made the zoonotic leap to us in 2019 by way of some yet unidentified bridging species, possibly pangolins. But what brought the bat into contact with that intermediary, and the latter into contact with us, is already clear: namely, the combined effects of global warming, on the one hand, and tropical deforestation on the other. What is also clear is that both of these are the progeny of capital, driven by an insatiable hunger for profit.[30]

While Fraser is certainly right to point the finger at capital's "insatiable hunger for profit" as the driver of zoonotic transmission, it's striking that she makes no mention of the central site of exchange that enables it, the wet markets whose "savage cruelty" materializes the commodification of sentient nonhuman animals. Indeed, for Fraser both bats and pangolins appear only as disease conduits; her opening reference to "nature" casts them as *de facto* data points along the trajectory of global warming, deforestation, and global pandemic.

Fraser does go on to make clear that the devastating impacts of global warming and deforestation have "eviscerated the habitats of innumerable species, triggering mass migrations, creating new proximities among previously distanced but now distressed organisms, and promotes novel transfers of pathogens among them." She mentions pigs, chimpanzees, and camels in addition to bats and pangolins as zoonotic hosts.[31] But it's very clear that the calamite that concerns Fraser is not that of the cruelty to any particular animal terrorized in a wet market cage, but rather the impacts of capital-fueled

Covid-19 on human beings for which some nonhuman animal species supply the vehicle of transmission. In other words, however otherwise sharp their analyses of the relationship between the commerce of wet markets and the Covid-19 viral crisis, both Scully and Fraser miss the element most crucial to understanding how this relationship could come about—and why it will happen again and again. On the one hand, while Scully astutely identifies "savage cruelty" as the root origin of the zoonotic transmission responsible for the pandemic, he fails to anchor that cruelty to its own ideological "justification" in the logic of commodification. On the other, while Fraser rightly condemns capitalism's predisposition to cannibalize its own existential conditions as a driving factor in the conditions that brought human beings into contact with pangolins and bats, she nonetheless fails to connect that cannibalism to its material effects—savage cruelty.

In short, if among our aims is to understand what role capitalism has played in the production of crises like the Covid-19 pandemic, a deeper conceptual excavation is clearly necessary concerning the logic that governs our relationship with nonhuman life and the ecologies we share. Scully's description of that relationship as "savage cruelty" should be read as a warning:

> We in the West don't eat pangolins, turtles, civets, peacocks, monkeys, horses, foxes, and wolf cubs—that's all a plus. But for the animals we do eat, we have sprawling, toxic, industrial "mass-confinement" farms that look like concentration camps. National "herds" and "flocks" that all would expire in their misery but for a massive use of antibiotics, among other techniques, to maintain their existence amid squalor and disease—an infectious "time bomb" closer to home as bacterial and viral pathogens gain in resistance. And a whole array of other standard practices like the "intensive confinement" of pigs, in gestation cages that look borrowed from Asia's bear-bile farms; the bulldozing of lame "downer cows"; and "maceration" of unwanted chicks, billions routinely tossed into grinders. All of which leave us very badly compromised as any model in the decent treatment of animals.[32]

Scully's doubtless right that we're "very badly compromised" with respect to our recognition that the treatment of nonhuman animals in Chinese wet markets is deplorable even as we deploy less violent-sounding euphemisms like "intensive confinement" or "maceration" as part of a strategy to ignore and deny horrific practices like bulldozing "downer cows" in American factory farms. But that it should take a global pandemic that threatens *human* life to get our attention, *even as we continue the hypocrisy*, raises precisely the question Scully doesn't address: what beyond the obvious savagery do these markets have in common? Scully offers a clue: "in general, we keep the sadness and desperation of those creatures as deeply suppressed from conscious thought as possible. An etiquette of denial pushes the subject away, leaving it all for others to bear." Indeed, but what Scully misses (or glosses over) is that insofar as this "etiquette of denial" very often comes cloaked in the appeal to cultural tradition, it functions not merely to "push the subject away," but make of it an affront to question whether the savagery is justified. It's impolite, even imperialist, to query whether an appeal to tradition suffices to justify barbarism, just as it's impolite, even disrespectful, to ask someone standing in a grocery line with their packages of hamburger why they haven't gone vegan. *So gaping, in other words, is the psychic distance between the fact of savagery and the possibility of moral outrage at the conditions that produce it that an appeal to little more than a caricature of "tradition" or "etiquette" is sufficient to push the subjugated away.* That is the genius of the logic of commodification: its capacity to *operationalize* those aspects, however significant or trivial, of cultural tradition that are *expedient* to it as a materialization of exchange value, a marketing gimmick, a revenue-generator.

The product of the wet market is not only the pangolin, the turtle, or the wolf cub slaughtered and taken home for dinner, but the image or *simulacrum* of cultural tradition that, albeit debauched, coopted, and caricatured, is represented *as* respected and preserved such that only the ill-mannered or boorish would question its significance. The ill-mannered thus becomes a dismissible object of righteous indignation. It can be ignored, denied, even scorned as if a violation of the etiquette respecting tradition is a worse thing than the savagery meted out in its name. Or: *irony is a savagery hidden behind an etiquette evinced in the name of tradition itself expropriated in the service of capital, but clothed in the language of "ought" or "respect," or "how dare you?"* This too is the genius of the logic of commodification: that *indignation can be exploited in the service of consumption*—made all the more effective by the righteous appeal to "food." That we *ought* to respect tradition at the cost of barbarity executed in the service of profits is the epitome not only of human chauvinism, but of the world system it mirrors: capitalism as kleptocracy. For like its analogue in the factory farm, the disarticulated product of the wet market is neither tradition nor culture, but a caricature of "tradition" and "culture" embodied literally and figuratively in the butchered bodies of pangolins or the carcasses of bludgeoned turtles.

Even the idea that tradition can be divorced from the capitalist forces that exploit it makes sense only *as* a marketing pitch, that is, as a product whose credibility as "culture" or "tradition" are advertised *as* exempt from their caricatures displayed on billboards, TV commercials, and travel brochures. To be clear, this is not to say that there's no such thing as culture or tradition; nor is it to suggest that culture and tradition play no active and important role in the life of a country. It is to say that insofar as economic development is driven by the logic of commodification, culture and tradition are as liable to the forces of conversion to exchange value as are the creatures sold at wet markets subject to the disarticulation of their bodies repackaged for consumption as food. Whether this assignment of value as "food" is tradition is largely irrelevant; the pangolin *now* counts as food because it's marketable as food. The turtle *now* counts as food because it commands a price. Once more: the rule of capital is neither chaotic nor excessive. It is simply the machinations of the logic of commodification grinding out "product," cannibalizing its own existential conditions, and ultimately, as Malm puts it, presenting us with the only decision left to make: militant opposition or watching it all go down the drain. Sometimes vigilant conceptual excavation hits the bedrock of molten irony: accusations of imperialism monetized to advance the commercial value of "tradition" or "culture" as products even though "as products" cancels the meaning of "tradition" and makes of culture a billboard, a TikTok, an Amazon deal.

SAVAGERY AND SIMULACRUM IN THE KLEPTOCENE

That culture and tradition can be commandeered as justification for savagery, *and* for ignoring the fact of savagery to profitable effect when packaged as "food," is emblematic of the *Kleptocene*—the age of unregulated increasingly vicious resource theft. Or better: having preempted the value of sentience as an obstacle, the logic of commodification is a logic of *regulated* resource theft insofar as regulation, or *apparent* regulation, serves its interests. Otherwise, all regulatory bets are off despite calving icebergs, viral outbreaks, and record-breaking heat in Death Valley—over and over.[33] The logic's *meaning* is always disclosed by what it seeks to monetize. The "age of the Kleptocene" thus signifies what is intrinsic to it materialized by conditions that expose its mercenary nature; for example, ExxonMobil's plans to drill in ANWR, or a defense of wet markets by appeal to culture or tradition regardless the toxic intersection between the geopolitical location of the markets in the global economy, the facts of zoonotic transmission, or the lethality of a novel coronavirus. Consider, for example, Christos Lynteris and Lyle Fearnley's argument for "why shutting down 'Chinese wet markets' would be a terrible mistake."[34] Certainly, the writers have a point when they argue that Western media reports concerning Chinese wet markets often depend on images that "communicate a sense of disgust toward the eating habits of the Chinese and at the same time reflect a fear of the interconnectedness of two types of 'emergence' in China: viral emergence and economic emergence," and that:

> "wet markets" are portrayed as emblems of Chinese otherness: chaotic versions of oriental bazaars, lawless areas where animals that should not be eaten are sold as food, and where what should not be mingled comes together (seafood

> and poultry, serpents and cattle). This fuels Sinophobia and anxieties of what anthropologists have long identified as "matter out of place": a symbolic system of pollution through which proscriptions and prescriptions of what foods or foodstuffs may be combined is held up.[35]

Lynteris and Fearnley are also right that the expectation China will conform to a Western model of economic development out of the desire to mimic Western ideals or out of economic vulnerability is little more than Sinophobic prejudice tinged with fear that China will do no such thing. They're right to point out that there's no one kind of "wet market," that assessing the risks posed to human health must be accompanied by a better understanding of the differences between them. Wet markets, they argue, "provided important livelihoods to independent smallholder farmers" especially given the history of the Agricultural Producers Co-operatives introduced in the 1950s by Mao Zedong,[36] the "post-Mao market reforms" that followed, and a "Second leap" that sought to greatly expand food production by building heavily capitalized supply chains "often centered on slaughter houses and processing facilities."

But, like Scully, what Lynteris and Fearnley miss is that the narrative against which they seek to defend small-scale farmers and farming traditions in China is the story of the expropriation of those very traditions in the interest of the country's capacity to compete in the global capitalist marketplace. The history of the post-Mao market reforms is not, other than as window-dressing, the history of a return to respect for small farmer traditions. It's the history of a culture commodified in a fashion most conducive to insuring the operations of capital under changing geopolitical and economic conditions The preservation of wet markets does not have as its first objective food, but rather merely the *simulacrum of the traditions of food* that can be exploited to sell nonhuman animals *as* food regardless the impact to habitat. Maintaining the wet market preserves the social order that helps to insure a steady reserve of labor, thereby helping to prevent disruption in the flow of goods and services even in the face of crises like viral outbreaks. As Lynteris and Fearnley hint:

> Anthropologists have discussed in some detail how the Chinese model of development . . . has been perceived in the West as a threat, both in political and cultural terms: China's economic development because of its rapid nature and the competition this might pose to the US or EU economies; and culturally, because reforms seem incompatible with western expectations of modernisation. In short, rather than China adapting to capitalism, capitalism (in China) is adapting to China.[37]

Indeed, but "capitalism is not adapting to China" because it operates on anything less or different than the logic of commodification, but because what makes the logic boundlessly adaptive is the absence of barriers that might otherwise be supplied by other values, first and foremost, sentience. Lynteris and Fearnley unwittingly concede this when they point out that "[w]here markets do contain what many western media portray as 'wild animals,' the majority of these are actually bred and farmed in captivity, such as mallard ducks, frogs, or snakes. Only a smaller proportion of animals are actually poached from the wild for sale."

What matters, in other words, is not the form that savagery takes; whether captured from the wild or bred in the misery of a factory farm, what concerns Lynteris and Fearnley is not the animal, but rather our perception of what counts as *as* food and whether the conditions under which food is produced and distributed can become vectors for viral transmission to human beings. That they can safely assume Westerners will be relieved to know that most of these animals are bred in captivity only reinforces the commodification of sentience that undergirds the market—Chinese or otherwise, a point reinforced by their claim that the reason wet markets should remain open is because the rule of capital by which they operate will merely reconstitute itself as a black market less regulable, and potentially more hazardous to human health:

> A permanent shutdown of "wet markets" would affect patterns of food consumption in ways that are unknowable but potentially harmful to public health. It would deprive Chinese consumers of a food sector that accounts for 30–59% of their food supplies. Due to the large number of farmers, traders and consumers involved, the abolition of "wet markets" is also likely to lead to an explosion of an uncontrollable black market, as it did when such a ban was attempted in 2003, in response to SARS, as well as in 2013–14, in response to avian influenza H7N9.[38]

While it might well be true that shutting down wet markets could lead to food shortages and the rise of black markets, the reasoning here remains circular and ultimately self-defeating. *It's precisely the absence of consideration for sentient life combined with the food insecurity of a human population whose growth is accelerated by the rise of industrial food production, itself driven by the super-power economic aspirations of the Chinese state, that makes the zoonotic transmission of deadly viruses more and more possible.* As Emma Gosalvez reports for North Carolina University, "[s]ix out of every 10 infectious diseases in people are zoonotic . . . Other zoonotic diseases to emerge in the past couple of decades have included SARS, H1N1, or the 'swine flu,' and AIDS," and "[s]ome of the worst diseases have emerged from illegal wildlife markets," . . . "The animals are sort of stacked on top of each other, they're usually still alive, they're still breathing and defecating, so it's a very good place for viruses to spread."[39] We might be tempted to characterize

Gosalvez's report as an example of Western prejudice and dismiss it as such. There could even be a kernel of truth in the criticism. We can defend the right to food for Chinese workers, and workers everywhere, and be on solid moral footing. We can raise the banner of tradition and culture, and of course find something of great value in doing so. We can insist on a nation-state's rightful place in the global competition for recognition. But insofar as viruses like Covid-19 are borne of the zoonotic interface that results from the habitat loss that inevitably results from the ambitions of farmers regardless the scale of their operation; insofar as such outbreaks are likely to be made more virulent and frequent by a climate crisis whose toll on our own existential condition is becoming clearer by the day; insofar as this entire chaotic world system of the social, economic, and environmental owes the suffering of its subjugates, human and nonhuman alike, to the radicle of capitalist exchange, the commodification of sentience, it does not matter whether Gosalvez's report is tinged with imperialism; it *can't* matter, as Fraser might agree, when the cannibalistic nature of this system threatens to bring it all down.

Put differently, whether a particular report, representation, image, or assignment of value reflects the imperialism of its origin *cannot* matter. The existential stakes at this perilous juncture in history are too high. Where our concern for the impacts of the climate crisis continue to be overruled by appeals to "culture" and "tradition" expropriated and fully capitalized, culture and tradition will themselves be the casualties, even if we're no longer in a position to recognize their intrinsic value. This isn't because culture and tradition lack such value, but because "intrinsic" will be defeated by hunger, violence, disease, and death. Self-defeat can, of course, appear in many guises: war, famine, hunger, human and nonhuman migration, terrorism, disease. But the lesson, as Dawson might point out, is in the Pangolin: just as this species faces extinction, so might we; as Elizabeth Kolbert suggests, *that* is the Sixth Extinction. Appeal to culture and tradition will no more save us from the anthropogenic monsters we've created than the Pangolin from the wet market.[40] This is the arrogance that defines the Kleptocene.

THE GEOPOLITICS OF FOOD SECURITY: GENETICS IN THE PROVINCE OF PROFIT

What wet markets and factory farms have in common is a logic of commodification that takes sentience to pose no obstacle to exchange value and, having crossed that Rubicon, has little incentive short of profit losses not to remain indifferent to savagery, whatever form it takes: being bludgeoned to death with a metal pipe or crushed to death at the bottom of a cage stuffed with other animals. Whether pigs or pangolins, chickens or peacocks, lambs or dogs, nonhuman animals delimit the commodifiable and thereby make the conversion to exchange value of everything possible. Naturalizing the cruelty required to carry out *and* ignore the bulldozing of sick cows, the grinding up of male chicks, or the selling of Pangolins for dinner, confers upon every other form of savagery the prospect of an acceptable price. What may have originated in culture is now fully the province of profit such that to defend it requires a divorce of the cultural from the capitalized that, while it may expose the extent to which culture can become commodified, can no more save it than it's possible to travel back in time. If what gains our attention to live animal markets, to the "unusual human-animal interface," as Anthony Fauci courteously puts it,[41] is reserved to the potentially calamitous impacts for *us*, it is hardly surprising that where no such consequences follow for *us* that can't be ignored, or our enculturated denial insures "we" can ignore such impacts so long as they fall on "others," business as usual will remain the order of the day; the logic of commodification will remain uninterrogated. Indeed, even where zoonotic transmission is acknowledged as the genetic source of viral outbreak, references to the welfare of the nonhuman animals identified as its conduits gets no more attention than whatever are the implications for human interests and health. Consider, for example, a recent piece from the esteemed medical journal, *The Lancet*, in defense of wet markets despite the Covid-19 pandemic:

> Severe acute respiratory syndrome coronavirus 2 (SARS-CoV-2), which causes COVID-19, may have emerged at a wet market in Wuhan, China. The term wet market denotes any place selling fresh produce, but global attention has focused on markets selling live, sometimes wild, animals. To avoid future pandemics of zoonotic diseases, leading international figures have called for an international ban on wet markets. However, from the perspective of planetary health, which draws a connection between the health of humans and their environment, engaging in small-scale animal husbandry—of which live-animal markets often form a part—while reducing global meat consumption and more rigorously enforcing a ban on illegal wildlife trade would be beneficial. Wet markets provide an important source of protein to populations in low-income regions and the food systems in which such markets are embedded, and they are more environmentally sustainable than industrial food systems. Banning markets with live animals is likely to disadvantage both human and planetary health; a more effective approach would be to improve hygiene and regulatory standards at such markets, eliminate industrial-scale movement of live animals, and outlaw sales of wild animals known to be of risk for disease spread.[42]

To be sure, there are vital issues here concerning food security in low-income regions, what constitutes an environmentally sustainable food system, what contributes to planetary and atmospheric stability, and how each of these bears on the industrialization of food. One thing, however, seems clear: the logic of commodification that takes advantage of food insecurity to insure low wages and high production is precisely the same as that which subjugates nonhuman animals as "food."

That what positions the wet market as a vital source of food, particularly during a crisis, is the same rule of capital that drives every extractivist enterprise at the cost of the environment and the atmosphere can only ultimately undermine the capacity of that node in the food supply chain to fulfill its role. It's thus self-contradictory to conclude, as the *Lancet* editors do, that the reason wet markets should not be banned is because they provide an "important source of protein." That can, in fact, no more remain true than, as Dawson shows, whale blubber could remain a source of oil regardless how important was its use or lucrative was its international exchange value,[43] or that coal wouldn't run out. Mark Stoll may put the point most clearly in his discussion of "conservationists":

> Conservationists never challenged industrial capitalism itself. Life without it had become unthinkable. Conservation meant only fixing the environmental problems that industrialization had caused. Industrial capitalism was [capitalist advocate, Stanley] Jevon's goose laying golden eggs, even if it was a sooty wheezing goose. Surely all the beast needed was a little fresh air, a wash, and a bit of uplifting greenspace, and it would produce eggs forever.[44]

Similarly, the Lancet writers seems to be arguing that a return to small-scale animal husbandry, enforcing a ban on illegal wildlife trade, and reducing global meat consumption will insure that we'll escape the next pandemic. But this is as naïve as the belief that there are golden gooses laying golden eggs. Insofar as the commodification of sentience animates domestic animal husbandry *and* the illegal wildlife trade, the *Lancet* claim that it's possible to enforce a ban on the latter is unlikely at best. In whatever form it takes—viral outbreak, extreme weather catastrophe, desertification, habitat collapse—need, especially need for food, will drive what ends up for sale at a wet market. As Dawson argues, even the prospect of extinction will be insufficiently persuasive:

> [n]o efforts were made by the Europeans and their North American competitors to conserve stocks of whales. Instead whalers acted as if their quarry were inexhaustible . . . Although it was clearly in the industry's interest to limit the accelerating predation, the competitive dynamic of industrial capitalism made such forms of conservation impossible. Instead whalers came up with far-fetched arguments to justify their monumentally short-sighted plunder of the oceans.[45]

While we might not describe the *Lancet* defense of wet markets as "far-fetched," the hope that a ban on wildlife trade is any more likely to avoid the extinction of the Pangolin in the 21st century than what became the near wholesale collapse of the Blue Whale by 1966 is a risky gamble. As the *Lancet* editors make clear, their priority is not species preservation but rather the prevention of zoonotic transmission. This too, however, only reiterates and reinforces the commodification of sentience that undermines their defense of wet markets: appeals to "environmental sustainability" that seek to justify a ban on wildlife trade primarily on the grounds of its potentially negative impacts for human health are unlikely to have substantive positive effects for achieving the goal of preventing zoonotic transmission since, absent any genuine concern for species diversity and conservation, environmental sustainability is also likely to suffer—driving even greater food insecurity, more wildlife hunting, more habitat encroachment—and more opportunities for zoonotic transmission.

One response here is to argue for the aggressive subsidizing of small-scale livestock farmers. But this strategy will also fail: although the *Lancet* editors are certainly right to take seriously food insecurities in human populations, the implicit assumption that rural animal husbandry can be sustained without a radical transformation of the economic conditions that gave rise to the crises that endanger it can only reinforce a logic of commodification that will hasten the demise of the small farm. First, and perhaps most obviously, the potential impacts of the climate crisis, itself intimately associated with the emergence of zoonotic viral transmission, did not originate with Covid-19, and will not expire with vaccine access. At every scale of production large and small, for example, China's pork industry "is still reeling from the 2019 outbreak of African swine fever that reduced the country's pig herd by more than 40% and drove up prices."[46] In this case, the supply chain from small farm to market survived, but not without serious impact bound to be repeated given that every link in that chain is forged out of hydrocarbons, including porcine bodies fed on corn, wheat and soy grown with the help of petroleum distillate pesticides.[47]

That the wet market supply chain is localized does not, in other words, render it immune from the same forces that impact larger industrial concerns; indeed, as the Swine fever case shows, precisely the opposite is the case. It thus stands to reason that being more ecologically sustainable in virtue of small size, cultural attractiveness, and the livelihood of millions of Chinese families won't protect wet market vendors from the health and economic impacts of Covid-19 or future viral outbreaks; again, the opposite is the case. Moreover, to whatever extent illegal trade in wildlife would likely continue in the face of a wet market ban, this is itself a *materialization* of the commodification of sentience, a preservation of tradition in name only since, as the *Lancet* editors implicitly acknowledge, the primary driver is the struggle for survival in a fully capitalized Chinese economy whose chain supermarkets compete with wet markets now more than ever. In fact, in at least one respect, the Covid-19 outbreak in Wuhan was a boon for supermarket chains:

> [Wet market] [s]tall owners in Wuhan said they were not optimistic after their business was badly hurt by the strict shutdowns in China, which ordered a temporary ban on trade and consumption of wildlife in January. "There is no business and no one is coming," said a worker chopping fish who only gave her surname, Zhang. "Everywhere is blocked and people cannot come in. Everyone is scared to go out and contract the virus." Wuhan will spend 200 million yuan ($28 million) to upgrade its 425 farmers' markets, in a campaign to improve hygiene, city officials said on Friday. Still, some worry they may not stay around long enough to see it. "We don't have any income and business," said Jin. "If it goes on like this, it will be very difficult for us to survive."[48]

Another wet-market vendor remarks that "[e]ven the supermarket is full of people," despite the fact that disease transmission is well understood to be person-to-person regardless locale (in fact, outdoor venues are less likely to pose a transmission hazard). In short, a defense of wet markets on the grounds that they're more ecologically sustainable, culturally significant, and offer a higher level of access to food security ignores precisely the logic of commodification that positions industries like "Big Agriculture" to take advantage of crises, especially as strictly enforced lock-down measures spur a rising tide of on-line shopping.[49] To the extent, moreover, that small farmers depend on the same pesticides and the same culturally exploitive advertising to compete, it's also just not true, and will likely be less true come the next crisis, that they're necessarily more ecologically sustainable, culturally preservative, or offer competitive access to food security.

It's not, in other words, merely pandemic that has the capacity to dramatically alter the Chinese food landscape; it's the shifting of economically advantaged position that, as Naki Mendoza observes in 2016, has already undergone significant change driven by the pressure to feed a growing Chinese population, maintain resistance to genetically modified fast-growing food commodities produced by global North companies like *Monsanto*, and sponsor the development of a Chinese GMO industry via state-owned *ChemChina* or *SinoChem Corp*. As Mendoza notes, wherever China goes with respect to GMO development the implications for global food markets will be immense. "Officially, Beijing has a strict stance against genetically modified products. China's farmers are barred from growing GMO crops and the government only allows imports of genetically altered grains for use in animal feed," she explains. "But unofficially the country has been shifting its position, most likely as it weighs the implications of its booming population growth and food security." In recent speeches President Xi Jinping has called on China to "boldly research, innovate and dominate the high points of GMO techniques,"[50] and, as it turns out, acquire competitor corporations like Swiss-based Syngenta. One reason for this shift is China's 1.4 billion people, a population outgrowing the capacity of its small farms, made more fearful of food shortages by the prospect of future pandemic. As David Fickling reports for Bloomberg, the "logic behind the 2016 acquisition [of Syngenta] was simple":

> The country has a fifth of the world's population and just 7% of its agricultural land, so has to use about a third of the globe's agricultural chemicals to feed itself. This is pushing its environment toward breaking point . . . Diplomatic relations with major food exporters such as the U.S., Australia, and Brazil are difficult, so China needs to build its expertise in crop technologies and genetically modified seeds if it's to have a hope of maintaining food security. The fate of the Soviet Union, which fell in part because of its dependence on imported grain, is a grim reminder of what could go wrong.[51]

Food security may be the primary driver, but it's certainly not the only motive for the "state-owned Chinese giants" Sinochem and ChemChina to merge, potentially risking "a fresh round of foreign-ownership investigations over their Swiss-based Syngenta unit."[52] As Fickling points out, among the reasons such a merger would fail are that 47% of Chinese consumers surveyed in 2018 were highly skeptical of GMO produced crops; indeed 14% associate GMOs with bioterrorism. He remarks that "[w]hile the country imports substantial volumes of GMO foods from overseas commercialization on domestic farms is still in its infancy, and attracts unusually strong public dissent." It would appear, then, that the strong preference of many Chinese for non-GMO food combined with the argument for the preservation of wet markets on grounds of culture and tradition would insure a future for the small farmers largely responsible for supplying vendors—but we cannot conclude that is the case.

As Fickling also points out, President Xi understands acutely that China's geopolitical position can also impact his country's food security, and with it the compliance of a growing population in a time of crisis, especially as the United States has now listed SinoChem and ChemChina as "Communist Chinese military companies." Despite its failure, in other words, the point of a possible merger of Sino-Chem and ChemChina was to gain greater clout over the international trade and development of GMOs. Could President Xi have gained that clout, *wet markets would not have stood in his way.* This is so not because he does or doesn't care about the food preferences of his countrymen, *and* it's not because Xi's worried at least in the first place about food insecurity. It's because *food insecurity is geopolitical insecurity* in a world dominated by an increasing number of crises driven directly or indirectly by climate change and its ancillary implications, including the prospect of zoonotic transmission of disease. Like most if not all of his fellow world leaders confronted by the economic impacts of future global pandemic, Xi's is an essentially kleptocratic point of view, thinly regulated by the laws and customs of international trade agreements. From this point of view, the life or death of the wet market signifies matters of market share, patterns of consumption, and consumer attitudes, but, contrary to the *Lancet* argument, its survival is no more *about* preserving culture or tradition or *about* environmental sustainability than the advantage a viral pandemic might present to a supermarket chain or a biotech corporation.

WEAPONIZING CHARGES OF "CULTURAL IMPERIALISM" IS THE IMPERIALISM OF THE KLEPTOCENE

A limited appreciation of the geopolitical dynamics governing the question whether criticism of wet markets constitutes a form of cultural imperialism is, I suggest, only the most obvious way in which the *Lancet* defense undermines its own best intentions. A second issue concerns the rather rosy picture it paints concerning the potential of wet markets to aid in reducing greenhouse emissions. To review: like Lynteris and Fearnley, the *Lancet* editors support avoiding the "tint" of "Western Imperialism." But their argument claims an additional benefit: the reduction of greenhouse gas emissions associated with large-scale animal agriculture. It might be better, they argue, to encourage, at least tolerate, wet markets since they're not an atmosphere-destroying polluter like, say, the animal agriculture giant, Smithfield Farms.[53] This may be true on the short-term, but it doesn't actually matter either for atmospheric integrity, the prevention of viral outbreak, or even the preservation of culture for the barely-more-than short term. First, while the Lancet's advice seems more sensitive to traditional dietary habits, or encourages less meat consumption, it fails to acknowledge that the demand for meat, domesticated or wild, is itself growing right along with the burgeoning human populations of the developing world.[54] Second, the same logic that normalizes and thereby ignores the commodification of sentient wildlife also normalizes and ignores the subjugation of vulnerable human beings; "one worker from a slaughterhouse in Sioux City, Iowa, unburdened himself: 'The worst thing, worse than the physical danger, is the emotional toll. Pigs down on the kill floor have come up and nuzzled me like a puppy. Two minutes later I had to kill them—beat them to death with a pipe. I can't care.'" Is it cultural imperialism to draw an analogy between this Tyson slaughterhouse worker and the Chinese slaughterhouse worker? Do benign-sounding references to the importance of small-scale farmers, regardless country, act as smokescreens to conceal the fact that the vast majority of workers confronted with the suffering of nonhuman animals work in slaughterhouses or meat processing plants? The logic of commodification draws no distinction other than whether the production of nonhuman animal bodies is scalable to mass consumption. To the extent that sentience is no obstacle to the conversion to exchange value, neither animal bodies, workers' capacity for labor, or worker's bodies are immune to disarticulation; one is called "processing," another "the division of labor," the last low wage replaceability of sick or injured workers. Insofar as the logic determines what enterprise will survive, both serve mass production, especially in growing developing world populations. Indeed, the attention drawn to wet markets during the Covid-19 pandemic has galvanized their defense as cultural tradition and national pride, and provided a rhetorical weapon to combat Western imperialism, even if "rhetorical weapon" is as deep as the appeal to culture actually goes.[55]

This leads directly, however, to a third point against the *Lancet* claim that the reason wet markets should be left alone is that their continued existence will help to slow the rise of greenhouse gas emissions: *cultural imperialism is a real thing, and the Lancet's argument is a prime example of it.* Why? Because we have to assume that were it the case that wet markets did not contribute to the curbing of greenhouse gas emissions, the *Lancet* editors would not defend them. Hence, the appeal to culture and tradition is, in fact, a smokescreen to advance the real objective: combatting the climate crisis. It's perhaps darkly ironic that the *Lancet* editors effectively resort to the same exploitive strategies as the capitalist to defend the wet markets. But the point is that despite the fact that the defense of culture and tradition is preemptively undermined by the appropriation of wet markets to the logic of commodification, that does not exonerate the *Lancet* against the accusation of cultural imperialism. If anything, that accusation sticks all the more given that, regardless whether their ostensive motives are defensible, the ulterior motive remains undisclosed and arguably nefarious: exploiting the appeal to culture or tradition as a weapon in the war against climate change. There is likely no better a motive than one contemplated to combat the climate crisis. But that cannot justify weaponizing a cultural institution, especially one intimate connected to food security, and especially since such a strategy would likely be summarily abandoned once it was no longer effective; *that is cultural imperialism*. Understood from the point of view of the logic of commodification, the *Lancet* conscripts the charge "cultural imperialism!" to the rule of capital.

Finally, the *Lancet's* appeal to "planetary health" is not only short-sighted and hypocritical, but yet another way in which their argument in defense of wet markets is self-defeating. Return for a moment to the story of ExxonMobil: the same logic that makes possible oil and gas extraction in highly sensitive environments like the Arctic or ANWR also drives a growing Chinese population's demand for "proteins." The rule of capital quantifies value according to the demand created by what consumers can be convinced they need. The actual value of gasoline and animal bodies, power grids and supply chains, cannot be determined by appeal to culture and tradition because the very culture and tradition they cite has already become fully appropriated, disarticulated, repurposed, and repackaged as capital—with a billboard veneer of "culture." There is, in other words, nothing to salvage as a backstop against increasing greenhouse gas emissions; the myth of endless resources has as its equally self-defeating analogue the myth of everlasting culture. Planetary resources and human cultures have suffered irreparable compromise via the logic of commodification. Both are subject to similar forms of denial, concealment, theft, and pretense; the claim to "endless" or "sustainable" in each case is as false as subterfuge mounted in their defense is transparently mercenary. To argue, as the *Lancet* editors do, that wet markets should remain open because they produce a lower quotient of greenhouse gas emissions is like arguing that grass fed beef is a morally permissible alternative to factory farmed meat: neither require any transformation in the way we think about consumption as an entitlement. Hence neither pose any significant challenge to the logic of commodification. The *Lancet* justification of wet markets is in fact a reinforcement of the central governing premise of capitalism: not only does its argument for reducing greenhouse gas emissions pose no challenge at all to the commodification of sentience, the argument actually advances the logic by effectively trading the continuing commodification of sentient life, including that of workers, for a reduction of greenhouse gas emissions—that will be short-lived at best. To be clear, the issues here are not merely whether good ends, like reducing carbon emissions, justify sketchy means; such reasoning permits us to ignore savagery on the grounds that the ends are worth it. Not only will the ends, ecological stability, reduction of disease transmission vectors, and atmospheric integrity, not be achieved, but more: reaffirming against its deleterious consequences the commodification of sentience will contribute to environmental and atmospheric erosion, coarsen ever-further our sense of entitlement, accelerate the likelihood of catastrophes like extreme weather events and pandemic outbreaks, aggravate geopolitical jockeying for access to food production technologies, invite war over water between nations who identify each other's biotech ventures as military-grade weaponry, and thereby hasten the march of the kleptocene to its nihilistic conclusion.

NOTES

1. Ashley Dawson. *Extinction: A Radical History*. (New York, NY: OR Books, 2016), 40–41.
2. Dawson, 43–6.
3. Kenny Torrella and Marina Bolotnikova. "Undercover Audio of a Tyson Employee Reveals 'Free-Range' Chicken is Meaningless." VOX, 8.2.23. https://www.vox.com/future-perfect/23724740/tyson-chicken-free-range-humanewashing-investigation-animal-cruelty.
4. Christopher Shields. "In the Shadows of Dominion: Anthropocentrism and the Continuance of the Culture of Oppression." Doctoral Dissertation, East Tennessee State University, 2015. https://dc.etsu.edu/etd/2474/, 28–48.
5. Christophe Bonneuil and Jean-Baptiste Fressoz. *The Shock of the Anthropocene*. (Brooklyn, NY: Verso, 2017), 154.
6. Bonneuil and Fressoz, 209.
7. Torrella and Bolotnikova, https://www.vox.com/future-perfect/23724740/tyson-chicken-free-range-humanewashing-investigation-animal-cruelty.
8. Simon Deakin and Wolfgang Meng. "The Governance of Covid-19: Anthropogenic Risk, Evolutionary Learning, and the Future of the Social State." https://academic.oup.com/ilj/article/49/4/539/6020142.
9. Torrella and Bolotnikova, https://www.vox.com/future-perfect/23724740/tyson-chicken-free-range-humanewashing-investigation-animal-cruelty.
10. Shannon Hall. "Exxon Knew about Climate Change Almost 40 Years Ago." *Scientific American*, 10.26.15. https://www.scientificamerican.com/article/exxon-knew-about-climate-change-almost-40-years-ago/.
11. Jennifer Dluohy. "Environmental Groups Warn Alaska Drillers Not to Pursue ANWR Leases." *World Oil*, 9.17.20. https://www.worldoil.com/news/2020/9/17/environmental-groups-warn-alaska-drillers-not-to-pursue-anwr-leases.
12. Andreas Malm. *The Progress of This Storm: Nature and Society in a Warming World*. (Brooklyn, NY: Verso, 2020), 106.
13. Bill Chapell. "Trump Administration Moves Closer to Allowing Oil Drilling in Arctic Refuge." *NPR*, 8.17.20. https://www.npr.org/2020/08/17/903239366/trump-administration-sets-plan-for-oil-drilling-in-arctic-refuge.
14. *United Nations Climate Ch*ange (UNFCCC). "The Paris Agreement." https://unfccc.int/process-and-meetings/the-paris-agreement/the-paris-agreement.
15. *United Nations Climate Ch*ange (UNFCCC). "The Paris Agreement." https://unfccc.int/process-and-meetings/the-paris-agreement/the-paris-agreement.
16. Alison Durkee. "Texas Governor Vows to Sue Biden Over Climate Change Orders." *Forbes*, 1.21.21. https://www.forbes.com/sites/alisondurkee/2021/01/28/texas-governor-abbott-vows-to-sue-biden-over-climate-change-orders/?sh=60ff86662db5.

17. ExxonMobil. "Growing the Gulf." https://corporate.exxonmobil.com/Locations/United-States/Growing-the-Gulf.

18. David Wallace-Wells,. *The Uninhabitable Earth*. (New York, NY: Tim Duggan Books, 2019), 161.

19. Wendy Lynne Lee. *Eco-Nihilism: The Philosophical Geopolitics of the Climate Change Apocalypse*. (Lanham, MD: Lexington Books (Rowman and Littlefield, 2016), 372–9.

20. ExxonMobil. "Sustainability at ExxonMobil." https://corporate.exxonmobil.com/news/reporting-and-publications/sustainability-report.

21. Karma Allen. "Polar Bears May Be Extinct by 2100 if Arctic Ice Melts at Projected Rate, According to New Study." *ABC News*, 7.22.20. https://abcnews.go.com/US/polar-bears-extinct-2100-arctic-ice-melts-projected/story?id=71895289.

22. *World Meteorological Association*. "United in Science Report: Climate Change has not Stopped for Covid-19." 9.9.20. https://public.wmo.int/en/media/press-release/united-science-report-climate-change-has-not-stopped-covid19.

23. Malm, 106–7.

24. Nancy Fraser. *Cannibal Capitalism*. (Brooklyn, NY: Verso, 2022), 108.

25. Carol Adams. *Neither Man nor Beast: Feminism and the Defense of Animals*. (Brooklyn, NY: Lantern Books, 2015).

26. *World Wildlife Federation*. "Beef." https://wwf.panda.org/discover/our_focus/food_practice/sustainable_production/beef/.

27. *Animal Asia*. "Cat and Dog Welfare." https://www.animalsasia.org/us/our-work/cat-and-dog-welfare/.

28. Matthew Scully. "China's Wet Markets, America's Factory Farming." *National Review*, 4.9.20. https://www.nationalreview.com/2020/04/chinas-wet-markets-americas-factory-farming-both-violate-moral-common-sense/.

29. *Centers for Disease Control and Prevention* (CDC). "Covid-19." https://www.cdc.gov/coronavirus/2019-ncov/index.html.

30. Fraser, 160.

31. Fraser, 160.

32. Scully. https://www.nationalreview.com/2020/04/chinas-wet-markets-americas-factory-farming-both-violate-moral-common-sense/.

33. Andrea Thompson. "Death Valley Could Set a World Record Hot Temperature." *Scientific American*, 7.14.23. https://www.scientificamerican.com/article/death-valley-could-set-a-world-record-hot-temperature/.

34. Christos Lynteris, and Lyle Fearnley. "Why Shutting Down Chinese Wet Markets Could Be a Terrible Mistake." *The Conversation*. https://theconversation.com/why-shutting-down-chinese-wet-markets-could-be-a-terrible-mistake-130625.

35. Lynteris and Fearnley. "Why Shutting Down Chinese Wet Markets Could Be a Terrible Mistake." *The Conversation*. https://theconversation.com/why-shutting-down-chinese-wet-markets-could-be-a-terrible-mistake-130625.

36. Robin Porter. *From Mao to Market: China Reconfigured*. (New York: Columbia University Press, 2011), 39.

37. Lynteris and Fearnley. "Why Shutting Down Chinese Wet Markets Could Be a Terrible Mistake." *The Conversation*. https://theconversation.com/why-shutting-down-chinese-wet-markets-could-be-a-terrible-mistake-130625.

38. Lynteris and Fearnley. "Why Shutting Down Chinese Wet Markets Could Be a Terrible Mistake." *The Conversation*. https://theconversation.com/why-shutting-down-chinese-wet-markets-could-be-a-terrible-mistake-130625.

39. Emma Gosalvez. "How Habitat Destruction Enables the Spread of Covid-19." *North Carolina State University: College of Natural Resources News*, 4.22.21. https://cnr.ncsu.edu/news/2020/04/habitat-destruction-covid19/.

40. *Mongabay.com*. "Three Pangolin Species Closer to Extinction: IUCN." 12.18.19. https://news.mongabay.com/2019/12/three-pangolin-species-closer-to-extinction-iucn/.

41. Scully. https://www.nationalreview.com/2020/04/chinas-wet-markets-americas-factory-farming-both-violate-moral-common-sense/.

42. *Lancet, The*. "Covid-19, Wet Markets, and Planetary Health." Vol. 4, June 2020. https://www.thelancet.com/pdfs/journals/lanplh/PIIS2542-5196(20)30122-4.pdf.

43. Dawson, 53.

44. Stoll, 139.

45. Dawson, 53–4.

46. Xiaobo Zhang. "Chinese Livestock Farms Struggle Under Covid Restrictions." *International Food Policy Research Institute*, 3.26.20. https://www.ifpri.org/blog/chinese-livestock-farms-struggle-under-covid-19-restrictions.

47. *National Pesticide Information Center*. http://npic.orst.edu/ingred/petroleum-distillates.html.

48. Thomas Suen and Brenda Goh. "Wet Markets in China's Wuhan Struggle to Survive Coronavirus Blow." Reuters, 4.12.20. https://www.reuters.com/article/us-health-coronavirus-china-wuhan-market/wet-markets-in-chinas-wuhan-struggle-to-survive-coronavirus-blow-idUSKCN21U03S.

49. *Nielsen.com*. "China's Shifting Retail Landscape Signals the Permanence of Change Post Covid-19." *Nielsen.com*, 12.16.20. https://www.nielsen.com/us/en/insights/article/2020/chinas-shifting-retail-landscape-signals-the-permanence-of-change-post-covid-19/.

50. Naki. B. Mendoza. "Will Big Agriculture Mergers Impact Smallholder Farmers?" *DEVEX*, 9.29.16. https://www.devex.com/news/will-big-agriculture-mergers-impact-smallholder-farmers-88820.

51. David Fickling. "China's Giant Crop Takeover Has Failed. Time to Admit It." *Bloomberg News*, 12.10.20. https://www.bloomberg.com/opinion/articles/2020-12-10/chemchina-s-syngenta-takeover-is-a-failure-time-to-admit-it.

52. Fickling. "China's Giant Crop Takeover Has Failed. Time to Admit It." *Bloomberg News*, 12.10.20. https://www.bloomberg.com/opinion/articles/2020-12-10/chemchina-s-syngenta-takeover-is-a-failure-time-to-admit-it.

53. Georgina Gustin. "As the Livestock Industry Touts Manure-to-Energy Projects, Environmentalists Cry 'Greenwashing.'" *Inside Climate News*, 12.7.20. https:

//insideclimatenews.org/news/07122020/livestock-industry-manure-energy-natural-gas/.

54. *Beef Magazine*. "Here's Why China is Going to Boom." https://www.beefmagazine.com/livestock-management/here-s-why-china-is-going-to-boom.

55. Kalinga Seneviratne. "'Wet Markets' a Crucial Part of Asian Economy." *China Daily*, 4.29.20. https://www.chinadaily.com.cn/a/202004/29/WS5ea8d13ca310a8b2411527c7.html.

Chapter 2

Normalizing the Disarticulation of Value Across Species

Response to David Wallace-Wells

"IF WE COULD WISH A SOLUTION INTO PLACE . . ."

In *The Uninhabitable Earth*, David Wallace-Wells speculates about whether "we," or some subset of "we," have sufficient imagination to "wish a solution into place" in the ever-more urgent effort to confront the climate crisis.[1] He disagrees with futurist Alex Steffen who, insisting on the enormity of the challenge, argues that the task of shifting to alternative forms of energy is dwarfed by that of reducing demand, itself dwarfed by the challenge of "reinventing how goods and services are provided—given that global supply chains are built with dirty infrastructure and labor markets everywhere are still powered by dirty energy."[2] For Steffen, however, "[a]ll of this" is made harder still by "the monumental cultural undertaking of imagining together a thriving dynamic sustainable future that feels not only possible, but worth fighting for."[3] Wallace-Wells pushes back, arguing, as he puts it just a bit later, against a "dour terminological competition among climate writers aiming to coin a new clarifying language":[4]

> [i]f we could wish a solution into place by imagination, we'd have solved the problem [of the climate crisis] already. In fact, we have imagined the solutions; more than that, we've even developed them, at least in the form of green energy. We just haven't yet discovered *the political will, economic might, and cultural flexibility* to install and activate them, because doing so requires something a lot bigger, and more concrete than imagination—it means nothing short of the complete overhaul of the world's energy systems, transportation, infrastructure and industry and agriculture.[5]

Getting to that sustainable future, in other words, is less about whether we have the know-how, the technology, or the right system of economic exchange, and more about will, "economic might," and whatever Wallace-Wells means by "cultural flexibility." As we've seen, this latter is a freighted notion that, even beyond issues concerning cultural imperialism and appropriation, raises difficult questions about who defines the "we" of those who benefit from such solutions. Who exactly is the "we" whose wishing reflects the right version of "political will"? How do "we" know who this is? Who bears the costs of the "solutions"? In short, whose wishing matters?

These are difficult questions, and we have little time to answer them. Nonetheless, their answers matter because the global, borderless, nature of the climate crisis inevitably intersects with the geopolitical: food security, geographical location, cultural and community identity, political conflict, and ecological deterioration. Whatever writers like Wallace-Wells mean by "solutions," none are exclusive to whether climate change can be mitigated, but bear directly on communities of human and nonhuman inhabitants in danger of being harmed, dispossessed, or even sacrificed. Consider, for example, the climate change mitigation project sponsored by the United Nations/World Bank: "Reducing Emissions from Deforestation and Forest Degradation" or REDD:

> Reducing Emissions from Deforestation and forest Degradation, plus the sustainable management of forests, and the conservation and enhancement of forest carbon stocks (REDD+), is an essential part of the global efforts to mitigate climate change. FAO [Food and Agriculture Organization of the United Nations] supports developing countries in their REDD+ processes and in turning their political commitments, as represented in their Nationally Determined Contributions, into action on the ground. At the core of this work are forests and the fundamental role they play in climate change mitigation, by removing CO_2 from the atmosphere and storing it in biomass and soils. This also means that when forests are cleared or degraded, they can become a source of greenhouse gas (GHG) emissions by releasing that stored carbon. It is estimated that globally, deforestation and forest degradation account for around 11 percent of CO_2 emissions. Halting deforestation is a cost-effective action that has a clear impact in reducing global GHG emissions. FAO's support also helps countries during the later implementation phase of REDD+.[6]

However benign REDD sounds in theory, in reality the program is notoriously controversial because it exploits social and economic inequalities in order to advance an environmental program from which global Northerners benefit at the expense of developing world peoples and their ecologies. Such programs are effectively advertised as if all the relevant parties have signed on as agents and beneficiaries. This is false. Both in description and execution the program significantly benefits the few while others suffer the dispossession of their very means of life. Indeed, the meaning of phrases like "cultural flexibility" functions as little more than a polite euphemism for cultural genocide made possible through forceable relocation in the name of reforestation. REDD's program not only requires the displacement of global South peoples like the Sengwer, but does so at the effective behest of global North consumers resistant to reducing what is already a grossly disproportionate volume of consumption. However less noble-sounding, the truth about REDD is: "move vulnerable peoples out of their communities and their traditional lands to make room to plant more trees that create more CO_2 storage so wealthy global Northerners can keep driving big cars and eating big steaks."

In other words, however outwardly reasonable the FAO description of REDD sounds, its place, to utilize Wallace-Wells' phrasing, in the "complete overhaul of the world's energy systems" isn't actually reasonable at all. REDD materializes the subjugating displacement of food insecure developing world peoples, their ecologies, and their communities. The global South already disproportionately shoulders climate crisis impacts particularly with respect to access to potable water.[7] Programs like REDD only exacerbate these grim conditions, making it all the clearer that what political will, economic might and cultural flexibility actually mean is "massive evictions and forced relocations" in the name of profit:

> According to the *No REDD in Africa Network* (NRAN), the *Sengwer Indigenous Peoples Programme*, and the *Indigenous Peoples' Biocultural Climate Change Assessment Initiative*, "massive evictions and forced relocations" of the Sengwer as "squatters" from their ancestral Kenyan lands in order to reforest it towards carbon emission off-sets is nothing more than another form of capitalist exploitation of the peoples of the global South by powerful profit-driven interests in the global North.[8]

To be clear, I'm not suggesting that Wallace-Wells would necessarily support programs like REDD. I'm also not suggesting that the phrase "cultural flexibility" necessarily maps neatly onto community displacement. But it is this second point that opens a Pandora's Box, and it's not clear, given his rather rosy reference to "our imagined solutions," that Wallace-Wells sees that his somewhat blithe reference to "we" conceals a litany of potential harms. There are at least four reasons why: first, as we've examined with respect to Chinese wet markets, while cultural preservation can be exploited to sustain practices and institutions already coopted to the service of profit, what follows from this isn't license to treat culture and tradition as exploitable or expendable. Rather, environmental writers including myself and Wallace-Wells have a duty to ask more probing questions about the intersection of culture, capitalism, and structural inequality. NRAN seeks to defend the Sengwer's inherently sustainable traditions such as bee-keeping, herb gathering, and small herd cattle grazing *against* the violent seizure of their lands. Yet, according to a 2018 *Euro News* report, "since 2009 the Sengwer tribe has been systematically targeted and violently evicted from Embobut forest by the Kenyan Forest Service guards (KFS) as part of the government's conservation efforts."[9] What NRAN recognizes is that something other or more than reforestation, more than merely wishing for a solution to the climate crisis, is what governs decision-making not only about the "where" such projects will be undertaken, but about "who" can be moved out of the way to make room, in the case of REDD and WaTER, for turning a swath of land into a *monetized planetary ventilator* capable of pumping out just enough oxygen to keep the "chaotic world system" and its sky-high levels of consumption by Westerners going for a bit longer. According to the *Euro News* report by Eileen Gbagbo:

> The Kenyan government, alongside the European Union (EU) embarked on a €31 million Water Tower Protection and Climate Change Mitigation and Adaptation Project (WaTER) in June 2016, expected to run for six years. The main aims of this project were to stimulate the productivity of the ecosystems around Embobut forest and Mount Elgon. The Embobut Forest is one of the most important areas of high forest land in Kenya as it supplies water to the surrounding region. But in the December, the KFS announced that the Sengwer tribe would be evicted by the end of the year in order to begin the project. It mirrored the failings of the World Bank's Natural Resources Management Project (NRMP) as they did not receive prior informed consent from the Sengwer community.[10]

The Kenyan government knew, of course, that it was unlikely to get this consent; it would have amounted to a cultural death wish. Moreover, what the evidence made clear was that the government didn't have to seek permission; the Sengwer command neither the numbers, the property claims, nor the weapons to mount a serious resistance against eviction on their own. "In March 2017," for example, "a man of the Sengwer community was shot dead by the KFS [Kenyan Military Police] and to this day, his widow and family wait to be acknowledged, much less compensated, by the Kenyan government." "'We really are nobodies to them!' says Winnie Kadoshy, a Human Rights Defender and member of Sengwer community, expressing how neglected the community feels by the government." In other words, even as the World Bank project fails, the "we" who remains empowered to wish solutions into place remains largely the same such that for whatever climate change mitigation might be achieved by projects like REDD or WaTER, the "we" who benefits is plainly not *we*.[11]

The second problem for Wallace-Wells claim to represent "we" is that for whatever lip service he pays to the way that other people besides global Northerners live on the planet when he reiterates the claim that "[t]his book is not about the science of warming; it is about what warming means to the way we live on this planet,"[12] he largely glosses over why it is that the *differing ways* people live on the planet matters, *greatly*. For example, what distinguishes the Sengwer's pastoralism from Wuhan, China wet markets as a means to economic survival is that the Sengwer graze herds, gather herbs, and cultivate bee colonies primarily for *subsistence*, not for surplus value in the interest of reinvestment and economic growth.[13] Pastoralist grazing aims to preserve the life of the herd, not fatten-to-slaughter-for-sale; its investment is not in animal bodies *as* food-to-market as swiftly and expediently as possible, but in what grazing cows and goats produce such as milk and as a representation of community wealth. The value of land for grazing is the living animal whose needs are not met through a calculus of the cost of feed, and whose own value is thus not reducible to that calculus. Subsistence livelihoods are not competitors for supermarket chains; they don't utilize billboards; they don't rent market space. The pastoralist works to repel wild animal predators that threaten the herd—not hunt them as "exotic" bush meat.

This is not to say that the Sengwer, their cultural traditions, their way of life, cannot be coopted by the logic of commodification; it can, and in ways that will likely weaken their resistance to eviction, solicit ambivalence with respect to defending capitalized versions of their cultural practices, and heighten their vulnerability to future environmental crisis, viral pandemic, or wage slavery. What must be said, however, is that arguments for the defense of culture and tradition made by the Sengwer are rooted in an importantly different history, in different economic and geopolitical conditions, than those made by the Chinese wet marketer—even if both have legitimate claims in support of families, are vulnerable to the expropriation of their lands, and are subjugated by the political will and economic might of others. Indeed, we needn't look back further than 1958's Great Leap Forward to discover that the roots of the contemporary wet market lay, at least in part, in reforms introduced to alleviate the staggering level of suffering caused by the government's "restructuring" of the Chinese countryside into Communes:

> It is now clear that very substantial suffering occurred during the years immediately following the Great Leap Forward. There has been much debate about the numbers who died of starvation in this period . . . All Chinese alive at the time remember it as a period of great bitterness, though not all believe that the Party was principally to blame.[14]

That reform toward what came to be called a "socialist market economy" was also driven in part by extreme weather in 1950–60, producing drought and flood in different regions of China,[15] only emphasizes the significance of the country's return, through a new contract system in the late 1970s, of farming to the family, making it "once again the prime unit of production in agriculture."[16] As historian Robin Porter makes the point: "[t]he new system was characterized by flourishing free markets in produce, diversification of production, and in many but not all parts of China a new rural prosperity."[17]

The return of farming to private landholders after the Cultural Revolution in China is, in other words, already the product of the rule of capital. Whatever claim might be made to culture and tradition, the "new system" of the "socialist market economy" that includes the wet market has already inscribed the "family farm" as a unit of production, simply one more economically resilient and less prone to generating the conditions of starvation than the 1950s Communes. This, however, hints at a third point largely absent from Wallace-Wells' universalizing use of "we," namely, that no story like that of the Great Leap Forward can be told about the Sengwer pastoralists. Whatever violence, environmental disaster, or other forms of pressure have confronted the Sengwer (for example, the introduction of modern technology or the encroachment of industrial enterprise), their culture and tradition had not been coopted or subjugated by ideological or economic objectives—until 2009. Consider, for instance, the story of David Kisang:

> One morning in May, David Kisang, 50, sat outside his tiny dome-shaped hut, with its walls made of sticks and black polythene for a roof, sipping tea. His two red calves grazed behind the hut while his cattle and merino sheep grazed further afield, outside the bamboo-stick enclosure surrounding his compound. From where he sat he could scan two grassy glades in Embobut Forest, where hundreds of cattle and merino sheep belonging to other Sengwer grazed. Kisang's compound wasn't always as humble as it is today, with just the one small hut inside. He once had two big, round mud-and-thatch houses and a granary full of maize and potatoes. His children attended school nearby. Then, in December 2013, forest guards with the Kenya Forest Service (KFS) descended on the entire Embobut, evicting everyone living in the forest and destroying their property. That included Kisang and many other Sengwer. Since then, Kisang's life has been a game of hide-and-seek. He said he has to be alert at all times lest the forest guards ambush him, beat him and arrest him for trespassing. Round pits are all that remain of his houses. He lives alone because the area is no longer safe for his family. "One can't stay here with family because of the KFS," he said. "Children can't even go to school from here and there isn't a house they can sleep in. There is no accommodation."[18]

As NRAN puts it, violently shaming the Sengwer as *squatters* on their grazing lands must be understood not only as a product of the logic of commodification, but as the imperialistic *debauchery* of their culture and tradition.

"Squatter" positions and demeans the Sengwer. Consigning them to the status of interloper, and as engaged in an action so otherwise foreign, namely, the theft of an economic asset, it solicits organized resistance. But this resistance is not rightly construed, at least in the first place, as "economic asset" to the Sengwer, but as something more precious: ancestral title and cultural heritage. "Squatter" is dis-placing; it casts the Sengwer not as legitimate land-holders, but as trespassers and thus disposable obstacles to what is now appropriated as an economic conquest, if however thinly veiled as an environmental imperative: restoring and stabilizing the planetary atmosphere in order to continue business as usual, including oil and gas production, corporate-scale farming, and animal agriculture. Projects like REDD and WaTER authorize the United Nations, the World Bank, and the Kenyan government as brokers to determine, in the interest of the rule of capital, who counts as a "squatter," namely, whomever is in the way of restoring the "lungs" that extractivist enterprise needs to absorb greenhouse gases and other pollutants. For however such governments and agencies represent themselves as a caring "we," for however programs like REDD or WaTER portend to solve the climate crisis, for however environmental writers like Wallace-Wells casually utilize the "restoration" vocabulary, what the evidence shows is that what is systemically ignored is the cost to those whose "wishes" aim at the resolution of other more immediate problems like food security and access to clean water. It's thus a particularly bitter irony that the resistance mounted by courageous activists like Winnie Kadoshy endanger the very culture she, like NRAN, seek to save. Technologies like the Internet, who use is made essential as a means of gaining international attention to the Sengwer's plight, but that also open the door to the larger world, can propel a culture to extinction even as it expropriates it as the next product for sale.

A last point, then, against Wallace-Wells' use of "we" is that insofar as references to "squatters" are deployed to distinguish the good "we" from the bad, the dutiful who want to do something about climate change from the selfish trespasser, "we" actually functions to fortify the power of those already well-positioned to take advantage of existing social and economic inequalities. It provides precisely the convincing cover story that sustains another version of the myth of endless resources, namely, that if "we" could wish a sustainable planet into being, we'd already have one—as if the "we" doing the wishing had the slightest interest in the fundamental social and economic transformation that would be required in order to cauterize at the root the advantage of the capitalist. In other words, among the myths central to the capitalized world order is not merely that fossil fuels, water, useable soil, animal bodies, and human labor are endless, but that the social and economic inequalities that make labor cheap, disposable, and substitutable are themselves morally defensible. That is what sustains a discourse where casting the Sengwer as squatters can be weaponized in the interest of their violent removal. That is what the "we" who remain empowered to do the wishing for the rest of "us" are not about to give up. That is the myth that "justifies" reforestation programs whose real aim is to preserve economic growth by expanding the atmosphere's capacity to absorb greenhouse gases and other pollutants, a commitment to economic growth rooted in the power to either annihilate or commodify indigenous peoples, or both—whatever propels economic growth. These are the myths that use the atmosphere as a toilet. It's thus no wonder that "we" must be solicited to maintain what is a subterfuge narrative, namely, that we're all benefitted by projects sold to us as noble, foresightful, good by authorized agents like the United Nations or a recognized government agency. Perhaps Wallace-Wells would cast analyses like this as "dour terminological competition among climate writers," but the note he strikes in his discussion of economic growth could hardly be classified as cheery:

> Climate change will accelerate two trends already undermining the promise of growth: first by producing a global economic stagnation that will play, in some areas, like a breathtaking and permanent recession; and second, by punishing the poor much more dramatically than the rich, both globally and within particular polities, showcasing an increasingly stark income inequality, unconscionable already to more and more.[19]

Wallace-Wells is right on both scores, but he's also missing what connects the two trends: the logic of commodification that animates projects like REDD to expand the planet's lungs is precisely the same that makes possible the evictions of those who pose an obstacle, and thus a threat to the rule of capital. Projects like REDD and WaTER reinforce the "punishment of the poor" behind a veil of environmental responsibility.

The real aim of projects like REDD and WaTER is to stave off economic stagnation in order to keep the global economy growing. The Sengwer are simply far-away casualties of that project. If this were a project of ExxonMobil's, we might condemn it, but we'd get it, and we wouldn't expect this corporation to go to much effort to conceal it. But that the evictions of the Sengwer pose no obstacle *even to the subterfuge narrative that projects like REDD are about good planetary and atmospheric stewardship* suggests that stark income equality is *not* becoming more unconscionable to more and more, but quite the opposite: "we" who benefit from the subterfuge narrative seem perfectly comfortable with the cultural decimation, material destruction, psychic and material dispossession of the "other" so long as "we" get to stand behind a "justification" that absolves us of guilt. We're then free to consume at the same levels we always have. The absolution of guilt, and therefore responsibility, is what locates the "squatter" at the heart of the subterfuge narrative. "We" think we're saving the planet by supporting the planting of trees, that the Sengwer are just selfish trespassers who refuse to see the "bigger picture." The trouble, however, is this: however attractive is the subterfuge narrative that absolves us of guilt and invites us to think we're "doing our part" to combat the climate crisis, the most REDD and WaTER are going to achieve is to buy some reforested time. Eventually economic stagnation and permanent recession will begin to catch up even to those protected by subterfuge; for denial is indeed a resource, but like most others, not an endless resource. What the climate crisis will herald is just how much of "unconscionable" "we" can stomach behind the ever-thinning appeal to notions like "cultural flexibility." A logic that ignores the value of sentience and suffering says: *a lot.*

"[I]N MOST CASES I'D PROBABLY GO FOR GROWTH"

If the development of "green" energy, argues Wallace-Wells, has not slowed down the pace of climate change, it's because the goals of the market have not changed:

> We are . . . billions of dollars and thousands of dramatic breakthroughs later, precisely where we started when hippies were affixing solar panels to their geodesic domes. That is because the market has not responded to these developments by seamlessly retiring dirty energy sources and replacing them with clean ones. It has responded by simply adding the new capacity to the same system.[20]

He's right, the market responds to the advent of "clean" energy in the same way it responds to the appearance of any potential commodifiable, by adding new capacity, expanding its corporate portfolios, advertising its existing products as if they were "green," insuring that new products appear "green," and working to advance a corporate image that takes full advantage of consumers' desire to "buy green." If the acceleration of the encroaching climate crisis has not been slowed, it's because, first, there's no necessary relationship between seeming green and being green; advertising can create its own "reality," and if consumers feel good about a product, they'll buy more of it. Second, there's no consensus about what being "green" means in the context of profit generation other than as an advertising strategy. Third, wherever green-washing—advertising made to appear "environmental"—will sell a product more effectively than actually working to reduce environmental damage associated with the company, the logic of commodification dictates greenwash, that is, until consumers forget to care again.

Wallace-Wells, however, aims for what is doubtless a tricky balance: realism about why we haven't done a better job of mitigating greenhouse gas emissions, and hope that new technologies may yet translate into reductions sufficient to pull us back from the edge without any radical overhaul of the capitalist system itself. This balance will be very hard, if not impossible, to pull off. On the one hand, he argues that "[s]hould anything save us, it will be technology," but on the other Wallace-Wells recognizes that at least among the "shamans" of tech-rich fantasy-lands like Silicon Valley that "conspicuously few . . . seem meaningfully concerned about climate change."[21] He wants to project hope, but quickly follows this up with the caution that what he doesn't mean by "hope" is blind faith or "hippies."[22] That Wallace-Wells wants to project hope is certainly a good thing. Of course, we must have hope. The issue is whether the arguments of *The Uninhabitable Earth* can substantiate that hope. And what we discover on a careful read is that they can't. Indeed, it's blind faith to believe that technology "if anything" can save us, and that's particularly true when we've not done the harder work of excavating the ideological and material causes of our current ecological dilemmas. To be clear, it's not that Wallace-Wells' view of the promise of new technologies is naïve, and it's not that he doesn't see that the road to hope is littered with landmines. It's that there's a critical misfire in the *way* Wallace-Wells casts his inquiry concerning *why* the propensity for capitalist enterprise is to simply "add capacity," a misfire that leads to a fundamental misdirection for the rest of his effort to ground any realistic hope. In short, you have to get the foundation right for the building to stand. But insofar as Wallace-Wells' foundation cleaves to the "rule of capital," including the commodification of sentience, he destines his argument to false hope—at best.

We get a first hint of misfire when Wallace-Wells admits that "while I always thought it was basically a good idea to keep streams clean, I also accepted the proposition that there was a trade-off between economic growth and the cost to nature—and figured, well, in most cases I'd probably go for growth."[23] He writes in past tense, as if perhaps he's changed his mind, but while the chronicle of climate crisis disaster that follows this claim plainly points in the direction of radical collective action, little argument follows to dissuade us that Wallace-Wells doesn't indeed put his faith in a system whose founding premises are false (the myth of endless resources), and self-defeating (the commodification of sentience). Toward the end of his ruminations, he writes that "[t]o the left are those who see no solution short of political revolution. And even those activists are being crowded for space, these days, by texts of climate alarmism, of which you may feel the book in your hands is one. That would be fair enough, because I am alarmed."[24]

It's notable that Wallace-Wells allows *and* discounts the alarm—all in one passage. He implies that the "revolutionary" critics of the capitalist system are the "alarmists" and tries to distance himself as the more sensible, if alarmed. He's already made his bed with the prospect of a technological solution to the climate crisis, one motivated by a profit motive Wallace-Wells appears to take for granted as if this were itself a feature of nature. He remarks, for example, that "[i]f we do succeed, and pull up short of two or even three degrees, the bigger bill will come due not in the name of liability but in the form of mitigation and adaptation—that is, the cost of building and then administering whatever systems we improvise to undo the damage a century of imperious industrial capitalism has wrought across the only planet on which we can all live."[25] Here, Wallace-Wells tacitly appeals to the rule of capital in the cost of building and ecological restoration *and* condemns capitalism as "imperious industrial." He heralds the possibility of a technological salvation, but cautions the reader about its expense. He uses "we" as if it were obvious that "we" who improvise will be driven by motives not structured by the social, economic, and political inequalities upon which "imperious industrial" capitalism depends, even as he acknowledges the damage this system has wrought "across the only planet on which we can all live." Upshot: Wallace-Wells is trying to have his capitalist "probably go for growth" cake and eat it—"we" can save the planet—too. He effectively commits himself to the view that capitalist Frankenstein, as he'll refer to it, can be rehabilitated knowing the monster operates not on conscience, but on cost/profit analyses. But, given the urgency of his confessed alarm, whether this techno-utopian Hail Mary can provide grounds for hope is surely a long-shot—that he both tacitly acknowledges, but embraces regardless.

The trouble is that Capital-Frankenstein cannot be rehabilitated even with better technology because what's necessary to oxygenate his circulatory system and sustain his need to grow is that nothing exist beyond the reach of the logic of commodification. This claim is neither anti-technological nor is it reductionist; it's grounded instead in the copious and compelling empirical evidence supplied by accounts like Wallace-Wells' even if he doesn't draw the moral of his story. The logic of commodification may grease the wheels of technological development, but this is no more the case now than when the new technologies of the late 18th century facilitated the near extinction of Right Whales:

> No efforts were made by the Europeans and their North American competitors to conserve stocks of whales. Instead whalers acted as if their quarry was inexhaustible. Competition led to increasingly sophisticated techniques of slaughter,

> from faster sailing ships . . . to the invention in the mid-nineteenth century of the explosive harpoon gun and huge steam-powered factory ships . . . Although it was clearly in the industry's interest to limit the accelerating predation, the competitive dynamic of industrial capitalism made such forms of conservation impossible.[26]

Of course, the market isn't going to retire dirty energy, and of course it's going to add green technologies *if* they're profitable. But the idea that the rule of capital operates on any other value than profitability, or that the capacity for sentience will matter more now than during the Golden Age of 18th and 19th century whaling, is not hope; it's delusion. Questions about why corporations like ExxonMobil or Smithfield Farms haven't shifted over to greener energy sources and technologies make no sense not because the logic of commodification cannot accommodate them, but because such questions *don't arise at all.* So long as nothing significantly disrupts the energy/product/service supply chain, adding capacity is simply attractive advertising that requires no actual change. Consider, for example, Wallace-Wells' alarming discussion of coral-bleaching:

> You have probably heard of "coral bleaching"—that is, coral dying—in which warmer ocean waters strip reefs of the protozoa, called zooxanthellae, that provide, through photosynthesis, up to 90% of the energy needs of the coral. Each reef is an ecosystem as complex as a modern city, and the zooxanthellae are its food supply . . . when they die, the whole complex is starved with military efficiency, a city under siege or a blockade. Since 2016, as much as half of Australia's Great Barrier Reef has been stripped in this way.[27]

As Wallace-Wells rightly points out, "[t]his is very bad news." Yet, the reason he offers—in the same sentence—is that "reefs support as much as a quarter of all marine life and supply food and income for half a billion people."[28] Without skipping a beat, in other words, he equates the ecological loss with the economic loss, going on to argue that what's "bad" is that coral reefs offer protection from storm surges, "a function that offers value in the many billions, with reefs worth at least $400,000 million annually to Indonesia, the Philippines, Malaysia, Cuba, and Mexico—$400,000 million annually to each."[29]

In short, Wallace-Wells reaffirms and reinforces the very "rule of capital" responsible for generating horrific environmental disasters like coral death, whale extinctions, and the climate crisis even as he seeks to hedge his bets by noting that coral reefs are more valuable alive than dead. But this is another version of the fundamental misfire that plagues *The Uninhabitable Earth* since, by Wallace-Well's own reasoning, if the Great Barrier Reef turned out to be worth more dead than alive—if some entrepreneur could make

$410,000 million offering "ghost" tours of a dead reef and its "twilight zone" ocean floor strewn with the debris of dead coral—absolutely nothing bars that revaluation. Insofar, in other words, as Wallace-Wells calculates value first and foremost as exchange value, whatever provides the greatest share of the latter *is* value. This is not to suggest that being alive, being beautiful, being vulnerable, being endangered are without value, but rather something worse: that the value of each of these is itself a calculus of what "we" are willing to pay for their conservation or restoration. What Wallace-Wells shows, perhaps unwittingly, is that this isn't very much: "[a]lready, coral life has declined so much that it has created an entirely new layer in the ocean . . . which scientists have taken to calling the 'twilight zone.'"[30]

Indeed. Consider Catrin Einhorn and Elena Shao's July 2023 *New York Times* report from what, as of this writing, is the hottest Summer yet recorded:

> Florida's coral reefs are facing what could be an unprecedented threat from a marine heat wave that is warming the Gulf of Mexico, pushing water temperatures into the 90s Fahrenheit. The biggest concern for coral isn't just the current sea surface temperatures in the Florida Keys, even though they are the hottest on record. The daily average surface temperature off the Keys on Monday was just over 90 degrees Fahrenheit, or 32.4 Celsius, according to the National Oceanic and Atmospheric Administration. The real worry, scientists say, is that it's only July. Corals typically experience the most heat stress in August and September. Coral reefs are natural wonders that support myriad species and blunt damage from storms. In the United States, reefs generate economic benefits to the tune of $3.4 billion annually for fisheries, tourism and coastal protection, according to NOAA. But oceans have absorbed some 90 percent of the additional heat caused by humans as we burn fossil fuels and destroy forests.[31]

Note that here too the benefits of coral reefs are measured according to an economic "tune" that, very much like Wallace-Wells, Einhorn and Shao treat as if it were a feature of nature: a natural wonder that generates huge economic benefits. Like Wallace-Wells, Einhorn and Shao are dead-on: it's alarming that waters off the coast of Florida are so hot that coral reefs are enduring the heat stress that causes bleaching and eventual death long before the arrival of the hottest months of the year. Yet, the appeal to a valuation of "$3.4 billion annually" undermines their claim to alarm since, like Wallace-Wells, did "we" not regard the reefs as "natural wonders," did "we" simply change our minds about this, "we'd presumably let the reefs bleach and die having little of the only value that matters: exchange value. In other words, despite the fact that Wallace-Wells, Einhorn, and Shao each express heartfelt concern for the environment they recognize as endangered, their reasoning exemplifies the human chauvinism that more often than not accompanies the profit motive. Coral reefs are pretty, but at bottom they're cash cows; whatever's a cash cow is worth preserving, otherwise not so much. This is no recipe for hope no matter what technology we throw at cooling the waters off the coast of Florida.

Wallace-Wells closes this chapter of *The Uninhabitable Earth* by pointing out that "[d]ramatic declines in ocean oxygen have played a role in many of the planet's worse extinctions, and this process by which dead zones grow . . . is already quite advanced not only in the Gulf of Mexico, but just off Namibia, where hydrogen-sulfide is bubbling out of the sea along a thousand-mile stretch of land known as the Skeleton Coast." He notes that while "Skeleton Coast" "originally referred to the detritus of wrecked ships," "today [the reference is] more apt than ever."[32] Indeed; but what connects ships to whales to coral to fossil fuel production to people to the climate (to wet markets to coronavirus to biotech companies to globalization) is a logic of commodification that, because it is inherently kleptocratic, is likely to bleach and skeletonize more and more of the planet, until it has nothing to consume. By then it's too late for a technological fix unless that includes a spaceship to a more habitable planet. I think Wallace-Wells sees this, but he's holding out for the techno-utopian fix, and thus, for all his hand-wringing about an uninhabitable earth, he ultimately turns his gaze away.[33]

"I'M NOT ABOUT TO PERSONALLY SLAUGHTER A COW TO EAT A HAMBURGER"

Wallace-Wells *is* right with respect to how much progress we've made, or not, addressing the climate crisis: we're right where we started with hippies and solar panels. The trouble is that while Wallace-Wells rightly comprehends that we've made precious little progress, because he fails to interrogate the ideology of capitalism as fundamentally kleptocratic, he's too easily wooed by the possibility that technological solutions made profitable will be the way out. Can the rule of capital can be rehabilitated? For Wallace-Wells, the answer is yes. Can mitigation technologies like carbon capture/offsets be made sufficiently profitable? Yes; indeed, these are the solutions Wallace-Wells offers as a "reason for optimism . . . which could bring the planet closer to a state we would today regard as merely grim, rather than apocalyptic."[34]

Nancy Fraser, however, provides at least one compelling reason for tempering this optimism: "neoliberalism is marketizing environmentalism: consider the brisk trade in carbon permits and offsets and in 'environmental derivatives' which draw capital away from the long-term large-scale investments needed to transform unsustainable forms of life premised on fossil fuels."[35] Consider: one form of what is often called *disaster capitalism* includes profit ventures that take advantage of more frequent and/or more catastrophic natural disasters like firenadoes or Category Five hurricanes to, for example, sell home owner's insurance at sky-high premiums or sell fire retardant foam. But although she doesn't use the phrase "disaster capitalism" Fraser alerts us to its crucial other form: that profit venture which exploits "environmentalism" or the desire to "go green" to sell other kinds of commodities like carbon permits—a license to pollute "offset" by "greening" efforts in another domain of company activity, for example, an oil and gas company that drills along caribou routes in Alaska, but plants trees in Ohio in order to advance a "green" advertising strategy. What Fraser recognizes, in other words, is that arguments that promote carbon permits/offsets as an albeit grim remedy for the climate crisis—arguments like Wallace-Wells'—illustrate this second form of disaster capitalism. But unlike Wallace-Wells, Fraser also sees the far-more-than-grim potential for this kind of gambit to undermine itself: insofar as carbon gambits draw "capital away from the long-term large-scale investments needed to transform unsustainable forms of life premised on fossil fuels" they not only take advantage of ecological crises as species of profitable commodity, they are highly unlikely to sustain even the optimism of "grim" since they syphon money away from the long-term investments necessary to realize sustainability.

Wallace-Wells might, of course, respond to this line of critique that, at a minimum, technologies such as ever-improving solar panels, electric cars, and wind turbines can help us imagine an environmentally sustainable world, and that's certainly true. But, as Fraser argues, insofar as that imagined world reproduces the structurally unequal and subjugating world that far too many already endure, "sustainable" will remain at best a term of leisure for the privileged:

> While some claim a "right to development," insisting that the burden of mitigation should fall on Northern powers that have been spewing greenhouse gases for two hundred years, other advocate communing or a social and solidary economy, while still others, donning the environmentalist mantle, utilize neoliberal carbon-offset schemes to enclose lands, dispossess those who live from them, and capture new forms of monopoly rent.[36]

This neoliberal version of the carbon-offset scheme raises the specter of programs like REDD (Ch. 1), and none are likely to see what Wallace-Wells has in mind when he speaks of "optimism." But some grim mix of "right to development" and "dispossession" is what we get from toss-off reflections that, in stark contrast with observations like Fraser's, suggest incredibly little sensitivity with respect to the complex and interconnected issues relevant to addressing the climate crisis:

> I'm not about to personally slaughter a cow to eat a hamburger, but I'm also not about to go vegan. I tend to think when you're at the top of the food chain it's ok to flaunt it, because I don't see anything complicated about drawing a moral boundary between us and other animals, and in fact find it offensive to women and people of color that all of a sudden there's talk of extending human-rights-like legal protections to chimps, apes, and octopuses, just a generation or two after we finally broke the white-male monopoly on legal personhood.[37]

That Wallace-Wells occupies a sufficiently comfortable economic and social position that he can choose whether to "go vegan," make jokes about cow slaughter, and take for granted the authority to express offense on behalf of women and people of color does not by itself discount the value of his arguments in *The Uninhabitable Earth*. But that he occupies this position without taking any meaningful account of the privilege it affords him does shed light on his failure to interrogate whether the rule of capital can achieve a sustainable world attractive to anyone other than beneficiaries of the logic of commodification—like himself.

The problem, in other words, is not that Wallace-Wells is wrong about who's at the top of the food chain (viruses), wrong about whether the extension of some legal rights to nonhuman animals is "all of the sudden" (Peter Singer has entertained this idea since at least 1973), and wrong about the end of the "white-male monopoly on legal personhood." He *is* wrong about all of these. The problem is that understanding why and how Wallace-Wells is wrong sheds a bright light on his unexamined but operative commitment to the logic of commodification, and thus on how a book titled *The Uninhabitable Earth* turns out to be an *apology* for the very system of capital that will not only render the planet uninhabitable, but effectively offer a pass to those most responsible for its plight. Wallace-Wells' argument for hope beyond hippies depends precisely on preserving a system whereby the moral impetus to "go vegan" is preempted by the assumption that human beings are the top of the food chain, that the extension of legal rights to some nonhuman animals is "offensive" because it somehow diminishes the struggle for equality undertaken by women and people of color. In other words, according to Wallace-Wells, the struggle for social justice can only be achieved on condition that the sentience of nonhuman animals can be *discounted*, that disarticulating nonhuman animal bodies can remain safely the stuff of jokes. "Human being," on this account, is affirmed *because* the value of other sentient life can be preemptively demoted, converted to exchange value, and remain defined as a thing to be consumed. This too is a species of the commodification of sentience, in this case, to make jokes that sell books.

Wallace-Wells doesn't merely need an argument to substantiate the "uncomplicated moral boundary" he blithely draws between human beings and nonhuman animals, he needs to show why the extension of rights to nonhuman animals should be perceived as "offensive" to women and people of color. Otherwise, the position he seems to assume, that sentience is no obstacle to commodification, is bound to become self-defeating since "sentience" applies just as well to people as to many species of nonhuman animal. *How is capitalism to be rehabilitated if the structural inequalities that insure the dispossession of human beings like the Sengwer are likely to continue to be reproduced on the grounds that sentience is no bar to commodification?* Are the Sengwer in a position to flaunt being at "the top of the food chain"? Migrant women and children at the U.S.-Mexico border? Wallace-Wells claims to want to end for good the "white male monopoly." But he tethers his support for that noble objective to the same faulty premise that institutions like slavery, wage slavery, heteropatriarchy, sex-trafficking, and segregation exploit to subjugate women, people of color, and those coded as "other," namely, the commodification of sentience. In so doing, he effectively annuls any morally defensible claim he might otherwise make to justify the "uncomplicated boundary" between human beings and nonhuman animals. Put simply: if the capacity for sentience is no bar to commodification, *it is no bar to commodification*; it doesn't matter whose sentience it is. Wallace-Wells unwittingly reinforces the domination of the very institutions he might otherwise condemn, thereby reinforcing the rule of capital advantaged by them, dooming his argument to endorse the system he himself recognizes is a danger to the climate and to the life of the planet.

Perhaps Wallace-Wells can counter by offering some other argument to support the claim that that the "moral boundary" between human and nonhuman is "uncomplicated." But his options here are scarce. He can argue that nonhuman animals are non-sentient, and thus do not suffer, but this is patently false. He can argue that while nonhuman animals suffer, they do not suffer as much or in the same ways, or both; but particularly with respect to higher primates and cetaceans, this too is a nonstarter. First, it raises thorny questions concerning how "as much" is to be qualified or quantified, and second, it requires a defense of an argument notoriously liable to the chauvinistic claim that "uncomplicated" means that some forms of suffering "count," namely ours, while others don't. Lastly, Wallace-Wells can argue that there's just something "special" about human beings, and thus human sentience. But here too he's on thin ice since the candidates for "special" are either false (we share virtually every feature of our sentience in common with other higher primates and cetaceans to some degree), or arbitrary (we're special because we say so). In short, had Wallace-Wells undertaken any of these routes, what we'd learn from his effort is likely to tell us more about *why* such a boundary is important to *him* than about whether any such boundary can be sustained. In Wallace-Wells case, this "why" turns out to illumine his underlying, if only tacitly disclosed, commitment not merely to the idea that capitalism can be rehabilitated, but that, by definition, it cannot be inherently kleptocratic since a rehabilitated capitalism surely prohibits resource theft, and is therefore not capitalism at all. The upshot seems to be that the rehabilitation of capital can be achieved without forfeiting our current forms or volume of consumption. No need to go vegan; the white male monopoly is nearly defeated; we human beings are all at the top of the food chain. Trouble is, the arbitrary moral boundary Wallace-Wells draws between human and nonhuman beings actually functions primarily to preserve power in the hands of the privileged, is itself an artifact of the rule of capital, an obstacle to realizing social and economic justice and, in the end, an accelerant to the climate crisis.

HOW THE COMMODIFICATION OF SENTIENCE NORMALIZES SLAVERY

We needn't look further than to the history of American slavery to see that the moral boundary Wallace-Wells treats as a feature of nature can be seen as uncomplicated—but not for the reasons he appears to think. The reasons why, moreover, lead us *to* the uninhabitable earth, not *away* from it. From the point of view of the rule of capital, "uncomplicated" has nothing to do with whether boundaries are natural or artifactual, but everything to do with the generation of profit. The claim to "natural" anchors a crucial narrative offered to justify the commodification of a particular incarnation of sentient life; whether bovine or Homo sapiens, porcine or people makes no difference to it. Iman Cooper, for example, makes the point this way:

> The horror of the institution of slavery during the late eighteenth century was not that it displaced millions of African people from their homes to the US, but rather that it laid the foundation for the commodification and dehumanization of the black body that was culturally, socially, and politically maintained for hundreds of years to come . . . White slave owners executed their perceived right under the creation of commoditized black bodies to sexually abuse their slaves, producing mixed race (mulatto) children.[38]

Wallace-Wells would doubtless condemn this institution, as would most, as morally decrepit. But what he doesn't see is that his tacit naturalizing of the "moral boundary" between human beings and nonhuman animals authorizes the same logic of commodification that offers *permission* to slavers to ignore the suffering of human beings in the name of profit. Such "boundaries" are thus rightly conceived as neither "natural" nor "artifactual," but rather as *instrumental and monetizable*. As Andreas Malm puts it, "[t]he branded body of the slave might be the ultimate example of how property relations and corporeal nature can be combined."[39] Capitalism can afford no boundary it must treat as fixed other than that which diminishes profit, and this is not because there are no differences between "human being" and "nonhuman animal," but because what matters to exchange value is not "difference" *per se*, but whether a resource is exploitable, extractible, disposable. As Cooper explains, following Stephanie Smallwood's argument in "Turning African Slaves into Atlantic Commodities":

> [T]he replication of individual choices to capture, buy, and trade African slaves created a societal structure that equalized the value of human life with a market value. The moment that these steps crossed over from simply the process used on a daily basis, to a rigid structural system of oppression was the moment that bodies became objectified for future use in slavery. When lives revolve around market values and are believed to be valuable only for the potential profitability they may bring, the very fabric that holds communities together shifts.[40]

The unexamined assumption that makes such crossover possible is not only that sentience is no bar to commodification, but that its commodification, regardless the animal, *facilitates* market value. Contrary to Wallace-Wells' intentions, the appeal to "uncomplicated moral boundaries" *authorizes* slavery; it functions to legitimate the presupposition that suffering in no way prohibits conversion to exchange value. And worse: insofar as the capacity for suffering either implies other capacities that can be capitalized, or can be made itself into theater or entertainment (for example, public lynching), it has its own exploitable market value.[41]

Wendy Lynne Lee makes a similar argument in in *Contemporary Feminist Theory and Activism* (2010), arguing that "to the same extent that language codes for race, it also codes for sex, and for the intersection of race and sex as these are hierarchically represented in the logic of domination . . . although black women are animalized, their place in the logic as female—and therefore as inferior to black men—locates them solely as the objects of sexual (and other forms) of exploitation by men—black and white."[42] In other words, the way race and sex have been represented in the logic—racialized, sexed, sexualized and animalized—offers advantage to the capitalist in the form of particular incarnations of sentience. By casting its subjugates as commodities no matter what kinds of sentient creatures they may be, the historically entrenched structural inequalities that advantage the carnivore, the slaver, the patriarch, the multinational CEO are appropriated to the rule of capital, and thereby enabled to achieve a profit-objective by instrumentalizing whatever narratives of inferiority, "uncomplicated moral boundary," or "nature" that can be put to service. As Mark Stoll makes the point: "[p]lantations were precursors of the factories of industrial capitalism,"[43] but as he also readily acknowledges particularly about the English who "often regarded sub-Saharan Africans as subhuman and bestial," slavery epitomizes the mercenary nature of the logic of commodification. Black bodies, male and female, are animalized in order to excuse the rape of black women cast as sexually licentious and insatiable, while at the same time, the bodies of black men are cast as violent and sexually predatory in order to "justify" unduly severe punishment, and sometimes entirely fabricated charges, for the rape of white and black women—but where the charges for the rape of white women carry a particularly high price for damaging the property of white men.[44]

Here too, Wallace-Wells might respond that while indeed the legacy of slavery is grim, we have, as he puts it, "finally broke the white-male monopoly on legal personhood." African Americans can vote, are no longer subject to the ugly laws that characterize segregation, and are better represented at every income, social, and political level in American life. But, as Michelle Alexander's *The New Jim Crow* (2005) documents in exquisite if painful detail, while progress has doubtless been made since the end of the Civil War, the monopoly of white male personhood remains alive and well in the American prison industry, itself rooted in the demeaning treatment of particularly black and brown men as subhuman. As Alexander explains:

> Although Northern Slavery had been abolished, every black person was still presumed a slave—by law—and could not testify or introduce evidence in court . . . Slavery may have died, but for thousands of blacks, the badge of slavery lived on . . . Today a criminal freed from prison has scarcely more rights, and arguably less respect, than a freed slave or a black person living "free" in Mississippi at the height of Jim Crow. Those released from prison on parole can be stopped and searched by the police for any reason—or no reason at all—and returned to prison for the most minor of infractions . . .[45]

As Alexander goes on to spell out, the U.S. prison industrial complex is a multi-million dollar enterprise that depends on a conception of black men as reckless, violent, and sexually predatory to justify the harsh conditions, length of sentence, and brutality of treatment meted out against its inmates. As early as 1998, Eric Schlosser wrote for *The Atlantic* that the "lure of big money is corrupting the nation's criminal-justice system, replacing notions of public service with a drive for higher profits," and that although conditions in private for-profit prisons are modestly better than in state penitentiaries, what the lucrative industry depends on is a steady and growing supply of incarcerable black and brown bodies.[46]

It's no surprise that images of violent and predatory behavior remain a staple at the racist and heterosexist intersection of the American prison narrative. The trouble is that it's as false as is the claim that the white male monopoly on legal personhood has largely gone to sunset. As Debbie Nathan documents for *The Appeal*, for example, although no more likely to commit sex-crimes than their white male counterparts, African American men are far more likely to be listed on sex offender registries. In fact, as of 2018 "one of every hundred black men [is] on a registry, a rate double that of white men."[47] Nathan argues that "[b]lack sexuality and racism have long been intertwined in the criminal justice system," and would likely agree with Patricia Hill Collins when she argues that

> To explain these [commodified] relations, White elites created the controlling image of the buck. Unlike images of African natives who roam their wild homelands like beasts untamed by civilization . . . The representation of the buck described a human animal that had achieved partial domestication through slavery . . . Because the vast majority of enslaved African women and men did agricultural labor, these controlling images of the mule, jezebel, breeder woman, and buck justified black economic exploitation.[48]

Just as the institution of slavery animalizes its subjugates while at the same time counting on the physical strength and stamina of it laboring bodies in order to maximize agricultural production, so too the prison industry animalizes its inmates while at the same time counting on the physical strength and stamina of its incarcerated bodies to justify, as Alexander explains, virtually permanent entrapment in a racist, but wildly lucrative, criminal justice system. "Once a person is labelled a felon, he or she is ushered into a parallel universe in which discrimination, stigma and exclusion are perfectly legal, and privileges of citizenship such as voting and jury service are off-limits."[49] The legacy of slavery is reiterated in "the New Jim Crow" as the relationship between race, the commodification of sentience, and the rule of capital. "Even beyond private prison companies," writes Alexander, "a whole range of prison profiteers must be reckoned with if mass incarceration is to be undone, including phone companies that gouge families of prisoners . . . ; gun manufacturers that sell taser guns, rifles, and pistols to prison guards and police; private health care providers contracted by the state; the U.S. military that relies on prison labor," and so on.[50]

It accomplishes little to insist that the remedy for racism is to reassert the moral boundary between human beings and nonhuman animals by relocating men and women of color on the "human" side. This failure is not because animalizing human beings remains far too lucrative for capital conquest to give up—though that's true. It's because, this "moral boundary" is itself a creation of capital wherever it's lucrative, as it is in distinguishing white men cast as fully human from black men cast as predatory, if controllable, "bucks," for the purpose of insuring that "the market for private prisons is as good as it's ever been."[51] Insofar as the capacity for sentience itself remains no obstacle to commodification, the claim that what is wrong with racism is that it perpetrates great harm to sentient beings cannot be asked in any way that doesn't expose it as a red herring. That is, Wallace-Wells' "moral boundary" functions to excuse the commodification of nonhuman animals, all the while concealing the fact that it operates just as perniciously to facilitate the continued exploitation of human beings. To query whether there actually exists such a boundary, or to insist that surely nature can be carved at these sorts of joints, is to open the door to precisely what cannot be acknowledged within the rule of capital, namely, that *sentience cannot matter to the logic of commodification.* If it did, the advantages afforded to capitalism at the intersection of racism, heterosexism, geography, indigenous status, and economic vulnerability could not be exploited with the kleptocratic fervor essential to its survival.

"FATALLY COMPLACENT"

However much effort philosophers and economists have undertaken to present capitalism as morally sound, its inherently kleptocratic character can make nothing more of "morality" than an advertising pitch. Sometimes it's greenwashing, sometimes it's less sugar, sometimes it's charitable donation, but beyond window-dressing for the sake of consumer reassurance, "conscience" is as foreign a concept to the quest for profit as circles are squares. Materialized as the disposition to extract fossil fuels, labor, animal proteins, clean water, arable soil, and geopolitical advantage, the driving narrative of capital conquest can only fortify admissions like Wallace-Wells' who writes that he's "like every other American who has spent their life *fatally complacent*, and willfully deluded, about climate change" even though it poses a threat on "the scale of human life itself."[52] He says he's "not about" to "go vegan" despite the contribution made by concentrated animal feeding operations (CAFOs) to greenhouse gas emissions of which he is fully aware. He defends his refusal by appeal to the "uncomplicated moral boundary" between human beings and nonhuman animals, and the idea that when you're on the top of the food chain it's okay to "flaunt" it. As we know, this argument cannot be sustained. On one side of it, the uncomplicated boundary is indeed, very complicated, as is made clear by the millions of animalized black and brown bodies incarcerated and commodified by many forms of slavery, including the prison-industrial complex. On another side are countless nonhuman animals consumed on behalf of "fatal complacency," a fact complicated by the countless ways in which that complacency translates into abject misery for them, disease for us, and crisis for the atmosphere. Whatever boundary we might try to erect, the idea that we can consume animal bodies without adding to the waste evaporating upwards from factory farm lagoons, or without absorbing the toxins to which they're treated to fatten, immunize, and speed their development, is demonstrably false. As Monica Nickelsburg reports for *The Week*, "[t]here is a near consensus among experts that overuse of antibiotics, crowded and unsanitary livestock conditions, unnatural feed diets, and a lack of diversification are responsible for some serious global health risks," including Covid-19.[53]

On a third side of Wallace-Wells' defense of an "uncomplicated" boundary, there's the self-serving unacknowledged privilege of those whose secure social and economic positions grant them the leisure to write books about uninhabitable planets without having to make the easy choices made possible by their affluence. "Going vegan" is one of the easiest, yet Wallace-Wells' isn't "about" to do that. He writes as if we're all in such a fortuitous position. We're not, of course, and given how early in his book he announces that he's a comfortable carnivore, he makes it clear that he's uninterested in setting an example of moral fortitude for his readers. Mirroring the rhetoric of the capitalist, Wallace-Wells justifies remaining an unapologetic, if fatally complacent, meat-consumer by appeal to a toss-off version of "might makes right," that we're on top, so we get to flaunt it. Such a position is morally bankrupt. If "flaunting it," meant calling out from the top of Mt. Everest to the frigid atmosphere that we humans are special, we could safely ignore it or write it off to altitude delirium. The trouble is twofold: first, the colossal suffering that "might makes right" actually produces is far more than could ever be justified short of the wholesale abandonment of moral principle by the desire to flaunt power. Second, insofar as we condemn "might makes right" *because* of the suffering it causes to other human beings, it's hypocritical to exempt nonhuman animals unless we can justify a distinction between us and them *other* than the desire to flaunt power. After all, institutions Wallace-Wells would doubtless condemn as immoral such as slavery and sex-trafficking have "might makes right" at their core, and *we* are the cause of the suffering these institutions produce just as we are the cause of factory farm suffering for human and nonhuman beings.

Indeed, the environmental consequences of "flaunting it" can impact the very human beings doing the "flaunting" as well as countless "others" that seem to remain largely unseen to Wallace-Wells. Consider, for example, cotton farming in the post-Civil War South. As Erin Stewart Maudlin recounts in *Unredeemed Land: An Environmental History of Civil War and Emancipation in the Cotton South*, one of the ugly byproducts of slavery is environmental deterioration:

> [E]manicipation had created a new class of mostly landless farmers who could not be supported without widespread changes in land use. Emancipation's subsequent entanglement of agricultural techniques with race and labor relations complicated poor southerner's access to vital subsistence resources and chained them to increasingly intensive cultivation techniques that were too expensive to be profitable. Thus, the region felt the Civil War's environmental impacts for decades after Sherman marched through Georgia.[54]

In other words, there are no uncomplicated boundaries that can offer a faithful picture of the post-Civil War South, or tell us what harm or suffering matters, and for whom. The "entanglements" of human need, agricultural methods, race and labor relations overlap and are mutually reinforcing. This is not to say no boundaries were drawn in the Reconstruction South; there certainly were. But their beneficiaries belong, unsurprisingly, to the same class of mostly white affluent men for whom "uncomplicated" readily translates into privilege.

Given this analysis, it's tempting to think that Wallace-Wells' failure on the nonhuman animal side of his moral boundary simply mirrors his failure on the human subjugation and slavery side; this is true to some extent. On both sides there exists a "we" who are responsible for immense and unnecessary harm and suffering directly implicated in how we all arrive at the uninhabitable earth. But there are also important differences that shed light on the ways in which the commodification of sentience comes to be implicated in this ultimately nihilistic trajectory, and these require an analysis focused squarely on how we come to naturalize what are otherwise contrived boundaries to which we appeal to justify not merely slavery, but what can only be described as a barbaric incarnation of "fatal complacency." Consider, for example, Cora Diamond's landmark essay, "Eating Meat and Eating People." Diamond argues that the reason we do not eat our own dead except in extreme circumstances is not because people have some set of capacities, like the capacity to suffer, that makes them something not to eat, but because, *regardless the capacity to suffer*, "human being" is *itself* defined as "something not to eat":

> There is not a class of beings, pets, whose nature, whose capacities, are such that we owe it to them to treat them in these ways [by not eating them]. Similarly, it is not out of respect for the interests of beings of the class to which we belong that we give names to each other, or that we treat human sexuality, or birth or death as we do, marking them—in their various ways—as significant or serious. . . . it is not out of respect for our interests which is involved in our not eating each other. These are all the things that go to determine what sort of concept "human being" is . . . And so too—very much so—with the idea of the difference between human beings and animals. We learn what a human being is

> in—among other ways—sitting at a table where we eat them. We are around the table and they are on it.[55]

For Diamond, arguments like Peter Singer's that extend the right to not be made to suffer (at least unnecessarily) to nonhuman animals, and ground that right in the capacity to suffer, are "a totally wrong way of beginning the discussion" of animal rights. But this is not because nonhuman animals do or don't have such capacities, but because the way we define "human being" precludes nonhuman animals *at the outset* from counting as something not to eat.[56]

Yet, Diamond argues, the way we identify nonhuman animals as "things to eat" and human beings as "things not to eat" is in fact entirely *arbitrary*, a matter simply of preference for our own, effectively another version of "might makes right," and thus ultimately morally insupportable. Consider her example of eating the dead or the amputated:

> It is in fact part of the way this point is usually missed that arguments are given for not eating animals, for respecting their rights to life and not making them suffer, which imply that there is absolutely nothing queer, nothing at all odd, in the vegetarian eating the cow that has obligingly been struck by lightning. That is to say, there is nothing in the discussion which suggests that a cow is *not* something to eat; it is only that one must not help the process along. One must not, that is, interfere with those rights with which we should usually have to interfere if we are to eat animals at all conveniently. But if the point of the Singer-Regan vegetarian's argument is to show that the eating of meat is, morally, in the same position as the eating of human flesh, he is not consistent unless he says that it is just squeamishness, or something like that, which stops us eating our dead. If he admitted that what underlies our attitude to dining on ourselves is the view that *a person is not something to eat,* he could not focus on the cow's right not to be killed or maltreated, as if that were the heart of it.[57]

In other words, that the vegetarian will eat the cow struck by lightning, but not the human being struck by lightning is not because cows or human beings have or don't have a capacity to suffer, but because *the cow is a cow*—preemptively classified as something to eat; the human being is not so classified—regardless the fact that, being dead, he/she will not suffer upon being eaten. If suffering enters into moral consideration it is because killing the cow might cause it pain—but not because it's not something to eat already dead. Yet, we'd not eat the person (any more than we'd eat an amputated human limb) regardless their metabolic status—because a *human is a human.*

Diamond argues that we arrive at this belief through enculturation that, among other things, introduces us to what counts as food: "[w]e learn what a human being is in—among other ways—sitting at a table where *we* eat *them.*

We are around the table and they are on it."[58] Such introductions are not arguments; they're simply parts of ordinary practices and traditions; we take them for granted until there's a reason not to or, in Wallace-Wells' case, even at the cost of fatal complacency. Yet it's these same practices and traditions that Wallace-Wells insists should be able to be taken for granted as a perfectly sensible moral boundary for women who, having only recently gotten past the male monopoly, should not have to contend with yet another class of creatures up for emancipation. Just as human beings are on top and get to flaunt it, women should be able to celebrate their liberation from heteropatriarchy without having to worry about who or what may be beneath them—at least if what's below is already classified as a "thing to eat." But there are at least two reasons why Wallace-Wells' argument cannot work even as a defense of the emancipation of women: first, the form of reasoning he takes for granted to justify the moral boundary between women and nonhuman animals is precisely the same as that to which the slaver appeals to justify the moral boundary between the (white) slaver and the (black) slave, namely, that there exists a hierarchical order of nature that puts white men on top where they're justified in flaunting it, and where flaunting it realizes itself in the subjugation of whatever falls below.

Ecofeminist philosopher Karen Warren calls this "the logic of domination"[59]: what is represented as an "uncomplicated moral boundary" is, in fact, a human artifice hierarchically structured to authorize human *and* heteropatriarchal domination. To confront the "male monopoly" is to confront the logic that facilitates commodification: of women, nonhuman nature, and nonhuman animals. For it's the logic *itself* that, however natural it feels to its beneficiaries, is exposed by analyses like Warren's as *naturalized* in the interest of the maintenance of power. Our privileged complacency permits us to ignore nonhuman animal suffering because we take for granted that they just are "what's for dinner." But this is precisely what will insure the continuation of a white male monopoly that remains authorized, for example, to erect oppressive laws governing women's reproductive lives,[60] or statutes that disenfranchise black voters.[61] "What's for dinner," in other words, has its analogue in "what's for (white) men." The second reason Wallace-Wells' argument fails is hinted at in Warren: his view does not square with what the majority of feminists would point out is alive and well, namely: the (white) male monopoly. Indeed, from "heartbeat" laws governing access to abortion, to unequal pay for female athletes,[62] to the gender wage gap,[63] to the disproportionate impacts of the climate crisis on indigenous women,[64] the evidence is not on Wallace-Wells' side.

Many of these feminists argue that there can be no reckoning with heteropatriarchal institutions without analyses of every other incarnation of structural, intersectional, and hierarchical inequality. In an essay widely regarded as a bulwark of ecological feminism, "The Power and the Promise of Ecological Feminism," Warren argues that, insofar as the logic of domination forms an entrenched structural feature of the social and economic order, tackling heteropatriarchy requires tackling racism, and tackling racism requires tackling human chauvinism.[65] Far from offended, then, by the extension of moral consideration to nonhuman animals, most ecofeminists insist that we are unlikely to make moral progress without it, and the idea implied by Wallace-Wells that it's somehow too much to ask to expect women to now go on to defend animal rights actually reiterates a sexist idea—that this is women's work. Wallace-Wells' argument thus finds itself in a conflict (if not a contradiction). He represents himself as a forward-looking, politically progressive, and environmentally responsible man. But once he adopts what amounts to a particularly crude version of "might makes right" in order to justify the continuing objectification of nonhuman animals his self-representation is stripped of its "Renaissance Man" veneer to expose the unearned privilege of his position—and his unwitting but nonetheless chummy alliance with the capitalist "Frankenstein" he presumes to critique.

NOTES

1. David Wallace-Wells. *The Uninhabitable Earth*. (New York, NY: Tim Duggan Books, 2019), 178.
2. Wallace-Wells, 178.
3. Wallace-Wells, 178.
4. Wallace-Wells, 214.
5. Wallace-Wells, 178–9 (my emphasis).
6. *Food and Agriculture Organization of the United States*. "Key Facts and Findings; By the Numbers: GHG Emissions by Livestock." http://www.fao.org/news/story/en/item/197623/icode/.
7. United Nations Climate Action. "Water—At the Center of the Climate Crisis." https://www.un.org/en/climatechange/science/climate-issues/water.
8. Wendy Lynne Lee. *Eco-Nihilism: The Philosophical Geopolitics of the Climate Change Apocalypse*. (Lanham, MD: Lexington Books, 2016), 284–5.
9. Eileen Gbagbo. "The Dark Side of Forest Conservation: The Sengwer Tribe and Embobut Forest." https://www.euronews.com/green/2020/07/20/the-dark-side-of-forest-conservation-the-sengwer-tribe-and-embobut-forest.
10. Gbagbo. "The Dark Side of Forest Conservation: The Sengwer Tribe and Embobut Forest." https://www.euronews.com/green/2020/07/20/the-dark-side-of-forest-conservation-the-sengwer-tribe-and-embobut-forest.
11. Gbagbo. "The Dark Side of Forest Conservation: The Sengwer Tribe and Embobut Forest." https://www.euronews.com/green/2020/07/20/the-dark-side-of-forest-conservation-the-sengwer-tribe-and-embobut-forest.

12. Wallace-Wells, 11.

13. ArcGIS. "The Sengwer."

14. Robin Porter. *From Mao to Market: China Reconfigured*. (New York: Columbia University Press, 2011), 45.

15. Porter, 45.

16. Porter, 55.

17. Porter, 59.

18. *Mongabay.com*. "Three Pangolin Species Closer to Extinction: IUCN." 12.18.19. https://news.mongabay.com/2019/12/three-pangolin-species-closer-to-extinction-iucn/.

19. Wallace-Wells, 165.

20. Wallace-Wells, 177.

21. Wallace-Wells, 171.

22. Wallace-Wells, 172.

23. Wallace-Wells, 6.

24. Wallace-Wells, 213.

25. Wallace-Wells, 169.

26. Ashley Dawson. Extinction: A Radical History. (New York, NY: OR Books, 2016), 53–4.

27. Wallace-Wells, 96.

28. Wallace-Wells, 96.

29. Wallace-Wells, 96.

30. Wallace-Wells, 96.

31. Catrin Einhorn and Elena Shao. "How Hot is the Sea Off Florida Right Now? Think 90s Fahrenheit." https://www.nytimes.com/2023/07/12/climate/florida-ocean-temperatures-reefs.html.

32. Wallace-Wells, 97.

33. Wendy Lynne Lee, Ch. 5.

34. Wallace-Wells, 31.

35. Nancy Fraser. *Cannibal Capitalism*. (Brooklyn, NY: Verso, 2022), 12.

36. Fraser, 76.

37. Wallace-Wells, 6.

38. Iman Cooper. "Commodification of the Black Body, Sexual Objectification and Social Hierarchies During Slavery." (https://earlham.edu/media/2544034/commodification-of-black-bodies-iman-cooper-spring-2015.pdf), 20.

39. Andreas Malm. *The Progress of This Storm: Nature and Society in a Warming World*. (Brooklyn, NY: Verso, 2020), 169.

40. Cooper, 22.

41. Paula Giddings. "The Origin of Lynching Culture in the United States." *Facing History and Ourselves*. https://www.facinghistory.org/resource-library/video/origins-lynching-culture-united-states.

42. Wendy Lynne Lee. *Contemporary Feminist Theory and Activism: Six Global Issues*. (Peterborough, Canada: Broadview Press, 2010), 208.

43. Mark Stoll. *Profit: An Environmental History*. (Cambridge, UK: Polity Press, 2023), 68.

44. Lee, 208–13.

45. Michelle Alexander. The New Jim Crow. (New York: New Press, 2020), 140–1.

46. Eric Schlosser. "The Prison-Industrial Complex." *The Atlantic*, December, 1998. https://www.theatlantic.com/magazine/archive/1998/12/the-prison-industrial-complex/304669/.

47. Debbie Nathan. "Black Men Disproportionately Represented on Sex Offender Registries." The Appeal, 11.15.18. https://theappeal.org/black-men-disproportionately-represented-on-sex-offender-registries/.

48. Patricia Hill Collins. *Black Sexual Politics: African Americans, Gender, and the New Racism*. (New York: Routledge, 2004), 56–7.

49. Alexander, 94–5.

50. Alexander, 231–2.

51. Alexander, 231.

52. Wallace-Wells, 7 (my emphasis).

53. Monica Nickelsburg. "5 Modern Diseases Grown by Factory Farming." The Week, 11.7.13. https://theweek.com/articles/457135/5-modern-diseases-grown-by-factory-farming.

54. Erin Stewart Maudlin. *Unredeemed Land: An Environmental History of Civil War and Emancipation in the Cotton South*. (Oxford: Oxford UP, 2018), 5.

55. Cora Diamond. "Eating Meat and Eating People." In *Animal Rights: Current Debates and New Directions*. Ed. Cass Sunstein and Martha Nussbaum. (Oxford: Oxford UP, 2004, 93–107), 97–8.

56. Diamond, 95.

57. Diamond, 95.

58. Diamond, 96.

59. Karen Warren. "The Power and the Promise of Ecological Feminism." (*Environmental Ethics*, 12.2, Summer 1990, 125–46).

60. Rebecca K.K Lai. "Abortion Bans: 9 States Have Passed Bills to Limit the Procedure This Year." *New York Times*, 5.29.19. https://www.nytimes.com/interactive/2019/us/abortion-laws-states.html.

61. Tessa Stuart. "Everything You Need to Know about Georgia's New Voting Law." *Rolling Stone*, 3.26.21. https://www.rollingstone.com/politics/politics-news/georgia-voting-bill-brian-kemp-voter-suppression-1147493/.

62. *Women's Sports Foundation*. https://www.womenssportsfoundation.org/education/fight-equal-pay-womens-sports/.

63. *American Progress*. "Act Now for Equal Pay." https://www.americanprogress.org/article/quick-facts-gender-wage-gap/.

64. Kyle Powys White. "Indigenous Women, Climate Change Impacts, and Collective Action. Hypatia, 29.3, 2014, 559–616.

65. Karen Warren. "The Power and the Promise of Ecological Feminism." (*Environmental Ethics*, 12.2, Summer 1990, 125–46).

Chapter 3

Commodification of Sentience in the Maintenance of Structural Inequality

More of David Wallace-Wells

"LEFTISTS . . . TECHNOCRATS . . . CONSERVATIVES"

For ecologically-oriented feminists like Karen Warren the logic of commodification cannot be fully understood without careful analysis of the deeply entrenched structures that govern the relationships between human institutions, nonhuman species life, and the ecologies upon which we all depend. Among their most important insights is that the structural devaluation of women, black and brown people, the economically vulnerable, indigenous peoples, and communities of the Global South is of a piece with the subjugation and disarticulation of nonhuman animal bodies. Yet, as we've seen, Wallace-Wells makes no such connections—other than to dismiss them. He scorns the relationship between racism, sexism, and meat-eating appealing to "might makes right," "flaunting" the domination of nonhuman animals as if it had no analogue in the structures that maintain heteropatriarchy and white supremacy. Indeed, he writes as if these campaigns for social equality have already been won. Wallace-Wells is just wrong, but we can ferret out the reason why he takes the dismissive tack he does: he needs to discount the relationship between the oppression of nonhuman animals and that of human beings in order to utilize the clichéd compartmentalizing of "Left" and "Right" to explain why so little progress has been made in the effort to combat the climate crisis. In other words, the reason for so little progress can't be because the deeply entrenched relationships between the subjugation of women, nonwhite folks, indigenous peoples, and nonhuman animals advantages the capitalist—that would require a more probing analysis that risks impugning the economic system Wallace-Wells ultimately favors—capitalism.

What provides an avenue to the "reformed" capitalism Wallace-Wells defends are easy-to-castigate scapegoats:

> And yet, perhaps in part because we see the way that perspectives on climate change map neatly onto existing perspectives on capitalism—from burn-it-all-down leftists to naively optimistic and blinkered technocrats, to rent-seeking, kleptocratic, growth-is-the-only-value conservatives—we need to think of climate as somehow being contained within, or governed by, capitalism. In fact, it is endangered by it.[1]

Wallace-Wells is right about one thing: the climate *is* endangered by capitalism. In fact, the climate is *so* endangered by the kleptocratic disposition of capital conquest that avoiding an Earth made uninhabitable by its impacts will require a commitment to radical change far beyond the wishing and hoping of those tasked with greening what Bruno Latour calls the New Climactic Regime. But that the climate is endangered by capitalism does not mean that capitalism is endangered by the climate crisis—*yet*. That is, while Wallace-Wells correctly identifies the kleptocratic character of capital conquest, his own defense of schemes like carbon offsets will only extend "growth-is-the-only-value" until these schemes fail and the planetary atmosphere collapses. In short, capitalism won't be endangered until it's ruinously so, and among its nemeses will be the very schemes implemented to (pretend to) "offset" the impacts of climate change. Make no mistake: the kleptocratic character of capital conquest will ensure that carbon offsets *will* fail. Here are two reasons why:

> A study covering almost 300 carbon offset projects found that the industry's top registries have consistently allowed developers to claim far more climate-saving benefits than justified. Researchers led by Barbara Haya from the University of Berkeley's Goldman School of Public Policy assessed the methods underpinning forestry projects responsible for 11% of all carbon offsets ever issued. They found shortcomings in each that resulted in bogus credits . . . Haya said her team's findings amount to a systemic failing in the market. The challenge of placing a precise number on how much carbon is saved to generate each offset sold impacts all projects, not just forest management. Last year, a Bloomberg investigation found that almost 40% of the offsets purchased in 2021 came from renewable energy projects that didn't actually avoid emissions.[2]

Wallace-Wells argues that "[y]ou do not have to believe that economic growth is a mirage produced by fossil fumes to worry that climate change is a threat to it,"[3] but it's hard to take him seriously when his own solutions only invoke the very profit regime he rebukes. It's as if Wallace-Wells echoes a sentiment from the Left he caricatures as "burn-it-all-down," while actually advertising for a strategy embraced by the "growth-is-the-only-value" right, namely, carbon offset schemes. He can't have this both ways. Either economic growth is a mirage or it's not; either carbon offset schemes are a mirage or they're not. The evidence not only points clearly to "mirage," but to the deliberate chimera of the oil and gas profiteers, and to the inevitable catastrophic failure of both growth and offsets—for the same reasons: growth is the only value, and that will ensure we burn it all down however we cleave to the pretense of offsets.

Wallace-Wells' Left versus Right scapegoat approach fails as an explanation for why so little progress has been made addressing the climate crisis because its effectively erects straw arguments in place of an analysis of the underlying drivers of capital conquest. Although Wallace-Wells does pay lip service to the fact that some communities, especially in the Global South, are impacted by climate change in more harmful ways than others, because his proposed carbon-scheme solutions are predictably destined for failure, it's hard to take his concern especially seriously. In addition to ecological feminist writers like Nancy Fraser and Karen Warren, a number of others do take the issues Wallace-Wells dismisses (or even scorns) to be vital to understanding the climate crisis as well as to articulating possible solutions. Consider, for example, Bruno Latour's discussion of the New Climactic Regime:

> We can understand nothing about the politics of the last 50 years if we do not put the question of climate change and its denial front and center. Without the idea that we have entered into a New Climactic Regime, we cannot understand the explosion of inequalities, the scope of deregulation, the critique of globalization, or, most importantly, the panicky desire to return to the old protections of the nation-state . . .[4]

Latour takes seriously the complex relationships between political inequality, deregulation, globalization, and the return of the authoritarian state—issues that cannot be reduced to "Left" and "Right" without a distortion of their impacts on the climate crisis. Yet Wallace-Wells consigns Latour to the chorus of "futilitarians," describing him as an "instinctive insubordinate,"[5] a kind of rebel without a cause. This is hardly surprising since Latour doesn't fit Wallace-Wells' scapegoat approach to "Left" and "Right." Both put climate change "front and center," but it's Latour who takes the brave step toward understanding *how* the complex relationships that advantage the capitalist have produced not only the climate crisis, but a wide range of responses to it—including those like Wallace-Wells' claim that analyses like Latour's end up in futility.

Both seek to reach the people Latour calls the "climate quietists," the many consumers who hope, that "everything will be alright in the end," while doing little or nothing to achieve that goal.[6] We might ask: what distinguishes these consumers who, *de facto*, "opt for growth" from those who claim that if we could wish sustainability into place "it'd be a done deal" if neither actually *do* anything? If Wallace-Wells' "fatal complacency" has no political identity, how can appeals to "Left" or "Right" capture what is surely the far greater threat to the climate, namely, the desire to consume forms an enculturated fixation that may be met at a brisker pace in the wealthy Global North, but has its analogues in the growing economies of the Global South, especially China and India. For Wallace-Wells, the "Left" is too weak and too fragmented to burn it all down; the "Right," especially given its resource mythologies, too beholden to its fossil fuel benefactors to blink. But both buy cars, go out for pizza, and make Amazon orders. What Latour shows is that the power of the New Climactic Regime derives not from Left or Right, but from the way in which the social and economic order is structured to maintain and grow the machinery of profit-generation regardless political ideology. That the primary defenders and beneficiaries of these structures occupy the "Right" is materially relevant, but only insofar as "burning it all down" is not a money-maker. As Latour observes, Donald Trump won the United States' presidency as a populist, ostensibly identified with the Right, but really as an *opportunist*,[7] As Latour argues, wryly:

> What the militancy of millions of ecologists, the warnings of thousands of scientists, the actions of hundreds of industrialists, even the efforts of Pope Francis, have not managed to do, Trump succeeded in doing: everyone now knows that the climate question is at the heart of all geopolitical issues and that it is directly tied to questions of injustice and inequality.[8]

Trump, in other words, succeeds in drawing our attention to the climate crisis via his very loud and very public effort to deny it, ridicule the science, or dimly acknowledge that climate change is a political football—but withdraw the U.S. from the Paris Climate Accord anyways because that is the action which most benefits his fans and donors. By sheer contrast with the reality of more and more extreme weather events, drought, flood, and food insecurity, Trump offers a glimpse into the "injustice and inequality" that advantages the capitalist.

The emergence of populist demagogues like Trump cannot be reduced to a conflict of caricatures like "burn-it-all-down" Left and "profit-is-the-only-value" Right. The reason is simple: the kleptocratic ontology of capital conquest—its logic of commodification—not only preempts political identity and aspiration, but defines the conditions under which they're made possible.

The failure to comprehend that fact is the substance of Wallace-Wells' misfire with respect to his appeal to "Left" and "Right." While, as Andreas Malm shows, there's plenty about which to be critical in Latour, he's only a "futilitarian" if we accept Wallace-Wells' faulty caricature that assigns Latour to the "Left." But this mischaracterizes Latour's position in ways that are instructive: Latour recognizes that "wishing and hoping" is less about one-dimensional categories like "Left" and "Right" and more about maintaining a social order of rich and poor, global North and South, migrant and citizen, black and white, male and female. Latour understands that the "quietism" of the many is less about political power and more about rent, paying utilities, buying food, and keeping a car running—the quiet forms of desperation that make populist figures attractive. Latour knows it's vital to an analysis of the impacts of climate change to include the "explosion of inequalities," deregulations, and populist narratives even though these don't map neatly onto straw references such as the "burn-it-all-down left," the "rent-seeking kleptocrats," and the "blinkered technocrats." Such references are scapegoats to blame for our current dilemma; but, contrary to the optimism Wallace-Wells hopes to rouse against the "futilitarians," the effect of his scapegoating is to create paralyzing cynicism. As Latour puts it, "[o]rdinary people already had a general tendency to be skeptical; now they have been incited, thanks to billions of dollars invested in disinformation, to be skeptical about one massive fact: the mutation of the climate."[9] To be clear, it's not that Wallace-Wells is guilty of the sort of climate change hiding-of-fact we can assign to ExxonMobil. But he is guilty of another, more misleading, and thus potentially more dangerous kind of disinformation, namely, that capitalism is capable of reform, and particularly reform to ends compatible with planetary integrity. And this leaves ordinary folks utterly in the lurch. By forcing a false choice of "burn-it-down" Left and "Profit-over-all" Right, Wallace-Wells leaves the very people who might be attracted to a demagogue like Trump cynical about what they're being asked to give up, unrelieved with respect to the inequality of their social and economic position. But worst of all, he leaves folks with the false hope that the multinational oil and gas behemoths responsible for the environmental crises that encumber their vulnerable lives with ever greater trauma can be trusted to offset their greenhouse gas emissions.

QUIETISM, HYBRIDISM, NIHILISM

Let's return once more to a concrete example, the reforestation project, REDD. As we've seen, the same enculturated "quietism" that sustains West Virginia coal companies also sustains REDD's "justification" for the eviction of Kenyan villagers. Both are empowered to turn a blind eye to the impacts of their operations on those most vulnerable, and whether those impacts are brown lung disease or displacement, mortal injury or starvation, it doesn't matter at least to the extent that *the rest of us are effectively invited not to look*. Quietism, in other words, is the enculturated apathy, the fatal complacency, that follows, as NRAN puts it, from the fact that the commodification of life has become a naturalized and normalized expectation. Once we recognize, however, that the beneficiaries of industry and those of programs like REDD are the same, one incarnation of "Left" and "Right" collapses because, whether in the name of strip-mining or reforestation, subjugation remains the rule. As NRAN makes the point:

> REDD+ is a neo-liberal, market-driven approach that leads to the *commodification of life* and undermines holistic community values and governance. It is . . . driven by economic processes such as trade liberalization and privatization and by actors like the World Bank whom have been responsible for the destruction of forests and livelihoods of Indigenous Peoples all over the world. The concept of "Green Economy" is a vehicle for promoting trends of commodification of nature.[10]

NRAN activists are certainly right that what we might call the "language games" of the "Green Economy" facilitate the "*commodification of life*," conceal its operations behind a façade of environmental responsibility, hide its doings behind a spate of slogans like "sustainability," "green," resilient," "restored," "offset," and exploit the worthy goal of mitigating the effects of climate change as justification to commodify displaced villagers as disposable. Indeed, in this version of the commodification of sentience we're invited to endorse the proposition that whatever volume of land is necessary to extract from the peoples of the developing world to support the growing consumption of more geopolitically powerful countries can be justified by appeal to "restorative" projects like REDD. Disarticulating the lives and livelihoods of Global Southerners is simply the cost of doing the business of off-setting greenhouse gas emissions. Affluent Global Northerners seem happy to play this game, even as we're dimly aware of the cognitive dissonance it requires, because it make us feel better about our plastic water bottles and our gas-guzzling SUVs. "We" get to believe that our support of the United Nations or the World Bank is helping to re-oxygenate the lungs of the world, so we don't have to see the peoples and the ecosystems bulldozed to make room for planting trees. "We" stand stalwartly behind justificatory references to "green," and our enculturated quietism does the rest.

Yet, although the point concerning hypocrisy and denial made by *Indigenous Peoples Reject REDD* is well-taken, they get backwards, along with Wallace-Wells, what is most vital to understanding how projects aimed at mitigating the impacts of the climate crisis in fact undermine the climate: the "market-driven approach" does not *lead* to the commodification of life; it *underwrites* it. The rule of capital doesn't *produce* commodities; it's *built into* the *ontology* of "commodity." It's the logic of commodification that facilitates the conversion of life, sentient or otherwise, into exchange value, authorizing the "economic might" wielded in largely the same way by the World Bank or ExxonMobil, by ChemChina or Smithfield Farms. When Wallace-Wells refers to "economic might" in the same sentence as "political will" and "cultural flexibility" he re-inscribes the rule of capital he otherwise depicts as a Frankenstein onto the mostly white affluent men this marriage of might, will, and flexibility empowers. He accedes the planet to the Frankenstein that will render it uninhabitable. It is thus quite ironic that, despite Wallace-Wells' reference to Latour as a "futilitarian," Latour makes a similar mistake; that is, *it's not the market that leads to commodification, but the reverse*; it's the ontology, *the logic of capital*, that materializes what constitutes "commodity," a logic of commodification that assumes there is a difference, as Malm argues, between the material world and the logic empowered to *convert* it to exchange value.

Recognizing this difference is fundamental to understanding how we have arrived at an historical juncture so ecologically perilous. Latour's mistake, argues Malm, is to collapse nonhuman nature and human society into a "*hybrid*" that, in virtue of its having nothing against which to form resistance, is rendered impotent. If "we" simply are "nature" and "nature" is "us," then whatever environmental alterations "we" produce are nothing more than "nature" producing itself, however catastrophic. In this case, the idea that we must act to mitigate against environmental disaster, including the climate crisis, makes no sense. How can we assign culpability to this hybrid? As Malm puts it: "[i]f there is nothing but us, then there is nothing to figure out."[11] That is, if human beings and the systems we create are materializations of "nature," and the "nature" of us, then how can it be anything other than nature running its hybridized course that produces the climate crisis? It's only in the case where we can assign *agency* to human beings distinct and apart from nonhuman nature that we can also assign culpability,[12] and hybridism offers no opportunity for that assignment. Moreover, if the logic of commodification, an artifice of human chauvinism, is merely an expression of the human/nature hybrid, and thus without any agency of its own, our hand-wringing over climate collapse signals no more than the fact of our helplessness.

Despite Latour's calls to resist neo-liberalism, it turns out that hybridism is a species of nihilism, or worse: an excuse for the cognitive dissonance that permits us to ignore the eviction of Kenyan villagers. As Malm makes the point:

> Latour, however, is unambiguous on this count: "Domination is an effect, not a cause." But to understand why there is so much domination in the world, one needs to see it *as a cause that has an effect that loops back to further strengthen that cause* . . . the kind of dialectic Latour loathes, and the key to understanding why certain relations of inequality seem to be etched in stone.[13]

"Contemporary hybridism," argues Malm, "comes in two main forms: constructionism and new materialism. If the former collapses nature into society, the latter does the reverse."[14] Both Wallace-Wells and Latour effectively treat *reality* as a *hybrid* of nature and society. Wallace-Wells does so by failing to interrogate the logic that defines capitalism as kleptocratic and thus ideologically impervious to regulatory modification; Latour through his insistence that the "social" and the "natural" are "utterly arbitrary poles on a mental map" having "no more existence than West and East," such that domination is no more than a particular configuration of the relationship between these poles destined to be displaced by some future configuration.[15]

The practical difficulty here is that neither Wallace-Wells' nor Latour's understanding of the way in which capitalism informs our understanding of the relationship between nature and society is remotely adequate to explain how we find ourselves in our current ecological dilemma. Wallace-Wells fears we may be tilting toward an uninhabitable earth, but thinks a re-engineered capitalism can save us—implicitly conceding to the logic of commodification that acting in accord with its dictates is our natural state. Latour appears to hold that we're simply living out the inevitable course of the hybrid reality we have constructed—effectively positing that we could not have done otherwise. Whether such a nature/society hybrid leads to throwing up our hands in futility. As Wallace-Wells puts it against Latour, there's not much reason to think that those empowered to make meaningful change will change their ways. Wallace-Wells and Latour arrive at the same conclusions by different roads (and perhaps some hand-wringing denial on Wallace-Well's part)—but the same ecological nihilism. Malm rejects Latour's fatalistic hybridism, but the same argument could be just as well deployed against Wallace-Wells' misplaced optimism:

> A superstorm does not strike a shoreline because of something that has happened there. Behind it is the totality of the fossil economy, and so we can briefly sum up three tenets of a socialist climate realism: 1.) social relations have real causal primacy in the development of fossil energy and technologies based on it; 2.) by recursive loops of reinforcement, these relations have been cemented into the obdurate structure of the fossil economy; 3.) that totality has in its turn fired up the totality of the earth system, so that (some) humans have real reasons to be afraid.[16]

A superstorm, in other words, has as its cause the entire history of the development of fossil fuels and the greenhouse gas emissions it produces, and the relationship of the "social," that is, the capitalists responsible for hydrocarbon extraction, and the "earth system," that is, the planetary conditions that make life on earth possible. But this relationship has now become "cemented," fixed and reinforced by a logic of commodification that jeopardizes that life. This is no hybrid; *it is a struggle*. Wallace-Wells is not mistaken merely because he fails to distinguish society from nature, but because he fails to see that the social has become cemented into the "obdurate structure of the fossil economy" in virtue of the ontology of capital that takes the commodity value of hydrocarbons for granted. Latour is not mistaken because he fails to see that the climate crisis presents an existential threat to life on Earth, but because he fails to identify the difference between the capitalized society and nature such that culpability can be squarely assigned to the former. Hence, neither can show why projects like REDD are immoral as well as self-defeating, and neither have much hope to offer to its indigenous casualties.

BABOONS, BADGERS, AND BATS

In his forceful argument against Latour's hybridism (and indirectly against Wallace-Wells propensity to treat capitalism as a state of nature), Andreas Malm argues that:

> Nature is real; nature and society form a unity of opposites; society is constructed; agency cannot be found in inanimate matter but may still appear among human collectives, which can potentially target the incumbent technology that embodies social power . . . Rejecting hybridism, and its two branches, then, is not a matter of staking out some bland third way or middle course. It is about recovering the theoretical basis for ecological militancy.[17]

Malm is certainly right to single out *human* agency, *human* chauvinism, as the responsible party with respect to the ecological destruction that can be traced to anthropogenic—capitalist—causes; he's right to distinguish a particular capacity for technology-producing human agency from that of nonhuman animals: "[a]s inexact as it is to blame humankind rather than capital for the warming condition, it would be fantastical to think of any other species than *Homo sapiens sapiens* hatching a capitalist mode of production. Baboons could not do it, nor badgers or bats."[18] Malm argues that "it would presumably be of some interest to understand how our species but no other could do this [create the warming condition] to the earth."[19] He then goes on to explore cognitive differences between human an nonhuman animals in the interest of assigning exclusive culpability to human beings for the climate crisis. Well and good; it's also at this juncture, however, that Malm sells himself short with respect to his stated aim of recovering the theoretical basis for "ecological militancy." For while it's likely the case that baboons are not cognitively equipped to replace Rex Tillerson at ExxonMobil, it is precisely the fact that the baboon's capacity for sentience poses no obstacle to its subjugation to the logic of commodification that must be recovered and theorized if we're to understand how *Homo sapiens sapiens*—or some of its members—could do this—impose the rapacious Kleptocene—upon the earth.

Put differently: Malm's view that human agency is distinct from that of nonhuman animals in ways that are morally relevant to the critique of capitalism is certainly right: human beings, individually and collectively bear the blame for catastrophes like the climate crisis. But there's more to this story: an additional and crucial bulwark that supports the "theoretical basis" for any meaningful form of "ecological militancy" must include an analysis of the extent to which the logic of commodification systematically nullifies values that pose an impediment to the pursuit of profit. The capacity for agency is relevant to capitalism *only* insofar it facilitates the advance of the profit motive. Whether an organism is sentient or not, cognitively capable or not, an agent or not, is irrelevant to capitalism with one exception: utility toward converting all value to exchange value. The value of agency is thus determined according to the enculturated social structures that maximally advantage the capitalist. The pursuit of profit authorizes some human agents as beneficiaries of capital and others as disposable labor, some as CEOs and others as resources. Human agency forms a critical part of the capitalist tool-set, but not *because* being human is a feature of capital's ontological bedrock, but rather *because* agency supplies the distinction between some human beings and "Other" human beings, as well as some human beings and all nonhuman beings, that "justifies" the subjugation of sentience to exchange value. In the hands of the capitalist, the crucial distinction is thus not between human agent and nonhuman non-agent, but between agency that can be utilized toward profit-seeking and everything else consigned to potential commodity. Indeed, if baboons, bats, or badgers somehow turned out to be better fossil fuel company CEOs, it's hard to see how their failure to be human beings would prevent their rise to power. Malm rightly takes to task human agency because it's the guilty party, but what he doesn't quite see is that it's not membership in *Homo sapiens sapiens* that matters to the capitalist; it's agency. And it's not just any agency—it's agency that can be put to the service of the kleptocratic objectives of capital.

If this modest critique of Malm is on the right track, we have to conclude that it's not the agent/non-agent distinction that creates the conditions for exploiting nonhuman animals as well as human beings whose sentience is preemptively discounted as labor. What creates the optimal condition for a capitalist enterprise is the opportunity to take full advantage of the capacity for agency *regardless its source*. Although Malm is right to argue that there is a distinction between human and nonhuman agency, and that this distinction forms the basis of human liability for the "warming condition," to comprehend how agency, human or nonhuman, becomes commodified as labor, we must appeal to an ontology for which there are no exemptions other than what a given entrenched social structure makes opportune. Any militant response aimed at abating ecological collapse must understand the role that agency plays as a culpable actor—but also as a commodity. Sentience can no more act as an exemption to the logic of commodification than the concept of labor rights, human rights, or animal rights can disrupt the machinations of profit-seeking. We can decry poor working conditions, child labor, and animal abuse. We can demand better regulation. But insofar as we believe, like Wallace-Wells, that the system itself is sound, or with Latour that the system is a hybrid that provides no agent to take responsibility, any effort at militancy will fail. But such efforts will also fail if we ignore a critical fact Malm hints at, but doesn't quite say: *the structural inequalities upon which capitalism depends are rooted in the nullification of the very value of that upon which agency itself depends, the capacity for sentience—the capacity for suffering.*

The capacity for agency does, of course, afford a tiny handful of structurally privileged human beings great power. As Christian Parenti puts it in *Tropic of Chaos*, there will continue for a time to be those who can afford "armed lifeboats" outfitted to survive the chaos of war over access to existential necessities like clean water.[20] These beneficiaries of capital come to be defined in terms of their agency by, for example, the regulatory schemas that appear environmentally responsible but actually conceal and advance a profit-motive. Consider, for example, that the regulations that govern the oil and gas industries are often drafted by the industry itself, are rarely followed, and virtually never conflict with the bottom line.[21] Countless and largely invisible social structures encourage consumers to think there's something unique or different, for example, about a business that sells live animals as food that makes it inferior, even immoral, compared to the franchise that sells hamburgers or tacos or fish sandwiches. Wet markets are represented in Western news stories about the Covid-19 outbreak as rogue enterprises rightly understood as radically different from the "normal" capitalism of factory farms. But such examples show only how selective we are concerning whose agency we elevate as credible, and whose we're willing to assign as suspect—reinforcing the social structures that support capitalist advantage. Malm *is* right to identify human agency as a crucial source of blame for environmental destruction, but in glossing over the structural inequalities that supply the capitalist with resources and labor regardless the sentience of the commodified, he's unable to mount a convincing case for the ecological militance that fuels his primary objective. The beneficiaries of capital who own the factory farms and lease the Arctic are unlikely mutineers, and the burger franchise worker can't afford to lose her job.

Consider once more the example of "what's for dinner." For those who can afford it, buying more of "what's for dinner" is made possible by the fact that it's identified as *our* "what's for dinner." "We" condemn the slaughter of Pangolins for wet market sale in China on our drive to McDonald's. Our agency is privileged and normalized with respect to what "we" get to count as food. "We" are not going to personally kill a cow, but "we're" comfortable hiding behind a "fatal complacency" made somehow more palatable when we buy "grass fed" beef at a Wholefoods. In short, "we" feel justified not because the suffering of what ends up as "what's for dinner" suffers any less on the way to our plate, and not because we don't know that this suffering occurs at the behest of our sense of entitled consumption of animal bodies, but because we're not *"them."* We're not this "Other" whose agency we regard as morally suspect. We might call this *fatally complacent Western chauvinism*, but it's also wedded to the structural inequalities that supply racism and cultural imperialism with their stereotypes. Whatever we call it, it's as much part and parcel of our "flaunting it" from some imagined "top of the food chain" as is "I'd probably choose growth." In fact, it's this complacency that, while literally fatal for many of those commodified *as* "other," reinforces the prerogatives of the systemically advantaged, like Wallace-Wells, effectively defining agency in terms of what is given to privilege.

Fatally complacent Western chauvinism—the agency of normalized inaction wedded to racist stereotype—has impact well-beyond "what's for dinner." As Sabrina Tavernise and Richard Oppel, Jr. report for the *New York Times*:

> As the coronavirus upends American life, Chinese-Americans face a double threat. Not only are they grappling like everyone else with how to avoid the virus itself, they are also contending with growing racism in the form of verbal and physical attacks. Other Asian-Americans . . . are facing threats, too, lumped together with Chinese-Americans by a bigotry that does not know the difference.[22]

On a cost/benefit analysis of what most advantages particular forms of the commodification of sentience, "lumping together" Korea, Myanmar, or the Philippines into a single package of "otherness" is an opportunity to exploit an imperialist narrative that advances Western economic interests. "Mr. Trump and his Republican allies, write Tavernise and Oppel, "are intent on calling the coronavirus 'the Chinese virus.'" Trump, in fact, rejects "*World Health*

Organization guidance against using geographic locations when naming illnesses," even though such names are widely understood to "[provoke] backlash." That the use of "China" or "Wuhan" virus is racist is obvious, but such reference also serve less obvious, more nefarious, purposes: to normalize and thus provide cover to a complacency that legitimates an "I'd probably choose growth" world view, including the "what's for dinner" conversation that damns the wet market between bites of pork chop. We might call this *fatal hypocrisy*—quite literally: Trump later insisted in a Tweet that "we totally protect our Asian American community" even as "he dismissed concerns that his language could lead to any harm."

The key point: however apparently different, Trump's Tweet sanctifies a disposition toward the planet, its resources, and inhabitants that is ultimately no different in substance or consequence than Wallace-Wells' "I'd probably go for growth." Wallace-Wells undermines the central thrust of *The Uninhabitable Earth* at least insofar as he intends to solicit the militance that brings us back from the climate crisis point of no return. Trump and Wallace-Wells enjoy the public recognition of a privileged agency that benefits them not merely as affluent, white, Western(ized) men, but at the direct and indirect expense of others whose capacity for agency, or at least sentience, is preemptively discounted and subjugated. Trump gets to withdraw from the Paris Climate Accord and claim he's an environmental president.[23] Wallace-Wells gets an audience for a provocatively named book that, in the end, "goes for growth." Both effectively, however unwittingly, conceal the commodification of sentience upon which their hypocrisy is dependent; neither have any excuse for this willful ignorance; both tacitly endorse the Western chauvinism that sustains the institutions that benefit them—white, heteropatriarchal, and affluent, wasteful, and carnivore. Trump makes no bones about his denial of the climate crisis. When asked in 2018 to comment on the thirteen federal agency *National Climate Assessment's* finding that "[b]ased on extensive evidence, it is extremely likely that human activities, especially emissions of greenhouse gases, are the dominant cause of the observed warming since the mid-20th century. For the warming over the last century, there is no convincing alternative explanation supported by the extent of the observational evidence," his response was only more blunt than short: "I don't believe it. No, no, I don't believe it . . . "[24] Yet, while Wallace-Wells' forthrightly acknowledges that what might be required to achieve a "decarbonized economy" is "a perfectly renewable energy system, a reimagined system of agriculture, and, perhaps, even a meatless planet," he rejects Trump's "I don't believe it," but leaves us to wonder what exactly *The Uninhabitable Earth* is for other than a eulogy.[25]

FREE RANGE CAPITAL CONQUEST AND ITS CONSEQUENCES

The enculturated denial that sustains most species of chauvinist imperialism, including Wallace-Wells,' is the fertile ground of capitalist exploitation—at least until it isn't. Consider just a few examples that reach beyond wet markets and factory farms: the regulatory failures that resulted in lawsuits over Johnson and Johnson's baby powder, the company's history of resisting regulatory oversight, and the cancer claims that resulted in preventable human suffering,[26] or BP's regulation-evading shortcuts that produced the Deep Water Horizon disaster in the Gulf of Mexico in 2010,[27] or massive Covid-19 outbreaks at U.S. meat-packing plants caused by CEOs who refused to purchase equipment or institute procedures to prevent super-spreader events inside the plants.[28] What each of these have in common is that they caused immense suffering *regardless* the product or service of their business; this suffering was preventable and unnecessary; casualties occurred primarily to either consumers or workers lacking the economic wherewithal to mount defense or evasion; the companies responsible continued to profit during and after the crises they caused and exist to the present day despite the fatalities they caused; each has successfully crafted an effective rehabilitation of its image and, lastly, their self-styled rehabilitations invite consumers to forget their toxic, violent, reckless histories; the capacity for agency played little role in the determination of who'd end up a casualty.

Johnson and Johnson offers a model example of these dynamics. The company has taken full advantage of the opportunity to rehabilitate its public image by creating a one dose Covid-19 vaccine that, despite reports of albeit rare blood-clots, is now poised to reclaim the limelight of its former prestige.[29] Yet, although the strategy is very different, the goal of the Chinese campaign to promote wet markets is substantially the same: to recuperate an image of "food" as safe, good, desirable.[30] Both, of course, do serve valuable purposes. What is of greatest advantage to Johnson and Johnson is that a vaccine that can slow the spread of a potentially fatal virus *is* a good thing. That Chinese families have access to sources of fresh food is a good thing. What Johnson and Johnson and the wet market have in common, however, are their primary motives: rehabilitating a public image requires appearing to be a good thing; it does not necessarily require being a good thing beyond what a fickle and often short-sighted public is likely to remember. It seems hard to imagine that we'd forget about a cancer-causing product Johnson and Johnson *knew* about, or that ExxonMobil hid what the company knew about climate change twenty years ago, or that wet markets are the probable source of viral transmission from nonhuman animals to human beings. But the very success of each advertising campaign suggests we will and we do forget.

Our mistake is to assume that "advantageous" and "good thing" mean the same thing; *they don't.* Where greater advantage accrues to ignoring toxicity, cruelty, neglect, or recklessness, that is the business as usual; where the *appearance* of concern for human health and welfare is of greater advantage, that is the plan. What could, moreover, have been a very costly venture for Johnson and Johnson's rehabilitation efforts turned out to have been a boon: a viral pandemic so deadly that the risk and expense of developing a vaccine could be shifted onto the shoulders of taxpayers in the interest of "warp speed," all the while the company erases the history of its product's causal role in ovarian cancer.[31] What each of these otherwise very different examples share in common is not only the capacity to profit while at the same time producing great harm, but the capacity to recover public trust without any fundamental alteration of their business models, in some cases on the public dime, a fact that evinces all the more clearly the extent to which exchange value exceeds all other, the very meaning of "[i]n most cases, I'd probably go for growth."

It is, however, on this point about exchange value that Naomi Klein offers significant insight—but only gets it half right. She argues that,

> [a] culture that places so little value on black and brown lives that it is willing to let human beings disappear beneath the waves, or set themselves on fire in detention centres, will also be willing to let the countries where black and brown people live disappear beneath the waves, or desiccate in the arid heat. When that happens, theories of human hierarchy—that we must take care of our own first—will be marshalled to rationalize these monstrous decisions. We are making this rationalization already, if only implicitly. Although climate change will ultimately be an existential threat to all of humanity, in the short term we know that it does discriminate, hitting the poor first and worst, whether they are abandoned on the rooftops of New Orleans during Hurricane Katrina or whether they are among the 36 million who according to the U.N. are facing hunger due to drought in Southern and East Africa.[32]

Klein's right that where a country's cultural values embody the racism of its hierarchical social and economic order, it's unlikely to embody much else in its relationships with other nations. She's right that the populist's "take care of our own," "America first," rhetoric is likely to be deployed to justify "monstrous decisions" to keep our own, or some of our own, as Parenti puts it, lifeboats afloat. But even though Klein calls out the "market logic" behind these decisions, what makes them "monstrous" in the first place is not their manifest racism, but the logic that *operationalizes* racism so effectively that black and brown people left on rooftops are the same as those who disappear beneath the waves or die in the arid heat, that the terrified animals sold at wet markets are no different than the terrified animals coming up to the stun gun in a factory farm cattle channel—namely a logic of commodification for which sentience is no obstacle.

Racism precedes exchange value to the extent that the capitalist takes advantage of it, but exchange value precedes racism in that the logic of commodification cares not at all *what* can become the material of its advantage, only *that* it can. Capitalism is thus neither racist, sexist, or speciesist *per se*; it's simply amoral and mercenary. For the capitalist, it cannot matter whether Chinese wet markets perpetrate cruelty, or become a source of viral outbreak, or are a critical source of food security except when any or all of these threaten to impact profitability. As Johnson and Johnson so richly illustrate, it's the image that matters. The Western chauvinism elicited in citing the cruelty of wet markets is contained not in the way nonhuman animals are treated at wet markets, and not even in the hypocrisy of calling out the wet market while ignoring the factory farm. The chauvinism lay in the faulty belief that somehow the Western capitalism of the factory farm is superior, or more regulable, or safer, or more civilized compared to the state capitalism of a Communist country. The racism of a "hierarchy—that we must take care of our own first—[that] will be marshalled to rationalize these monstrous decisions," wholly ignoring the suffering of black and brown people, reflects not merely a "culture that places so little value on black and brown lives," but a logic of commodification for whom the fact that these are sentient lives has already been either converted to exchange value as labor, or ignored as "disposable." Klein rightly calls out culture, but the picture she paints is distorted by what it leaves unacknowledged: the capitalist enculturation that implicitly invites us to condemn "bad" capitalism as if there were a "normal" capitalism that could function without its hierarchies. This is false: insofar as the survival of capitalist enterprise depends first and foremost on the premise that sentience is no bar to commodification, it will reproduce whatever hierarchies are necessary to sustain that premise. This is made easier, moreover, by the very fact that all the while we rightly decry racism, we ignore speciesism. Like Wallace-Wells, Klein not only leaves largely intact the logic that insures the continuing devaluation of the people she defends, but, also like Wallace-Wells, dooms her own clarion call for change to little more than the reforms creative capitalists see as a profit opportunity.

It's not hard to see that, given the complex cultural, geopolitical, and economic factors of which we must take account in sharp analyses like Klein's, references to tropes like "left" and "right" have limited utility. If Klein only gets it half right, Wallace-Wells' may be in a yet worse position. The logic of commodification is no more vulnerable to political identity than are, for example, viruses likely to avoid mutation. And just as a virus will adapt to insure continuing replication, so too a capitalist enterprise will adapt through the corruption of elected representatives, the efforts of lobbyists, the evasion of evidence, the creation of effective ad-campaigns, or the calculation of the cost of doing business as usual—including shirking or ignoring regulation. Regulation will not prevent an enterprise from depleting its resources, even if it can slow it down, or from lying about these facts. Like a virus, the logic of commodification isn't immoral; it's amoral; it isn't "left" or "right," though it can become politicized. A company can "green" its image to meet the demands of a more "left" leaning consumer, but it cannot evade the environmental consequences of its actions; though it can ignore them and lie about them, for a while. Insofar as left-oriented reform measures assume capitalism can be rehabilitated, their boards of directors remain as committed to the myth of endless resources as do their rightward counterparts; regulation may slow the inevitable propensity for a particular enterprise to undermine its own existential conditions, but it cannot stop it. The deregulatory mania on the kleptocratic right simply speeds up the process, but it doesn't alter its fundamental character.

The self-defeat of a capitalist enterprise is also not, as Ashley Dawson might see it, chaos; it's simply the logical outcome of the assumption that the body of capital can grow without end. Indeed, As Dawson shows, even the deliberate annihilation of a species can be put to service in the interest of capitalist objectives:

> In some cases, ecocide is a conscious strategy of imperialism, generating what might be termed ecological warfare. For example, the destruction of the great herds of bison that roamed the Great Plains of North America was a calculated military strategy designed to deprive Native Americans of the environmental resources on which they depended . . . Commercial hunting began in the 1830s, soon reaching a toll of two million animals a year. By 1891, there were less than 1000 bison left on the continent, and the native Americans had been crushed—defeated militarily and forced onto a series of isolated barren reservations.[33]

Allied with private capital interests, American military might drive nearly to extinction both the American Bison and the indigenous peoples who depended on these herds. Corporate interests such as Hudson Bay traded 75,000 bison hides in their zenith year, 1844; wealthy trophy hunters responsible for the slaughter of more than 5000 animals a day as late as 1872—even as legislation in states like Kansas began to seek the preservation of the last remaining animals; a railway engineer was quoted as having remarked in 1873 that you could "walk a 100 miles along the Santa Fe railroad right-of-way by stepping from one bison carcass to another."[34]

But, as Dawson's example shows, regulatory restraint seems extremely unlikely to be accomplished even where there exists a promise of strict enforcement: the momentum to annihilate the American Bison herds was not the product of the potential profitability of bison hides (bones, tongues) alone, but derived first and foremost from the desire to claim land for settlers, a desire which necessitated the removal, in fact, the genocide of the indigenous peoples who occupied these lands. That one revenue generator—the acquisition of bison hides—became unsustainable did not mean that the primary objectives—land for settlers, the construction of railroads, defeat of an enemy demonized as "savage"—was unachieved. Put differently: Wallace-Wells argues that with careful planning, capitalist enterprise can be corralled as a sustainable generator of goods and services; Dawson argues that what makes capitalism un-regulable is its propensity to chaos. Both are mistaken. Capitalism is not the chaotic world system Dawson proposes because chaos is not useful to capitalism *unless* it advances a profit motive: while being hunted nearly to extinction solicited sufficient alarm among some elected, for example in the Idaho State Legislature "after they were gone from the state," this "chaos" allied with the profit motives of railroad engineers, hide traders, and homesteaders, among many others. But capitalism is also not the regulable system of global trade to which the capitalist aspires: the fact that by 1902 only 23 American Bison remained at Yellowstone, just over 1000 in all of North America, and a reservation system which remains a source of food insecurity and misery for its effectively imprisoned peoples today, attests to the chauvinism, racism, and the logic that governed Westward expansion. The stealthy profiteer takes advantage of whatever can be commodified: species of animal, population of human beings, natural disaster, geopolitical crisis, pandemic to advance a new market. The slaughter of the American Bison might be described as a manufacture of "chaos," but the product was a Westward expansion whose drive, like its railroads, would not be stopped, or slowed, or regulated.

When an industry faces self-defeat, its efforts at survival can threaten our existential conditions. As Dawson explains, such was the case with the near extinction of whales and the consequent loss of whale oil, and it's not hard to imagine what the end of Big Oil or Big Gas might look like without renewable replacements.[35] But, contrary to any promise toward regulation and/or Dawson's view of chaos, such threats can themselves be transformed into novel business opportunities: *disaster capitalism*. Up to the tipping point of environmental collapse, crises can be re-purposed by capital as opportunities simply because the appeal to need, especially the need for energy, is so easily exploited. What the logic of commodification predicts, in other words, is that there are likely no forms of regulation that will either prevent resource exhaustion or discourage taking advantage of crises, *and* there are no convincing reasons to believe, short of global environmental catastrophe, that chaos cannot in most cases be re-purposed to profitability. Consider for example businesses that sell private fire-fighting services to wealthy California homeowners bracing for the next climate change fueled firenado,[36] brokers who arrange access for their wealthy clients to the Covid-19 vaccine.[37] or contractors who take advantage of racist political projects like "Build the Wall!"[38] On the one hand, in each of these cases the logic of commodification is likely to result in the destruction of the conditions of its profitability not only because resources are themselves limited, but because some resources—like anxiety, fear, or even panic—have limited lifespans. There are only so many California homeowners with the means to contract private fire fighters; there are only so many acres of California forest to burn. The same goes for wealthy families looking to skip to the head of the Covid-19 vaccine waiting line; the U.S.-Mexico border is long, but it's not infinite, especially as technological surveillance is poised to replace steel and concrete. On the other hand, however, taking advantage of the opportunity created by fear and the need to placate it is not a reflection of chaos, but its opposite: it's *because* the logic confronts no unconquerable obstacle in its relentless pursuit of exchange value, including its own complicity in fear, that it destines itself to consume *every* resource—including fear itself.

All capitalism is thus, at bottom, disaster capitalism for the same reasons that all capitalist enterprise is kleptocratic. No circumstance, no matter how challenging, presents itself to the logic as chaos, but rather as opportunity, obstacle, disposable, or all three at differing times, under different circumstances. This is capitalism's genius: what originates as an obstacle, for example, not having a drill bit big enough to drill deeper into the Earth, becomes an opportunity to build bigger drill bits; what shale deposits are spent or chemically dirtied in the process of hydraulic fracturing may result in drill bits abandoned as too big to be worth the cost to move. If a species of animal needs to be exterminated in order to starve the people who depend on it either to submission or death, make jokes about walking on the carcasses. It's not the capitalist system that's chaotic, it's the impacts it imposes on the capacity of the planet to recuperate, impacts often experienced by human and nonhuman beings as suffering and misery. Yet, because the logic of commodification is immune to considerations of sentience, it's not relevant *to it* to be able to distinguish its environmental impacts from the resources it exploits: a resource is a *resource*.

What disaster capitalism shows is that the logic of commodification cannot be captured without significant distortion in the easy tropes of "left" or "right," technocrat or hippy; it's not itself *a* culture, though exchange value forms one of our earliest enculturated values. It is inherently kleptocratic, but theft for it is merely a species of resource exploitation; it is psychopathological, not in any hyperbolic sense, but according to the clinical definition: it acts in a fashion internally coherent, dogged, and systemically insensible to the prospect of its own self-defeat. The logic acts on the presupposition that, having preempted even the most burdensome of moral obstacles, namely, any consideration owed to sentience, commodifiable resources really are endless, until they're not. But that last moment only arrives when exchange value has been reduced to rubble, *literally*; that is, when capitalism is exposed not as chaotic, but relentless, environmentally annihilating, and intrinsically nihilistic. Thus "left" and "right" can only be correctly understood as barometers of the speed with which we advance toward "uninhabitable." We are already "burning-it-all-down."

STRUCTURAL INEQUALITY UP AND DOWN THE FOOD (SUPPLY) CHAIN

David Wallace-Wells puts it roughly this way in *The Uninhabitable Earth*: the rule of capital is a Frankenstein, that is, a monstrous creation that personifies human chauvinism and arrogance. This may well be, but unlike the original figure of Mary Shelly's *Frankenstein* who is misunderstood by the local torch-wielding villagers, and in the end solicits more empathy than horror, the Frankenstein of capitalism is a monster without conscience or distraction in its relentless conquest for profit.[39] So long as the "rule of capital" rules the day, what can be disarticulated, rearranged, reassembled, repackaged, and advertised as exchange value will be, or better: will be until it can't, that is, until there remain none who can be convinced through manipulation, extortion, or fear, that the rubble can be in some way monetized.[40] As an example, Wallace-Wells offers us Naomi Klein's account of the shock doctrine applied to Puerto Rico:

> [The shock doctrine] does give a very clear account of what kind of strategy to expect from the world's money elite in a time of rolling ecological crisis . . . Here is an island endowed with abundant green energy nevertheless importing all its oil, and an ecological paradise nevertheless importing all its food, importing both from a quasi-colonial mainland power that sees it merely as a market . . . It is hard to imagine a better illustration of the empire of capital in a time of climate change . . . This did not prompt a dramatic expansion of social spending or the extension of a Marshall Plan across the Caribbean; instead Donald Trump tossed a few rolls of paper towels to the citizens of San Juan, then left them to plead with the outsiders who now controlled public coffers for mercy, which did not come.[41]

What comes instead, argues Wallace-Wells, are new opportunities to create exchange value: " . . . here, too, even relatively fractional adjustments to the West's basic orientation toward business and financial capitalism are likely to arrive like earthquakes, so much has that orientation produced the culture's collective sense of what is thinkable and what is not."[42] It's hard to know exactly whose "collective sense" Wallace-Wells is referring to given that the impacts of Hurricane Maria (2017) were felt very differently by those whose daily lives were profoundly disrupted than by those for whom it was just another report of an extreme weather event somewhere else. But for the capitalist "in the scramble for shrinking profits" on a planet whose endless resources turn out to be far less than endless, the rush to extract, refine, grow, harvest, slaughter, process, and transport fuel and food will likely "only intensify," argues Wallace-Wells, "a further self-entrenchment of the rule of capital."[43]

Wallace-Wells makes starkly clear that those whose corporate or government power reinforces their position as the overwhelming beneficiaries of shock doctrine profit ventures have "much to answer for, to say the least."[44] He recognizes the long-normalized structural inequality that the rule of capital exploits and reproduces: "[t]he market has justified inequality for generations by pointing to opportunity and invoking the mantra of new prosperity, which it promised would benefit all. This was probably always less credible as a truth claim than it was as propaganda."[45] Offering the stock market crash of 2007, the Great Recession that followed, and a recovery whose benefits fell "almost entirely to the very wealthiest" as an example, Wallace-Wells observes that "this [form of recovery] itself represents a crisis of the entire system." It's "clear not just from the raging populism, on both left and right, sweeping Europe and the United States in the aftermath of the crash," he writes, "but by skepticism and lacerating self-doubt beaming out from the highest free market citadels" like the *International Monetary Fund*.[46] IMF anxiety, however, does not appear to offer much hope that the capitalist Frankenstein will turn back from the path of "further self-entrenchment." In fact, quite the opposite, with apocalyptic consequences:

> More than 140 million people in just three regions of the world will be made climate migrants by 2050 . . . assuming current warming and emissions trends: 86 million in sub-Saharan Africa, 40 million in South Asia, and 17 million in Latin America . . . [C]limate change may unleash as many as a billion migrants on the world by 2050. One billion—that is about as many people as live today in North and South America combined. Imagine the two continents suddenly drowned by the sea, the whole New World submerged, and everyone left bobbing at the surface now fighting for a foothold, somewhere, anywhere,

> and if someone else is scrambling for the same dry spot, scrambling to get there first.[47]

In short, Wallace-Wells paints a very dark picture of the impacts that the rule of capital has for the future of the planet, its cultures, and its inhabitants, making it that much more perplexing that he apparently plans to remain among those who'd "probably go for growth."

Indeed, there seem to be two Wallace-Wells: the one who has no intention of going vegan, and the one who recognizes the suffering caused by business as usual. This perplexing inconsistency (of which Wallace-Wells is by no means the only example) is made graphically clear with respect to the consequences of "business as usual" in Michael Grabell's and Bernice Yeung's *ProPublica* investigation of a Covid-19 outbreak at a *Smithfield Farms* meat-packing plant, Summer 2020. Despite repeated warning that a pandemic-level virus could spread with potentially devastating effects in what Smithfield CEO Kenneth Sullivan calls its "harvesting facilities," the company not only neglected to institute proactive safety protocols, but, consistent with the logic of commodification, sought to displace blame for the virtually inevitable Covid-19 outbreak on what Wallace-Wells describes as the all-absolving "bigness": "What no one anticipated, and has never happened in our lifetimes, is the scenario we are living through today," Sullivan wrote. "That is, our harvest facilities, which are the critical linchpin in the supply chain, could be threatened, *en masse*, by a global pandemic that threatens our ability to produce food"[48] No amount of warning, claims Sullivan, could have prepared the meat-packing industry for coronavirus. A global pandemic is just too big to plan for. As *ProPublica* shows, however, planning for just this scenario was what the meat-packing industry had been urged to do for over a decade:

> [A] *ProPublica* investigation has found that for more than a dozen years, critical businesses like meatpackers have been warned that a pandemic was coming. With eerie prescience, infectious disease experts and emergency planners had modeled scenarios in which a highly contagious virus would cause rampant absenteeism at processing plants, leading to food shortages and potential closures. The experts had repeatedly urged companies and government agencies to prepare for exactly the things that Smithfield's CEO now claims were unrealistic.[49]

It's hard to imagine a scenario more chaotic, indeed, terrifying and destabilizing than a global pandemic. But to comprehend how a virus could wreak havoc for the meat industry's supply chain, and thus how the resort to the "just too big" excuse plays a lead role in industry decision-making, we must look to the underlying logic that drives its cost-benefit analyses of action versus inaction (or action versus cosmetic pretense to action). What we discover is that, at least at one meat-packing plant, the chaos experienced by workers as a terrifying, even deadly, illness became sport for managers who placed bets on the spread of infection, a display condemned at higher ranks in the plant, but only after public disclosure threatened translation into financial losses.

Smithfield CEO Sullivan certainly knows that the Smithfield supply chain contributes mightily to greenhouse gas emissions, accelerating the climate crisis, adding fuel to the fire of its ancillary consequences—like the zoonotic transmission of coronaviruses. Yet, even as Covid-19 spread throughout several Smithfield plants, even as it became clear that the origin of transmission could be traced to the commodification of nonhuman animals in Chinese Wet Markets, the question whether sentient creatures should count as food registered in no way whatsoever in decisions about how the meat industry should manage the pandemic within its plants. To be clear, this is not at least in the first place a point about the fact that horseshoe bats,[50] Yorkshire pigs,[51] Black Angus Cattle[52] or Jersey Giant chickens,[53] are all capable of suffering, or that they may have a right to consideration of their capacity for sentience. The central point is that the logic of commodification so fully, even mechanically, preempts the way animal body industrialists conceive their business models, that whether Chinese wet markets and the American meat industry are both examples of the same subjugation of sentience to exchange value neither registers to conscience nor even arises to consciousness. Sullivan's goal in appealing to bigness is to displace blame, and thus responsibility, all the while carrying-on with business as usual. Pandemic makes "business as usual" harder, but that's not a point about rights. Indeed, for the rule of capital, nonhuman animal rights make about as much sense as do square circles or red greens. But neither do human rights or the capacity for agency retain much value, as is made clear by the 929 Covid-19 infections at Smithfield's Sioux Falls, South Dakota plant, or the 40,000 industry cases across the country. That sanitation measures to protect workers has come only after absenteeism, bad press, and preventable deaths began to outweigh the expense of more aggressive sanitation is also telling,[54] and even here Sullivan's *modus operandi* remains excuse-giving appeals to bigness: "For better or worse, our plants are what they are . . . Four walls, engineered design, efficient use of space, Spread out? Okay. Where?" It's hard to imagine a more concise claim consistent with the logic of commodification, or one that makes less room for rights.

What the disarticulated animal body supply chain illustrates in microcosm is just how deeply the logic of commodification is woven into the enculturation of capitalist exchange value, particularly with respect to what counts as "what's for dinner," or—and not the same—as food. Confronted with the kind of crisis for which the logic can either create new opportunities for profit-generation, or meet its limit in the exhaustion of resources, it's not surprising that the response of CEOs like Sullivan is to reaffirm the meat industry's vital role in food production all the while running interference against a tsunami of bad press concerning viral outbreaks in its plants. Given Sullivan's strategy was successful enough to persuade then President Donald Trump to "issue an executive order to keep facilities open" to preserve supply chains, it's also hardly surprising that it takes more than, for example, PETA (*People for the Ethical Treatment of Animals*) videos to raise any real concern for animal rights. It's not that the commodification of sentience is buried under mountains of chaos—though pandemic, pollution, resource exhaustion, and the climate crisis supply plenty of this; it's that the value of sentience is extinguished by the rule of capital such that there's nothing to unearth, such that even environmentally conscientious writers like Wallace-Wells can throw off one-liners like that "when you're on top of the food chain, it's okay to flaunt it." It's one thing, in other words, to evince concern, even to lay out in graphic detail how much worse things are going to get if "we" fail to act; but it's another to actually call for militant resistance against capitalist forms of exchange whose inherently kleptocratic impulses not only depend on either false or perverse premises, but are essentially nihilistic. Wallace-Wells does the first—but languishes on the second.

It's this failure of more probing analyses of the ontology of capital, analyses that show the way toward revolutionary change, that leave the vast majority of human and nonhuman beings at the mercy of those who fancy themselves at the "top of the food chain," especially affluent global Northerners and the rising middle classes of developing world countries like China. The denial and cognitive dissonance that saturates Western(ized) cultural narratives solicits consent to fake "news" stories like this one: President Biden plans to combat the climate crisis calls for a dramatic reduction in meat-eating.[55]

This story is entirely false. As Stephanie Feldstein, *Washington Post*, argues, however, what's absurd about the fact that a reduction of meat-eating is not on the president's climate agenda isn't that far right media outlets made up the story; they did. It's that meat-consumption *should* be on the agenda:

> It didn't take long for fact-checkers to expose that right-wing media outlets, including Fox News, were wrong to claim that President Biden is plotting to ban or cut back on beef consumption to address climate change. The administration was just as quick to distance itself from the idea that it had any plans to even suggest people eat less meat. That's a shame. Lowering meat consumption *should* be in the president's climate agenda. In return, Americans would get more delicious plant-based foods and a more sustainable future . . . In fact, Biden has yet to release any specific climate plans related to food and agriculture.[56]

What stories like this one illustrate is the genuine absurdity of false dichotomous positions like the one Wallace-Wells appears to take. He acknowledges we may have to move to a "meatless planet,"[57] but undermines this claim by reaffirming our (false) place at the "top of the food chain." He argues that we won't get to any meaningful reduction of greenhouse gas emissions "through the dietary choices of individuals," but fails to recognize that his insistence on "policy changes," as Feldstein argues, must include what counts as food. "Eating organic is nice," writes Wallace-Wells, "but if your goal is to save the climate your vote is much more important."[58] In effect, Wallace-Wells appears to want to have his animal body cake and eat his policy reform too. That is, he deploys false dichotomy: personal choice versus policy, eating organic versus voting, to the ends of insisting that we might as well go ahead with our enculturated habits of consumption, but vote for policies that will fix the climate.

This is, of course, ludicrous. Animal agriculture is the heavy hitter of greenhouse gas emissions. Policy that does not include significant behavioral change with respect to meat consumption, particularly in the global North, is vacuous, or worse: a lie. As Feldstein shows:

> [R]eplacing 50 percent of animal products with plant-based foods could prevent more than 1.4 billion metric tons of greenhouse gas pollution by 2030, or a quarter of current U.S. annual emissions. The climate savings were even greater with steeper reductions: If beef consumption were reduced by 90 percent alongside a 50 percent reduction in other animal products, more than 2 billion metric tons of greenhouse gas emissions could be prevented by 2030 . . . Dietary changes won't solve the climate crisis on their own. But the [IPCC] study also found that if we continue along our current trajectory, diet-related emissions will increase by 9 percent by 2030, pushing us further away from the emission reductions needed to avoid the worst impacts of climate change.[59]

In short, what Wallace-Wells offers us is a false dichotomy designed to solicit *resignation* to continuing our current nihilistic trajectory along which the commodification of sentience will generate not only greenhouse gas emissions, but the reinforcement of gross social and economic inequality. Returning once more to Smithfield Farms, consider three examples of the intersection between the industrial causes of the climate crisis, the emergence of viral pandemic, and what constitutes effective wage slavery in the service of animal production and slaughter. Smithfield's CEO, Kenneth Sullivan's stated concerns during the Covid-19 pandemic did not reflect those of workers, even as 25.6% of the Smithfield workforce at its Sioux Fall, South Dakota plant became infected, and two died by early August, 2020.[60] Confronted by the accusation that the industry had responded too slowly, or that plants should introduce wider work-station spacing as a precaution to help slow transmission, Sullivan bristled, referring to the "revisionist historians" who would chronicle Covid-19's impact on food production as refusing to be "bound to reality." Second, Sullivan makes clear that what *is* his primary concern is the Smithfield supply chain, a fact that becomes clear by comparing industry protocols for preventing the spread of viral infection between workers with that of preventing infection between animals: "[w]e were probably more prepared for animal pandemic issues than we were for human pandemics," said one former meat industry executive.[61] It might be tempting to interpret such protocols as concern for animal health or welfare; true, but only insofar as sick or dying animals reduce the number available for slaughter, thereby disrupting the supply chain. It's tempting to grant Sullivan's claim that no one could have been prepared for Covid-19, that becoming overwhelmed by absenteeism and the scramble to find masks, PPE, and plexiglass dividers was just too big to respond to adequately. But what's equally clear is that the cost of doing nothing to protect workers is, in the long run, still less than the cost of valuing their lives. As Nancy Cleeland reports for SHRM:

> The Department of Labor's Occupational Safety and Health Administration (OSHA) on Sept. 10 issued its first citation against a meatpacking plant for failing to protect workers against the novel coronavirus that causes COVID-19. The Smithfield Packaged Meats Corp. in Sioux Falls, S.D., was cited after more than a thousand workers became ill and four died. A second plant was cited the following day . . . OSHA proposed a penalty of $13,494, which it said is the maximum allowed by law, for the Smithfield plant. Based on a coronavirus-related inspection, OSHA cited the company for one violation of the general duty clause for failing to provide a workplace free from recognized hazards that can cause death or serious harm. At least 1,294 Smithfield workers contracted coronavirus, and four employees died from the virus in the spring of 2020.[62]

That the cost of doing business is, in this case, high is no more a point about the welfare, much less the rights, of workers than, say, it was for mercury poisoned silver miners in Petosi, Bolivia or Huancavelica, Peru in 1564.[63] "High cost" simply reflects the one thing the logic of commodification cannot accommodate, and therefore ignores, until it can't: resource exhaustion. That is, insofar as mass production of animal bodies, silver bars, plastic water bottles, diamonds, rare earth metals, or rubber truck tires reflexively assumes the myth of endless resources, the rule of capital will remain inured against obstacles that could disrupt it. In 1564 such "obstacles" were the bodies of the poisoned indigenous peoples recruited through the effective slavery of the Mita system; in 2020 they're the bodies of the meat-packing plant workers who, like their earlier analogues, are made even more vulnerable to exploitation by the racism that advantages the capitalist whose quest for profits, also like labor in silver mines, results in one of the most dangerous jobs in the world even before coronavirus: meat-packing.[64]

The "fatal complacency" to which Wallace-Wells confesses is precisely what insures the conditions of meat-packing plants under any circumstances; Covid-19 merely intensifies these conditions and brings them into stark relief. The women and people of color for whom he insists he's concerned, indeed, so much so he writes that, having conquered the "white male monopoly," it's simply too much to ask to extend rights to nonhuman animals, are precisely the people most vulnerable to injury and infection at these plants. Regardless Wallace-Wells' assurances that women and persons of color are doing okay, it is precisely the same structural inequalities that "justify" the stun gun aimed at the cow's head that expose the meat-processing plant worker to Covid-19: the commodification of sentience. As is made clear in analyses of the actions of CEOs like Kenneth Sullivan, the white male monopoly is directly benefitted by complacency. The climate crisis that "is not just the biggest threat human life on the planet has ever faced but a threat of an entirely different category and scale" is driven precisely by the logic of commodification Sullivan defends—and to which Wallace-Wells effectively accedes. Perhaps, given the magnitude of the crisis about which Wallace-Wells is rightly alarmed, going vegan is hardly even a drop in the bucket to confront it. But that is neither the point nor is it Wallace-Wells' position. His is "I'm not about to personally slaughter a cow to eat a hamburger, but I'm also not about to go vegan." That is, Wallace-Wells wants to participate in the commodification of sentience—so long as he doesn't have to see the bloody consequences of his self-interest. He wants to proclaim the end of the patriarchy, all the while enjoying the fruits of wage slavery and nonhuman animal butchery. That is not merely complacency; it is denial, and it is hypocrisy given an entire book devoted to "the biggest threat." He doesn't have to personally slaughter a cow. He has an entire industry—one central to the very story of apocalypse he tells—to do it for him.

THE UN-SEEN KLEPTOCENE AND THE UNINHABITABLE UTOPIA

That disarticulated animal bodies count, more or less reflexively, as food epitomizes the logic of commodification not only because sentience, much less agency, plays no role in decision-making that could compromise profits, but because its *preemptive omission* functions as the paradigmatic example of the value assigned to any sentient entity, including packing plant, BP and wet market workers, baby-powder consumers and vaccine recipients. What makes the "cognitive deficits" Wallace-Wells identifies, somewhat unwittingly, as defense mechanisms *and* enculturated responses to capitalism possible is not lack of concern for worker health and safety, but rather a logic that redrafts and subordinates all forms of concern to a cost/benefit analysis of productivity and profit margins. Given this cognitive infrastructure, it's hardly surprising that managers at a *Tyson* pork processing plant in Waterloo, Iowa placed bets on how many of their workers would become ill with Covid-19, or that CEO Dean Banks would rush to defend the company reputation, and it's bottom line, by suspending the offending managers once the scheme came to light,[65] As Vanessa Romo reports for NPR, "[a]round this time [mid-April, 2020], defendant Tom Hart, the plant manager of the Waterloo facility, organized a cash buy-in, winner-take-all betting pool for supervisors and managers to wager how many employees would test positive for Covid-19." Doubtless, the number of infected workers was amplified by the fact that the plant "did not have sufficient personal protective equipment [PPE], had too few nurses, and many of the plant workers are not native English speakers. That "at least one worker vomited on the production line and management allowed him to continue to work," and that supervisors were explicitly ordered to continue working even if they began to exhibit symptom of the virus, may have fortified the bet pool, but it also led to a temporary plant closure after "two dozen employees were admitted into a local emergency room," moving the Iowa governor, Kim Richards to lobby the Trump administration for relief not from pressure to keep the plant open, but "from Covid-19 mitigation efforts."[66] It doesn't take a pandemic to show that complacency has its casualties, but it certainly clarifies Wallace-Wells' reference to "fatal."

The wagers and the suspensions are simply two reflections of the same judgment, namely, that the cost of exposing workers to Covid-19 is outweighed by the profits that accrue to the "processing" of disarticulated pig bodies. That this calculus is at least partly culpable for the death of a worker is calculated as a cost of doing business and, as such, merely one more example of sentience commodified, elided, and discarded once its value as a resource is exhausted. Like Dawson, Wallace-Wells decries our lurch toward calamite, taking capitalism to task for its contribution to greenhouse gas emissions and other forms of environmental erosion. Yet, also like Dawson, Wallace-Wells doesn't identify what it is *in* capitalism that insures its consequences are "worse, much worse" than we think. Dawson does, however, come much closer when, concerning the rapidly growing pace of extinction, he observes that:

> Although many cultures recognize and celebrate this rich interdependency of species, the capitalist system that has come to dominate the world over the last five centuries is grounded in and thrives on dispossession. When viewed

> through the lens of extinction, it is an economic system founded on a drive to annihilate everything in its path.[67]

What Dawson gets right are the consequences of capitalism—annihilation. But this cannot be because capitalism is founded on a drive to that end. Capitalism is nihilistic because it is kleptocratic; that is, capitalism is nihilistic because there is nothing—not even the capacity for sentience—that raises a stop-sign to its logic of commodification. While the inevitable consequences are destruction and extinction, this is not because capitalism is suicidal, but because at its core, it's *utopian* in the most perverse way possible: it relies on the pretense that the earth, its species, and its atmosphere are *inexhaustible*, and then acts accordingly. Nothing in Wallace-Wells' riveting descriptions of how we arrived at the climate crisis are likely to move us, any more than him, beyond complacency simply because we've already acceded to the utopian premises of capitalism. While the fact that sentience is no obstacle to commodification is the first and crucial step into kleptocratic theft of resources, capitalism is devoted to a bounty of myths concerning, for example, techno-utopian replacements for dwindling oil and gas reserves, the equality of opportunity available to those who work hard, that nonhuman animals exist for human exploitation, that some people (woman and/or brown folks) are suited to certain sorts of wage labor, that women's work is merely a supplement to male head-of-households.

Wallace-Wells argues that "[o]ne possibility [for worse, much worse] is that the scramble for shrinking profits by the powerful will only intensify, a further self-entrenchment of the rule of capital."[68] No doubt true. Indeed, evidence of "scramble" abounds, as he observes:

> Climate change will accelerate two trends already undermining that promise of growth: first, by producing a global economic stagnation that will play, in some areas, like a breathtaking and permanent recession; and second, by punishing the poor much more dramatically than the rich . . . showcasing an increasingly stark income inequality, unconscionable to more and more.[69]

But while he's right that the scramble for profits will *appear* more and more kleptocratic, exposing "growth" for what it really is, namely, "theft," Wallace-Wells mistakes a cause for an effect: the "rule of capital" is only as entrenched as is the commodification of whatever facilitates the conversion of all value to exchange value. But because that "whatever" is the desertion of any concern for sentience, events like economic stagnation, recession, and the widening gap between the rich and the poor are not merely predictable from the outset, but facilitated by the rule itself.

In short, calamite is not the effect of the rule of capital; it's built into its execution as a *mirror* of what it values: profit at any cost—including the planet and its inhabitants. Similarly, grossly inequitable access to wealth and resources is not an effect of capitalism; it's a fortuitous advantage incorporated into the logic of commodification to sustain (some) competition, preserve the division of unskilled labor, and maximize revenue. It's also not the scramble for profit that is itself the accelerant of the climate crisis; it's the logic that, like any fire, "seeks" material to burn not because it is ravenous, but simply because it is *fire* (a virus seeks to replicate not because it desires to replicate, but because it is a *virus*). Likewise, the "rule of capital" is not "entrenched," implying that it could be more or less so; it's just *the* rule that, like fire, consumes whatever is combustible, and for which classifications like living or nonliving, sentient or insentient, stable or endangered, human or nonhuman, register no intrinsic significance. The transition, then, from the Capitalocene to the Kleptocene is a chimera. Capitalism is not "intensified" or "excessive" in its confrontation with diminishing resources, but rather simply the ostensibly utopian vision of profit for profit's sake, that is, "capitalism," running its course; fires can become firenadoes. The difference, of course, is that (for the moment) we can still deploy flame retardants, dump water, dig trenches to slow a fire, but such regulatory efforts deployed against capitalism are not merely "drops in the bucket" against kleptocratic theft, their "fire fighters" are convinced that the fire's too big to conquer *and* that there's really no fire at all; such is the nihilistic utopia—contradiction notwithstanding—of the logic of commodification once sentience is cast off as an obstacle to profit But, as Dawson might put it, while such contradictions are chaos-inducing for those harmed by the policies of industrialists and their elected political benefactors, they lead, conveniently for capitalism, to the same dead end: do nothing. But, consume.

To what we might depict as the psyche of consumption, Wallace-Wells provides a very instructive example. He begins the chapter titled "Crisis Capitalism" with an illuminating set of cognitive deficits, biases, and distortions that sustain the myths and falsehoods upon which capitalism depends: that endless resources will support insatiable consumption and guiltless waste.[70] But although he rightly identifies the practiced denial needed to navigate a world destabilized by environmental damage, because he fails to interrogate the logic whose consequences generate the *perception* that responsibility lay not in capitalism itself, but lax or absent regulation over its tendency to excess, Wallace-Wells effectively misidentifies the real drivers of denial—a logic of commodification for which denial is not ancillary, not merely a byproduct, but an opportunity to advance new forms of consumption. Think about it this way: we don't blame the fire for its laxity in regulating its penchant for excess burning. Fires burn, and ignoring the cause makes little headway dousing the flames. Indeed, we might make headway for *this* fire, but until we understand the causes of fires, our efforts will never be more than reactionary, and eventually we may meet a firenado we can't put out. The same can be said about Wallace-Wells' discussion of the psyche of consumption. While he's certainly right with respect to the role that denial, along with a range of other cognitive distortions, play in our effort to cope with precarious environmental conditions, he unwittingly reinforces the rule of capital by consigning our inaction to paralysis that derives from the sheer "bigness" of crises like climate change,[71] but not to the underlying logic.

Here, Wallace-Wells ironically echoes Smithfield CEO Sullivan. Both are like a fire-fighter who, confronted with a firenado and throwing up her hands in resignation, insists that since the bigness of this fire makes it impossible to put out, all fires are impossible to put out, that perhaps we should go get hotdogs to roast. Both effectively deny that there are ways to prevent fires from starting in the first place because neither want to give up the advantage the status quo provides to them. "[T]he scope of the climate threat is so large," write Wallace-Wells, "and its menace so intense, we reflexively avert our eyes, as we would with the sun."[72] Bigness, in other words, is an excuse for the inaction we describe as "paralysis," plus we like to save face. He's right, of course: the perception of "bigness" can be paralyzing, but if paralysis only serves to drive us deeper into denial, ignoring the real causes of the climate threat, perception will likely do little more than fuel consumption. We're like the fire-fighter who, detecting the flames over the hills in Paradise, California, turns the fire truck back toward the station, calls a friend to talk about "how bad things are," and pulls up to a burger drive thru.

This is Wallace-Well's "Frankenstein problem." He claims "we are more intimidated by the monsters we create than by those we inherit."[73] But what he leaves uncharted is that the havoc wreaked by this "Frankenstein" isn't monstrous because its actions are excessive, but because what we created *is a monster*. The logic of commodification is not excessive; it's *uncompromising*. Capitalism is nihilistic *because* it is utopian. The havoc is the product of the clash of the uncompromising and the limited. If denial, resignation, and hypocrisy are the only responses made possible by the capitalist "world system," it's not because environmental crises like climate change are, at least in the first place, too big; it's because no other responses, however much an implicit recognition that something in the "chaotic world system" is horribly wrong, are made available for our *consumption*. Make no mistake: denial, right along with the deficits, biases and distortions that inform our cognitive dispositions as laborers and consumers is a *product*. We purchase it every time we fill up our gas tanks, buy sneakers made in Vietnam, or eat fast food. That's one way, as Wallace-Wells might put it, we avert our eyes.

Another is the delusion that capitalism can be "renovated," that its excesses can be reigned in through stricter regulation.[74] But this too presupposes that Frankenstein can somehow be tamed without having to be killed, true in the original Boris Karloff movie, but not the Frankenstein of *The Uninhabitable Earth*. It's precisely our commitment to this vision of regulable excess that that sustains cognitive deficits like our capacity for denial, a tendency to deflect blame as well as the job of "fixing it" onto others, or onto the utopian hope that technology can save us from disaster.[75] Denial, blame-shifting, hypocrisy, false dichotomy, the resort to imperialist bigotries, and distortion of fact have become as naturalized to our complacent resignation as is the belief that corporations like Smithfield Farms can somehow be excused for the unnecessary deaths of its workers, because (again, somehow) having access to disarticulated animal bodies is more important than life; full stop.

Wallace-Wells rightly observes that things will get worse. Yet he argues that personal choices like becoming a vegan are unlikely to make much of a difference in the reduction of greenhouse gas emissions. Personal choices, however, can have mammoth impacts, for good or bad. Consider an example of "worse" that plainly accrues to personal choice: Americans who deny the climate crisis are also more likely to insist that "freedom" is rightly signaled by the refusal to wear a mask to avoid becoming infected and/or spreading Covid-19 to others during the pandemic. As Jenessa Duncombe reports for *EOS*:

> In an online survey of 2,200 adults on 14–16 April, a little over half of respondents who said climate change was a concern and caused by human activity said they "always" wear masks in public. In contrast, a little under a third of respondents "not too concerned" or "not concerned at all" with climate change said the same. There was a 24-percentage point difference between the two (54% versus 30%).[76]

Duncombe points out that the primary source of this correlation can be traced to the fossil fuel industry's effort to undermine trust in science: "[f]or decades, fossil fuel companies spent hundreds of millions of dollars to spread misinformation about climate change, and this undermined public confidence in science," yet the roots likely go even deeper. As Wallace-Wells argues, quoting critical theorist Fredric Jameson, "[i]t is easier to imagine the end of the world than it is to imagine the end of capitalism." And, for some, it's apparently easier to deny that mask-wearing isn't about "freedom" than it is to imagine gasping to death from a lung-compromising viral infection.

It's at this juncture that Wallace-Wells perhaps comes closest to recognizing the role of the logic of commodification when he remarks that "we tend to think of climate as somehow being contained within or governed by capitalism. In fact, it is endangered by it."[77] Yet, while he makes starkly clear that that the climate *is* endangered by capitalism, insofar as he remains committed to the false dichotomy of personal decision versus policy development, he's destined to remain mired in the blinkered utopian hope for a capitalist rehabilitation. Put differently: "the problem is that the climate is *not* endangered by capitalism *because* the 'conservative' is greed-driven, the techno-utopian 'blinkered,' the 'leftist' self-defeating; the climate is endangered because the logic of commodification is as deeply enculturated into the cognitive dispositions of human agents as do our needs, real or created, affect and propel our actions"—including the disposition Wallace-Wells himself personifies, namely, "the fatal complacency that excuses the 'personal' from moral responsibility." Walllace-Wells asks whether "capitalism [can] survive climate change?" But he preemptively deflates the force of his question by insisting that such queries are "now merely rhetorical on the Left."[78] This is deeply misguided. The question isn't whether capitalism can survive climate change; it's whether the capacity of the planet to recuperate from the assault of capital is a rational prospect given the logic that drives it, a point no more "Left" or "Right" than someone who says aloud that suffering does not concern them. No one would say this, and *that* fact is the substance of the deficits, biases and distortions—the cognitive dissonances—that underwrite the commodification of sentience.

NOTES

1. David Wallace-Wells. *The Uninhabitable Earth.* (New York, NY: Tim Duggan Books, 2019), 162.
2. Natasha White. "Bogus Carbon Credits Are a "Pervasive 'Problem,' Scientists Warn," Bloomberg, 3.21.23. https://time.com/6264772/study-most-carbon-credits-are-bogus/.
3. Wallace-Wells, 117.
4. Bruno Latour. *Down to Earth: Politics in the New Climate Regime*. (Paris: Polity Books, 2018), 2.
5. Wallace-Wells, 214.
6. Latour, 6.
7. Latour, 3.
8. Latour, 3.
9. Latour, 24.
10. REDD. "Reducing Emissions from Deforestation and Forest Degradation." UN. REDD Programme. https://www.un-redd.org, my emphasis.
11. Andreas Malm. *The Progress of This Storm: Nature and Society in a Warming World*. (Brooklyn, NY: Verso, 2020), 252.
12. Malm, 44–77.

13. Malm, 147.
14. Malm, 149.
15. Malm, 46.
16. Malm, 148–9.
17. Malm, 156.
18. Malm, 164.
19. Malm, 164.
20. Christian Parenti. *Tropic of Chaos: Climate Change and the New Geography of Violence*. (New York: Nation Books, 2011), 9.
21. Client Earth. "Greenwashing Files: ExxonMobil." https://www.clientearth.org/projects/the-greenwashing-files/exxonmobil/.
22. Sabrina Tavernise and Richard A. Oppel, Jr. "Spit on, Yelled at, Attacked: Chinese Americans Fear for Their Safety." *New York Times*, 3.23.20. https://www.nytimes.com/2020/03/23/us/chinese-coronavirus-racist-attacks.html.
23. Bess Levin. "Trump Declares Himself 'The No. 1 Environmental President.'" (*Vanity Fair*, 9.8.20). https://www.vanityfair.com/news/2020/09/donald-trump-environment-roosevelt.
24. Akshit Sangomla. "US Elections 2020: A History of Trump's Climate Change Denial." Down to Earth, 11.3.20. https://www.downtoearth.org.in/news/climate-change/us-elections-2020-a-history-of-trump-s-climate-change-denial-74075.
25. Wallace-Wells, 369.
26. Peg Brickley. "J&J Opposes Former Talc Suppliers Bankruptcy Plan to Resolve Cancer Claims." https://www.wsj.com/articles/j-j-opposes-former-talc-suppliers-bankruptcy-plan-to-resolve-cancer-claims-11610499939.
27. Jonathan Broder. "BP Shortcuts Led to Gulf Oil Spill." *New York Times*, 9.15.11, https://www.nytimes.com/2011/09/15/science/earth/15spill.html.
28. Rachel Axon, Rachel, Kyle Bagenstose, and Sky Chadde. "Coronavirus Outbreaks Climb at U.S. Meatpacking Plants Despite Protections, Trump Order." https://www.usatoday.com/story/news/investigations/2020/06/06/meatpacking-plants-cant-shake-covid-19-cases-despite-trump-order/3137400001/.
29. *Centers for Disease Control and Prevention* (CDC). "Janssen Covid-19 Vaccine (Johnson and Johnson)." https://www.cdc.gov/vaccines/covid-19/info-by-product/janssen/index.html.
30. Bloomberg Green. "Wuhan is Returning to Life. So are its Wet Markets." Bloomberg News, 4.8.20. https://www.bloomberg.com/news/articles/2020-04-08/wuhan-is-returning-to-life-so-are-its-disputed-wet-markets.
31. Jennifer Jacobs and Drew Armstrong. "Trump's 'Warp Speed'" Aims to Rush Coronavirus Vaccine." Bloomberg News, 4.29.20. https://www.bloomberg.com/news/articles/2020-04-29/trump-s-operation-warp-speed-aims-to-rush-coronavirus-vaccine.
32. Naomi Klein. "Let Them Drown: The Violence of Othering on a Warming World." *London Review of Books*, 38.11, June 2016. http://www.lrb.co.uk/v38/n11/naomi-klein/let-them-drow.
33. Ashley Dawson. *Extinction: A Radical History*. (New York, NY: OR Books, 2016), 57–8.

34. Bison Timeline. *All About Bison.* https://allaboutbison.com/bison-in-history/bison-timeline/.

35. Dawson, 53–5.

36. Susie Cagle and Vivian Ho. "'Not Our Mission': Private Fire Crews Protect the Insured, Not the Public." *The Guardian*, 11.3.19. https://www.theguardian.com/us-news/2019/nov/03/not-our-mission-private-fire-crews-protect-the-insured-not-the-public.

37. Olivia Goldhill and Nicholas St. Fleur. *STAT*, 12.3.20. https://www.statnews.com/2020/12/03/how-rich-and-privileged-can-skip-the-line-for-covid19-vaccines/.

38. Victor Reklaitis. "Here are the Companies Poised to Profit from the Trump Border Wall." *Market Watch*, 2.25.19.

39. Wallace-Wells, 161.

40. Wallace-Wells, 164.

41. Wallace-Wells, 164–5.

42. Wallace-Wells, 164.

43. Wallace-Wells, 164.

44. Wallace-Wells, 165.

45. Wallace-Wells, 165.

46. Wallace-Wells, 165.

47. Wallace-Wells, 133.

48. Michael Grabell and Bernice Yeung. "Meatpacking Companies Dismissed Years of Warnings but Now Say Nobody Could Have Prepared for Covid-19." *Propublica*, 8.20.20. https://www.propublica.org/article/meatpacking-companies-dismissed-years-of-warnings-but-now-say-nobody-could-have-prepared-for-covid-19.

49. Grabell and Yeung.

50. Matt Ridley. "The Bats Behind the Pandemic." *The Wall Street Journal*, 4.9.20. https://www.wsj.com/articles/the-bats-behind-the-pandemic-11586440959.

51. Mary Bates. "Thinking Like a Pig." *Psychology Today*, 2.16.21. https://www.psychologytoday.com/us/blog/animal-minds/202102/thinking-pig.

52. *Ag Daily*. "Top Ten Most Popular Cattle Breeds in the United States." https://www.agdaily.com/livestock/top-10-cattle-breeds-united-states/.

53. Jason Roberts. "15 Best Meat Chickens." *Know Your Chickens*, 6.17.21.

54. Lillianna Byington. "Smithfield Food Posts Q2 Loss After Spending 350 Million on Coronavirus." *Food Dive*, 8.12.20. https://www.fooddive.com/news/smithfield-foods-posts-q2-loss-after-spending-350m-on-coronavirus/583341/.

55. Bill McCarthy. "Joe Biden Banning Burgers? FOX News, GOP Politicians Fuerl False Narrative." *Politifact*, 4.26.21. https://www.politifact.com/factchecks/2021/apr/26/fox-news-channel/joe-biden-banning-burgers-fox-news-gop-politicians/

56. Stephanie Feldstein. "Opinion: Biden Isn't Trying to Cut Meat Consumption. But He Should." *Washington Post*, 4.29.21. https://www.washingtonpost.com/opinions/2021/04/29/biden-isnt-trying-cut-meat-consumption-he-should/

57. Wallace-Wells, 169.

58. Wallace-Wells, 187.

59. Feldstein.

60. Byington.

61. Michael Grabell and Bernice Yeung.

62. Nancy Cleeland. "OSHA Cite Meatpacking Plants for Coronavirus Failures." *SHRM*, 9.12.20.

63. Nicholas Robins and Nicole Hagen. "Mercury Production and Use in Colonial Andean Silver Production: Emissions and health Implications." *NIH: National Library of Medicine*, May, 2012. https://www.ncbi.nlm.nih.gov/pmc/articles/PMC3346781/.

64. Ben Schiller. "The Gruesome Statistics Behind One of America's Most Dangerous Jobs." *Fast Company*, 3.1.16. https://www.fastcompany.com/3057169/the-gruesome-statistics-behind-one-of-americas-most-dangerous-jobs

65. Vanessa Romo. "Tyson managers Suspended After Allegedly Betting If Workers Would Contract COVID." *National Public Radio*, 11.19.20. https://www.npr.org/2020/11/19/936905707/tyson-managers-suspended-after-allegedly-betting-if-workers-would-contract-covid.

66. Romo.

67. Dawson, 96.

68. Wallace-Wells, 164.

69. Wallace-Wells, 169.

70. Wallace-Wells, 159–60.

71. Wallace-Wells, 160.

72. Wallace-Wells, 160.

73. Wallace-Wells, 161.

74. Wallace-Wells, 161.

75. Wallace-Wells, 160–61.

76. Jenessa Duncombe. "No Mask? You May Not Worry about Climate Change, Either." EOS, 4.14.20. https://eos.org/articles/no-mask-you-may-not-worry-about-climate-change-either.

77. Wallace-Wells, 162.

78. Wallace-Wells, 162.

Chapter 4

Paving the Road to the Kleptocene

The Salvation Capitalism of Michael Mann's The New Climate War

HOW MICHAEL MANN'S *THE NEW CLIMATE WAR* UNDERMINES ITS OWN BEST INTENTIONS

Professor of Atmospheric Science Michael Mann certainly knows what he's talking about with respect to the fossil fuel industry's role in climate change and the mammoth efforts of corporations like ExxonMobil to deflect, downplay, and redirect blame for the crisis—all the while the fossil-fuel industry plays the green-washing game, but in action denies that there *is* a crisis. Mann argues that even where the fossil fuel industry acknowledges, however belatedly and reluctantly, the fact of climate change, culpability for the crisis is often shifted onto the shoulders of individual consumers, shaming, for example, folks who fly on planes as hypocrites.[1] The real hypocrisy, of course, lays squarely with the industry itself, in its use, as Bill McKibbon puts it, of the atmosphere as "the greatest market subsidy ever,"[2] a free greenhouse gas repository. Well-known public figures are, unsurprisingly, up for a particularly egregious form of "It's YOUR fault." "Take Al Gore," writes Mann, "the public figure most closely associated with the climate crisis. Gore has for years been pilloried by the right wing press, including FOX News . . . for the size of his home, his electricity bills, and even his weight. It's all part of an effort to portray him as a gluttonous hypocrite who doesn't practice what he preaches when it comes to his personal carbon footprint."[3]

The "it's YOUR fault" strategy is, argues Mann, part of the "fossil fuel disinformation machine," a suite of strategies adapted from the nefarious efforts of, for example, cigarette companies and pesticide manufacturers. Where flat denial that cigarettes cause cancer, or that DDT thins the shells of bird's eggs fails,[4] shifting blame to the consumer, as if their purported hypocrisy somehow shows the product isn't really a hazard after all, offers an easy excuse to continue production. The message is clear: If you want to believe you're a morally decent human being, *and* you're driving, smoking, eating, wearing, or spreading fossil fuel-based products, then either you're immoral, or they're OK. You're not immoral; ergo, inaction or, perhaps more to the point: suspension of conscience for the sake of sustaining one's self-image, itself a highly lucrative commodity advertised into unthinking consumption, and thus the status quo that brought us the climate crisis.

Whatever the strategy, the goal of the fossil fuel industry, its lobbyists and donor-dependent legislators, argues Mann, is the preservation of the "larger system" that sustains each of its subsidiary concerns. Although Mann seems reluctant to name it (it doesn't appear in the index), this larger system is multinational capitalism and its central assumptions: the myth of endless resources, that all value is reducible to exchange value, and that the capacity for sentience is no hurdle to commodification. Mann offers a cornucopia of examples of this "system" at work, ranging from attacks on Gore to the sexist character assassination of *Silent Spring's* Rachel Carson,[5] from Koch Brother misinformation campaigns to *Heartland Institute* "think tanks." Each deploys its own version of "it's THEIR fault," designed to reassure you that, so long as you're not "THEM," you're OK; eat, drive, wear, spread as "YOU" always have—fatal complacency, ignoring "fatal."[6] The picture Mann paints of the "larger system" is one of a mercenary, carefully orchestrated, survival-oriented, profit-seeking behemoth (Wallace-Wells' Frankenstein) driven by a logic of commodification, whose goal is to facilitate industry growth despite dwindling hydrocarbon reserves, competition from renewables, and the ever-louder voices of environmentalists cast as hypocrites, "tree-huggers," even "anti-American."[7]

That this logic is rooted in a *divide and conquer* that pits consumers shamed as likely hypocrites against Big Oil, Big Gas, and Big Agriculture cast as the heroes of energy and food isn't surprising; it's gaslighting tailored to identify the "friends" and "enemies" of fossil fuel cast as the friends and enemies of energy and food. Gaslighting is the psychic-gasoline that, ironically, produces active "inaction." It keeps pumps running, makes "Meat on the Menu" day a patriotic event, and inspires legislation to "bar plant-based meat-substitutes from using the words 'meat' and 'burger' on their labels."[8] Enculturated devotion to consumption serves both as the driver of industry growth, *and* an opportunity to shift blame; it offers an opportunity for patriotic sloganeering, *and* absolution to greenhouse gas polluters. It provides celebrity scape-goats *and* limitless opportunities for climate change denial. Unites, divides: conquers. Banning "burger" from veggie-burger ads may seem absurd; it's not. It's calculated. Like the campaign to dirty the image of an American hero like Rachel Carson, it epitomizes the kleptocratic character of the "larger system." The meat industry hijack of "burger" reminds us that meat-eaters and airline-travelers are as much a product of the fossil fuel industry as is "It's YOUR fault" a product of advertising *against* the hypocrite "YOU" don't want to be. If figures like Gore and Carson can be cast as hypocrites, but also as "Un-American" (Carson was smeared as a "Communist"), then burgers and airplanes become, effectively, ways to wave the flag—and then use it to wipe away "YOUR" complicity in the climate crisis.

Mark Stoll locates this "self-conscious consumerism" along with its environmental implications in its historical context, remarking that:

> By 1970, consumer capitalism had captured almost everything in American society and was on the march out of the U.S. into the wider world. From fast food to packed processed food on supermarket shelves, food had become a packaged, advertised, cheap, quick, and easily purchased item, like soap or deodorant was back in the 1920's. Environmental impacts were hidden but huge. Fast-food franchises each demanded great quantities of hamburgers, buns, French fries, condiments, milkshakes . . . Farmers had to produce animals and grains to suit corporate bulk buyers, which mean mass production of meat using hormones, antibiotics, and grain-fed feedlots and of grain with pesticides and herbicides and identical strains of wheat . . . The 1960's would be self-consciously consumerist like never before.[9]

What the sheer volume of fast-food consumed from the 1960s onwards shows is that the last thing a self-conscious consumer wants to feel self-conscious about are the "hidden but huge" environmental impacts of their consumption. Making the environmentalist out to be the boogyman, argues Mann, is one effective way to achieve self-conscious unconsciousness, active inaction, or "inactivism." The consumerist status quo thereby preserved has, however, other nefarious incarnations besides divide and conquer, each its own avatar for the logic of commodification, each aimed at gaslighting the consumer to ensure compliance with the "larger system" of endless consumption. While the first shames the "hypocrite," a second makes "YOU" a victim of the environmentalist who'd rob "YOU" of access to an entitled commodity like gasoline or meat. Consider, for example, Jennifer Jacquet's "The Meat Industry is Doing Exactly What Big Oil Does to Fight Climate Action":

> This spring [2021], politicians stampeded to defend the centrality of meat in the American diet. When Colorado's governor issued a proclamation encouraging people to avoid eating meat on March 20, Nebraska's governor called it "a direct attack on our way of life" and countered by declaring "Meat on the Menu Day" on the same date. In response to a false story that President Biden planned to limit Americans' meat consumption, Rep. Lauren Boebert (R-Colo.) told him to "stay out of my kitchen." The Texas House just passed a measure

> to bar plant-based meat substitutes from using the words "meat" and "burgers" on their labels.[10]

In this version of divide and conquer, "YOU" are not only a potential hypocrite for taking seriously the Colorado governor's proposal to avoid meat for one day, "YOU" are also a victim of the allegedly pernicious idea that "YOU" aren't entitled to eat meat every day. There is a divide and conquer here that advantages the fossil fuel industry: want to avoid hypocrisy? Eat a *beef* burger. Want to stick it to the "greenies"? Eat a *pork* hot dog. Yet, by making "YOU" the victim of the environmentalist, even worse, a vegetarian-for-a day, this strategy achieves something more than divide and conquer alone; it galvanizes "YOUR" resolve *against* the environmentalist and *for* Big Oil, Big Gas, and Big Animal Manufacture. Not only needn't "YOU" feel guilty, "YOUR" celebration of "meat on the menu" is a blow to the enemy trying to get into "YOUR" kitchen. "YOU" are a patriot *because* from the burger to the antibiotics to the hormones to the herbicides to the pesticides to the can-see-it-from-space animal waste lagoon to the transports trains and trucks, "YOU" are a patriotic fossil fuel consumer.

Whether "YOU" are shamed as a hypocrite or made out a victim of environmentalists, neither detract from the fact that the underlying premise of this argument for animal body consumption as essential to the right "way of life" is *ludicrous*: there's nothing "central" to any diet, including the American diet, that necessitates meat-eating. Yet, as Cora Diamond shows, even arguments that purport to defend nonhuman animal rights effectively concede to the "what's for dinner" myth at least insofar as we see "nothing at all odd in the vegetarian eating the cow that has obligingly been struck by lightning."[11] There's also no obligatory relationship between being a patriot and the consumption of fossil fuel products; not, at least, unless "being a patriot" means "submitting to the will of ExxonMobil or Tyson Foods." Factory farm animal bodies are no more an endless resource than are the fossil fuels required for their production, slaughter, processing, waste disposal, transport, marketing, and consumption. Consumers *are* victims—not of environmentalists, but of gaslighting fossil fuel dependent industries, and their allies. The pervasive enculturation of the myth that meat is nutritionally crucial, its consumption a right, that it's the cultural glue of American identity and patriotism, and that it's production is safe and endless advantages none but the fossil fuel industries at the expense of consumers, workers, democratic-decision-making, the planet, its species life, and its atmosphere. The climate crisis is as real as the facts of greenhouse gas emissions from factory farms.[12]

There's plenty of hypocrisy to go around, but none more calculated to conceal itself than that of the fossil fuel dependent companies who, as Mann shows, will go to great lengths to control or avoid regulation, oversight or policy that, in slowing the pace of climate change, also mutes the "cha-ching" of profit. In short, Mann suffers no delusions about the facts of capitalism: hydrocarbons are the corpuscles of the Kleptocene, consumption its oxygenating propulsion, and the climate crisis the ultimate expiration date of capital conquest. Indeed, he would seem to be on-board with Andreas Malm when the latter observes that "independent nature is the only thing that cannot come to an end. The paradox of climate change is that it makes it [nature] appear more strangely alive than ever."[13]

Yet, while Mann is right to focus attention on the fossil fuel producers, he seems to take a page from Wallace-Wells with respect to the role of animal agriculture in the climate crisis, and the lengths that this fossil fuel dependent industry will go to avoid regulatory intervention or environmental policy with respect to the prickly subject of food. He doesn't want to talk about "what's for dinner." Mann claims instead that he "shares the concern and bewilderment" his fellow climate scientists who have "chosen to devote our lives to raising awareness about the climate crisis" only to be antagonized by climate activists who'd "gladly throw us under the bus because we're not living as off-the-grid vegan hermits."[14] There are at least two problems here. First, it does Mann's argument against the industry machinations of "It's YOUR fault" little good to avoid the facts about factory farm greenhouse gas emissions by consigning any discussion of meat consumption to "victim-blaming." Just because people eat meat *as* individuals and not *as* groups does not necessarily imply that they are (or aren't) victims. Institutions, agencies and corporation do not eat; people do. To evade this fact as an instance of "It's YOUR fault" (as if it could be otherwise) is to ignore a crucial difference between the consumption of fossil fuel as gasoline and fossil fuel as food: the survival of some human beings may require both—but *all* living things require food as an existential necessity—so, of course what individual consumers eat matters.

Second, the dismissive hyperbole of "off the grid vegan hermits" is not an argument. Indeed, even if we accept the claim that it's neither nice nor fair to treat climate scientists as hypocrites unless they become "off-the-grid vegan hermits," it's still question-begging and commits straw fallacy: it's question-begging because it assumes without argument or evidence that living as an environmentally responsible vegan is lonely and brutish; it's straw fallacy because it pits a caricature of vegans against the heroic climate scientist in order to make the latter look morally superior, inviting us again to ignore the fact that discussion about what counts as food is substantively different than discussion about what counts as energy. Both are energy and neither require fossil fuel—but that cannot detract from the fact that food forms an *existential* condition for living things. In short, an indignant complaint about the ostensibly unfair treatment of climate scientists isn't an argument; it's a "how dare you" sort of cover-story intended to shut down the intrepid critic who'd dare to point out that there is no meaningful discussion of reducing greenhouse gas emissions without talking about food, particularly but not only: meat. And it's a cover-story that undermines itself: by blaming environmentalists who insist the discussion of food is vital to mitigating greenhouse gas emissions, Mann reproduces precisely the "IT'S YOUR FAULT" strategy, deploying it against a made-up enemy, the vegan hermit, and unwittingly helping to support an industry, Big Animal Agriculture, that spends *more* to support candidates who oppose emission regulations and other policies to slow climate change than even its closest fossil fuel competitor, ExxonMobil:

> Between 2000 and 2019, nine of the top 10 U.S. meat and dairy companies spent a combined $26 million on federal political campaigns, largely supporting Republican candidates, who typically oppose interventions designed to slow climate change. When we analyzed such expenditures as a share of revenue, we found that Tyson, the largest emitter of the U.S. meat and dairy companies, *spent twice as much as Exxon on political campaigns and 33 percent more on lobbying.*[15]

It's no surprise that the meat and dairy industry spend so much on federal campaigns to oppose regulation. What's striking is *how much more* they spend than ExxonMobil; but it shouldn't be.

The "America First" big truck enthusiast consumes hydrocarbons not only when she/he fills their tank, but as burgers, hot dogs, plastics, fertilizers, pesticides, just to name a few. Given the fossil fuel, water, grain, and labor required to produce a pound of meat, it's doubtless of paramount importance to Smithfield Farms or Tyson to do everything possible to keep costs down, particularly as demand increases. As Mark Bittman reports for the *New York Times* as far back as 2008:

> A sea change in the consumption of a resource that people take for granted may be in store: something cheap, plentiful, widely enjoyed and a part of daily life. And it isn't oil. It's meat. The two commodities have a great deal in common: Like oil, meat receives government subsidies in the U.S. marketplace. Like oil, meat is subject to accelerating demand as nations become wealthier, and this, in turn, sends prices higher. Finally, like oil, meat is something people are encouraged to consume less of, as the toll exacted by industrial production increases and becomes increasingly visible. Global demand for meat has multiplied in recent years, encouraged by growing affluence and nourished by the proliferation of huge, confined animal feeding operations. These assembly-line meat factories consume enormous amounts of energy, pollute water supplies, generate significant greenhouse gases and require ever-increasing amounts of corn, soy and other grains, a dependency that has led to the destruction of vast swaths of the world's tropical rain forests . . . The world's total meat supply was 71 million tons in 1961. In 2007, it was estimated to be 284 million tons. Per

> capita consumption has more than doubled over that period. (In the developing world, it rose twice as fast, doubling in the past 20 years.) World meat consumption is expected to double again by 2050, a projection that one expert, Henning Steinfeld of the United Nations, said was resulting in a "relentless growth in livestock production." Americans eat about the same amount of meat daily as they have for some time, about 8 ounces, or 230 grams, roughly twice the global average. At about 5 percent of the world's population, Americans grow and kill nearly 10 billion animals a year, more than 15 percent of the world's total.[16]

Given these facts concerning water pollution, grain dependency, growing demand, rainforest destruction, and the generation of greenhouse gases, it's not at all surprising that the animal agriculture industry would resort to red herring and straw caricatures of vegans as a way to maintain growth against a backdrop of impending calamite. What is surprising is that Mann doubtless understands these facts and makes a compelling case for resisting "It's YOUR fault" in the case of fossil fuel corporations like ExxonMobil. Yet, by resorting to this same divide and conquer strategy with respect to "personal decision" and "larger system" against the "off-the-grid vegan hermits," Mann undermines his argument that the only way to effectively combat the climate crisis is though policy, and not individual decision-making. Would the meat industry go to so much trouble and expense to ban the vegan food industry from using the word "burger" were vegan burgers *and therefore the vegans who eat them* not a threat?

The inescapable conclusion is that, however unwittingly, Mann helps to sustain the favored narrative of the fossil fuel industry—not merely as animal agriculture, but across the board. Because food is an existential necessity, Mann cannot make animal agriculture fit the "It's YOUR fault" strategy (short of evincing indignance on behalf of climate scientists). He's thus compelled to ignore a major source of greenhouse gas emissions in an industry wholly dependent on fossil fuels for the production of feed, slaughter, processing, transport, and waste disposal. But once we see this serious failing in the very way Mann draws the "personal decision" versus regulation and policy distinction, two more problems emerge, each of which show that his strategy commits fallacy of false dichotomy. Mann's argument:

> In short, scientists and communicators absorb the bad faith criticisms of hypocrisy leveled against them by their adversaries and make dramatic changes in their lifestyle, unwittingly affirming the flawed and misleading premise that it's all about personal action rather than policy. Leonardo DiCaprio—a hero in my book—has nonetheless spearheaded a global publicity campaign pointing the finger at the eating of meat. A whole bevy of climate scientists and advocates now advertise the fact that they no longer fly, have turned to vegan diets, or have chosen not to have children. These individuals are trying to do what they believe

> is the right thing, and attempting to lead by example. But they seem surprisingly unaware that when they seem to make it all about personal choices and the need for sacrifice, they are in fact playing into the inactivist agenda.[17]

For Mann, folks who make it "all about personal choices" with respect to combatting the climate crisis may express an honorable moral sentiment, but they won't accomplish much, and it distracts from the real work of articulating policy. If Leonardo DiCaprio wants to become a "vegan hermit," that's fine. But a campaign to encourage others to do the same is bound to fail; it wastes time, squanders resources, and takes attention away from a bigger picture that demands bigger policy players who can do the heavy-lifting of the climate war. Moreover, Mann continues, "[r]equiring climate activists to live ascetic lives gives the appearance that they expect everyone to give up meat, or travel, or other pleasures. And that is politically dangerous: it plays right into the hands of the inactivists who want to portray climate champions as freedom-hating totalitarians."[18]

The obvious rebuttal to this politicized version of the "off-the-grid vegan hermit" claim is that, insofar as it traffics not only in question-begging, straw fallacy, and red herring, but also in a *fear-mongering falsehood*—"freedom-hating totalitarians"—it "plays right into the hands of the inactivists." Indeed, we might add fallacy of projection to the ways in which Mann misses the point; this iteration of the false dichotomy is exactly what the fossil fuel companies want us to think not only about what we eat, but what a human being *is*. Of course, the fossil fuel industries would have us subscribe to what, at bottom, is an atomistic view of human nature that reduces human relationships to the transactional or the competitive, or both, and that's it. But this view of human nature is simply false, and would be false even if human beings are the rather loathsome creatures of Mann's cynical description. "Off-Grid Vegan Hermit" is a caricature; "freedom-hating totalitarian" is an extortive straw; the reference to "ascetic" as a descriptor of a plant-based diet is simply silly. It makes sense to conceive human relationships as atomistic and transactional only as support for the claim that "personal choice" is governed solely by self-interest, having little positive influence beyond the chooser. Such a conception of human nature does make sense within Mann's "larger system," but only because this larger system is the capitalism he appears to take for granted as human society's natural state, and only because capitalism takes as given a human nature *naturalized* to justify it: *human chauvinism normalized*. In short, what Mann leaves uninterrogated is the logic of commodification that's built into the conception of human nature and relationships he tacitly endorses. He thereby leaves unchallenged the logic's most critical operative premises, including a mercenary chauvinism that organizes the world into self-interested stereotypes: "consumers," "hypocrites," "vegan hermits," "totalitarians," and "meat-eating patriots," the very players Mann deploys to defend his argument for a reformed capitalism—and the first clue about how and why his proposals are destined to fail.

The *Leonardo DiCaprio Foundation* acts on a very different view of human nature, one modelled on the dedication of scientists, philanthropists, and activists to "protect the well-being of all Earth's inhabitants,"[19] one that aspires to goals similar to other movements past and present: "Leonardo's website and social media platforms are also dedicated to inspiring the public to take action on key environmental issues. Growing in reach from just 500,000 followers in 2007 to over 50 million today, Leonardo's fans have engaged on an array of issues protecting key species—sharks in California, tigers in Asia, elephants in Africa—and calling on world leaders to address the global climate crisis."[20] The foundation's aim is to make a substantive difference precisely because, at least for DiCaprio, *setting an example is not merely "personal choice."* What DiCaprio clearly recognizes is that he occupies an ideal position to challenge negative fear-mongering images weaponized by an industry whose history of deceit and denial—as Mann spells out—makes abundantly clear that regulatory interventions have had little real impact on "business as usual." From a perspective like DiCaprio's, the image of a "freedom-hating totalitarian" is likely to reflect the economic desperation of an industry losing market share to alternative energies and food options and its resort to increasingly absurd images to maintain its consumer base. Although DiCaprio would likely grant that measuring the success of a foundation can be dicey business, Mann's investment in the false dichotomy that fuels these images effectively discounts such philanthropic ventures as naïve, "surprisingly unaware," especially with respect to encouraging less meat consumption.

Malm makes a similar point in starker terms, writing that "[b]y force of temperatures, there will be more famines in a considerably hotter world whether or not institutions are democratic":

> Egalitarian adaptation might ameliorate the worst effects, but even if the world were a perfect democracy, it would still at some point become very hungry insofar as it allowed CO_2 emissions to continue. The first precondition for minimizing that risk is the destruction of business as usual—a matter of political content, which might very well require a certain democratic form *but cannot be reduced to it.*[21]

Foundations like DiCaprio's aim at "minimizing that risk," that is, slowing the impacts of the climate catastrophe by working to avoid species extinction and by setting an example for human consumers to participate less in animal agriculture. The foundation adroitly avoids mention of capitalism, much less the "destruction of business as usual." But it's also clear that the personal choices it advocates are intended for as large an audience as DiCaprio's name recognition can muster, that this audience is not the chauvinistic consumers Mann appears to take for granted, and that if the foundation met its democratically organized environmental goals, real change could be made.

On the other hand, if CO_2 emissions continue, as Malm points out, what will follow will not rise to DiCaprio's hopeful expectations. Rather, extinction and hunger will. Weighed, in other words, against not only the advertising Juggernaut of the fossil fuel and animal agriculture industries, but the chauvinistic view of human nature it takes as given, DiCaprio's efforts are likely to seem exactly as Mann describes them: well-intentioned, a "hero" even, but nonetheless naïve. But this criticism holds *only if* human chauvinism *is* an accurate and exhaustive reflection of human nature. That Mann *needs* this to be the case in order to distinguish "personal choice" from policy, however, is neither evidence that it *is* the case nor, as DiCaprio seems to recognize, can we afford to accede to a view of human nature so narrow. Mann claims that DiCaprio plays into the hands of the "inactivists" for having "spearheaded a global publicity campaign pointing the finger at the eating of meat." Yet, any doubt that Mann is committed to precisely the view of human being that provides the justificatory pretext to the capitalist excess he would otherwise take to task dissolves when we read that he's "very wary of individuals who seem to be trying to hijack the climate discourse for the cause of worldwide veganism (or, for that matter, the abandonment of market economics)."[22]

The only conceptual framework within which the claim that vegans are plotting to "hijack the climate discourse" makes sense is one where "personal choice" is animated by the nefarious motive to foist that choice on others, one that fits the fossil fuel company narrative that meat-eaters are patriots and vegans are "freedom-hating totalitarians." In other words, while Mann plainly knows this narrative traffics in absurd stereotypes, he in fact subscribes to it. Mann exploits the same scapegoat created by the fossil fuel industries. The difference is that whereas the industry needs to shift blame for the climate crisis away from itself, Mann needs a party he can hold culpable for "deflection," that is, someone to blame for distracting us from the real causes of the climate crisis, namely, the failure of policy—the failure Mann insists he can fix. What's important here is not merely that Mann is guilty of hypocrisy, he's also just wrong, as Mark Bittmann shows (and DiCaprio hopes), that meat-eating plays no substantive role in the climate crisis. To be clear, this is not to suggest the climate crisis provides justification for some world-wide totalitarian vegan regime: that's a boogeyman for which no one argues. It is to say that Mann's use of "hijack," is itself intended as a fear-mongering distraction from facts relevant to the contribution of meat-eating to the climate crisis—another clue to an argument that can only be made to look plausible on the basis of a pretext that does not hold up under interrogation.

Why, then, does Mann effectively authorize a view of human nature that supports the false dichotomy between the value of personal choice and that of policy-making? A view that lends itself to ridiculous and dangerous caricatures of environmentalists and vegans? That has as its main beneficiary the industry Mann rightly holds responsible for the climate crisis? *Because it's only where "personal choice" fails that a fundamentally reformist argument for regulation and policy can be made to look more plausible than it is, and thereby preserve the market economics Mann himself favors.* That Mann has to go to these lengths to defend his version of salvation capitalism more than hints at the possibility that the "larger system" he seeks to reform may be resistant, and that the time, energy, and resources spent on turning the capitalist ship full throttle toward regulatory reform might have been better spent on encouraging a view of human nature and moral responsibility less cynical—more hopeful, like DiCaprio's. "[W]hat is needed," argues Malm, "is an affirmation of nature as something other than the commodity."[23] Yet, he goes on to insist that "[T]he warming condition spells the death of affirmative politics" and that "[n]egativity is our only chance now."[24] We must "dare to feel the panic."[25] Still, Malm remarks, a bit closer to DiCaprio, that although "the climate movement is still struggling to constitute themselves as a demolition crew, [this] is not a reason to give up on them."[26]

For Malm, it's all hands on deck with respect to addressing the climate crisis, and its "[s]upport for existing social hierarchies [that] strongly predisposes people to denial," as opposed to a human agency destined to the feckless struggle to constitute a movement. Personal decisions such as becoming a committed vegan may be difficult, but, as Mann overlooks in his quest to make policy the hero of his sustainability story, the collective impact of personal daring to "feel the panic" is what gave rise to major historical movements—the American Civil Rights movement, for example. Mann needs the false dichotomy, personal versus policy, to preserve a cynical "inactivist" view of human nature that helps to support his argument for a reformed "larger system." But from the point of view of critics like Malm, defenders of the capitalist status quo do a lot of work to reform the un-reformable, save the unsalvageable, have a capitalist cake and eat it too.[27]

Maybe, however, this critique of Mann is unfair. Let's try another approach: perhaps Mann thinks he's using the fossil fuel industry's own weapons against it, that his argument for cap and trade, carbon-trading, and carbon credits is a 3X-punch that will land, creating real and substantive mitigation. This, however, seems unlikely given the extent to which his affirmations of caricature facilitates the interests of ExxonMobil, undermining Mann's own best intentions, sustaining a view of human nature implicit to the logic of commodification. Perhaps he thinks that by showing how the fossil fuel companies shift blame onto celebrity consumers like Al Gore, he can blame their failure to address climate change on particular companies, but not the capitalist system itself that makes their kleptocratic business models possible. But this also seems unlikely given that the success of ExxonMobil is modelled by multinationals across the globe, epitomizing a logic for which there exists no value irreducible to exchange, including sentient human and nonhuman beings. It comes to this: Mann's reasons for defending "the larger system" without any substantive examination of its logic don't really matter once we see that what matters to him, first and foremost, isn't actually the climate crisis, but rather preserving the "market economy" itself. Or: insofar as Mann takes capitalism to mirror human nature, no other system of economic exchange is imaginable. In either case, for Mann, whatever solution to the climate crisis is possible, it is so because it reflects and advances an albeit reformed market economy; no other form of economic exchange is plausible or worth articulating. The first of these reasons is disingenuous; Mann tells us his priority is to propose real solutions to the climate crisis—but not if these fall outside capitalism. The second amounts to resignation—unless Mann can show his solutions stand a realistic chance of thwarting the legion of strategies utilized by the fossil fuel industries to skirt, obstruct, undermine, and evade the law. Both cross the same Rubicon insofar as it's the logic of commodification that will define what counts as reform, and that according only to whether "reform" can be made to oxygenate the circulatory system of profit—until the planet and its atmosphere are choked to death.

"CRYING INDIANS," REFORM-CAPITALISM, AND THE COST OF A FALSE DICHOTOMY

While there are many forms of "salvation capitalism" none take quite the route Michael Mann takes in *The New Climate War*. Although the view of human nature implicit to his defense of market economies is as old as Adam Smith's claim in *Wealth of Nations* that among the primary drivers of labor is the desire for "Opulence,"[28] it's the dichotomy Mann contrives to segregate "personal choice" from "policy-making," in the pursuit of legitimating the latter as a mechanism of capitalist reform, that sets his approach apart. But that Mann resorts to a contrivance readily exposed *as* a contrivance reveals something more: that the war to save capitalism from the consequences of its kleptocratic logic is losing ground. Or: every day that ratchets up the need for some new market solution against a backdrop of more frequent and extreme weather events, more climate crisis refugees, zoonotic disease-transmission, or species extinctions, is a day we waltz further out onto the minefield of irrecoverable loss. So long as the first order of business is to save business, the first order of solutions will be to make the implausible look plausible—all the more so where the crisis is urgent, but the "larger system" is paramount.

Hence, Mann's resort to an especially distorted account of the "personal choice" dichotomy, the "Crying Indian." His story begins benignly enough:

> A chiseled traditionally clothed Native American is paddling his canoe down a river. Slightly ominous music plays in the background, accompanied by a steady drum beat. As he proceeds don the river he encounters an increasing volume of flotsam and jetsam. Behind him factories belch smog into the air. The music grows louder and more foreboding. He finally lands his canoe along the river's edge, where it is inundated with more strewn litter.[29]

Mann then goes on to describe how effective the ad was at getting us to stop littering: "*Were we willing to change*? You *bet* we were . . . No scrap of litter would escape our seizure. Thus was born a new generation of *litter* scoopers . . . That commercial changed me—and so many people of my generation—for the better, it would seem reasonable to argue."[30] But notice the hedge, "it would seem reasonable to argue." Mann doesn't keep us waiting: "if you're looking for a feel good story here, you'd better get used to disappointment. Some things aren't quite what they seem. Scratch beneath the surface of the Crying Indian . . . and a different picture—indeed a dramatically different picture—begins to emerge."[31]

Mann is exactly right—about one aspect of this picture. Following historian Finis Dunaway, it turns out that "Iron Eyes Cody [the Crying Indian] was not a member of a Native American tribe. He wasn't even Native American at all . . . He was an Italian American who often portrayed Indians in Hollywood films."[32] This is certainly disillusioning, and deserves the careful attention Finis gives it. But Mann's aims are very different. He effectively exploits this disillusion to launch and legitimate grounds for another, namely, his view of the inevitable failure of "personal choice," and hence support for the false dichotomy. As Mann rightly continues, the Crying Indian PSA helped give rise to consumer advocate Ralph Nader's *Public Interest Research Groups* (PIRGs) who, in the interest of addressing at least one form of litter, bottle and cans, worked to sponsor and advance "Bottle Bill" legislation,

> that placed a deposit on bottles and cans . . . that would be refunded to consumers upon their return, promoting returnable and refillable bottles and encouraging consumers to recycle rather than toss . . . [T]he beverage industry would bear the brunt of the responsibility and costs, as they would be required to process the returned bottles and cans. That would add to their expenses and decrease their profits.[33]

Unsurprisingly, as Mann recounts, the beverage industry fought the bottle legislation tooth and nail, recruiting politicians, industry lobbyists, and governors to their cause, ultimately offering a responsibility shifting "alternative" "through an industry front group calling itself the *Corporation for a Cleaner Commonwealth* (CCC). It involved hiring kids to pick up bottle and can litter."[34] "The solution, you see, isn't regulation of the industry. It's individual action," argues Mann—as a set up for deliberately conflating "hiring kids" with "individual action."[35]

This interpretation of the CCC alternative to the passage of Nader's bottle bill makes sense only if we accept Mann's dichotomous premises: legislated policy or "personal choice," where the latter means the forfeiture of the former. But we have no good reason to accept the slide from "hiring kids" to "individual action." This is a ploy, an artifice to legitimate Mann's view that the only effective way to address environmental problems is through policy and regulation, that is, via reform of the "larger system" whose industries are responsible for the pollution. Of course, the beverage industry tries to shift responsibility onto consumers to save money and increase profits. That is capitalism. But CCC's motives notwithstanding, "kids picking up litter" is not reducible to "individual action" because it's *not* individual action; the latter is not necessarily or solely self-interested, and it's not individual—it's a deliberately organized group action for a purpose other than the pay that presumably goes with "hire." That individuals participate in a group action does not mean the action is reducible to a collection of individual agents working for money (fallacy of composition). Imagine such an analysis of the Civil Rights Movement: whatever the motives, no organized action would be effective were group actions reducible to a collection of "individual actions" for hire. Moreover, whether or not the paid litter pick-up project was successful is beside the point; the work Mann needs the CCC alternative to do is exemplify a "deflection campaign."[36] That is, all Mann needs from the litter pick-up project is to be able to represent it as a deflection away from the bottle bill legislation in order to show that only legislation will be successful. But insofar as he's willing to resort to distortion to achieve that goal, what his example actually shows are the lengths Mann's willing to go to defend his version of salvation capitalism.

To be clear, my aim is not to support the CCC alternative; it's to argue that Mann's misrepresentation of it, whatever CCC's motives, is contrived to save capitalism by pitting policy and regulation against "personal choice." That the beverage industry (like fossil fuel, factory farms, and cigarettes) was going to resist any regulatory effort that compromised its bottom line, and deploy virtually any strategy to that end, is a given. Indeed, the industry's use of kids may be particularly despicable precisely because kids may not have sufficient judgment to assign "personal" to their actions; they're paid, and kids are *kids*. The fact that the bottle bill did eventually pass, was signed into law November 1981, and managed to thwart efforts at repeal does not imply that its success was due to the failure of any action taken by citizens, individually or collectively, whether set up by CCC or by one of Ralph Nader's PIRGs. Mann's strategy might thus be described as a straw argument appealing to a false dichotomy set up to generate a *reductio ad absurdam*: it's the policy way or the highway to climate hell. But the reason the legislation passed was not because only policy can effect change; it passed in virtue of the pressure exerted through the collective efforts of organized citizens acting on something more than self-interest, namely, an emergent environmental conscience. That "only a limited number of Blue states passed bottle bills, "or that "[m]eanwhile the growing mass of discarded plastic bottles has given rise to another great environmental crisis of our time—global plastic pollution," are red herrings intended to deflect from the fact that bottle bills were enacted, and the public pressure of organized individual agents played a vital role.[37] Mann introduces these important issues concerning plastic pollution as if they illustrate the case for more aggressive regulation—and they might be, but this isn't because coordinated citizen action fails. Without organized collective action, there would have been no bottle bills to begin with.

Yet, Mann would have us believe that contemporary PSAs like the 2006 *The Little Mermaid* encouraging us not to dump plastic bottles in the ocean are themselves reducible to nothing more than "the deflection campaign."[38] It's true that this PSA makes no mention of "the beverage industry's role in plastic pollution."[39] But, as Mann doesn't tell us, this is more an example of the moral compromise made by Big Greens like the *Environmental Defense Fund* (EDF) to maintain their "partnerships" with fossil fuel multinational corporations than a verdict on the effectiveness of coordinated citizen action.[40] Indeed, appealing to EDF as if the environment were its main objective, instead of its donor base, is like appealing to ExxonMobil as a conscientious steward of the climate, instead of it market share. With respect to climate action, in fact, the two organizations are essentially one: as recently as May, 2021 EDF's President Fred Krupp congratulates ExxonMobil for the company's pledge to "decarbonize" the economy to combat the climate crisis.[41] Sounds great, until we discover that he leaves out the backstory:

> It was a stunning moment for Exxon Mobil Corp. and the wider corporate world: a tiny activist fund had succeeded in changing the company's board. But in the hours leading up to this week's annual shareholders meeting, *Exxon went to extraordinary lengths to head off the threat from a campaign about which it had been largely dismissive months earlier*. Exxon telephoned investors the morning of the ballot—and even during an unscheduled, hour-long pause during the virtual meeting—asking them to reconsider their votes . . . Some said they

> found the last-ditch outreach and halt to the meeting unorthodox and troubling. "It was a very unusual annual general meeting," said Aeisha Mastagni, a fund manager at the California State Teachers' Retirement System, a major Exxon investor that backed the activist campaign from the beginning . . . The May 26 meeting concluded with Exxon stating that two of the dissident's four director nominees had been elected, a coup for Engine No. 1, a little-known investment firm calling for the company overhaul its strategy, cut costs and come up with a plan to address climate change. Its victory is widely seen as a warning to the rest of the industry that investors will now hold energy companies to account for environmental concerns. *Exxon opposed Engine No. 1 from the outset.* The fund holds a stake in Exxon of just 0.02%, valued at about $54 million. The oil company described the fund's four candidates as unqualified and said its proposals would *imperil Exxon's dividend*.[42]

EDF's Fred Krupp no more tells us the whole story with respect to ExxonMobil's pitched resistance to the "tiny activist fund," Engine No. 1, than does Mann with respect to the *Crying Indian* or *The Little Mermaid*. While Krupp would have us believe that corporations like ExxonMobil are ready and willing to do their part in curbing greenhouse gas emissions, and Mann would have us assume EDF is an environmental organization—both pitch arguments that omit crucial facts, and do so in the interest of advancing effectively the same narrative: that multinationals like ExxonMobil can be made into good environmental citizens.

Krupp's narrative represents ExxonMobil as if its pledge to decarbonize derived from some environmental epiphany; Mann argues that achieving this goal requires regulation and policy. But both ignore ExxonMobil's priorities: profit, obviously at any cost to the planet and its ecosystems. That ExxonMobil "*went to extraordinary lengths to head off the threat from*" Engine No. 1, including calling board members to pressure them during the annual board meeting shows us at least three things: first, that EDF's priorities are not, at least in the first place, the environment, but rather sustaining its corporate partnerships even if its president resorts to gross misrepresentation of the facts about ExxonMobil's real intentions; second, ExxonMobil has no plan to become a responsible environmental steward, and has learnt little from public condemnation over the company's effort to hide its own research into climate change; third, ExxonMobil can be counted on to resist any gambit that "imperils" its dividends, and we have no reason to think the company would see regulatory measures or policy any differently than board members like Engine No. 1. Each is a threat that must be neutralized as incompatible with the kleptocratic demands of profit. For the very reasons, however, that Mann's "personal choice" contrivance is misleading, the "tiny activist fund" represents a greater threat to the fossil fuel companies than does regulation or policy. Whatever Engine No. 1's motives, it's impact on the ExxonMobil board is not reducible to "individual action." Like Nader's PIRGs, Engine No. 1's objectives reach beyond chauvinistic self-interest. That Engine No. 1 is itself a profit-oriented enterprise, an investment fund, is irrelevant: it's power on the fossil fuel company's board derives from its investors' collective commitment to a conception of value: "We share an emerging view of value creation. One that takes into account a company's impact and the ways that impact drives shareholder value."[43] While ExxonMobil will doubtless work to undermine the activist fund, the fact that Engine No. 1 could force the company to produce a climate change plan testifies to the power of its investment, literally and figuratively.

In light of this analysis of the "personal choice" dichotomy, Mann's lamentation that he feels "*personally* betrayed" by the *Crying Indian* (and presumably *The Little Mermaid*) "as if the innocence of our youth was an illusion" feels itself contrived. Yet he persists claiming that it's "as if I—and everyone else of my generation—was led astray by a false prophet, for the motive of corporate profit."[44] Mann's right that he was "led astray" by the false prophet of profit, but not for the reasons he would convince his reader. That Mann conflates collective citizen action like Nader's PIRGs with Big Green corporations like EDF seems either disingenuous or deluded—or simply necessary to achieve the radical segregation of "individual action" and system-salvaging policy. Would Mann applaud Engine No. 1? On the one hand, the activist fund embraces the "larger system" Mann seeks to save:

> We are Engine No. 1—an investment firm purpose-built to create long-term value by harnessing the power of capitalism. We believe a company's performance is greatly enhanced by the investments it makes in workers, communities, and the environment. We believe that over time the interests of Main Street and Wall Street align, and we can engage as active owners to create value by focusing on this alignment.[45]

On the other, Mann himself refers to the "false prophet" of "corporate profits," casting doubt on whether any multinational, including presumably Engine No. 1's "activist investor" "It's Time to Reenergize Exxon" campaign, can succeed in "transforming America's largest oil company."[46] Engine No. 1 isn't a Public Service Ad; it's an investment firm. But what it nonetheless has in common with Nader's PIRGS is that it's not a regulatory agency or a federal policy. Like Nader's PIRGs and DiCaprio's foundation, Engine No. 1 is an NGO—a non-government organization composed of self-defined *activist agents*. Is the power that Engine No. 1 wields on the ExxonMobil board another example, given Mann's argument, of a "deflection campaign"? Do environmentally oriented investment firm board members waste time that would be better spent at agencies like the Environmental Protection Agency, the Department of the Interior, the Bureau of Land Management? Even if Engine No. 1's board gambit ultimately fails, like bottle bills restricted to blue states, this is far from obvious.

In short, the virtue of Nader's PIRGs, the Leonardo DiCaprio Foundation, or Engine No. 1, is not that they're anti-capitalist; *they're not*, and this fact lends itself to critique like that offered by Andreas Malm. But this is beside the point with respect to the false dichotomy Mann defends since what each confirm, in albeit different ways, is that collective action, whatever the underlying motives, can have real impact composed by but not reducible to "personal choice." None can be reduced to "deflection" from the job of policy, and the work citizens do for these each of these organizations is not merely a convenient way for the industry to see the time and energy of potential protesters frittered away. And there's this: there is nothing to guarantee that policy, even policy explicitly aimed at tackling the climate crisis, won't produce harmful consequences—often predictably. Consider once more projects like the United Nations/World Bank's *Reducing Emissions from Deforestation and Forest Degradation*, REDD. Because its primary if unspoken objective remains saving capitalism, not forest ecosystems, not their inhabitants, there is nothing in REDD to protect against casualties.[47] Indeed, the casualties of this climate war are the indigenous Sengwer who occupy land designated for reforestation toward the kind of new green global economy Mann's argument for cap and trade, carbon credits, and carbon trading would seem to embrace. Evicted as "squatters," itself a reference to land as property and the Sengwer as unlawful tenants, what REDD illustrates is the pitiless nature of the logic of commodification. Mann's optimism about the capacity of capitalism to heed the kind of regulatory regime capable of averting climate collapse seems itself to derive from his false dichotomy. Yet, although the example he makes of himself illuminates what Mann means by "personal choice," it also reveals something of the privileged position he occupies with respect to choosing, and the absurd position he has taken to defend the market economics he favors:

> As I frequently point out, I get my electricity from renewables, have one child, drive a hybrid vehicle, and don't eat meat. I have chosen a meat-free lifestyle for several reasons—solidarity with my daughter . . . ethical considerations, and a desire to minimize my environmental footprint. I think it's important to set a good example. *But I do not attempt to police others' lifestyles.*[48]

That as he "frequently points out," Mann feels the need to document his own "personal choices," in "solidarity with his daughter," and to "minimize his environmental footprint," suggests that Mann is himself sensitive to the "hypocrisy accusation" leveled at others, like Al Gore. This seems odd on its face since Mann defends Al Gore's airplane travel. If waging the climate war is about policy and not personal choices, why worry about what we eat? Why, given Mann's view of "individual action," isn't it a better example, a better illustration of solidarity, to thumb our noses at those who'd call us hypocrites for flying on airplanes?

In other words, it's great that Mann wants to set a good example, acting in solidarity with his daughter. But casting that noble aspiration against "policing others" as if "setting an example" and "policing others" were the only two options not only epitomizes Mann's false dichotomy, it shows just how narrow and stilted his definition of "personal choice" must be to make it the nemesis of policy. Consider "policing others" in a different context, the Covid-19 pandemic. Would Mann be comfortable with this analogy?

> As I frequently point out, I wear a mask, use hand-sanitizer, and socially distance. I do this for several reasons—solidarity with my daughter . . . ethical considerations, and a desire to avoid Covid-19 infection or infecting other people. I think it's important to set a good example. *But I do not attempt to police others' lifestyles.*

Really? Is the potential for infection by a deadly virus merely a matter of personal choice? Should we avoid asking others to put on masks *despite the clear danger of infection* because it's a worse thing to "police others' lifestyles" than it is to avoid this danger? Do we set a good example for our kids by modelling for them the value of not impinging on others even at the potential cost of our own health—or our children's? Aren't regulations that mandate mask wearing, for example, on mass transit buses "policing others"? Would Mann reject these?

Mann might respond, of course, that comparing the actions we might undertake to do our part toward reducing greenhouse gas emissions to asking people to mask-up is odious: the Coronavirus pandemic poses an immediate threat to human health, and the climate crisis does not. But this is, of course, for many, plainly false. Indeed, it leads to the second problem with Mann's solidarity disclaimer: for the Sengwer, the climate crisis is, in fact, an immediate threat to their community health insofar as it sanctions policies that have direct negative impact on their capacity to care for their children. Eviction, moreover, puts the lie to "personal choice." It is precisely the evictions, a grotesque violation of the choices, lifestyle, and even the *lives* of the Sengwer, that makes possible the privileged "lifestyle" of an academic whose own argument for "policy" helps to give rise to programs like REDD. It is the violation of the choices of the Sengwer that sustains the choices of affluent entitled global Northerners. Such programs preserve the "larger system" by exploiting the structural inequalities that leave the "other" voiceless. It's an easy thing to claim that "we" don't want to "police others' lifestyles" when we are required neither to hear nor see them. But it's as disingenuous as the idea that "we" have no connection to that "other." We do; *their loss is our gain.* Yet, it is this fact—that the planet, its resources, atmosphere, and its species are as intimately connected as food, energy, water, soil, seed, and the capacity for harm—that the logic of commodification cannot tolerate. By making a choice of the "larger system" over the climate, policy over the life of the "other," Mann has cast his lot with the logic. An appeal to respect for "lifestyle" may provide thin cover for the "personal choice" dichotomy and the argument for reform it scaffolds, but its real purpose in the case of the climate crisis (or pandemic) is either to excuse inaction or to reinforce a view of "personal choice" that legitimates policy as the only effective way to wage war, ignore the casualties, and look like you're setting a good example.

"THE TRUTH IS BAD ENOUGH," BUT NOT REALLY

It seems that the primary reason Mann erects a dichotomy between personal action and the creation of policy is so that he can make a convincing argument for the kinds of policies and regulatory devices he thinks suited to slow climate change. That he is forced to resort to caricature, straw fallacy, and *reductio ad absurdum* in order to make "personal action" seem an inevitable failure is cause not only for suspicion about the strength of his argument going forward, but a clarion call to examine the premises of his reformist proposals that leave the "larger system" fully in place. Mann's own failure to probe precisely in what this "larger system," *capitalism,* consists helps him to create superficially plausible arguments for cap and trade, carbon taxes, and carbon credits, but insofar as these proposals ignore the inherently kleptocratic character of the logic of commodification, they are bound not only to fail—but to hasten some of the worst consequences of the climate crisis, for example, food insecurity, future pandemic, human and nonhuman migration, extreme weather events, and war over potable water. Indeed, as Mann's (like Wallace-Wells') own panoramic and detailed accounts show, nothing other than "kleptocratic" can describe a "system" whose *raison d'étre* is power and profit, whose business model is extractivist and mythological, and for which the capacity for suffering is no obstacle to commodification. Premised on the extraction of hydrocarbons, animal proteins, precious metals, water, labor, all of which are conceived as inexhaustible, the very idea that regulatory schemes, even schemes that include "credits," pose anything more than a temporary obstacle to business as usual, including using the atmosphere as "the greatest market subsidy ever," ignores the very reality Mann so carefully lays out.

Mann acknowledges that we'd not be at war, much less engaged in a "new war" were past regulatory strategies or policies reliable. He writes that "[t]here is no one well-defined threshold that defines dangerous human interference with our climate. There is no cliff that we fall off of at 1.5C (2.7F) warming . . . A far better analogy is that we're walking our onto a minefield, and the farther we go the greater the risk. Conversely, the sooner we cease our forward lurch, the better off we are."[49] That we're walking onto a minefield at all testifies to the failures of past regulation and policy. Moreover, policies erected by one administration can be undone by the next: a slower "lurch" onto the minefield by President Obama sped to a gallop during President Trump's fossil-fueled efforts to repeal environmental protections in the interest of the oil and gas industry, its wealthy donors, and the fortunes of its preferred electeds.[50] Investment firms like Engine No. 1 may be best understood as one form of coordinated response to the environmental hazards of the Trump administration. As Mann's many examples show, the real problem is that once you're out onto the minefield, stepping in any direction is a gingerly business, and there may be no way to trace your steps back to safety. Eventually you'll step on a mine and blow stuff up. And while some are in a better position to avoid the mines, some are born in the field itself. Some can afford luxuries like private residence solar panels and protective fire foam; others come home at night to neighborhoods next to landfills or waste incinerators, factory farm lagoons, or acid mine run-off. Some can buy electric cars, most can't.

As Mann makes clear, we're already blowing stuff up. Hurricane Maria's devastation of Puerto Rico in 2017, deforestation of the Amazon, wildfires in the Arctic and in California, Biblical scale drought, flood, and even plagues of locusts in Africa, Mann remarks that "[d]angerous climate change has in fact already arrived for many."[51] He makes no bones, moreover, about the fact that its causes are anthropogenic: the first reference of Mann's "Introduction," cites a 2015 *Inside Climate News* report concerning what ExxonMobil's own research scientists knew about the contribution of fossil fuels to global warming as early as 1977 and the disinformation machine the company deployed to hide the facts from the public.[52] That ExxonMobil spent at least 30 million dollars to promote climate change denial is only one barometer of its efforts to protect the profitability of its product, but one that makes starkly clear the company's view of consumers who might demand alternative forms of energy if they understood the threat to the existential conditions of their grandchildren, but could be shamed into "fatal complacency," as Wallace-Wells might put it, by the hypocrisy modern life makes virtually unavoidable. It's in this straightforward sense that Mann's example of ExxonMobil acts as the posterchild for the claim that, in the context of capital venture, "anthropogenic" means "kleptocratic." A company that goes as far as to create a disinformation-front called *The Global Climate Coalition* whose sole aim was to sow doubt about climate change is plainly willing to go to great, indeed, planetary lengths to protect its bottom line, and perpetuate the myth that the atmosphere is a bottomless toilet.[53]

As Mann puts it, things are "bad enough," to consider joining forces with, for example, Naomi Klein's brutal critique of capitalism in *This Changes Everything*.[54] But instead of taking Klein's critique seriously, he exploits a caricature deployed by far right climate change deniers to demonize her as a means of promoting his own version of salvation capitalism:

> [Klein's] thesis is that neo-liberalism—the prevailing global policy model, predicated on privatization and free market capitalism—must be overthrown through mass resistance [and that] climate change can't be separated from other pressing social problems . . . Such framing fans the flames of the conservative fever swamps, reinforcing the right wing tropes that environmentalists are "watermelons" (green on the outside, red on the inside) who secretly want to use environmental sustainability as an excuse for overthrowing capitalism and ending economic growth.[55]

There are, in the first place, a number of reasons to dispute Mann's interpretation of Klein's argument for overthrowing capitalism, including her own reluctance to confront Animal Agriculture, a "lacuna," as *Climate Change N*ews reporter Alan Lockwood puts it, "at the heart of *This Changes Everything*."[56] Mann is doubtless aware of this criticism (among others), and surely knows he shares this reluctance concerning Animal Agriculture with Klein—and a number of others, including otherwise progressive 2020 presidential candidates like Elizabeth Warren, Cory Booker, and current Vice President, Kamala Harris:

> At this fall's "Climate Crisis" town hall forum on CNN, Democratic front-runner Senator Elizabeth Warren dismissed the idea of reduced meat consumption as a simple distraction: "This is exactly what the fossil fuel industry hopes we're all talking about . . . [They want to make this] your problem. They want to be able to stir up a lot of controversy around your lightbulbs, straws, and cheeseburgers." Senator Cory Booker, the only vegan running for office, did not wish to draw more attention to his dinner plate: "Freedom is one of our most sacred values. Whatever you want to eat, go ahead and eat it." When asked if she would support dietary guideline changes that would lower greenhouse gas emissions caused by meat heavy diets, Senator Kamala Harris responded that she loves cheeseburgers: "I mean I—I just do."[57]

The point, however, is not merely that Mann shares with presidential candidates and climate activists what *Journal of International Affairs* writer

Christina Sewell describes as a variety of cognitive dissonance. The point is that what makes possible the magnitude of dissonance required to ignore Animal Agriculture's 14.5% contribution to greenhouse gas emissions is the commodification of sentience.[58] Once the capacity for sentience and suffering no longer registers as a moral hurdle to commodification and consumption, ignoring the causes of that suffering becomes normal—or normalized. Once that bridge is burned, the climate activist, the elected representative, the scientist, the presidential candidate, and most of the rest of us are effectively issued a pass to ignore the horrific consequences of animal agriculture in all of its incarnations—from pollution to institutionalized cruelty.

Cognitive dissonance is thus not about "personal choice" at all. It's an enculturated disposition that benefits the fossil fuel industry at the expense of the planet, its populations, and its atmosphere. Animal agriculture is no more exempt from analysis of its greenhouse gas emissions than are other extractivist enterprises, tar sands mining, hydraulic fracturing, or mountain-top removal coal mining. Arguments like Mann's simply permit us to evade the touchy discussion of what should count as food. But the strategy is disingenuous. That is, it's not merely fallacious; it embodies the very cognitive dissonance that fuels the consumption of hydrocarbons, reinforces the logic of commodification—and exposes Mann's reformism as at least naïve if not deluded. To consign meat-eating to "personal choice" is not merely to endorse the commodification of sentient creatures, but to endorse the cognitive dissonance required to maintain the illusion that meat-eating *is* a merely personal choice, as opposed to an enculturated behavior whose purpose is to oxygenate the circulatory system of capital. The factory farm is thus itself the most damning indictment of Mann's false dichotomy in that it exposes "personal choice" as a fiction of capital:

> Consider: meat and other animal-derived products constitute the third-largest source of greenhouse gas emissions globally, following the energy and industrial sectors. They have a larger carbon footprint than the world's entire transportation sector . . . The meat and dairy industries alone account for 78% of all agricultural GHG emissions . . . These emissions aren't derived simply from fossil fuels used to plant, fertilize, and harvest the feed to fatten livestock for market, but due largely to cows, sheep, and other animals' especially potent methane gas. And while this gas doesn't linger in the atmosphere as long as carbon dioxide, in the first 20 years after release, its greenhouse effect is *25 times* more effective at trapping the heat of the sun and warming the planet . . . More than a quarter of humanity's water footprint goes toward the meat and dairy industries due to the incredible amount of water needed to produce food for livestock . . . Beef—the second most consumed meat in the United States—has the largest water footprint of all types of meat, requiring a whopping 1,800–2,500 gallons of water per pound, more water than is used to shower every day

> for six months. . . . Likewise, one gallon of dairy milk requires 2,000 gallons of water inputs, roughly twice what is needed for a gallon of almond milk, the most water-intensive dairy substitute. Animal agriculture also drives unprecedented levels of deforestation as forests are cleared to make way for livestock grazing and growing crops for animal feed, which now accounts for more than one-third of the Earth's total landmass . . . Across the countries of Amazonia . . . livestock accounts for roughly 80% of current deforestation rates . . . This is especially alarming considering that tropical rainforests are a major carbon sink.[59]

This is not merely a lot to assign to "personal choice," *it puts the lie to it.* What this level of cognitive dissonance requires is a mythology about the planet and its "endless resources," a human chauvinism readily put to consumption and repackaged as "freedom," the willingness to deny the consequences for the planet's atmosphere, and the suspension of belief about the suffering caused to human and nonhuman beings in the production of a single cheeseburger. What it requires is the normalizing of a fatal complacency that sustains the façade of personal choice without any risk to the industries in the "what's for dinner?" supply chain.

Mann knows, as do vegans like Cory Booker and climate activists like Naomi Klein, that the market-based solutions he favors concerning cap and trade, carbon taxes, and other incentives won't get a hearing if they point a finger at animal agriculture. But this is simply irrelevant in light of the fact that what 14.5% of greenhouse gas emissions means is that there is no meaningful climate action without addressing animal agriculture's contribution to the crisis. To accuse the vegan who points this out of victim-blaming is thus particularly absurd, especially in light of the fact that being deprived of something we merely like or want no more makes Kamala Harris a victim than depriving a child molester of access to little girls makes him a victim. Want is not need—however much we're encouraged to conflate the two in the interest of promoting more consumption. Yet the conclusion we're invited to draw from Mann's caricature of Klein is that either you're with the anti-capitalist insurrectionists or the sensible market-reformists—another faulty dichotomy. You don't want to be Klein, Mann implies, and thereby risk being demonized by FOX News pundits like Sean Hannity who, pandering to his far right audience, claims that environmentalists would impose "government-forced vegetarianism" through a regime resembling "what Stalin dreamt about."[60] Instead you want to be the sensible cap and trade reformist who "puts a price on it," that is, retains capitalism through regulatory mechanisms and policies that can save capitalism from itself.

What's important to recognize here is that Mann claims to reject these demonizing stereotypes of Klein (Al Gore, Rachel Carson), but that does not prevent him from exploiting these images to his own ends. Put differently: Mann cannot raise the question whether capitalism is worth preserving because this would utterly undermine the premises of his own argument for regulation and policy. So, instead he decries "conservative" "firebrands" like Hannity as mean, but then effectively endorses their demonizing rhetoric as a means to cauterize *any* critique of capitalism inconsistent with his reformist program. Thus, the stage is set for Mann's argument for Cap and Trade, carbon taxes, and carbon credits, all of which embrace the logic of commodification:

> We need mechanisms that force polluters to pay for the climate damage done by their product—fossil fuels—tilting the advantage to those forms of energy that aren't destroying our planetary home . . . Such mechanisms can take the form of tradable emissions permits, also known as *cap and trade*. In this policy, government allocates or sells a limited number of permits to pollute, and the polluters can buy and sell these permits. This strategy limits pollution by providing economic incentives for polluters to reduce emissions. Another policy is a *carbon tax*, wherein a tax is levied at the point of sale on the carbon content of fuels or any other product yielding greenhouse gas emissions. Additionally, *carbon credits* can be granted for activities that take carbon out of the atmosphere and bury it or store it thus offsetting carbon emissions.[61]

Should we adopt the right policies and enforcement mechanisms, in other words, we can remain free from having to worry too much about changing what we eat, what we drive, or our "lifestyles" because the real issues are "with the larger system and its incentives."[62] While we must be prepared to engage in a "war" for truth about the climate crisis and its real "Frankenstein," the energy industry and its "vested interests," the "shift away from fossil fuel burning towards a clean, green global economy" is not only within reach, contrary to the hand-wringing divinations of the "doomsayers,"[63] but no radical transformation of how we eat, drive, or live will be required.

Unfortunately, as we've already seen with the Sengwer, while these strategies benefit some, especially the fossil fuel industries that survive and continue to profit, their success comes at great cost to others, especially those least able to defend themselves against the expropriation of farmland, consequent loss of livelihood, and expulsion. Indeed, the same cognitive dissonance that attends the exemption of animal agriculture from greenhouse gas mitigation efforts also exempts car-driving meat-eating global Northerners from having to take responsibility for the consequences of reforestation programs like REDD. To be clear, this is not to say that reforestation is not important to slowing the pace of climate change; it's to say that until we confront the cognitive dissonance that makes false dichotomies and the salvation capitalisms that depend on them appear sensible, we will neither slow that pace nor mitigate the harm done to the climate crisis' real victims, namely, all those human beings and nonhuman animals who pay the real cost of "put a price on it." Perhaps, then, the most charitable reading of Mann is that regardless what strategy has to be adopted to implement cap and trade, carbon credits, and carbon taxes, the ends, slowing the pace, justify the means even if it means resorting to false dichotomy, evasion, straw fallacy, or other shady rhetorical tactics. The trouble is that even if we could accept this mercenary version of the principle of utility, we have no good reason to think the ends will actually be achieved. Indeed, not only will these strategies fail in virtue of the exemption made for animal agriculture—they fail on their own.

"THE RIGHT MARKET INCENTIVES": HARBINGER OF THE KLEPTOCENE

When Mann argues that "[w]e need mechanisms that force polluters to pay for the climate damage done by their product—fossil fuels—tilting the advantage to those forms of energy that aren't destroying our planetary home," he doubtless hopes, as he puts it, that with the right mix of "supply-side and demand-side measures" the market can provide the vehicle for the "fundamental transition in our global economy and [the] massive new infrastructure" needed to avoid climate disaster.[64] Mann goes on to detail an ambitious set of supply-side measures that include "banning fracking, stopping mountain-top removal coal mining, divesting in fossil fuel companies, and putting a halt to most new fossil fuel infrastructure—including the 1700 mile, tar sands exporting Keystone XL Pipeline" blocked by President Obama, revived by President Trump, and terminated by President Biden after thirteen years of coordinated citizen action.[65] Yet, despite his recognition that "blocking Keystone XL gave Obama a strong hand in negotiating a bilateral climate agreement with China in 2015 that would, in turn, lay the groundwork for the monumental Paris Agreement later that year," and likely positioned Biden to cancel Keystone XL's building permits in an early executive order,[66] Mann consigns the work of organized protesters to pressure Obama to mere "personal action":

> But, just as personal action is no substitute for systemic change, supply side efforts are no substitute for demand-side approaches. Demand-side measures attempt to level the playing field so that climate-friendly energy, transportation, and agricultural practices outcompete fossil fuels in the marketplace. Carbon pricing is one of the most powerful tools we have to do that. Taking it off the table would constitute unilateral disarmament in the climate wars.[67]

The trouble here is that it's absurd to characterize the coordinated efforts of organizations like *Bold Nebraska*[68] as an assembly of "personal actions." Even more vexing, however, is that this argument is demonstrably circular. Mann deploys the market to consign "personal action" to "supply-side efforts" that, he insists, cannot be sufficient to do battle in the "climate wars." Yet, he appeals to a false dichotomy pitting "personal action" against "demand-side measures" to defend carbon pricing as a "powerful tool." He reduces "personal action," in other words, to a market activity in order to dismiss it as inadequately effective, in order to claim that it would be a "disarmament" disaster to "take off the table" its (equally contrived) "demand-side" opposite.

This isn't merely an exercise in bad logic; the issue is the worldview Mann's bad logic reinforces, one that effectively authorizes the market-domination that, in turn, insures the survival of the fossil fuel industry and its largely uninterrupted kleptocratic conquest. Mann argues, for example, that had the Australian Prime Minister, Tony Abbott, not cancelled what Mann insists would have been a successful carbon-pricing program, a "shining example of climate leadership," the country might not have become a "dystopian hellscape resembling a scene from the 1979 Australian film, Mad Max."[69] But Mann doesn't offer criteria to determine what would count as "successful" for a program in existence only since 2012, and we have little reason to think that Australia's largest oil producer, Woodside Petroleum, would behave differently than its competitors, including ExxonMobil. In fact, because Australia is dependent on oil imports to make up for domestic shortfalls, 2019/2020 saw a sizable uptick in oil exploration off the country's southern coast, the Great Australian Bight, cast by the Prime Minister as vital to "energy security," the catch-all cover language for nearly any fossil fuel gambit.[70] Yet, the Prime Minister hardly needs an excuse to continue drilling. What even a cursory look at the brief history of the *Australian Clean Energy Act, 2011*[71] shows is that the goal of a 5% reduction of greenhouse gas emissions was greeted with momentary fanfare that gave way quickly to a new, climate change denying, administration that would repeal it altogether.[72]

Put philosophically: by treating the planet's atmosphere as just another commodity or transactional asset, "demand-side" market schemes like carbon-pricing are bound to propel the disarticulation of value and accelerate the ecological impacts of kleptocratic capitalism even as the same schemes offer false hope that fossil fuel extraction can continue without environmental catastrophe. It is in the sense of this false hope that we opt for the less terrifying signifier "Anthropocene" as a euphemism for the "Kleptocene" whose logic of commodification tells the truth about what we count as value—despite our disclaimers. So deeply enculturated is the idea that all value is reducible to exchange-value, the fact that carbon-pricing effectively *monetizes our existential conditions* goes unremarked. Still, what could monetize our existential conditions more transparently than putting a price on the *atmosphere*? And how do we know when the price we have paid, a price far higher for some than for others, is too high? In *The Critique of Commodification*, Christoph Hermann reminds us that "nature creates an ultimate boundary for commodification and accumulation":

> Yet the elastic nature of the barrier also presents a major risk: precisely because we do not know how much depletion, pollution, and destruction nature can take and what the cumulative effects of the various forms of ecological degeneration are, there is a real possibility that the limit will be overstepped and ecological devastation will reach a point of no return.[73]

It is precisely what we do not know, this *epistemic opacity*, that creates the conditions for market schemes like those advocated by Mann to appear reasonable. But this exploitation of ignorance is also what the fossil fuel industries bank on, literally; "not knowing," "probably not today," "2050, or thereabout" give us permission to use benign-sounding references like "Anthropocene" because it's so easy to mistake "not right now" for "maybe never." But, as Hermann makes clear, the elastic nature of a barrier does not negate the fact that there exists a barrier, and that we are at great risk of breaching it beyond a "point of no return."

What the fossil fuel companies see in carbon pricing legislation is the opportunity to take perverse advantage of the "elastic nature" of the planetary and atmospheric barrier along with the epistemic opacity that goes with it to continue their pursuit of profit. What schemes like carbon-pricing tacitly promise as a bribe is that planetary barriers need not be barriers to capital accumulation since, after all, it's all "elastic." Proposals like Mann's thereby facilitate the advance of the Kleptocene's worst possible climate impacts because they depend on the same exploitation of ignorance about the limits of the planet as do the fossil fuel behemoths. His argument for carbon pricing offers a "powerful tool" not for legislatures, but for an industry fully prepared to weaponize the threat of regulation as a justification for going on offense. The road for this strategy is well-paved: why would Woodside Petroleum recognize "mechanisms that force polluters to pay for the climate damage done by their product" as anything other than an obstacle to neutralize, green-wash, or both? Insofar as carbon-pricing schemes depend on the same logic of commodification, they're aimed at the same ultimate objective: profit. The election of "climate skeptics" like Tony Abbott is thus better understood not as a cause of environmental catastrophe; but merely as a symptom.[74]

Abbott's policies so undercut the *Australian Clean Energy Act* that any constraint it might have imposed on the fossil fuel companies could be expeditiously undone by ginning-up public anxiety over "energy security," an anxiety made possible by the same epistemic opacity that attends our inability to predict the ultimate limits of the planet's ecologies. We don't know exactly how much more abuse the planet and its atmosphere can take, so how can we know to what lengths we can go to insure "energy security" before we, as Malm puts it, "burn it all down"? "Energy security," moreover, turns out to have wide application, including, as Alexander White reports for *The Guardian*, the expenditure of tax dollars on "charco-state" mining company subsidies:

> Tony Abbott and his government seem intent on turning Australia into a reckless "charco-state" (the coal equivalent of a petro-state). These fossil fuel subsidies don't just pay companies to pollute our air, water and atmosphere. They also distort our markets by making fossil fuels, like diesel and gas, artificially cheap. Special tax treatment for big oil, gas and coal projects allows fossil fuel companies to rapidly depreciate their assets, like drilling rigs. This means they get away with not paying taxes that other companies are forced to. Finally, fossil fuel subsidies are socially dangerous because many pension and superannuation funds have fossil fuel investments, risking tens or hundreds of billions in retirement savings in a carbon bubble.[75]

A public dependent on fossil fuels, in other words, is itself a lucrative commodity. And this is especially true, hence even more effectively weaponized, when the aging members of this same public don't know when the climate crisis will turn climate catastrophe. What such folks do know is that they're particularly vulnerable insofar as their retirement savings are floating in a "carbon bubble." It's precisely this sort of epistemic opacity combined with age-heightened vulnerability that empowers the "charco-state." With the right advertising, fear-mongering, and appeal to patriotism, even critical social guarantees like pensions can be deployed as variables subordinated to the quest for profit. Like many of its fossil fuel analogues, Woodside Energy plays the "long game," greening its image when such advertising serves its purposes,[76] conjuring the enemies of national security when patriotic defense of country seems more profitable, planning for an oil revenue bonanza as lockdown-weary travelers hit the post-pandemic vacation road. But every one of these gambits depend on the same thing: our willingness to suspend judgment about the potential for climate apocalypse on the grounds that we don't know when its coming. This is a very dangerous game.

But not, apparently, dangerous enough for Mann whose claim that we can "force polluters to pay for the climate damage done by their product" simply defies the fact that time is running out. Hermann once again puts this crucial point succinctly:

> [Ecological] limits follow from the fact that certain natural resources which are critical for the capitalist accumulation process are of a finite nature and will therefore run out at some point in the future . . . Another challenge stems from the tension between the speed-up in accumulation and the stagnating or increasing time necessary for nature to reproduce itself. Because nature increasingly lacks the time to reproduce itself, accumulation does more than deplete non-renewable resources; it destroys renewable inputs into the accumulation process. Finally, the complexity of nature and natural processes means that human interference can have unintended consequences and can cause chain reactions with dangerous outcomes . . . humanity can easily overstep the ecological limit without realizing it.[77]

In short, Mann's dream of capitalist rehabilitation requires us to forget the history *and* the ongoing criminality of the fossil fuel industry; it requires to wear the epistemic opacity built into the "run out at some point" nature of the planet's resources as a shield against having to undergo radical change. We have, however, no reason to think that ExxonMobil wouldn't go to the same lengths to conceal, obfuscate, down-play, or deny what their scientists know about greenhouse gases now just as the company had in the past because we are as unsure now about when "run out" will come as we were then—even though we know that clock is ticking.

Indeed, were it not for brave whistle-blowers, we'd not likely know ExxonMobil's criminal history at all, including the 32.2 million the company was required to pay out in 2010 to compensate for "underpaid natural gas royalties on federal and American Indian leases,"[78] and, more recently, an SEC (*Security and Exchange Commission*) investigation into the overvaluation of an oil field asset in West Texas:

> The whistleblower complaint concerns Exxon's valuation of a key asset in the Permian Basin, which, located in West Texas and New Mexico, is currently the highest-producing oil field in the United States. According to the complaint, in order to reach a higher valuation of the asset, Exxon employees were forced to use unrealistic assumptions about the speed at which the company could drill wells there. The complaint states that several people involved in the valuation complained about these practices during an internal assessment in 2019.[79]

This is not the ExxonMobil of the 1970s, or even the ExxonMobil of the early 21st century pretending to be sorry for hiding what it knew about climate change. This is ExxonMobil 2019. Similarly, Mann claims that Australia has become a "poster child for the cost of climate inaction," but ignores the fact that this "inaction" is the predictable result of fossil fuel industry inspired action. What he ignores, in other words, is a logic of commodification that defies history, or better: whose history testifies to its utter lack of concern for the past or the future, other than as investment opportunity. Consider once more Tony Abbott:

> [Tony] Abbott came to power last September promising to abolish the country's landmark carbon and mining taxes, and cut "green tape" that he said hindered development. Brendan Pearson, CEO of the Minerals Council of Australia (MCA), said the abolition of these two industry taxes would secure future investment and jobs, help regional communities, increase tax revenues, reduce energy prices, and boost Australia's international competitiveness. But Professor Bill Laurance . . . is astounded by the pace and scope of the environmental rollbacks. He said the proposal to abolish the carbon tax and replace it with a "direct action plan" was just one of a "whole avalanche" of issues that worry Australia's leading environmental scientists.
>
> The list of issues includes:
>
> - culling sharks off the coast of Western Australia,
> - approving cattle grazing in highland National Parks,
> - wholesale cutting of green energy initiatives, and
> - appointing a climate change skeptic to review renewable energy targets.

This was just the beginning of what, contrary to "inaction," might be far better to describe as the nullification of resistance through capitalist enculturation, "national security" pandering, and the vilification of "green tape," complete with an unrelenting and irrecoverable assault on fragile ecologies, cultural heritage, endangered species, and biodiversity, all of it "justified" by appeal to concern for the burden of the regulation of "communities":

> Even more controversially, Abbott's government has permitted a coal port to dredge up and dump millions of cubic feet of sand into the iconic Great Barrier Reef Marine Park . . . And in another unprecedented move, the government has asked UNESCO to remove 74,000 hectares of Tasmanian forest from its World Heritage List. A prime ministerial statement has also effectively banned the creation of new National Parks, with Prime Minister Abbott announcing that too much forest was already "locked away." Laurance . . . says Abbott's National Parks decision had come at a "very bad time," with some ecosystems in desperate need of protection, such as the Mountain Ash forests in Victoria, home to the critically endangered native Leadbeater's possum, decimated by logging and wildfires. Fulton laments Abbott's rolling back of the Environment Protection and Biodiversity Conservation (EPBC) Act, Australia's seminal legislative tool used to measure whether a development is environmentally sound. New offshore oil and gas exploration permits, for example, are now being approved by the National Offshore Petroleum Safety and Environmental Management Authority, says Fulton, the same agency that's responsible for enforcing safety regulations . . . Pearson, of the MCA, said the amount of time and effort being

> wasted on the duplication of regulations was undermining industry and community confidence, while adding little value to environmental or heritage protection. "The mining industry isn't seeking to duck or dodge scientific scrutiny—quite the opposite . . . "[80]

Abbott's "green tape cutting" initiatives and rollbacks are rightly described as "climate inaction" only in the utterly misleading sense that the removal of regulation liberates fossil fuel companies to continue, even accelerate, their greenhouse gas emissions. Such a notion of "inaction" is built for the fossil fuel industry. But this isn't merely because the distortion of fact concerning the industry's role in the climate crisis is irreducible to "inaction." It's that many of Abbott's policies diminish the significance of the industry's potentially devastating environmental impacts even if we ignore the climate crisis. The potential extinction of the Leadbeater's Possum, irreversible damage to fragile coral reefs, and deforestation are just a few of these, endangering not only the planetary ecology, but its biodiversity well beyond Australia.

The lengths, moreover, that the Abbott administration was willing to go to intercept and cauterize resistance to his policies aren't hard to find. We need look no further that the Minerals Mining Commission. Effectively, a tactical campaign pitch for Abbott's conservative party and its fossil fuel allies, the MMC sought to pit communities against their own ecologies and those who would defend them arguing that too much regulation would undermine "confidence" without adding "value" to environmental or heritage protections. Many indigenous Australians, however, found this line of argument unconvincing given the extent to which industry talking points tended to reflect Abbott's own demonstrably racist attitude toward indigenous communities. Abbott claimed, for example, that if climate change is a real thing it's "probably doing good," and that environmental regulation was like "primitive people once killing goats to appease the volcano gods." He "backed a plan to shut down 150 Aboriginal communities" in 2015, arguing that Australian taxpayers can't be expected to pay for Aboriginal "lifestyle choices,"[81] and insisted "that Australia was unoccupied at the time of white invasion." Abbott described pre-invasion Australia as "extraordinarily basic and raw"; stated precolonial Sydney was "nothing but bush" before the arrival of the First Fleet in 1788; and suggested [that] white invasion was a positive, "defining moment."[82]

It's thus unsurprising that the appointment of Abbott in 2018 as Special Envoy to Australia's Indigenous communities would be greeted with displeasure:

> Abbott's previous policies on Indigenous issues had been characterised by funding cuts, exclusions and silencing. His Indigenous Advancement Strategy

> was criticised for its destructive consequences to governance within Indigenous communities. Someone who had caused such injury and grief in the past, stripped communities of their capacity for self-determination and seemed so lacking of respect in their own community was largely unwelcome.[83]

Mann might respond, of course, that criticism of Abbott's racism is a red herring—that it has little more than tangential bearing on whether the 2011 *Australian Clean Energy Act* would have been successful had Abbott not been elected as Prime Minister. But the fact is that the structural inequalities maintained by Abbott's policies are precisely those that advantage companies like Woodside by insuring that claims concerning ecological and community destruction can be ignored or papered over without significant cost to the company's public image and bottom line. The same structural inequalities that advantage the oil industry are, moreover, at least partly responsible for the election not only of Abbott, but also, just a few years later, Scott Morrison. Comparing the two men, *Guardian* columnist Jack Lattimore remarks that "Abbott is wrong for the job [of Special Envoy], but his boss, Morrison, is himself too paternalistic to bother much about it." He continues: "in both men there is a hulking paternal arrogance." Indeed, Morrison's "neocolonialism is right on par with Abbott's," both climate change "skeptics," although it's Morrison's theatrical flare that has him toting lumps of coal to work "to boast his party's commitment to coal-fired power over renewables."[84]

Put simply, the machinations of institutionalized inequality can no more be reduced to a province of "inaction" than can the advantages it makes possible—*and for whom*. While the "inactivists" may help Mann frame the opposition he needs to argue that "action" is the exclusive domain of policy, this straw argument is really just a preemptive smokescreen behind which clamors a throng of invested parties empowered to make decisions that serve the interests of mostly white Western(ized) men and their corporate allies at the expense of those discounted by elected leaders like Abbott and Morrison. "Discounted," moreover, has impacts generational as well as immediate: "Vulnerable people in detention died during Morrison's watch as minister for immigration. Vulnerable people experienced added hardship and distress due to his welfare system overhaul as minister for social services."[85] Mann does reference "intergenerational inequity," but only as a "baleful aspect" of what he calls "doomism," namely, the prospect that the climate crisis might doom the hope of a good life for future generations of human beings.[86] In other words, he deploys intergenerational inequity as a weapon against those who would expose the failures of *policy*.

To be clear, the point is not whether Mann's right or wrong to criticize, for example, Rupert Read,[87] Roy Scranton,[88] or "Doctor Doom" Guy McPherson,[89] as "doomists." The point is that we can make no objective assessment of their "Doomist" positions at all given the false dichotomies and straw characterizations that premise Mann's arguments. Indeed, even if Mann's right that these "Doomists" paint a picture of the future that's too dark, we'd do well to consider critically the short shrift he offers to generational inequity. Carbon-pricing and regulation are thin reeds upon which to hang the hope that the future will be more equitable than the past. And it's not clear that the structural inequalities that help sustain the fossil fuel industry are more significant to Mann than as another avenue for dismissing the "doomists." But if this latter is the case, it serves as one more example of how Mann, however unwittingly, does the work of the fossil fuel industry sparing it from having to defend its contribution not only to the climate crisis, but to impacts that will harm some more than others, and that will maintain structural inequality well onto the future.

"DOOMISTS," REALISTS, AND THE HISTORY OF HORSES AND CARS

Recent Australian history makes a compelling example of the challenges of slowing the pace of climate change—but not for the reasons Mann would have us think. Indeed, once we have a clearer picture of this history and its players, Mann's claim that "it is not too late for Australians to reclaim leadership by voting in a government that promises to act on the climate in the next election" seems more fantasy than realistic possibility.[90] A reclamation of leadership that ignores damage already done resulting in species extinction, the destruction of coral reefs, loss of forest habitat, and the rights of the country's Aboriginal peoples seems not only an anemic view of leadership, but a paradigmatic example of the commodification of sentience. Why, given the suffering generated by the Abbott and Morrison administrations should we accept any approach to the climate crisis that fails to aggressively pursue social and environmental justice? Does Leadbeater's possum count in Mann's calculus of climate action more than it does for the industry that would drive it to extinction? This is not obvious, at least in *The New Climate War*. Given Mann's stated faith in market mechanisms, the value of an endangered species seems unlikely to be greater than its value as a commodity, and we have no reason to think that's very much for a possum, or a species of grouse, or a forest, or an aboriginal people. By insisting that "the right market incentives" combined with "demand-side measures" such as carbon-pricing can achieve significant reductions of greenhouse gases, Mann effectively endorses the disarticulation of value upon which all such schemes are premised; after all, capitalist solutions are as much indebted to the ontology of capital as their capitalist-generated crises. Insofar as all value is reducible to carbon-based exchange value, traits like being a living thing, a living sentient thing, a vulnerable thing are preempted and systemically erased as irrelevant to the determination of exchange value. Hence, a carbon-pricing regime is no more likely to save the Leadbeater Possum than it is to promote generational equity for aboriginal Australians.

Lastly, there's the difficult question whether, setting aside issues of environmental or social justice, Mann's argument for carbon pricing policy as the road to greenhouse gas reductions will actually work. This is really two questions. The first is whether, on the assumption that such policies might work, the fossil fuel industry can be trusted not to circumvent them, lie about their implementation, or ignore them altogether. The second is whether such policies will work, or work in time even if implemented faithfully. But these questions boil-down to the same concern: even a slim chance such policies could have a positive effect reducing greenhouse gas emissions before we "burn it all down" depends not only on whether the fossil fuel industries can be trusted generally, but whether their policy implementation can be trusted. Are we in any position to know whether ExxonMobil or any of its corporate analogues are worthy of this moral investment? The epistemic opacity that attends our understanding of nonhuman nature and its tipping points to radical change may be, as Malm argues, built into natural laws and processes—however affected by human action. Not knowing what a corporation is up to is perhaps a rather more prosaic species of ignorance. But it would be folly to assume that fossil fuel CEOs like Rex Tillerson are not entirely comfortable with exploiting every scrap of doubt fed to consumers along with our gasoline and hamburgers: that is the *modus operandi* of disaster capitalism.

Consider: given a public better acquainted with the implications of climate change in 2021 than in 2012, it's no surprise that Mann's promotion of a carbon tax might solicit a different response from the fossil fuel companies now than a decade ago. But it would be naïve to think that a more apparently positive response to regulation reflects some honest reckoning with the damage these companies have effected for the planet and its atmosphere. The *American Petroleum Institute* offers a textbook example. Nimble in the protection of its industry members, API has responded to carbon pricing not with rejection, but with savvy strategies for circumvention, advertising, and portfolio expansion. As Jennifer A Dlouhy and Leslie Kaufman report for *Bloomberg Green*:

> A carbon price—whether in the form of an emissions trading scheme or a tax on planet-warming pollution—seems antithetical to the fossil fuel industry's interests, as it would effectively make their core product more expensive for consumers. Large oil and gas companies are likely worried that any other potential action from the Biden administration would be worse for them, said

> Joe Aldy, a public policy professor at the Harvard Kennedy School . . . "They think the alternative climate policy may be a lot of regulations they would view as burdensome and inefficient." . . . *But the policy itself has a number of silver linings for polluters*. For starters, unlike regulations restricting drilling or mandating clean energy, a carbon tax wouldn't bar companies from extracting natural gas or force the fossil fuel out of the nation's electricity mix. It could also drive investments in direct-air carbon capture and other technologies that would prolong the use of fossil fuels as a power source. In the short run, putting a price on greenhouse gas emissions could give natural gas an even greater edge over dirtier-burning coal. "All of the oil majors have natural gas assets they are trying to protect, and this is a way to do that," said Mike McKenna, a former deputy director of the White House Office of Legislative Affairs. "Once they became natural gas companies and started competing in the electricity space, it was just a matter of time till they wanted to rub coal out."[91]

To be clear, the "oil majors" are not interested in "rubbing out coal" because it's dirty, or because it contributes to climate change. Were that their interest, they'd not look to methane whose greenhouse gas footprint is, in the long run, far more hazardous to the atmosphere, particularly given recent technologies such as hydraulic fracturing. As *Unpopular Science* reports: "[t]he US coal industry is dying. The technologies of hydraulic fracturing and horizontal drilling have flooded energy markets with cheap methane fuel. Methane is a hydrocarbon with 72 times the atmospheric heat-trapping potential as the carbon dioxide molecule in a 20-year time frame."[92] The "oil majors" want to "rub out coal" because there are new, potentially more profitable, games in town. Indeed, even Woodside Petroleum has joined with several other "mining giants" claiming that "the companies would benefit from putting a higher price on carbon" because, as Chief Executive Peter Colman makes the point, "We don't want to have perversive outcomes where lowest-cost energy suppliers are competing against renewables, and we end up in a situation where we've invested a lot in renewables but in fact see no benefit from a carbon point of view."[93] Whatever promotes company "sustainability," say, touting natural gas as a "bridge fuel," conforms to the logic of commodification. It's thus predictable that companies like Woodside will pursue it, call it "green," and continue to support carbon-friendly electeds like Tony Abbott. But company sustainability, that is, "grow or die," is not atmospheric sustainability.

The challenge for the oil majors is to exploit what Stephanie LeMenager, in *Living Oil: Petroleum Culture in the American Century,* shows is the deep-rooted conceptual, economic, and technological *culture of petroleum*[94]—but in a fashion that can take advantage of the "silver linings" of a carbon tax. Indeed, if LeMenager is correct, the fossil fuel behemoths are unlikely to see such a tax as a "make them pay" because, insofar as they can count on the fact that "[w]e experience ourselves, as moderns, and most especially as modern Americans, every day in oil, breathing it and registering it with our senses,"[95] they don't have to contend with any of the strategies Mann defends as a threat to business as usual. They simply have to get more creative in order to circumvent, suppress, camouflage, and greenwash, *just as they always have*. Stoll's historical account also sheds light on the long journey to experiencing ourselves "in oil":

> Early humans dug shallow open-pit mines to get to un-weathered flint, which flaked better . . . In Swaziland at least 43,000 and perhaps 80,000 years ago, miners extracted tons of specularite (a source of red ocher). By 35,000 years ago, people in Poland and Hungary had dug pits and sometime subteranian mines for colored ores, while in Paleolithic Egypt, Australia, France, Spain, Belgium, Poland, and (later) in Texas, they dug up flint.[96]

To be clear, situating the human love-affair with mining in its historical context is not to suggest that digging up flint or colored ore is somehow endemic to human nature; it's not to imply that human chauvinism is inevitable. Were that the case, pleas like Malm's concerning our choice to mount militant resistance would be futile. We have to assume that if we are still capable of "feeling the panic," there's still hope that we can save ourselves. The point then is that there are historically salient events that cast the die for the ways in which capitalism has become enculturated and naturalized such that we experience the world "in oil" *as if* this was our natural state.

We can go further: to whatever extent "we experience ourselves . . . in oil," that is, to whatever extent petroleum fuels not only our machines but our concept of ourselves as social agents, this process of enculturation exposes the atomism of Mann's "personal choice" dichotomy as not merely ahistorical, but contrived for the sake of pitting personal against policy. And we *do* experience ourselves, as LeMenager puts it, as citizens of "petrotopia," as members of a utopia made possible by fossil fuels: "[a]s utopia, petrotopia represents itself as an ideal end-state, the service economy made flesh, repressing the violence that it has performed upon South Bronx neighborhoods leveled for freeway development or the wetlands below New Orleans, which were filled to build suburban homes."[97] In short, our experience as social beings is rooted in social institutions like gas stations and automobiles, smart phones and Spotify—not self-contained nodes for whom "feeling the panic" is doomed to inaction.

The challenge, then, for the oil majors is not whether there are ways to undermine, circumvent, or turn to advantage regulatory schemes like carbon pricing. The challenge is to maintain the from-the-cradle enculturation of the capitalist worldview that makes each of these ways possible and convincing. It's in this specific respect that disaster capitalism is simply one of the fresher-looking faces of the Kleptocene. Put differently: so long as it remains viable to repress the violence necessary to the maintenance of the petrotopia such that, as Wallace-Wells puts it, "we can't see anything but through the cataracts of self-deception,"[98] and we're convinced that what's "made flesh" is what we want, that it manifests the utopia, the kleptocratic logic that "justifies" levelling the South Bronx to build a freeway or bull-dozing Louisiana wetlands to build suburbia goes uninterrogated and uninterrupted. Moreover, the fact that we don't know when it's all going to burn down supplies a powerful epistemic narcotic to our capacity for denial and cognitive dissonance. The key to petrotopia is the unexamined belief that freeways, shopping malls, and suburbia represent the natural evolution of human societies—that they instantiate progress and the good life to which "we," or at least some affluent subset of "we," are entitled. Buttressed by the myth of endless resources, itself sustained by colossal violence done to ecosystemic integrity on behalf of profit-driven technological innovation, the most perilous danger to petrotopia is obvious: its governing mythologies are false, and the potential that more of us will come to "feel the panic" as we're confronted more frequently and viscerally by the impacts of climate change makes the utopian illusion harder to keep up.

As Stoll and LeMenager also show, a key strategy for maintaining the have-cake-eat-too illusion of a world of endless petro-consumption *and* environmental stability depends on creating the mirage of an unsullied nature. Consider, for example, LeMenager's example of the creation of a road-accessible state park system:

> Up through the 1920s, when California voters approved a road-accessible state park system, the car was conceived as a means of achieving a premodern vision of nature that had been lost to the railroad. Like preindustrial transport by horse, cars allowed closer, slower viewing than had been possible in trains. Auto tourism captured the U.S. middle class in the early twentieth century and was boosted by auto club campaigns to "See American First," before visiting Europe. By the 1950s, the fact that automobiles could reach speeds up to one hundred miles per hour and that more than forty thousand miles of freeway were in the making shifted the ecological significance of cars. The car "problem" received articulation in the Wilderness Act of 1964, which prohibited vehicles from federally designated wilderness—a promise not clearly met, as Edward Abbey famously notes in his manifesto on industrial tourism. Abby chides the park system for road-building that caters to "the indolent millions born on wheels and suckled on gasoline."[99]

What's important to recognize here is that what the "indolent millions" to whom petrotopia caters believe about the interface of the automobile and the "nature" created by the state park system is that a "road accessible state park system" is a chance to experience nature "slowly," as if on horseback—and, as William Cronin explains, the illusion that there *is* such a thing as "wilderness" to be experienced as escape, vacation, refuge. But insofar as this experience, *auto-tourism*, is orchestrated as a drive-through park system to facilitate a concept of "nature" that advances fossil fuel industry interests, "experience" is made-over into a product, a commodity for consumption:

> Wilderness had once been the antithesis of all that was orderly and good-it had been the darkness, one might say, on the far side of the garden wall-and yet now it was frequently likened to Eden itself . . . One by one, various corners of the American map came to be designated as sites whose wild beauty was so spectacular that a growing number of citizens had to visit and see them for themselves. Niagara Falls was the first to undergo this transformation but it was soon followed by the Catskills, the Adirondacks, Yosemite, Yellowstone, and others. Yosemite was deeded by the U.S. government to the state of California in 1864 as the nation's first wildland park, and Yellowstone became the first true national park in 1872.[100]

The way "wilderness" is packaged and sold may be coincident with what is the spectacular beauty and vastness of places like Yosemite but, as Cronon goes on to explain, the way the idea of "national park" comes into being promotes objectives that exploit "wild beauty" as advertising for interests commercial, territorial, nationalist, racist, and classist—all rolled up into an effectively genocidal displacement of the indigenous peoples for whom these places were home. Nancy Fraser makes this point succinctly:

> [T]he chunks of nature that capital appropriates are virtually always the life conditions of some human group: their habitat and meaning-laden place of social interaction; their means of livelihood and material basis of social reproduction. Moreover, the human groups in capital's crosshairs are virtually always those that have been stripped of the power to defend themselves, and often those relegated to the wrong side of the global color line.[101]

Whatever the century, "wilderness" is a lucrative commodity for those who can afford it, and more often than not is acquired at the expense of those human and nonhuman beings who haven't the resources to put up resistance, militant or otherwise. Indeed, it's hard to imagine an example of capitalism as resource theft more transparent than the creation of a National Park system for wealthy mostly white consumers looking for opportunities to materialize their cognitive dissonance concerning the real cost of a drive-through experience of "nature."

Hence, it appears that our experience of ourselves "in oil" is, at the same time, an aspiration to create experience that denies or at least ignores its cost. As Cronon recounts, "the decades following the Civil War saw more and more of the nation's wealthiest citizens seeking out wilderness for themselves. The elite passion for wild land took many forms: enormous estates in the Adirondacks and elsewhere . . . cattle ranches for would-be roughriders on the Great Plains, guided big-game hunting trips in the Rockies, and luxurious resort hotels wherever railroads pushed their way into sublime landscape."[102]

However romanticized in movies and newspaper stories, rough riders and big game hunters also serve as reminders of some very dark aspects of this history including the near annihilation of the American Bison. Yet the bleak contradiction of this particular incarnation of the commodification of sentience—hunting for the sake of entertainment—juxtaposed against the idea of "wild beauty" is even more instructive. The idea of the "wild beauty" of bison thundering across the plain is at once promoted as an advertising strategy to get consumers to buy more gas for their "wilderness" adventure and destroyed by the roads that need to be built for the cars that have mostly replaced the trains and railroads. There are, of course, no longer any bison to see thundering across the plain, and this presents a dilemma: how to make convincing the fiction of a wilderness uninhabited and wild, one where we may not see the bison, but that invites us to imagine they're just over the next horizon. What this requires, argues Cronin, is the perverse "thorough-going erasure of the history from which it sprang," that is the displacement, eviction, or slaughter of those for whom wilderness was home in order to remake it for the affluent consumer of "wilderness":

> The movement to set aside national parks and wilderness areas followed hard on the heels of the final Indian wars, in which the prior human inhabitants of these areas were rounded up and moved onto reservations. The myth of the wilderness as "virgin, uninhabited land" had always been especially cruel when seen from the perspective of the Indians who had once called that land home. Now they were forced to move elsewhere, with the result that tourists could safely enjoy the illusion that they were seeing their nation in its pristine original state, in the new morning of God's own creation.[103]

Whereas Bison were commodified as a form of recreation, the indigenous peoples for whom "wilderness" was home are subjugated as an obstacle to the experience of the "sublime." But just as the sentience of the bison elicits no moment of conscience, no pause in the conversion to "big game," the sentience of the indigenous means only that the brutal evacuation of entire tribal regions becomes essential if the creation of "wilderness" is to be a marketable fiction sufficiently convincing to lure the capital investment of the elite.

Given this kleptocratic template, it's unsurprising that "wilderness" just a few decades later is fully incorporated into state park systems designed not merely to accommodate, but facilitate the build-out of auto tourism. What more illuminating example of outright theft could we imagine than the exile of whole cultures and peoples of their lands and lives for the sake of creating a fiction for the "elite"? "Wild" is at once a critical feature of advertising to attract wealthy adventurers, and fully contained to insure against its potential for disruption. "Wilderness" becomes a thing to be consumed as a variety of recreation at first accessible only to the very few who could afford the "big game" hunts, but later to anyone who could afford a car and put gas in it: "[o] ne went to wilderness as a consumer, not as a producer," argues Cronon "hiring guides and other backcountry residents who could serve as romantic surrogates for the rough riders and hunters of the frontier if one was willing to overlook their new status as employees and servants of the rich."[104] By the time the early 20th century dawns, replacing the train with the automobile as a surrogate for the rough rider's horse, the enculturation of the petrotopia feels as natural to an adventure seeking middle class as did an earlier generation feel entitled to maintain its hegemony through the violence of removal and extermination. It is precisely this template upon which the fossil fuel industries rely now just as they did in the invention of "wilderness" or the digging up of colored ore. Indeed, what Cronon demonstrates with respect to the history of the post-Civil War Westward expansion and LeMenager expands through her discussion of auto tourism and the creation of state parks is that while "wilderness" may not be the specific handiwork of the fossil fuel majors, as its primary beneficiaries, it might as well have been.

Cronin argues that "the trouble with wilderness is that it quietly expresses and reproduces the very values its devotees seek to reject. The flight from history that is very nearly the core of wilderness represents the false hope of an escape from responsibility, the illusion that we can somehow wipe clean the slate of our past and return to the tabula rasa that supposedly existed before we began to leave our marks on the world."[105] Yet, it's just this willful forgetting that Mann's optimism concerning carbon pricing counts on to convince us that our "fatal complacency" can be overcome, that the consumption we take to be the virtual birthright of the petrotopia can be maintained—with just some tinkering in the form of "greener" alternatives, modest conservation, but nothing "radical" like putting an end to animal agriculture. Thus the powerful, if simple, point is this: refusing to forget is not doomism. *It is realism.* Indeed, the refusal to remember—that is doom.

NOTES

1. Michael Mann. *The New Climate War: The Fight to Take Back Our Climate.* (Scribe, 2021), 77–87.

2. Mann, 99.
3. Mann, 83.
4. Mann, 10–11.
5. Mann, 11.
6. Man, Ch. 1.
7. Jennifer Jacquet. "The Meat Industry is Doing Exactly What Big Oil Does to Fight Climate Action." *Washington Post*, 5.14.21. https://www.washingtonpost.com/outlook/the-meat-industry-is-doing-exactly-what-big-oil-does-to-fight-climate-action/2021/05/14/831e14be-b3fe-11eb-ab43-bebddc5a0f65_story.html.
8. Jacquet.
9. Mark Stoll. *Profit: An Environmental History*. (Cambridge, UK: Polity Press, 2023), 171–2.
10. Jacquet.
11. Cora Diamond. "Eating Meat and Eating People." In *Animal Rights: Current Debates and New Directions*. Ed. Cass Sunstein and Martha Nussbaum. (Oxford: Oxford UP, 2004, 93–107), 3.
12. *Food and Agriculture Organization of the United States*. "Key Facts and Findings; By the Numbers: GHG Emissions by Livestock." http://www.fao.org/news/story/en/item/197623/icode/.
13. Andreas Malm. *The Progress of This Storm: Nature and Society in a Warming World*. (Brooklyn, NY: Verso, 2020), 77.
14. Mann, 80.
15. Jacquet (my emphasis).
16. Mark Bittman. "The Staggering Cost of Rising World Meat Production." *New York Times*, 1.28.08. https://www.nytimes.com/2008/01/27/business/worldbusiness/27iht-meat.1.9525251.html.
17. Mann, 88.
18. Mann, 90.
19. *Leonardo DiCaprio Foundation*. https://www.leonardodicaprio.org.
20. *Leonardo DiCaprio Foundation.*
21. Malm, 152.
22. Mann, 78.
23. Malm, 218.
24. Malm, 223.
25. Malm, 224.
26. Malm, 231.
27. Malm, 134.
28. Adam Smith. "Wealth of Nations, Ch. 1." *Adam Smith Works*. https://www.adamsmithworks.org/documents/chapter-i-of-the-natural-progress-of-opulence.
29. Mann, 53.
30. Mann, 53.
31. Mann, 54.
32. Mann, 55.
33. Mann, 56.
34. Mann, 57.

35. Mann, 57.
36. Mann, 57.
37. Mann, 59.
38. Mann, 61.
39. Mann, 60.
40. Wendy Lynne Lee. *Eco-Nihilism: The Philosophical Geopolitics of the Climate Change Apocalypse*. (Lanham, MD: Lexington Books, 2016), 367–76.
41. Fred Krupp. "Exxon Investors Vote for Change in a Watershed Moment for the Climate." *Environmental Defense Fund*, 5.26.21. https://www.edf.org/media/exxon-investors-vote-change-watershed-moment-climate.
42. Scott Deveau, Saijel Kishan, and Joe Carroll. "ExxonMobil's Last Ditch Attempt to Stave Off a Climate Coup." *Bloomberg News*, 5.29.21. https://www.bloomberg.com/news/articles/2021-05-29/exxon-mobil-s-last-ditch-attempt-to-stave-off-a-climate-coup#xj4y7vzkg.
43. *Engine No. 1*. https://engine1.com.
44. Mann, 60.
45. *Engine No. 1*.
46. *Engine No. 1*.
47. Lee, 285.
48. Mann, 78 (my emphasis).
49. Mann, 179–80.
50. Cayli Baker. "The Trump Administration's Major Environmental Deregulations." *Brookings*, 12.15.20. https://www.brookings.edu/blog/up-front/2020/12/15/the-trump-administrations-major-environmental-deregulations/.
51. Mann, 180.
52. Neela Banergee, "Exxon: The Road Not Taken." *Inside Climate News*, 2015. https://insideclimatenews.org/book/exxon-the-road-not-taken/.
53. Shannon Hall. "Exxon Knew about Climate Change Almost 40 Years Ago." Scientific American, 10.26.15. https://www.scientificamerican.com/article/exxon-knew-about-climate-change-almost-40-years-ago/.
54. Mann, 95.
55. Mann, 95.
56. Lee, 365.
57. Christina Sewell. "Removing the Meat Subsidy: Our Cognitive Dissonance Around Animal Agriculture." *Columbia University: Journal of International Affairs*, 2.11.20. https://jia.sipa.columbia.edu/removing-meat-subsidy-our-cognitive-dissonance-around-animal-agriculture.
58. *Food and Agriculture Organization of the United States*. "Key Facts and Findings; By the Numbers: GHG Emissions by Livestock." http://www.fao.org/news/story/en/item/197623/icode/.
59. Sewell.
60. Mann, 95–6.
61. Mann, 99.
62. Mann, 6.
63. Mann, 6.

64. Mann, 120.

65. Marianne Lavelle. "Requiem for a Pipeline: Keystone XL Transformed the Environmental Movement and Shifted the Debate over Energy and Climate." *Inside Climate News*, 6.20.21. https://insideclimatenews.org/news/20062021/keystone-xl-pipeline-environmental-movement-energy-climate/.

66. Rob Gillies. "Keystone XL Pipeline Halted as Biden Revokes Permit." Associated Press, 1.20.21. https://apnews.com/article/joe-biden-alberta-2fbcce48372f5c29c3ae6f6f93907a6d.

67. Mann, 121.

68. *Bold Nebraska*. https://boldnebraska.org.

69. Mann, 121.

70. Sonali Paul. "Australia Explorers step up Hunt for Oil After Big Find." *Reuters*, 10.1.19. https://www.reuters.com/article/us-australia-oil/australias-explorers-step-up-hunt-for-oil-after-big-find-idUSKBN1WG2ZM.

71. *Center for Climate and Energy Solutions*. "Australia's Carbon Pricing Mechanisms." https://www.c2es.org/document/australias-carbon-pricing-mechanism/.

72. Sophie Vorrath. "Australia Dumps Carbon Price, as Repeal Passes Senate." *Renew Economy*, 7.17.14. https://reneweconomy.com.au/australia-dumps-carbon-price-as-repeal-passes-senate-22018/.

73. Christoph Hermann. *The Critique of Commodification*. (New York, NY: Oxford University Press, 2021), 115.

74. *The World*. "Scientists Say Australia's Tony Abbott is Engineering an "Environmental Trainwreck.'" Global Post, 4.8.14. https://theworld.org/stories/2014-04-08/scientists-say-australias-tony-abbott-engineering-environmental-train-wreck

75. Alexander White. "Why Does Australian PM Tony Abbott Support Fossil Fuel Subsidies?" *The Guardian*, 2.2.14. https://www.theguardian.com/environment/southern-crossroads/2014/feb/02/fossil-fuel-subsidies-tony-abbott-spc-ardmona-corporate-welfare#_=_.

76. *Woodside Petroleum, Ltd*. "2019 Sustainable Development Report." https://files.woodside/docs/default-source/investor-documents/major-reports-(static-pdfs)/2019-sd-report/sustainable-development-report-2019.pdf?sfvrsn=73cea616_14.

77. Hermann, 117–8.

78. Nick Snow. "ExxonMobil to Pay 32.2 Million to Resolve Whistleblower's Suit." *Oil and Gas Journal*. 4.6.10. https://www.ogj.com/general-interest/article/17284815/exxonmobil-to-pay-322-million-to-resolve-whistleblowers-suit.

79. Geoff Schweller. "Whistleblower Complaint Leads to SEC Investigation of Exxon." *Whistleblower Network News*, 1.20.21. https://whistleblowersblog.org/2021/01/articles/whistleblower-news/whistleblower-complaint-leads-to-sec-investigation-of-exxon/.

80. *The World*.

81. *Sky News, Australia*. "Tony Abbott: 10 Controversial Things Former Australian PM Has Said." https://news.sky.com/story/tony-abbott-ten-controversial-things-former-australian-pm-has-said-12063946.

82. Jack Latimore. "Abbott as Indigenous Affairs Envoy? Be Disturbed. Be Very Disturbed." *The Guardian*, 8.28.18. https://www.theguardian.com/commentisfree/2018/aug/29/abbott-as-indigenous-affairs-envoy-be-disturbed-be-very-disturbed.

83. *The Conversation*. "Why Tony Abbott's Appointment as Indigenous Envoy was a Diplomatic Blunder and Policy Failure." 11.29.18. https://theconversation.com/why-tony-abbotts-appointment-as-indigenous-envoy-was-a-diplomatic-blunder-and-policy-failure-106345.

84. *The Conversation.*

85. Latimore.

86. Mann, 190.

87. Mann, 190.

88. Mann, 190–1.

89. Mann, 191–2.

90. Mann, 121.

91. Jennifer Dlouhy and Leslie Kaufman. "How the Oil Lobby Learned to Love Carbon Taxes," Bloomberg Green, 3.4.21. https://www.bloomberg.com/news/articles/2021-03-04/how-the-oil-lobby-learned-to-love-carbon-taxes.

92. *Unpopular Science*. "Why Fracking is Worse than Coal." https://medium.com/@unpopularscience/why-fracking-is-worse-than-coal-578515a004f8.

93. Guardian Staff. "Woodside Petroleum Joins GHP and Rio Tinto to Call For Carbon Price." *The Guardian*, 11.13.18. https://www.theguardian.com/environment/2018/nov/14/woodside-petroleum-joins-bhp-and-rio-tinto-to-call-for-carbon-price.

94. Stephanie LeMenager. *Living Oil: Petroleum Culture in the American Century*. (Oxford: Oxford University Press, 2014), 6.

95. LeMenager, 6.

96. Stoll, 12.

97. LeMenager, 75.

98. David Wallace-Wells. The Uninhabitable Earth. (New York, NY: Tim Duggan Books, 2019), 160.

99. LeMenager, 82.

100. William Cronin. "The Trouble with Wilderness." *Environmental History*, Vol 1.1 (Jan. 1996, 7–28), 9. http://www.jstor.org/stable/3985059.

101. Nancy Fraser. *Cannibal Capitalism*. (Brooklyn, NY: Verso, 2022), 108.

102. Cronin, 15.

103. Cronin, 15.

104. Cronin, 15.

105. Cronin, 16.

Chapter 5

How Animal Rights Ethics Sustains the Commodification of Sentience

Response to Gary Francione and Richard Epstein

"MORAL SCHIZOPHRENIA," ANIMAL RIGHTS, AND THE LOGIC OF COMMODIFICATION

Intended as a robust defense of individual nonhuman animal rights, Gary Francione argues that "[w]hen it comes to other animals, we humans exhibit what can best be described as moral schizophrenia,"[1] a moral disorder "related to the status of animals as property, which means that animals are nothing more than *things* despite the many laws that supposedly protect them."[2] Although it serves the aims of human chauvinism to treat nonhuman animals as property, argues Francione, we erect laws to preserve an illusion to the contrary—that nonhuman animals can be our "companions" or "partners," instead of our dinners, entertainments, tools, or scapegoats. Our behavior, in other words, is not only inconsistent, but *schizophrenic* in virtue of the lengths we're willing to go to conceal our self-interested intentions, even from ourselves, behind laws that evince respect for nonhuman life. This schizophrenia runs even deeper, however, in that such statutes are themselves chauvinistic. Behind a rhetorical veneer of "protection" and "regulation" continues not only the grim reality of the industrialized production, commodification, and disarticulation of nonhuman animal bodies, but the active recognition that this reality must be concealed in order to maintain a view of human beings as moral agents capable of humane treatment. What remains uninterrogated, in other words, is *whether* the conversion of nonhuman animal bodies into milk machines, dinner entrées, belts and shoes, and all the other countless products into which bone and sinew, muscle and organ find their way is *itself* defensible. What remains uninterrogated, as Cora Diamond might put it, is *whether* we are the moral agents represented in the language of our statutes. Francione's diagnosis of "moral disorder" suggests we are not. But until we confront *that* question moral schizophrenia will be our only defense against hypocrisy, even as its cost to nonhuman animals, human beings, and the planet's capacity to support life grows as relentlessly as tornadoes that now "annihilate" entire towns like Mayfield, Kentucky—in Winter.[3]

Although Francione offers a compelling profile that traces the historical development of our schizophrenic disposition, he stops short of raising the crucial question concerning whether, given that history, we occupy *an epistemic position* sufficiently undeluded to make morally defensible judgments concerning our relationship to nonhuman animals. Francione supports his diagnosis of our "moral disorder" by situating its development in, for example, Rene Descartes's theological argument that nonhuman animals are soulless "machines created by God," deserving of no consideration beyond human use. Francione then turns to Immanuel Kant's defense of indirect duties. According to Kant, refraining from the abuse of nonhuman animals, effectively using them as tools to demonstrate acceptable behavior, sets a good example for other people, especially children, of our moral duties to human beings. But as instrumental value is not intrinsic value, duty goes no further than this display. Nonhuman animals are simply instructional devices for the inculcation of appropriate moral sentiments. Kant can discourage cruelty as corrosive to building good character, but there's nothing to deter the objectification of nonhuman animals, including their experimental use involving vivisection[4] for the sake of expanding human knowledge.[5] Moreover, as setting a good example requires the audience for whom the example is intended, acts of cruelty perpetrated without witness would seem to raise no red flag. Can one set a poor example for the development of one's own character? Perhaps; but even in this case the value of the animal remains purely instrumental. While it might then be tempting to applaud Kant as more humane than Descartes, his view is actually the more schizophrenic: it purports to encourage compassion, but in fact leaves everything largely as it is—other than offering plausible deniability to those whose harm to nonhuman animals can be cloaked in the rhetoric of crucial human interests. At least Descartes avoids subterfuge.

Following some of his utilitarian forerunners in the refutation of this view, Francione champions the *humane treatment principle*, grounding it in Jeremy Bentham's argument that "despite any differences, humans and animals are similar in that they both can suffer, and it is only the capacity to suffer and not the capacity for speech or reason or anything else that is required for animals to matter morally and to have legal protection."[6] For Francione, in other words, it's not merely morally inconsistent or hypocritical that laws drafted to protect human beings from unnecessary suffering are not extended to nonhuman animals who share that capacity; it's schizophrenic because what objectification requires is an enculturated cognitive dissonance aimed at denying what, for Bentham, was obvious: nonhuman animals can suffer physically, emotionally, and psychologically; many human activities cause or contribute substantially to this suffering; these activities are often if not always unnecessary to meet human needs.

However, while Francione and Bentham are right about the capacity for suffering, reacquainting us with this fact via the humane treatment principle is bound to fail (indeed, *has* failed) as an avenue for substantive change in the treatment of nonhuman animals precisely because it fails to probe the question whether we're in an epistemic position to define "necessary" as anything other than "self-interested." As Diamond might put it, so long as nonhuman animals remain things that can be *on* the table, but not seated *at* the table, "necessary" will remain an arbitrary measure of human desire. Indeed, there could be no better evidence for this assessment than the fact that, despite calls by organizations like the *American Humane Society*, "there are no federal laws that set humane care standards for animals in factory farms."[7] But even if there were, we have little reason to believe that such statues would make a meaningful difference in the lives of entities whose value remains strictly instrumental. Instead, even sincere efforts at making such laws have inspired "right to farm" legislation that seeks "to preserve the status quo by greatly limiting the ability of states to regulate the conditions on farms, including the cruel confinement of farm animals."[8]

To be clear: I take it at face value that raising attention to cruel treatment is virtually without exception a good. The trouble for Francione is that he invests the humane treatment principle with the power to inspire more than fleeting recognition despite the fact that it is itself situated, as LeMenager might put it, in a world experienced "in oil." The humane treatment principle is, in other words, grounded in a worldview that encourages a sober assessment of the difference between need and want, the truly necessary and the merely self-interested. But that is not the world as we experience it. And while we can "dare to feel the panic" of a more objective view of our anthropogenic destruction, that will require a transformative moral reclamation of value in the struggle to wrestle it back from exchange. Francione argues as if by adding a new principle to our moral toolbox the crucial distinction between need and want will be made clear, and will thereby transform the way we solve conflicts concerning suffering:

> In sum, the principle assumes that we may use animals when it is necessary to do so—when we are faced with a conflict between animal and human

> interests—and that we should impose only the minimum amount of pain and suffering necessary to achieve our purpose . . . If there is a feasible alternative to our use of animals in a particular situation, then the principle would seem to proscribe such use.[9]

Insofar as "necessary to do so" remains a function of the uninterrogated "what's for dinner" we have virtually no reason to believe the humane treatment principle will have any impact whatever on a status quo where the value of nonhuman animal is systemically preempted by the logic of commodification. Put differently: until we come to terms with the prospect that the capacity for sentience *is* a morally relevant bar to commodification—that *on* the table and *at* the table are mutually exclusive properties of things—we will have no principled way to adjudicate "necessary."

For consumers the difference between "necessary" and "desired" is itself the product of advertising campaigns aimed at conflating that difference beyond recognition. Sensitive to recent demands by consumers for better treatment of "food" animals, we now see commercials that feature rolling green pasture and happy-looking cows, chickens, and pigs. But, contrary to Francione's aspirations, few rise to question whether it counts as "humane treatment" to commodify the value and disarticulate the bodies of nonhuman animals. Instead, Francione effectively offers a green-washing strategy to animal agriculture perfectly consistent with the moral schizophrenia he rightly condemns. Francione might respond, of course, that upon being introduced to the humane treatment principle some might watch a *People for the Ethical Treatment of Animals* video and it will move them to write to their elected representative to "do something" about the CAFO in their region. Perhaps they'll order the veggie-burger at Red Robbin upscale burger restaurant, or applaud a friend who buys their meat "free range." But insofar as none of these "humane" actions lead us to interrogate whether nonhuman animals should count as food—at least for wealthy Westerners for whom "necessity" is a thin reed upon which to hang justification—Francione's claim to a *principle*, let alone a transformative principle, is largely vacuous.

In short, without a deeper interrogation concerning whether sentience counts as a bar to commodification, we won't get to Francione's "feasible alternatives." This is true for at least three reasons directly relevant to the ontology of capital. First, insofar as "necessary" is defined in terms of human interests, the solution to any human/animal conflict requires little more than the assertion of human prerogative. What particular individual consumers count as necessary varies widely, rendering "necessary" reducible to desire plus a demand likely scaffolded by advertising. Perhaps we could import Kant's directive that we seek to set good examples as opposed to observably cruel ones as a brake against truly arbitrary appeals to "necessary," but even

Kant allowed for bottomless suffering such as vivisection if it served human interests. Second, only the abolition of factory farming, including the disingenuous "cage-free" and "free range," could solve the conflict between the desire to treat nonhuman animals as disposable commodities and the cruelty institutionalized in animal agriculture. Yet, abolition seems highly unlikely since, although, false, the belief that animal proteins are necessary to a healthy diet is a staple of animal agriculture advertising. Neither Francione, Wallace-Wells, nor Mann appear to have any interest in highlighting this falsehood. And whether we *really* belief this myth about the "necessity" of animal proteins is itself suspect; do we really believe diamonds are rare? We might appeal to Kant's indirect duties to defend the free range "ranch" against the warehouse conditions of the factory farm. But this seems at best impractical unless we can show folks watching us eat meat that the humane treatment principle was deployed in the birth, rearing, and painless slaughter of our holiday roast. Perhaps, of course, we could demonstrate this humane treatment—if we raised the animal ourselves. But this gets us no closer to interrogating *whether* the sentience of a living thing excludes it from the category of "food." As Diamond makes implicitly clear, if it doesn't we have little reason to spare the anencephalic baby from the dinner menu.

Third, insofar as Francione's account of capitalism is largely limited to references to "property," absent any sustained critique of how sentient creatures become "property," he is bound to miss the extent to which regulatory statutes, themselves drafted by the very corporations they're intended to police, reinforce and conceal conditions driven by the profit motive. This crucial omission leaves no principled way to distinguish a "feasible alternative" from a "more profitable" one. Neither Descartes's consignment of nonhuman animal life to soulless machine nor Kant's defense of indirect duties address commodification, much less that of sentience, *per se*, even if we can safely assume neither would raise an objection. Francione's discussion of wrongful objectification represented by reference to nonhuman animals as "things" goes some ways toward the moral reclamation of the value of nonhuman life, but "thing" does not and cannot capture "*commodity*." Insofar, moreover, as "feasible alternative" often means "more expensive," what it solicits from the animal agriculture industries is not regulatory enthusiasm, but rather the incentive to shield their operations through whatever avenues are available: right to farm legislation, appeals to the "necessity" of animal proteins, aggressive "what's for dinner" advertising campaigns, and green-washing the conditions of the factory farm floor.

Francione is right when he argues "[t]here are several specific ways in which animal welfare laws ensure that there will never be a meaningful balance of human and animal interests."[10] Current law, for example, "explicitly exclude[s] most forms of institutionalized property use." Anticruelty statutes are interpreted by most courts to permit "common use" even if it generates "extreme suffering." Because anti-cruelty laws are criminal statutes, the criteria to prove intent to harm is difficult to achieve—making actual convictions very rare.[11] Francione also points out that penalties for animal cruelty, are "wholly inadequate."[12] But what Francione misses are the very premises that make sense of *why* the law excludes forms of property use such as industrialized food animal production, *how* "extreme suffering" comes to be cast as "common use," *why* culpability for cruelty requires proof of intent to harm, and not merely gross negligence, and finally *how* nonhuman animals come to be seen as mere "things" whose destruction does not justify severe penalty, namely, the capitalism enculturated as foundational to our view of the world and our agency in it. What he misses is the ontology of capitalism and its logic of commodification.

It's somewhat ironic that Francione misses precisely that which justifies his depiction of our treatment of nonhuman animals as morally *schizophrenic*, not "merely" callous or inconsistent—but morally and psychically deranged—namely, the commodification of sentience. Yet it's the foundational (civilizational) decision to accede moral valuation and judgment to economic expediency that casts the die against the value of sentience and suffering, and thus against the sorts of moral compass that might keep us from the nihilism of human chauvinism. Diagnoses of cruelty to nonhuman animals that constrain themselves, as Francione's does, to finding a "meaningful balance" between human and nonhuman animal interests are in fact vacuous: first because it remains human beings who get to decide what counts as nonhuman animals interests; second because we have no good reason to think such decisions will not privilege human interests; third because the ontology of capital systemically conflates need with want, and thereby renders "interest" not only privileged but ultimately arbitrary. "[T]hat we may use animals when it is necessary to do" must thus be read as an *excuse* for cruelty since it effectively liberates the pursuit of profit regardless suffering, justified by whatever version of "necessary" can be made to sound plausible. So without substance is his application of moral principle that the vocabulary of "humane," "necessary," "feasible," "alternative," "sustainable," and "minimum amount of pain," must be understood as negligible by the capitalist, or worse: as language that can be conscripted to excuse cruelty and neglect. Images of plump chickens and chipper pigs preserve the *illusion* of humane treatment without the necessity of going any further than the regulatory letter of the law concerning, for example, cage size, feed regimen, or slaughter protocol. Although his intentions in the defense of animal rights are no doubt laudable, Francione's appeal to humane treatment *contributes* to the objectification of nonhuman animals by providing cover to an industry that appropriates this jingoistic moral vocabulary as fodder for advertising in the same way that other extractivist enterprise seeks to leverage "green."

"SPECULATIVE FABULATION" AND ZOMBIE PIGS

Nominally reformist but hardly militant or revolutionary, Francione's humane treatment principle is no more a barrier to the commodification of nonhuman animals than Michael Mann's or David Wallace-Wells' market-based solutions to the climate crisis are likely to curb greenhouse gas emissions sufficiently to avoid disaster. Just as corporations like ExxonMobil appropriate the language of "sustainability" to green their image while they continue to drill, the humane treatment principle offers vocabulary for advertising campaign slogans that sanctify the desire for meat by inviting the consumer into a fiction that sanitizes and window-dresses the life of the animal, dissociating it from "what's for dinner." Highly deceptive pictures of chickens roaming a yard depicted as "cage free," or calves frolicking in a pasture with the slogan "free range," are created to vindicate and mollify consumers, to insure consumers remain consumers with access to "necessary" proteins. The "meat" eater is thus co-created *as* a consumer with the animal body *as* food; neither could *be* without the other, and this is true despite (or because of) the fictions that define their relationship: human health requires animal proteins, advertising captures the natural lives and painless deaths of "food" animals, nonhuman animals are treated as the sentient beings they are. All of these claims are demonstrably false.

Consider an object of comparison: in a 2011 essay featuring the work of installation artist, Patricia Piccinini, philosopher Donna Haraway explores one of the Nature-Culture intersections we see in much of her theorizing, namely, the technologically mediated, rapidly evolving, endlessly complex relationship between human beings and nonhuman animals:

> From the start, I knew Piccinini lived and worked in Australia; like me, she is the offspring of white settler colonies, their frontier practices, their ongoing immigrations, and their bad memories and troubled discourses of indigeneity, belonging, appropriation, wastelands, progress and exclusion. Twenty-first century technoscience and technoculture are nothing if not frontier practices, always announcing new worlds, proposing the novel as the solution to the old, figuring creation as radical invention and replacement, rushing toward a future that wobbles between ultimate salvation and destruction but has little truck with thick pasts or presents (Kenney). But in her sensuous sculptural and graphic stories of terran critters who were not on earth before now and whose evolutionary and ecological habitats are the installation, the mall, the website and the lab, Piccinini seems to me to be proposing not another frontier, but rather something

> more akin to a decolonizing ethic indebted to Australian Aboriginal practices of taking care of country and accounting for generations of entangled human and nonhuman entities.[13]

Haraway treats the transgenic "speculative fabulations" of Piccinini's artworks—human-looking wombats, motorbikes with attributes of human affection, the "African meerkat-like beings" of a work called "The Leather Landscape" (2003), as the "critters" made possible by "Twenty-first century technoscience and technoculture," whose "evolutionary and ecological habitats are the installation, the mall, the website and the lab." Like Piccinini, Haraway's aim is to explore the transgenic conceptual landscape in light of the challenges it poses to the ways in which we understand the relationships of human beings, nonhuman animals, and the ecologies—many technoculturally mediated—"we"/they inhabit.

Although Haraway's approach to "trans" is highly sensitive to the possibility that, in light of new technologies such as gene editing, this relationship may experience significant change of the sort explored in Piccinini's artwork, she doesn't lose sight of the material realities that define a *relationship* as opposed to an assimilation of one species by another, or a transmogrification of each into something new. As Haraway remarks, Piccinini's "speculative fabulations" are not so much "frontiers" as allusions to a "decolonizing ethic"; her terran creatures elicit delight and dread because they resemble human beings; they look at us, reminding us of our difference, but also of our intimate relationships to "others." Yet, it's at this juncture that, casting Haraway as a "postmodernist" in the same mold as Bruno Latour, Andreas Malm overlooks an aspect of Haraway's view of "trans" that can shed important light on Malm's critique of capital, namely, that technoculture is itself an instantiation of the exchange value invested in technologies like gene editing that promise gargantuan profits to biotechnology companies.

Consider, for example, the introduction of gene-editing to animal agriculture. Kenny Torella and Marina Bolotnikova report for VOX that:

> The promise of the technology is obvious for agribusiness, which naturally wants to use these new tools to boost profits by designing bigger, faster-growing animals with higher fertility rates. But that's not the only use of the technology. It could also be deployed to eliminate many sources of animal suffering on today's factory farms by editing genes in ways that would make painful procedures unnecessary. Hornless calves are just the start. For instance, male piglets are castrated, usually without pain relief, shortly after birth. If they aren't, their meat will emit a terrible odor when cooked, leading to what the pork industry calls "boar taint." So scientists are working on a male pig that never reaches puberty, eliminating the need for castration. A similar advance could be made with poultry. Each year at America's egg hatcheries, as many

> as 300 million male chicks are gruesomely killed—usually by being ground up alive or gassed—since they can't lay eggs and have been bred to be too small to be worth the effort of raising for meat. Researchers around the world are using transgenic engineering and gene-editing tools in an attempt to solve this chicken and egg dilemma.[14]

There is a great deal more to be said about the relationship between factory farms, gene edited "food" animal production, the humane treatment principle, the role of regulation, advertising, and consumption. The point most relevant to Malm's analysis of the warming condition, however, may be this: while manufacturing an animal insensitive to pain might circumvent Francione's concerns over humane treatment, transgenic animal agriculture offers precisely nothing toward mitigating the emission of greenhouse gasses from waste lagoons; in fact the opposite is more likely to be true for a conscience liberated from worries about "humane."

Given the acceleration in demand for conscience-free meat predicted by the industry, we could expect a parallel hastening toward climate apocalypse. After all, a gene-edited animal presumably produces waste just like its predecessor. Or think about it this way: given the "hall pass" of "necessity," nothing in Francione's argument for the humane treatment principle prevents male chicks from being dumped in grinders now. Hence, we have every reason to believe that the logic of commodification operative in maximizing the profitability of animal agriculture in the present will only be enhanced through its marriage to a gene-editing that can spot male chicks before they hatch and, in so doing, alleviate the conscience of would-be consumers. In effect, gene-edited factory farming epitomizes a very dark version of Piccinini's "speculative fabulation" except that it's only marginally speculative, presenting us with a potential reality that, by conforming to the ontology of capital, disarticulates not only the bodies of nonhuman animals, but their genetic identity as living things. Indeed, it's truly hard to imagine a state of affairs that more fully illuminates the Kleptocene than the commodification of genes. And because this is the case, it's equally hard to imagine a more terrifying version of Malm's "burn it all down" where "speculative fabulation" meets zombie pigs floating in greenhouse gas emitting waste lagoons visible from space.

NO, WE'RE NOT "ALL HYBRIDS NOW"

Andreas Malm worries that Donna Haraway's objective is to "liquify" the "wall between human and nonhuman,"[15] but he's mistaken—and in ways that are instructive with respect to a fuller understanding of the ontology of capital. What Haraway's analysis of Piccinini's work shows is that the technologies of, for example, gene editing assume the very real materiality of species, genes, chemistry, biology. While "technoscience" raises issues concerning the relationship of human to nonhuman beings, it does not deny their distinct and separate existence. Art works like Piccinini's take advantage of this difference in order to explore the potential implications and meanings of "transgenic." Indeed, if we find her "speculative fabulations" disturbing, it's likely because Piccinini's "terran" creatures are like us—*and not*. Malm, however, argues that according to "posthumanists" like Haraway:

> But are we not all hybrids now? We have pacemakers and amalgam fillings and contraceptive implants in us and use screens as our extended selves . . . We call ourselves human, but we flow in and out of our presumes opposites: machines, animals, medical technologies, digital circuitry in whose absence we would not be the sort of beings we are. This is the observation at the heart of posthumanism . . . chiefly preoccupied with liquefying the wall between the human and the nonhuman. In her classic "cyborg" and "companion species" manifestos, Donna Haraway revels in the sight of the boundaries—between organism and machine, physical and nonphysical, dog and master, nature and culture—leaking away: "nothing," she exults "really convincingly settles the separation of human and animal."[16]

In short, Malm rightly worries that relegating nonhuman nature to the status of constructed fiction threatens to seriously undermine efforts to combat the climate crisis by draining it of its reality. But this isn't what's afoot in Haraway or in Piccinini's installation artwork. In fact, it's precisely the material reality of difference between human and nonhuman, nature and culture, that inform "*The Leather Landscape*."

Piccinini captures our attention precisely *because* her work explores boundaries already given between human and nonhuman being. While these boundaries may not be those stipulated by Descartes or Kant, they're also not so fluid that we'd mistake our toddler for the "terran's." Malm's mistake is to conflate a conceptual investigation concerning what we *mean* by "boundaries" with the imputed posthumanist desire to "liquify" the boundaries themselves. But were there no boundaries to begin with, the conceptual investigation of "boundaries" would have no content. Put differently: Haraway no more denies the reality of the nature represented in Piccinini's work than she'd deny that specific references to *Homo sapiens* as a species are meaningful *on their own*. This doesn't mean that technologies like gene editing don't have the potential to alter and complicate the *relationship* between human and nonhuman beings; they do precisely in virtue of the materiality of differing species and their evolutionary histories. As LeMenager or Stoll might put it, our experience of living in oil has utterly transformed our relationship to the planet and its atmosphere materially *and* conceptually—but this doesn't mean the material and the conceptual are the same things.

Malm clearly recognizes both the difference between the material and the conceptual *and* the import of locating concepts that can capture the material impact of the technologies that have altered our relationship with nonhuman nature. He argues that "[t]he warming condition is hyper-human. It might perhaps usher in a posthuman moment, in a slightly different sense, if the average temperature is allows to increase by 8 degrees celsius or more and push the last sweltering humans—unlikely to forget who brought the demise upon them—off the edge of the planet, but until then the ontological centre will hold."[17] The ontological center that will hold until it doesn't is, of course, a reference to the temperature range within which human life is possible. After that comes the posthuman or, very possibly, extinction. Malm utilizes concepts like "hyper-human" and "posthuman" in a fashion similar to Haraway to describe the relationship of the "warming condition" to our existential fate—and to those whom we rightly blame for our demise. Indeed, Malm stands in closer agreement to Haraway than he appears to think. In a recent interview, for example, Haraway observes that:

> The pandemic, global warming, and the crises of extraction are profoundly co-constitutive and interrelated. I think I would start from the Brazilian Amazon for this moment, for example, where the Bolsonaro government—but much longer than Bolsonaro, backed by all kinds of international forces—has been involved in the long term conversion of the Brazilian Amazon into settlements and ranches, the clearing and the fires, and the extraordinary destruction of the Amazon forest and its peoples, so that the extinction crisis is an extermination crisis, and a genocide crisis, for many many Amazonian Indigenous groups. Clearly, this was going on before COVID-19 hit the scene, before the second coronavirus. But that said, the spread of infection into Amazonia and into Indigenous communities is frankly genocidal, and is accompanied by even stronger pushes from the Bolsonaro government toward yet further extraction and cutting and fires, so that the fires are expected to be worse this year than last. This intersects with the extinction crisis—the degree to which lifeways of human and non-human beings are, in this moment, in the heart of the storm.[18]

Contrary to Malm's view that by "co-constitutive" Haraway denies that nonhuman nature has existence independent of human reference, it's clear that Haraway affirms the separate existence of nature in its very destruction. She affirms nature as global warming, as Covid-19, as extinction. She affirms nature in the contrast she evokes in her condemnation of Brazilian President Balsonaro's "frankly genocidal" policies that allow for the decimation of Amazonian rainforest in the interest of profit-seeking extractivist activities. That these activities co-constitute the dire existential condition of Brazil's indigenous peoples is not a denial of their separate identities, but rather an acknowledgement of the profound impacts of Balsonaro's authoritarian regime. Similarly, that Piccinini's work co-constitutes the existential condition of a possible creature does not negate the fact that its human-like features still identify a separate species by contrast—*Homo sapiens*. Nonetheless, her work explores and interrogates boundaries in light of the potential impacts of technologies like gene editing for what we might, along with Haraway and Malm, call posthuman "in a slightly different sense."

Put differently: while it's doubtless true that the gene editing made possible through "technoscience" heralds an expanded frontier for transgenic creation, we have already crossed the transgenic Rubicon—altered our relationship to nonhuman nature—in at least two ways. First, we cross this Rubicon every time we accede to an interpretation of principles like Francione's humane treatment that leaves "necessity" open to the insertion of human self-interest, that allows "plausible alternatives" to "wobble" between the "ultimate salvation[s] and destruction[s]" we define as "conflicts." Perhaps producing a kind of pig that cannot feel physical pain solves, however superficially, a moral conflict, even as it still denies the sentient psychological lives of nonhuman animals. Indeed, from the point of view of the logic of commodification there really are no conflicts: making human chauvinism the arbiter of "necessity" drains "conflict" of its meaning, effectively filling the void with, at best, laws governing the treatment of nonhuman animals rife with exceptions. This isn't to suggest that the concept of "conflict" is entirely useless to the capitalist; it serves as an opportunity for principles like humane treatment to function *as if* they could offer "solutions," effectively strengthening the case for the appeal to "necessity." Consider, for example, the current *American Guide for the Care and use of Laboratory Animals*:

> According to the Guide, researchers must minimize the distress and pain inflicted to research animals, sedate or anesthetize animals if the procedures cause relevant pain or distress, and provide living conditions that are appropriate for the species and that guarantee health and well-being to the animals . . . However, the Guide also introduces several exceptions when these exceptions are justified for scientific purposes (e.g., sedation or anaesthesia may be not used during painful or distressful procedures if necessary for reaching the project's goals).[19]

In other words, if sedation interferes with a research goal that includes pain or suffering as part of the research itself, then "scientific" is permitted to function as a suitable analogue for "necessary." Or, "if researchers aim to specifically test for the effects of social deprivation on NHPs, [nonhuman primates] the obligation of ensuring the social well-being of the study subjects does not have to be fulfilled," despite the fact that this research, *if any*, seems wholly unnecessary.[20]

The second way we cross the trans Rubicon is this: nothing in Francione's expansion of the principle of utility precludes the use of biotechnology (or any technology) to advance human interests. Whether such uses are trans*genic* depends on the context, but the baseline assumption that knowledge gained from using nonhuman animals is transferable to human cases is certainly trans. Here too "necessity" functions as the operative justification. Consider, for example, the Trump administration's *Operation Warp Speed* development of mRNA vaccines to combat Covid-19. The primary research subjects here are our close evolutionary relatives, Rhesus monkeys.[21] Few deliberate the urgency of developing safe, effective, vaccines. Yet for however "urgency" seems the operative justification, it cannot be so because it is preempted by a "necessity" defined as *any* "human interest." The question, in other words, *whether* the use of Rhesus monkeys can be justified doesn't arise because the question *whether* it is morally acceptable to use *any* species of nonhuman animal in *any* experiment benefitting human beings doesn't arise. There is no "special justification" tethered to the urgency of coronavirus because appeal to it is redundant; "the ends justify the means" is all that's required. As Maria Padrell, Miquel Llorente, and Federica Amici make the point in their *National Institutes of Health* (NIH) piece, "Invasive Research on Nonhuman Primates—Time to Turn the Page":

> Even if the costs and benefits of invasive research could be objectively measured, the utilitarian approach may have intrinsic limits because it assumes the potential ethical validity of invasive research as long as the benefits to humans outweigh the costs to NHP . . . Such an approach is not used in human research and has been rightly strongly condemned, both ethically and legally . . . Given that species other than humans have a complex perceptual, emotional, and cognitive life (see above), they should also be granted the right not to be harmed or killed for the benefit of others.[22]

Francione may respond, of course, that the concept of "humane treatment" gives voice to this notion of a "right not to be harmed or killed for the benefit of others." But given the inherently *trans* nature of the reasons given for using higher primates in medical research—that they're like us in ways physiologically, socially, and psychologically relevant to our goals—"humane" is likely to take a back seat to "necessity." This too is trans: just as we're likely to recognize something of ourselves in Piccinini's fabulations, so too they look back at us—even if we turn away. Just as "the warming condition is hyper-human," its firenadoes, hurricanes, and viral outbreaks reflect upon our actions—even if we turn away from the thing that is the mirror of our chauvinism.

What even a fleeting survey of the evidence that "invasive research implies huge costs for NHPs [nonhuman primates]," shows is that while artworks like Piccinini's raise crucial moral questions about human-nonhuman relationships, "trans" need not be trans*genic* to lay bare the limits of at least Francione's version of the principle of utility. Piccinini's critters personify a technologically mediated world that is, at one level, fantastical, but at another a perfectly realistic vision of the human chauvinism required to bring creatures of the lab and the mall into existence. Whatever Piccinini's intentions, and whatever her objections, her critters are commodities: a creation of human interest informed by the values of a deeply enculturated and naturalized capitalism. Why? Because everything is a potential commodity. That "informed by" can also (and often does) incite the resistance we interpret in Piccinini's work doesn't detract from this context; it makes the artistic instantiation of things like malls and labs that much more potent. It makes the capacity of her critters to inhabit contexts capitalized as malls and labs that much more telling; in looking back at us, they invite Malm's appeal to militance—maybe.

What underwrites the limits of the humane treatment principle is thus not only the limits of what ends justify what means, but the logic of commodification, including profit as its preeminent goal. Quite literally any combination of elements from the genetic to the plastic, the organ to the machine, the cell to the clone, the primal soup to the shopping mall, can be materialized as exchange value. To acknowledge this isn't to deny the independent reality of nature, but rather to recognize its power since, whatever becomes our existential fate over the course of the warming condition, planetary nature will persist—long after we're gone. What seals this fate is kleptocratic capitalism; indeed, the concept of exchange value is the *original transgenic* because it is exchange value that determines what *is*, that is: what counts as what *is* according to capital. Once the moral barrier represented by the capacity for sentience has been thrown over and replaced by exchange value, differences that accrue to origin, species, genetic identity, technological intervention signify only insofar as they represent particular sites for exchange. "As food" is one such site, "as research subject" another, "speculative fabulation" yet another. Insofar as it is sufficient from the point of view of the logic to identify "as food" as "angus beef," "cage free" eggs, or "free range bantams," we don't need the transgenic "fabulations" of Piccinini's imagination to signify the transient character of value. *We are already these creatures.* We eat them; they eat us. They can be infected with Covid-19, as can we. Their pain-free zombies could just as well be ours in some dystopian future. Whether the food market features beef from cattle-clones or wild-caught pangolins is as irrelevant as whether Piccinini's terran creatures evolved or are techno-cultural inventions, whether they have histories that reach back into primordial time or show up for sale at the mall.

What is relevant is that as human populations are compelled to confront the impacts and implications of a capitalist techno-culture ultimately unable to control the Frankensteins it creates, the schizophrenia of its claim to morality is bound to collide with its capacity for denial and self-delusion. And whether these Frankensteins are melting arctic ice shelves, the 100th variant of Covid-19, wars over access to clean water, mass megafauna extinctions, or the evolution of microscopic clone versions of Piccinini's fabulations who'll stop at nothing in their drive to replicate—the road to these catastrophes will have been paved by the same perhaps uniquely human form of moral blindness, namely, that while the suffering of (some) human beings is supremely important, that of nonhuman animals is of so little consequence, it can be ignored for any but the most idiosyncratic of reasons. And these reasons include neither what's for dinner, who counts as an object of experimental research, nor—as Piccinini's explores in her artwork—fabulations other than those we can imagine as pets.

DE-BEAKED, DE-GUILTED; TRANSGENIC, TRANSGRESSIVE

Gary Francione is certainly onto something when he refers to our moral schizophrenia with respect to nonhuman animals. Unfortunately the "necessary" exception he includes in his argument for animal rights offers a loophole for nonhuman animal commodification, neglect, and cruelty thinly concealed behind animal welfare laws that function more as a balm to conscience than protection for the vulnerable, including human laborers at factory farms, slaughter houses, and meat processing plants. Ultimately, Francione not only undermines his argument for humane treatment, he personifies the cognitive dissonance at the core of our enculturated moral schizophrenia. The appeal to "necessity" lets us forget that the bodies that end up in our circuses and zoos, in our labs, as our shoes, and on our plates are the direct, often genetically manipulated product of the commodification of sentience. However we window-dress it, the necessary exception invites conversion to exchange value consistent with insuring that *everything*, human, nonhuman, evolved, transgenic, living, nonliving, and dead are commodifiable; the very things Francione seeks to defend. As Haraway argues, consumers, human and nonhuman, are not themselves immune to the logic that determines the ways in which "things" like "food animals" and the people who eat them are materially, psychically, culturally, and economically co-created out of relationships defined in terms of production and consumption. The same worldview that de-beaks the factory farm chicken divests consumers of responsibility for its misery. "Necessity" exempts us from considering what's in our Happy Meals. Hence, the best Francione's humane treatment principle can do is to remind us of what we already know: *not* that nonhuman animals can suffer, *but that we do not care*, and are not required to care. Indeed, the appeal to "necessity" can keep us even from that dim recognition by allowing us to believe that, of course we do care, *but*. . . .

Let us return once more to Piccinini's artwork in light of Haraway's argument for a radically alternative ethic, namely, an ethic whose aim is to "decolonize," that is, examine the conceptual structures that shape the ways in which we're enculturated to conceive of human and nonhuman nature, as well as what counts as habitat, society, moral status, and the boundaries of the human-nonhuman relationship. Haraway writes that "in her [Piccinini's] sensuous sculptural and graphic stories of terran critters who were not on earth before now and whose evolutionary and ecological habitats are the installation, the mall, the website and the lab, Piccinini seems to me to be proposing not another frontier, but rather something more akin to a decolonizing ethic."[23] The possibility, in other words, of such "critters" is not just an imaginative product of the techno-cultural frontier; its relevance is not merely novelty, like a new version of the popular video game *Zelda*. For Haraway the possibility of the creation of beings who are us/not us, the result of a gene-edited fantasy, raises vital questions about *boundaries*—of species, of indigeneity (such as Australian Aboriginals), of geography (such as Australia), and of technology (gene editing). These boundary questions are not important because they blur or discount the difference between the way we conceive reality and reality itself. Haraway is, after all, no less committed than is Malm to the independent reality of nonhuman nature. They're important because only an independent nature subject to the physical laws that make change possible provide material for the sort of transformative modification that is gene editing; indeed, that is species extinction, the evolution of viral strains, the destabilizing alteration of the planet's atmosphere.

Malm's right: "power does not stem from notional [conceptual] dichotomies; it is of a far more earthly nature, the tracing and dislodging of which might require both hammers and sickles." Nancy Fraser makes a similar point, but situates the visceral "practice" of power in the history of "modernity," itself cast in the terms of capitalist venture: "its [capitalism's] practitioners disclose a hidden barbaric underside of capitalist modernity: beneath surface niceties of consent and contract lie brute violence and overt theft."[24] In casting "violence and theft" against the conceptual backdrop of modernity, Fraser underlines the kleptocratic relationship of society and nonhuman nature—a conceptual "dichotomy" from which capital draws its force and direction.

She makes this point even more forcefully when she argues that "[c]apitalism brutally separated human beings from material, seasonal rhythms, conscripting them into industrial manufacturing powered by fossil fuels, and profit-driven agriculture, bulked by chemical fertilizers."[25] While power can only be made possible given specific material conditions for its exercise, this does not preclude a "notional" component that authorizes that exercise. If the power wielded by the capitalist requires the "hammers and sickles" of a militant opposition to dismantle it, this is precisely because its promise of "modernity" is soaked in violence and theft—but advertised as progress and affluence. Haraway is also right: power is ineradicably "notional" in that what makes its exercise possible are the social and economic structures through which it is accorded and maintained. The stability of such structures may be challenged by "notional" fabulations like Piccinini's terran creatures, but also advantaged by the exploitation of the transgenic in the hands of the capitalist in whose barbaric zombie chicken is "what's for dinner."

The technologically mediated transgenic is thus inevitably *transgressive* despite the necessity for capital to keep it constrained to exchange value. What works like Piccinini's illustrate is that the very real boundaries of species, geography, and identity can be disrupted through the introduction of technocultural tools like gene editing. The subjugation of such technologies to the logic of commodification is thus a task requiring vigilance. Fortunately for the biotechnology capitalist, the preemption of sentience as a barrier to commodification authorizes the appropriation of the transgressive to the pursuit of profit. That Piccinini's fabulations may be sentient, capable of intimate relationships, and able to experience pain is no more a bar to commodification than it is for factory farmed pigs right now, and gene-editing our way to a pain-free porcine simply makes what was once a "fabulation" real and arguably barbaric. Against this backdrop, articulating a "decolonizing ethic," or any morally defensible form of opposition, is a tall order. What, then, might such an ethic look like? At its most basic, the objective of a decolonizing ethic is to gain insight about what we're doing with technologies that have the capacity to alter features crucial to defining species, whether a particular use such as producing a species of chicken immune to physical pain is morally defensible, and what the implications of a technology like gene-editing imply for the future of a deeply problematic industry like animal agriculture.

Haraway offers a glimpse of what "decolonizing" implies for the ways in which the boundaries that advantage the capitalist might be *de-naturalized*, that is, revealed as the created power wielded by the white, Western(ized), and patriarchal—but not ordained by nature. What she appears to have in mind mirrors what feminists like Maria Lugones argue with respect to the ways in which gender, race, and indigeneity are colonized to preserve the cultural and economic hegemony of white male conquerors. Gettering clear on this history is the first step toward decolonizing, that is, *undermining* it:

> [m]odernity organizes the world ontologically in terms of atomic, homogeneous, separable categories. Contemporary women of color and third-world women's critique of feminist universalism centers the claim that the intersection of race, class, sexuality, and gender exceeds the categories of modernity. If *woman* and *black* are terms for homogeneous, atomic, separable categories, then their intersection shows us the absence of black women rather than their presence. So, to see non-white women is to exceed "categorial" logic.[26]

Piccinini's artworks invite us to see nonhuman "critters" in a fashion similar to the way Lugones invites us to see non-white women; each works to disrupt the uninterrogated "universal" by exposing the ways in which "modernity" organizes the world to benefit some through the systemic subjugation or even erasure of others.

Lugones goes on to argue that she "want[s] to emphasize categorial, dichotomous, hierarchical logic as central to modern, colonial, capitalists thinking about race, gender, and sexuality. This permits me to search for organizations from which people have resisted modern, capitalist modernity that are in tension with its logic."[27] While Lugones' focus is reserved to human beings, it's not a stretch to add "species" to "thinking about race, gender, and sexuality." In fact, if Haraway's reading of Piccinini's artwork is correct, we must: "The Leather Landscape" not only signifies a marked tension with the logic of commodification, its critters *exceed* its boundaries, and thereby challenge its legitimacy, decolonizing its claim to naturalized categories of gender, race, history, locale, *and* species. Analyses like Lugones' also expose the limits of Francione's humane treatment principle. The principle assumes the same hierarchical logic that defines "necessity" in terms of human prerogative without interrogating whether it's justified, or whose "necessity" matters. A world organized in terms of "atomic, homogeneous, separable categories" "assumes that we may use animals when it is necessary to do so" because it assumes the hierarchical array that defines gender, race, sexuality, and species in the interest of its beneficiaries: mostly white, male, Western(ized) men who helm the ship of capital. Francione might reject this view of the humane treatment principle, but there is no nonarbitrary way to segregate one level of this hierarchy without disruption to every other level. Just as the principle takes for granted that humans may use nonhuman animals, so too it sanctions the use of women by men, the use of non-white men and women by some white men, and so on. In reproducing these fixed categories, Francione reproduces the conceptual structure of which they are an essential feature, and thereby reproduces the oppressive social and economic order the humane treatment principle is intended to challenge—but can't.

To be clear, the logic of commodification does not itself require any particular social order. What it requires is the governing presupposition that sentience is no obstacle to commodification such that the conversion of everything to exchange value is made possible. On the one hand, transgressive entities like Piccinini's fabulations pose no real challenge to the logic of commodification because, although such creatures do threaten to disrupt the boundaries that advantage the capitalist, they're no more disruptive than, for example, the horrific August 2023 wildfires in Maui—change presents opportunity to market something new. On the other hand, rigid hierarchies structured by gender, race, sexuality and species form the bread and butter of capitalism, but, as Lugones argues, these are not artifacts of nature; a decolonizing ethic might provide ammunition to the militant. That such hierarchies become institutionalized certainly pave the road for fatal complacency concerning what we take for granted, but this only makes the work of a decolonizing ethic more urgent and important. The transgenic may be transgressive, but transgressive has meaning only when it can be put to the service of materializing opposition to the subjugation of sentience as having value that transcends commodification. That technologies like gene-editing are even now conceived in terms of creating zombie animals who cannot feel physical pain testifies only to the utter domination of a capitalism that will undertake any means necessary to grow the profit margins of its animal agricultural industries. We have little grounds for being disgusted however; such is the character of the kleptocene.

A couple of examples will underscore this point: it's not mere metaphor to suggest that SARS-CoV-2 and its multiplying variants epitomize the *unintentionally* transgenic. Though unlike Piccinini's fabulations which embody characteristics we might wish were in greater supply among human beings, compassion, kindness, patience, her critters and Covid-19 nonetheless share in common at least one crucial feature: *monstrosity*. The possibility of their existence decolonizes the ways in which neoliberal "modernity organizes the world" by exposing the stability it promises as a *lie*. Both disrupt the hierarchy of sex, gender, race, and species through the exposure of vulnerabilities, that is, disruptions of the capitalist social order necessary to maintain its kleptocratic authority. Both transgress across barriers of skin and organ, identity and locality. Both appear excessive, at least when compared to a world organized "in terms of atomic, homogeneous, and separable categories" of power and wealth. Both threaten to upend the human chauvinism of the status quo, however unintentionally. And both can be appropriated via the mechanisms of disaster capitalism, or better: just like climate change, both present opportunities for novel forms of exploitation; fear of monsters can be a highly lucrative venture.

The xenotransplantation of a porcine heart valve to save the life of a human person may not count as trans*genic*, but CRISPR, gene editing technology recently used to treat an inheritable form of blindness, surely does.[28] So too the use of CRISPR to develop DNA-based enhancers for Covid-19 vaccines.[29] Yet here too, we needn't go as exotic as biotechnological intervention. That SARS-CoV-2 is the result of zoonotic transmission from bats or Pangolins or perhaps some other species of creature made into "what's for dinner" at a wet market or caught trespassing on farmland recently created out of forest—is sufficient to qualify as a variety of *trans* capable of radically altering the critter that becomes its infected host. Just as insurance companies capitalize on the climate crisis by assessing higher premiums for building in a flood or fire zone, so too will biotech and pharmaceutical companies capitalize on Covid-19, and the next virus, and the next. In short, kleptocratic capitalism has no boundaries, moral or otherwise, and this leaves principles like Francione's humane treatment mute on the question of what counts as a morally defensible end. The "ends" of "what ends justify what means?" are preemptively conscripted by the demands of capital just as the "trans" of zoonotic transmission can be conscripted to new profit opportunity. Without a critique of capitalism capable of embracing "trans" as "transgressive," ethicists like Francione have no grounds for the judgment that, for example, the millions upon millions of human and nonhuman deaths that have resulted from Covid-19 are bad, or that pharmaceutical companies that donate vaccine doses to developing world countries is good. "Necessityy" is already itself conscripted to commodification and consumption. Francione has nowhere to go but silence on questions like whether it counts as necessary to use, for example, Rhesus Monkeys in Covid-19 vaccine trials, regardless the suffering.[30] He has nothing to say about the creation of zombie chickens because the appeal to "necessity" eviscerates the transgressive.

FATAL COMPLACENCY AS THE PERFORMANCE OF DENIAL[2]

Understood in light of Haraway, Piccinini, Lugones, and the logic of commodification, the strengths and weaknesses of Francione's view of moral schizophrenia return us, with a sharpened blade, to David Wallace-Wells' discussion of "fatal complacency." A species of cognitive dissonance, but more perilous in virtue of having become a fully naturalized feature of global North capitalist culture, complacency is *the performance of denial*, or more specifically: it's the fully internalized, largely forgotten, denial that there is anything to deny. As opposed to being targeted to specific phenomena or events, for example, that Northern California fires are becoming more ferocious and frequent, that "atmospheric rivers" of snow are gradually replacing ordinary blizzards, or that Thwaites Glacier may shatter by 2027 due to climate change,[31] complacency's purpose is to deny that there is anything to deny, or as Wendy Lynne Lee makes the point in "Dewey and Climate Denial^2,"

> [D]enial^2 demands we be convinced not merely that the capitalist worldview mirrors facts about the planet, but that what the world it presents offers is what we (ought to) want—that the world it offers us is the aesthetically desirable world, and that consumption of goods is the highest form of aesthetic experience.[32]

The only way to become convinced that the world is just as capitalism presents it to us is to have internalized a form of denial that not only licenses the capacity to ignore stories about melting glaciers, atmospheric rivers, firenados, viral outbreaks, and the like, but permits us to forego knowing *that* we've chosen to ignore these crises.

Complacency is thus an inherently *epistemic* activity. It disposes us not to resignation, but to something far more dangerous: smug oblivion. Resignation acknowledges possible catastrophe; willful oblivion authorizes the decision to *not* know: denial^2. Resignation comprehends the revolting prospect of an uninhabitable earth; complacency is the product of a bribe. Seduced by a social-media/advertising saturated world depicted as beautiful, clean, fun, adventure-filled, safe, reliable, comfortable, and cool, we're sold a manufactured aesthetic whose price is the denial that it's premised on a lie; whose cost is the complacency borne of forgetting that denial. Complacency is the price we pay for a fiction that cannot be sustained, yet made to be experienced as if it were the crucial scaffolding of what philosopher John Dewey called the aesthetic *in* experience. Created out of the enculturated belief that happiness is the product of endless consumption, the capitalist aesthetic *in* experience is facilitated through the internalized erasure of facts that threaten to disrupt it. We are, in other words, effectively compelled to silence about the facts concerning our dispossession of the planet, its living inhabitants, and the futures of our successors, but we are bribed by the promise of endless consumption to forget the silence, or experience it only as the news story that conflicts with the "aesthetically desirable world" of the mall—where perhaps we gaze at one of Piccinini's installed fabulations. But we cannot understand it, and it cannot replace the attention we need to shop. This is denial^2, and given the consequences the very need to maintain it foreshadows, it's easy to see why Wallace-Wells would call it fatal; it is nihilism regardless whether he looks away.

Denial^2 needn't, however, itself be silent in order to sustain the manufactured halcyon of the status quo; the maintenance of complacency isn't itself necessarily complacent. It can be as vulgar as death threats to public health officials who support consumption-retarding lockdowns during a pandemic,[33] as deceptive as ads for "clean natural gas,"[34] or as moral-seeming as Smithfield Farms "Helping Hungry Homes" program to donate factory farm hams to low-income Americans.[35] But make no mistake: it's fatal complacency that makes the hamburger taste good; it's why we're "not about to go vegan." It's why "fabulations" like Piccinini's, though cuddly-looking, make us vaguely uncomfortable: they're us, and not. The aesthetic experience of complacency is the comfort we feel when we can evade guilt, when commercials tell us everything's ok, especially when we make that order for Omaha Steaks, by that new SUV, book that cruise. Complacency is among the principle products of capitalist enculturation; it normalizes acquiescence to the commodification of sentience by making it easy to not look, to not know "what's for dinner." While Francione is unlikely to have the critique of capital so squarely in mind when he references moral schizophrenia, it is denial^2 that makes possible the maintenance of the psychic chasm between the human consumption responsible for factory farm brutality and the predictable failure of policies erected on the humane treatment principle. Indeed, the humane treatment principle is itself an incarnation of denial^2: while laws made to embody this principle have had little positive effect protecting the nonhuman animals for whom they're intended, they offer a powerful moral tranquilizer for those who don't want to be seen as fatally complacent, but cannot see beyond reform.

On one side of denial^2 is an aesthetic *in* experience curated for us by multinational corporate interests dependent on the myth of endless resources and the commodification of sentience. On the other side are shattering glaciers, the daily terror of slaughter chutes, dying coral reefs, story-high snow "rivers," pig birthing crates, accelerated extinctions, debeaking, deforestation, firenados, and, as Wallace-Wells puts it, the uninhabitable earth. On the one hand, we know that this other side is very real; it's what makes enculturated denial^2 critical to the survival of capitalism. On the other, however constrained by the human chauvinism of their ultimate objectives—more judicious use of planetary resources, including nonhuman animals—Francione, Mann, and Wallace-Wells are sounding an alarm, if not very loudly. The issue here is not that their arguments are uninspired, or that they need to be augmented to make real progress toward getting us to see the error of our ways. The issue is that in their failure to take the critique of capitalism seriously, especially with respect to its foundational premises concerning the commodification of sentient life, they end up bedded down with those they'd likely cast as the opposition. Consider, for example, Richard Epstein's "Animals as Objects, or Subjects of Rights." Epstein argues that "systems of human ownership" have been more a benefit to nonhuman animals than a loss,[36] that "[i]n the end, even the proponents of animal rights must adopt a speciesist approach, complete with arbitrary distinctions" about, for example, whose suffering matters.[37] Epstein explicitly defends the objectification of nonhuman animals against Francione, arguing that because "[a]nimals counts as assets with positive economic value,"[38] their appropriate care could be entrusted to their owners who, governed by law and common practice, would seek to avoid liability by insuring their property did not become a hazard or nuisance.[39] In short, because nonhuman animals count as an economic commodity in the form of food, labor, or even companionship that contributes to the advance of human initiatives, their owners could be entrusted with their care:

> They [nonhuman animals] received the extensive protection of the law because they were valuable to the human beings who owned them. To imagine an ancient society in which animals had rights against human beings solely because they were sentient creatures is to envision a society in which human beings would be prepared to put themselves and their families at risk for the sake of brute sentient creatures . . . [The ancients] never denied the agency of animals. Yet at no time did they talk themselves into thinking that animals should be holders of legal rights. Those altruistic sentiments are the rich and secure.[40]

No doubt Francione would respond that whatever narrow notion of rights the Ancients had, it need not apply to the present, especially given how much more we now know about the sentience of nonhuman animals. As Epstein acknowledges, moreover, arguments that seek to justify the reduction of nonhuman animals to economic assets have been made in defense of commodifying other sentient creatures, including human beings forced into slavery and women forced into the servitude of marriage.

Epstein, however, rejects this comparison, arguing that, for example, Roman law recognized a number of more subtle and specific distinctions:

> The Roman rules for men within the power of their fathers and for women and for the insane persons all differed from each other in important particulars. Men within the power of their father could become heads of their own families at the death of their father; they had full rights to participate in political life even while consigned to a subordinate position within the family . . . marriage for its part was a consensual union . . . Animals did not marry . . . With a nod toward modernity, the woman, as well as the man, was free to renounce the marriage at any time. Women, slaves (not to mention sons), and animals were each subject to distinct rules tailored to their own distinct status.[41]

The trouble here is that whatever were the complexities of Roman law, these neither conflict with nor obviate the fact that slaves, women, and nonhuman animals occupied a subjugated status. While women, as opposed to nonhuman animals, could marry, the "nod to modernity" Epstein references was far more a formality in the law than a realistic choice in women's lives since, although they could inherit and own property, women had no right to vote, hold elected office, or participate in civic life. Epstein goes on, like Wallace-Wells, to insist that because women and slaves are human beings, their gradual enfranchisement into economic and public life was bound to come to fruition, and that "the status quo ante on slaves and women slowly crumbled precisely because they were human beings and not animals."[42] But, again, we have only to look toward the oppressive patriarchal regimes of, for example, the Taliban,[43] misogynist statutes like the Texas abortion laws,[44] or the sheer scale of human trafficking,[45] to see that much is yet left to crumble before we arrive at any full appreciation of human rights. Epstein argues that laws favoring patriarchy had eventually to fail, yet he undermines this claim by insisting that "it is easier to maintain the line against women because of the prominence of sex differences."[46]

In short, Epstein's defense of the argument that, despite their comparable capacity for sentience, nonhuman animals are justly counted as property but women and the enslaved are not—at least as we move toward the present era—fails abysmally because the reason he offers, "because women and slaves were human beings and nonhuman animals are not," merely restates his premise: human beings have rights and nonhuman animals do not. That is, his reasoning is circular. But the failure of Epstein's argument does little to help bolster Francione's moral extensionism since, as Epstein acknowledges, the extension of rights under evolving human law aimed to benefit property holders and their progeny—and was only begrudgingly extended even to some women. To the extent that "extension" privileges "human being" as its model of value, it will remain human interests that determine who or what has "rights." And, as we can see in the case of the Taliban or the Texas abortion laws, "human interests" still too often means "some men's interests." Just as in the Ancient Rome Epstein defends, in the fully capitalized world rights are recognized only insofar as appeal to them is economically expedient. We've thus little reason to think that even seemingly robust defenses of nonhuman animal rights, like Francione's, will translate into the end of animal agriculture or the preservation of habitat; in work to protect critically endangered species or a reconsideration of what counts as a research subject. Francione's argument can't compel us to reconsider whether pets are property or even whether women should be permitted to vote because the "humane treatment" principle can no more be extracted from the context of its primary beneficiaries, property owners, than can the commodification of sentience distinguish slaves, dogs, or wives.

In the end, arguments like Francione's actually help to sustain the status quo they portend to disrupt: they function as opportunities to market vegan alternatives, sponsor endangered species wings at zoos, show off bigger cages at primate research facilities, and market pet toys. Instead of revolutionizing our disposition toward our nonhuman fellows, the humane treatment principle hints at products aimed at disgorging and dissolving guilt, if not hypocrisy; it sanctifies denial[2]. This is not to say that going vegan, refusing to visit a zoo, protesting outside a research facility, or treating nonhuman animals as companions instead of property has no value. It is to say that insofar as the "ends justify the means," the trajectory of the principle of utility remains uninterrogated, and insofar as these ends are given by capital as profit and the power that accrues to profit, Francione's plea for the humane treatment of nonhuman animals is unlikely to be realized beyond utility; that is, beyond human chauvinism steeped in the myth of endless resources.

In fact, there's at least one way in which Epstein's explicit human chauvinism is preferable to Francione's moral extensionism. Epstein skips the moralizing; nonhuman animals are assets, and to whatever extent they merit human protection, it is because they have economic value—and that's it. The view that systems of human ownership are what's best for nonhuman animals invites not complacency, but rather ratification of the status quo—without the guilt, and therefore with the need for denial, moral schizophrenia, or any other form of self-deception. Epstein takes the commodification of sentience as given, and argues that where, for example, saving human lives from disease is at issue, there's no morally relevant question to consider even if the pursuit of treatment or vaccine requires a research subject that's also our closest living relative, the chimpanzee: "[l]et it be shown that the only way to develop an AIDS vaccine that would save thousands of lives is through painful or lethal tests on chimpanzees. People will clamor for those tests."[47] Put simply: such a research program is made easy to justify by the fact that it derives from "human being," the epicenter of value from which all other value is extended, or not; and for thinkers like Epstein for whom "extended or not" is entirely arbitrary, bearing no moral weight other than what advances (some) human interests.

THE PATH WE HAVE ALREADY TROD AND THE "NECESSITY" EXCEPTION

A comparison of Francione and Epstein raises fundamental questions about whether and how we ought to assign value to nonhuman entities. But it also equips us with a clearer, more transgressive and potentially decolonizing view of the planet Wallace-Wells' calls home, a view whose central objectives—to sound the climate crisis alarm and offer realistic solutions—is undermined through his implicit adoption of the logic of commodification. Wallace-Wells argues that the climate crisis is "worse, much worse" than we think, and that his aim in *The Uninhabitable Earth* is to shake us out of the paralysis created by the fact that "[t]he path we are on as a planet should terrify anyone living on it."[48] Yet, he goes on to insist that "all the relevant inputs are in our control," that "there is no mysticism required to interpret or command the fate of the earth,"[49] and that "[o]nly an acceptance of responsibility is required" to see that "the solutions are obvious and available."[50] The only solutions that Wallace-Wells seriously considers, however, are those that leave uninterrogated the presupposition that "when you're at the top of the food chain, it's ok to flaunt it," an iteration of human chauvinism consistent with Epstein's support for the commodification of sentience: "all human beings are in one category; animals fall into another."[51] The only solutions Wallace-Wells doesn't consign to "mysticism" or "fatalism"[52] are those which reaffirm his view that "[i]f humans are responsible for the problem, they must be capable of undoing it,"[53] in other words, if free marketeers, lobbyists, government agents, elected officials, and ordinary consumers are the cause of the climate crisis, "they" must be capable of undoing it—no substantive or transgressive militance required.

In a 2019 piece for the *Intelligencer*, "The Cautious Case for Climate Optimism," for example, Wallace-Wells argues that

> Let's consider the tools at hand. First: a carbon tax. . . . The premise is simple: Legislate a high enough cost on the stuff and the market will respond by producing less, then eventually none, of it. It is also an appealing proposition to those who don't want to see the economy truly upended; to those who trust that market forces will deliver the outcomes they are predicted to; to those who believe that the world would trust action on climate only if it came for free or, better yet, with economic benefits; and to those who believe that action would otherwise involve, invariably, a trade-off—that climate action of any meaningful scale would be expensive, probably too expensive for any growth-minded country to countenance.[54]

To be clear, Wallace-Wells concedes that limited efforts thus far to institute a carbon tax have produced disappointing results:

> A carbon tax is hypothetical for Americans, which may be one reason they tend to be optimistic about it. But there are already, today, many places with existing carbon pricing—South Korea, Japan, the E.U. None of their emissions are declining fast enough to meet a goal of two degrees, according to the

> carbon-watchdog site Climate Action Tracker. It is conceivable, even probable, that at much higher levels of taxation, the impact would be clearer. But as Jay Inslee, the governor of bright-green Washington State, which tried and failed to enact such a tax in 2018, recently put it, "To actually get carbon savings, you have to jack up the price so high that it becomes politically untenable."[55]

But neither the political nor the economic short-falls of a carbon tax deter him, or move him to consider the possibility that capitalism may itself be "the problem." Indeed, Wallace-Wells grants that proposals like the massive investment in "replacing dirty energy sources with clean ones and producing, along the way, an entirely renewable economy" built into the Green New Deal are "worthy, invigorating, and—believe it or not—popular." He claims to be "all for them." Yet, as we have seen in our discussion of Michael Mann, the likelihood that such state-sponsored investments will do more than "buy ourselves some time," even in combination with regulatory incentives, fails to move Wallace-Wells to reconsider whether more transgressive options might at least defray or slow some of the most devastating impacts he knows will be borne by the most vulnerable. There *are* other options: policies drafted on a global scale that prioritize the systemic conservation and restoration of land, waterways, ocean ecosystems, and endangered species, bringing a complete end to animal agriculture, support for the educations of girls, to name just a few. What each of have in common, of course, is that they find themselves in direct conflict with applications for drilling leases, logging permits, corporate scale fishing rights, subdivision construction, and consumer demand.

Insofar as Wallace-Wells appeals to the logic of commodification, his plea for "taking responsibility" doesn't move us much beyond the Roman law Epstein defends: both seek to facilitate human advantage, and neither see sentience or the capacity for suffering as an obstacle to that pursuit. Indeed, Wallace-Wells' commitments aren't, in the end, the planet, its nonhuman species or ecologies other than in so far as sustaining them is necessary to insure against catastrophe for the "we" he actually cares about: "[i]nstead, we assign the task [of combatting the climate crisis] to future generations . . . This is why this book is also studded so oppressively with 'we,' however imperious it may seem. The fact that climate change is all-enveloping means it targets all of us, and that we must all share in the responsibility so we do not all share in the suffering—at least not all share in so suffocatingly much of it."[56] In other words, although Wallace-Wells knows his use of "we" is "imperious," he calculates that its faux-universalizing is worth the risk because it allows him to argue that "we" must all take responsibility so a few can escape the worst impacts of the climate crisis. Imperious—yes, but also revealing. Setting aside the dubious proposition that "we must all share in the responsibility" for a crisis that epitomizes the structural inequalities characteristic of global capitalist culture, this glittering generalization is really just a hollow defense of the status quo that protects those most responsible for the suffering of those least able to evade the environmental crises of the present, let alone the catastrophic future. Wallace-Wells' follow up observation that "[w]e do not know the precise shape such suffering would take"[57] is also disappointing. Such claims would be trite were they not evasive: we may not know precisely, but we certainly do know who and what will bear the brunt of a future swallowed up by environmental disaster—the same human and nonhuman populations who do most of the suffering now. These are the sorts of claims we expect from corporate CEOs looking to limit their liability by pleading ignorance, or from proud human chauvinists like Epstein, not from the work of those who claim to be committed to preventing catastrophe and to supporting social and environmental justice.

What is deeply, sadly, ironic is that in their failure to examine the crucial assumptions that ground the logic of commodification, Francione, Epstein, and Wallace-Wells each miss the very real prospect that at the end of capital's emerging incarnation as unconcealed resource theft is an *uninhabitable*, nearly unimaginable earth. While Francione's right about moral schizophrenia, his argument that "necessity" can justify the exploitation of nonhuman animals even though "we" ought not to treat them as mere things, is fully consistent with the commodification of sentience. This "necessity" exception makes it possible for Wallace-Wells and Epstein to applaud calls for humane treatment because they cost precisely nothing; such calls demand nothing; they change nothing. In other words, *subterfuge offers a pass*. "Necessity" enables Wallace-Wells' "when you're at the top of the food chain, it's ok to flaunt it" because it grants license not only to ignore suffering for the sake of, say, "proteins," but ignore the greenhouse gas emissions produced in the manufacture of this "necessity"; the justification of the first offers cover to the second. Francione's exception excuses the inconsistency in Wallace-Well's claim that moral complacency is at fault for the climate crisis, even as he stops short of any remedial strategy that threatens to topple us from the top of the meat-eating food chain. Wallace-Wells acknowledges that "environmental panic is growing, and so is despair," but grouses that some environmental writers, including Bruno Latour, Wendy Lynne Lee, and Stuart Parker, are responsible for a "dour terminological competition [that] has sprung up among climate writers, aiming to coin new clarifying language . . . " as if the work to be more humane has given way to a petty race over whose dark lexicon makes the most convincing case for the bleak future "we" face.[58]

"Bleak," however, may be more fittingly assigned to the likelihood that Wallace-Wells' defense of arguments grounded in the logic of commodification can make capitalism a willing and honest ally in the effort to reduce greenhouse gas emissions. In fact, capitalism *can't* become this ally.

Consider: Wallace-Wells comprehends the peril climate change poses to the planet's ecosystems; he understands that fossil fuel extractivism plays a starring role. But what he fails to grasp is that *the very logic of capital is inherently incompatible with the long-term thinking and strategizing required to make good on carbon-trade or carbon tax*. This is not merely because the logic operates on the presupposition that planetary resources are endless, but because, given that it knows that presupposition is both *necessary and false, it cannot think long-term at all*. To argue that strategies which retain the basic structure of capitalist markets are the solution toward blunting the impacts of the climate crisis is a paradigmatic example of denial^2 at its most nihilistic: while Wallace-Wells does not deny that the climate crisis *is a crisis*, the effect of his *de facto* defense of an economic system whose survival requires an inexhaustible planet and atmosphere—*that it knows it does not have*—is the denial of the planet and atmosphere as it really is: exhaustible. It is to deny that the trajectory of capitalism is kleptocratic, that resource scarcity will inevitably incite a race to expropriate, pilfer, rob by whatever means necessary, fuel, clean(able) water, arable land, and exploitable bodies—even if it has to genetically engineer them to make their "painless" exploitation more palatable to consumers. To then insist that "the solutions [to the climate crisis] are obvious"[59] because that economic system can be corralled toward the right course is to effectively deny not only that the planet and its atmosphere cannot sustain this economic system, but that there is any real crisis at all. How can there be a crisis if the planet and its atmosphere is the one that the favored system of economic exchange can be deployed to repair?

The logic of commodification assumes a planet of inexhaustible resources that can always be fixed—or never needs to be. Denial^2 thus effectively relieves fossil fuel companies from having to think long-term long enough to assume the financial expenses entailed, or to plan according to the profit-limitations implicit in these carbon schemes. And even though, as ExxonMobil's extensive efforts to conceal the evidence makes clear, we know *they know better*, the point is that they cannot be required to do better because doing better would require acknowledging what cannot be acknowledged: that the planet and its atmosphere are resources that, no matter the techno-wizardry of the interim, will still eventually *run out of the capacity to sustain life*. In short, strategies that demand a capitalist enterprise make its objective something other than profit, thus demanding it conceive of the world as something other than a limitless resource for profit, effectively solicit its suicide. To deny this essential characteristic of the logic of commodification is to deny that capitalism is capitalism, that is, of necessity kleptocratic. Still, Wallace-Wells' argues we can have the capitalist-cake and eat it too:

> The threat from climate change is more total than the bomb. It is also more pervasive . . . Half of the Great Barrier Reef has already died, methane is leaking from Arctic permafrost that may never freeze again, and the high-end estimates for what warming will mean for cereal crops suggest that just four degrees of warming could reduce yields by 50 percent. If this strikes you as tragic, which it should, consider that we have all the tools we need, today, to stop it all: a carbon tax and the political apparatus to aggressively phase out dirty energy; a new approach to agricultural practices and a shift away from beef and dairy in the global diet; and public investment in green energy and carbon capture.[60]

The threat posed by climate change "is more total than the bomb," yet the tools of capital can be put to the service of staving off this catastrophe; *it need only cease to be capitalism.*

The only question left here is how Wallace-Wells misses this conundrum. There are (at least) three reasons for this: first up is his myopic focus on energy production. Given his command of the facts about the climate crisis and its implications it seems that, even if nonhuman animal suffering doesn't concern him, factory farm emissions and waste lagoons should—until we realize that Wallace-Wells can't afford to include animal agriculture in his analysis of the climate crisis because it would detract from his optimistic assessment of the potential benefits of carbon-trading, *an assessment focused solely on energy production.* Carbon trade policies, in other words, can be made to look like they'll work only if the sole industries for which we have to account are the fossil fuel extraction industries. The trouble, of course, is that this is false. Insofar as animal agriculture is a major contributor to greenhouse gas emissions, excluding it from assessment produces a highly distorted picture of what carbon trade policies can achieve, even were they otherwise plausible. Indeed, it reveals more about Wallace-Wells' commitments—the maintenance of his "it's ok to flaunt it" human chauvinism—that it does about possible solutions to the climate crisis.

Second: although Wallace-Wells' reference to "top of the food chain" is, like Epstein's, question-begging insofar as he provides no argument for it, he cannot forfeit the hierarchy it exemplifies. The commodification of sentience is as structurally essential to Wallace-Wells' market-oriented solutions to the climate crisis as it is to Epstein's insistence that the value of nonhuman animals is strictly instrumental. Carbon trade initiatives only make sense from within this structure because their primary aim is a habitable future for human beings. Indeed, the hierarchical nature of these initiatives is reinforced on human and nonhuman populations in reforestation projects like REDD that, in the name of curbing the impacts of climate change, displace entire villages and uproot whole ecosystems. Moreover, human beings are not the top of the food chain. We may be apex predators, but unless what Wallace-Wells means by "top" is our capacity to manufacture animal bodies *en masse*, or wipe out entire species via trophy-hunting, or genetically engineer pain-free monstrosities, or drive whole species to extinction through the domination of land and access to water, the award for senior apex predator goes to Lions, Great White Sharks, and more recently to the increasing volatility of viral outbreaks whose capacity to kill knows no bounds of class, geography, sex, or race.

Third, although Wallace-Wells provides innumerable and compelling accounts of the human suffering caused by the climate crisis and its impacts on the way to making his case for market-oriented solutions, he offers little reason to believe that human behavior will change in the direction of environmental sustainability. Why? Because he offers no reasons to care about any other species than our own. In fact, the structural inequalities that "justify" the commodification of nonhuman animals reinforce all of the ways we commodify human beings. Insofar, then, as Wallace-Wells' myopic focus on the fossil fuel industry reinforces this commodification of sentience, it reinforces by default a mercenary and pitiless disposition toward the planet and its inhabitants that hardly bodes well for a future worth wanting. While Wallace-Wells' claim that we're entitled to flaunt our position at the top of the food chain may seem innocuous, even funny, it's actually camouflage for the dark reality we're invited to ignore, but also reinvent, in the name of greenhouse gas reduction schemes that take no account of industries whose emissions we ignore—*so that we can ignore the suffering they cause*. Reinforcing this disposition foreshadows a future that, while it may be sustainable (barely), cannot be one that any but the few equipped to protect themselves from its endemic barbarity and violence would want. The enculturated callousness to suffering necessitated by the determination that sentience is no bar to commodification may put human beings at the top of the food chain, but it also normalizes cruelty and viciousness in all of its incarnations. Wallace-Wells is right, "[t]he path we are on as a planet should terrify anyone living on it," but it is the path we have already trod, and that we are recklessly reproducing.

"HIS FACE WAS HACKED OFF"

Ashley Dawson's opening description of elephant tusk poaching should terrify us all. It brings home at least one of the consequences of flaunting our position at the top of the food chain: a cautionary tale about a world that only a few, equipped with weapons, food reserves, and callous disregard, would be in a position to survive at the end of the Kleptocene—for a while. That this particular incarnation of the commodification of sentience transpires in the global South instead of the global North is no cause for comfort. In fact, just the opposite:

> His face was hacked off. Left prostrate in the red dust, to be preyed on by vultures, his body remained intact except for the obscene hole where his magnificent six foot long tusks used to be. Satao was a so-called tusker, an African elephant with a rare genetic strain that produced tusks so long that they dangled to the ground, making him a prime attraction in Kenya's Tsavo East National Park.[61]

Although Wallace-Wells, Francione, Epstein, and Mann would surely condemn this sickening act of ivory poaching, their arguments have little to offer beyond evincing moral outrage, pique floating on the hypocrisy of a largely unsupported optimism concerning the aptitude of markets to be regulated against mercenary profiteers. The logic of commodification that taints Francione's "necessary" is the same as that which subsidizes Wallace-Wells, Epstein's, and Mann's plea for a kinder, gentler capitalism. We might like to think butchering tuskers assumed to be protected in national parks is an aberration; it's not. If there's "nothing complicated" about drawing a boundary that relegates nonhuman animals to the status of things other than a nebulous indirect duty to avoid setting poor examples for children by hacking off an elephant's face *in front of them*, notions like "moral boundaries," "necessity," or even humane treatment laws have little enforceable value. As much of human history illustrates, it's just too easy to "justify" exceptions. Unwittingly, Wallace-Wells' joke that he's "not personally about to slaughter a cow to eat a hamburger," but he's "not about to go vegan," reinforces just this point.[62] Just because Wallace-Wells doesn't dirty his hands in hacking up a cow doesn't mean he has clean hands. It's precisely fatal complacency that slaughtered Satao.

"Nothing complicated" epitomizes the history of the commodification of sentience at its most terrifying and irrecoverably destructive. Where little more is required than for those in power to simply assert their prerogative as if there was "nothing complicated" about what counts as a tool, a disposable, or a marketable, then "natural boundaries" can just as well be drawn, as did the American slavers, in whatever way most lucrative to their profit objectives. Consider, for example, a letter to the editor by S. Trott, 1842:

> It requires but little acquaintance with the blacks as a people, to be convinced that by nature, they are fitted for greater usefulness, and the enjoyment of more comfort, in a state of bondage than in a state of freedom. In this state the providence of God had placed them among us, before we became a nation, and the same providence which brought us into existence as a nation, and gave us

> the most perfect and favorable form of government on earth, left them in their bondage, with the masters control over them guaranteed by the Constitution.[63]

For the slavers, there was little significant difference among justifications for bondage; God's providence manifests itself toward its fulfillment in the provision of fertile fields, cattle and human chattel, each realizing its end as the property of the tobacco or cotton plantation. Yet, the force of this appeal to providence seems lost on Epstein who insists that "even before the change in formal legal status, it would be a mistake to assume that slaves were treated like women, or that animals were treated like either. The variations in social status were just too great."[64] The issue here is not only that Epstein misfires on the slaver's justifications or that, regardless legal status, social position could be regarded as valuable only where it advantaged the slaver's ends. The issue is that the institutions upon which the success of the slaver's profit venture depend, property, slavery, and marriage, could not acknowledge any such boundaries—and survive. The logic of commodification ordains the enforcement *and* the transgression of boundaries, whichever serves to generate exchange value.

Consider, for example, the advantage conferred on the slaver in Carol Adams's analysis of concepts like the "rapacious black man," the virginal white woman, the licentious black woman, and the supposed sexual appetites of male apes:

> By viewing African-Americans as black beasts, Euro-American men created two pornographic scenarios, one about rapacious black men, and one about lascivious black women available to anyone, man or beast. Both concepts interacted with the notion of white women as pure, virginal and sexless. . . . Black men were seen as beasts sexually threatening white womanhood, a white womanhood defined to aggrandize the sense of white manhood. Black women were seen as sexed, as not able to be violated because they would enjoy anything—including sex with animals. . . . Indeed, Winthrop Jordan concludes that "[t]he sexual union of apes and Negroes was always conceived as involving *female Negroes* and *male apes*."[65]

Whether we see these "variations in social status" as complicated is beside the point. The point is that the animalizing of black men and black women functions to reinforce the privileged, *humanized*, social status of white men and white women, and of white men over white women, black men, black women, nonhuman animals, and nonhuman nature—in each case for largely the same reasons: the maintenance of a social order, including its relations of resource, labor, and property, that empowers some by demonizing and sexualizing others, that "justifies" the commodification of the subjugated to the profit-advantage of the master.

According to Nancy Fraser the best way to describe the relationship between the enslaved and their overseers is as a form of *expropriation*:

> Expropriation works by *confiscating* human capacities and natural resources and conscripting them into the circuits of capital expansion. The confiscation may be blatant and violent, as in New World slavery; or it may be veiled by a cloak of commerce, as in the predatory loans and debt foreclosures of the present era. The expropriated subjects may be rural or indigenous communities in the capitalist periphery—or member of subject or subordinated groups in the capitalist core.[66]

In short, expropriation is theft, and theft veiled behind the assumed legitimacy of a capitalist venture such as a plantation, an auction block, or a factory is not merely predatory, but fundamentally kleptocratic. The social position of the master empowered over his property represents the plantation not only materially in the form of cultivation, harvest, and market, but, consistent with the logic of commodification, as a maximally productive factory for both commodities and for future producers of commodities: white women are sexualized and commodified as an asset that must be kept pure to retain value invested as property rights in the master and *his* offspring. Black men are sexualized and demonized as "beasts" in order to justify the violence meted out against them as punishment for resisting the whip and to control their imputed uncontrollable sexual urges, strengths best corralled like those of laboring brutes. Black women are sexualized and associated with nonhuman farm animals as well as apes—themselves compared to black men—with whom they're alleged to consort, justifying their status as chattel that cannot be raped in virtue of their inherent promiscuity, yet effectively mechanized as incubators of enslaved offspring that, however their existence is denied, can be sold at auction. Mark Stoll argues that the expropriation of human beings into plantation slavery was the "precursor of the factories of industrial capitalism."[67] But in truth the confiscation of enslaved labor wasn't really a *precursor* at all, but rather simply an incarnation of the ontology of capital, as is made clear in its environmental as well as its human implications:

> Plantation capitalism transformed environments on French Martinique, Guadeloupe, and Saint-Domingue (Haiti) . . . Deforestation caused sheet erosion and gullies and sent native plants and birds into extinction. Erosion silted up the harbor of Bridgetown, Barbados, in the 1660s . . . By the 1660s, soil depletion had forced plantation owners to increase their slave force to collect the dung of sheep and draft animals and fertilize fields with it.[68]

Imbricated throughout the history of capital, relationships premised on their expropriation as resource affect a kind of flow between labor, soil, bodies, reproductive capacities, dung, and commodity production determined by a logic that defines value as exchange. That the prevailing racialized and sexual hierarchies to which men and women, but also nonhuman animals, were consigned authorized plantation owners to effectively conceive of labor, soil, bodies, reproductive capacities, dung, and commodity production in more or less the same way—as the components of a factory that produced a highly fungible commodity like cotton, sugar, or tobacco, but that ultimately produced the plantation owner *as* the *plantation owner*.

Going even further, in *Contemporary Feminist Theory and Activism: Six Global Issues* Wendy Lynne Lee argues that animalizing black men and women formed a crucial feature of their commodification *as* enslaved because it served to naturalize and reinforce a social order whose beneficiaries, in this case white male plantation owners, were authorized not only *as* plantation owners, but *as* fully human by sheer contrast with their property—a distinction vitally important to maintaining the "moral" justification for institutions like slavery. Slavers saw as "nothing complicated" a natural boundary between those "fitted for greater usefulness in bondage" and those ordained by the "providence of God" because they saw themselves as paradigmatic of creation in God's image, and therefore rightful masters of those whose status as "human" was either ambiguous or at least intended as subjugate.[69] Even if white women were counted as human, this in no way barred the commodification of their reproductive sexuality in marriage, itself an institution whose primary function was the preservation of property and inheritable wealth through primarily male bloodlines. In *This is Environmental Ethics*, Lee makes a point well-established by Friedrich Engels long ago:

> In *The Origin of the Family, Private Property and the State*, Engels argues that the primary beneficiaries of institutions like private property, the commodification of women's reproductive sexuality, and marriage (compulsory monogamy) are men whose control of women's bodies act as a conduit of inherited wealth to male offspring through male bloodlines. He argues that just as land and livestock came to signify human domination of nonhuman nature, so too women's reproductive capacities came to signify another kind of property: the progeny in which future labor, property, and wealth could be invested and consolidated.[70]

Human chauvinism, in other words, "is demonstrably *not* generic, but rather relies on the maintenance of social institutions whose privileges and prerogatives are defined according to a logic that evokes patterns of comparison and identity between specific . . . categories of human being and equally specific images of nonhuman animals and nature, patterns that establish otherness, but also commodifiability."[71] Human chauvinism is fundamentally masculinist, patriarchal, racist—and capitalist.

What feminist analysis shows is that however "boundaries" may be represented as fixed by nature, the pursuit of profit dictates that they're made to be transgressed in the interest of expediency. Black and white, human and nonhuman, male and female—these boundaries *and* their potential for transgression are crucial to maintaining a capitalism nimble enough to capitalize on *anything* that fends off "grow or die." Among capital's key objectives is to "invoke patterns of identity and comparison" conducive to maximizing marketability in the service of creating surplus value. Capital creates (or identifies) in each new market boundaries it may well transgress in the next, empowering its beneficiaries by establishing their status as authorized by God or nature, reshuffling the subjugated toward the next profit venture. To be clear, this is not to say that the structural hierarchies of race, sex, gender, and species don't retain their relative stability over the course of time. It is to say that what undergirds this stability *is* the advantage it guarantees, and that if some other configuration of the social order were of greater utility to the capitalist, we'd likely see some form of justification for it—however tortured. The point is that transgression preserves ostensibly "moral" boundaries in virtue of being in a position to violate them; acts of transgression provide reminders that whoever is authorized, for instance, to rape the slave, sell her offspring, or yoke her husband to a plow, is reaffirmed *as* a human being, ordained by providence to determine the status of the "other." It is, moreover, precisely this history of boundary violation that recent efforts to ban the teaching of *Critical Race Theory* seek to expunge from public education.[72] It's the controversy over what counts as a boundary that evokes outrage in Bud Light consumers over the appearance of transgender celebrity Dylan Mulvaney in a "woke" beer commercial, tanking sales.[73] Yet it's also the more frequent appearance of gay and/or interracial couples in ads that sell everything from automobiles to hamburgers—maintaining the fossil fuel economy. Boundary transgression epitomizes another incarnation of denial^2: denying that institutions such as slavery form a foundational bulwark of American economic growth requires denying that slavery is *slavery*. Consider, for example, Florida governor and Republican presidential candidate Ron DeSantis' approval of an African American history that instructs students to believe that slavery was good for the enslaved because it taught "resourcefulness" and "useful skills."[74]

Theorists like Epstein might respond that it's simply not necessary to engage the feminist or anti-racist literature in order to show that nonhuman animals have no rights. This approach begs the question, however, by assuming some defining distinction between human and nonhuman that sets the oppression of people apart from the exploitation of nonhuman animals. As we've seen, Epstein would be hard-pressed to locate this distinction. Epstein is also not alone in ignoring the considerable anti-racist, feminist, and ecofeminist literature on these issues; Wallace-Wells, Mann, and Francione occupy the same company, raising the important question: to what extent, if any, are contemporary writers on the status of nonhuman animals, environmental crises, rights, or human welfare responsible to engage arguments that feature analyses of the role that structural inequality plays in environmental crisis? Why don't we see more of the feminist and anti-racist literature in their work—especially since it shows how deeply imbricated inequality and oppression are in the causes of environmental deterioration?

We know, for example, that corporate advertising can vary significantly with respect to consumer response to particular marketing campaigns. Rising and often violent bigotry against the LGBTQ+ community encouraged some companies such as Budweiser to devote ad revenue to a greater emphasis on diversity among their potential consumers. But the beer producer quickly shriveled under the backlash of its conservative transphobic consumers.[75] Similarly, being accused of "rainbow-washing" in light of the company's support for LGBTQ+ Pride month, Target swiftly caved to criticism.[76] What both cases illustrate is that an objective critique of capitalism requires close attention paid to the drivers of company decision-making. Capitalist enterprise is advantaged by structural inequality such that product development and advertising will always exploit that inequality one way or another to attract consumers. Caught between consumers they hoped to recruit and those already loyal to their brand, Budweiser and Target simply chose the audience upon whom they count to sell their product. Analyses like these are crucial to an understanding of capitalism as kleptocratic, yet we see relatively little focus on what structural inequality actually means to capitalism in Wallace-Wells, Mann, Epstein, and Francione. Governments, moreover, are not immune, as Malm puts it, to the pathologies that ally policy-creation with profit venture:

> If current trends are anything to go by, the warming condition looks set to be an era of retrogression, ecologically and politically. One of the greatest pathologies is surely the superabundance of energy thrown into the demonization of refugees. Muslims, Mexicans, various otherwise coded others in advanced capitalist countries, while climate change receives barely a sliver of attention . . . fossil energy is a bane entirely internal to the system, but immigrants and other others can be framed as external enemies, so much more convenient a target of aggression.[77]

The logic that provokes Budweiser and Target to abandon their albeit shallow commitment to the LGBTQ+ community is no different than the logic to which governments appeal to demonize racialized immigrants in the service of distracting us from actual crises—like climate change. Malm's inclusion of refugees—many looking to escape the impacts of the "warming condition"—aligns him with legions of feminist scholars such as Kathryn Yusoff who theorize precisely these "pathological" dynamics and their impacts.

Consider one more particularly egregious example of the failure to consult the anti-racist or feminist literature relevant to, in this case, an analysis of animal rights. Epstein argues that insofar as differences of intelligence between human beings and nonhuman animals are obvious, "[i]t follows . . . that we should resist any effort to extrapolate legal rights for animals from the change in legal rights of women and slaves."[78] Any question about whether nonhuman animals have rights is thus moot: "What animal can be given the right to contract? To testify in court? To vote?"[79] Yet, Epstein's narrow formulation of rights-bearing as "right to" but not "right from" excludes children, the intellectually disabled, Alzheimer's' victims, and other human beings who suffer cognitive or psychological impairment. This is bad enough, but perhaps even worse: the logic Epstein deploys can be (and has been) used to exclude countless human beings from the status of rights-bearers. Not only the obvious cases such as those kidnapped or born to slavery, but those demonized as immigrants, refused entry to the country as Muslims, allowed to die in childbirth under obscenely cruel and misogynist abortion laws—all are dehumanized through the application of the same logic Epstein uses to refuse rights of any kind to nonhuman animals. For him, the only creatures who have rights are those *deemed to have* the cognitive wherewithal to *do* a thing—like vote, enter a contract, or refuse to be an experimental test subject or a dinner entré, namely, fully capable human adults.

But what we know from careful feminist and anti-racist analyses is that "deemed to have" has a checkered and violent history closely allied with the ontology of capital and its instantiations as slavery, human trafficking, racial profiling, and misogynist law. Moreover, Epstein's view embodies the intimate relationship of denial^2 to the commodification of sentience: to deny that a sentient creature has at least some right not to be made to suffer merely to fulfill a human interest requires denying that it shares any relevant quality in common with those human beings who, as children, disabled persons, or elderly—as black or brown or female or poor or indigenous or Muslim—would also have to be denied the exercise of a right on the same grounds, namely, that they can't exercise a right because they do not occupy the relevant epistemic position, like affluent global North white men do.

Put differently: while most children will develop the intellectual wherewithal to vote, not all will—some are still counted as human. While nearly all Alzheimer's victims will lose their intellectual capacity to vote, we do not thereby, as Diamond might put it, consign them to "what's for dinner." Whatever contortions of reason Epstein deploys to justify denying the right to avoid human-caused suffering to nonhuman animals, he cannot maintain that view without also denying *that there is anything to deny* in the analogue cases of people who share the same cognitive wherewithal: denial². To deny that nonhuman animals have at least some right not to suffer is to effectively deny that there exist human beings whose cognitive capacities are similar; but of course, this is both false, an arbitrary assertion to power, and the stuff of bigotry exploitable by the capitalist. Once we see this, we see that Epstein's commitment to the commodification of sentience is no more than a "might makes right" claim to power girded by an indignant rejection of the possibility that the categories he asserts are vulnerable to transgression. Insofar then as the premise of his argument to deny rights to nonhuman animals retains these "natural boundaries," he can defend neither the claim that nonhuman animals have no rights nor the claim that (some) human beings do—nor the reverse of either. For, a bit like the statues of Daedalus, neither will hold still long enough to avoid transgression.

"ANTHROPODENIALISM": "VAIN BEINGS SUCH AS OURSELVES" AND THE ANXIOUS APPEAL TO FREE WILL

Slavery is just one example of a "nothing complicated" woven out of denial². Indeed, once we comprehend "nothing complicated" as part of the logic of commodification, we gain a clearer view of why sentience is no obstacle to the emergence of kleptocracy, and why a number of contemporary environmental writers seem to avoid engagement with animal rights, just as they seem to avoid engagement with feminist and anti-racist literature. Consider once more David Wallace-Wells. He appeals to a "moral boundary" distinguishing human beings and nonhuman animals in order to justify ignoring an industry—animal agriculture—that doesn't fit his market-oriented climate crisis fix, yet is responsible for colossal greenhouse gas emissions. To this end, he exploits a demonstrable fiction to support his version of "moral boundary," namely, that women and people of color are offended by talk of animal rights so soon after the women's liberation and Civil Rights movements because talk of "liberation" appears to compare the status of women and people of color to that of nonhuman animals.[80] This claim is not merely false, it's aimed at producing false outrage; it's a straw argument that creates a fake boogyman comparison. It also betrays just how little of the contemporary feminist, anti-racist, and environmental theory Wallace-Wells has actually sought to engage. In his apparent rush to show he's "like every other American," Wallace-Wells ignores the tidal wave of feminist theorists who, like Karen Warren, Carol Adams, Josephine Donovan, Greta Gaard, Lori

Gruen, Chris Cuomo, Donna Haraway, Wendy Lynne Lee, Cora Diamond, Val Plumwood, Martha Nussbaum, Julie Sze, Nancy Tuana, Nancy Fraser, and many others, have provided a cornucopia of analysis demonstrating the links between the liberation of women, indigenous, brown, and black people and the recognition of rights as they apply to nonhuman animals. Ecological feminism is routinely credited for spelling out the ways in which women, nonhuman animals, and nonhuman nature are similarly objectified and commodified, how some forms of institutionalized violence impact women and nonhuman animals in analogous ways, and how the struggle to end oppression depends, as Karen Warren argued in "The Power and the Promise of Ecological Feminism" structural inequality must be tackled at all of its levels, not merely those which impact some human beings.

Wallace-Wells also makes no mention of the many ways in which these movements have sought proactive alliances for decades.[81] The issue, however, is not merely that Wallace-Wells' ignores the feminist and anti-racist contribution to discourse concerning moral boundaries. It's that, by ignoring these contributions, he signals that he's not interested, despite his disclaimers, in whether his market based solutions to the climate crisis might disproportionately impact women, particularly developing world women, or whether CAFOs built in predominantly minority communities are a moral issue, or whether talk of nonhuman animal rights might be essential to the struggle for human rights under repressive regimes (or emergent autocracies). Despite his thoughtful and comprehensive discussion of the impacts of the climate crisis for the developing world generally, Wallace-Wells doesn't connect the causes of the crisis, namely, kleptocratic capitalism, to other society-altering contemporary issues. What role, for example, might the commodification of sentience play in the return to the use of torture during the Iraq War? Police brutality against black men? The often dehumanizing treatment of inmates incarcerated in the American prison-industrial complex?

A compelling argument can be made that what each of these cases have in common is the animalizing of their subjects—POWs, black men, inmates—made possible originally by the demotion of sentient life to mere exchange value. But, as I have argued throughout, it is the room made in the ontology of capital for the commodification of sentient beings that casts the die for the commodification of *everything*. Wallace-Wells tells us he "began collecting stories of climate change, many of them terrifying, gripping, uncanny narratives." He goes on to profile the plight of climate refugees, but his aerial discussion of United Nations numbers—200 million climate refugees by 2050, for example—seem mostly a gratuitous nod in the direction of a genuine concern for suffering: He's already hedged it via the admission that he too, white, male, Western, and economically comfortable, suffers from "fatal complacency," as if his confession somehow absolves him the responsibility to probe any further the causes of this incalculable suffering.

The failure to consider any of the arguments relevant to the causes of suffering, arguments that surely bear on the conditions of the climate crisis, is itself a form of denial. Long before Wallace-Wells, Francione, Mann, and Epstein take up their positions in the ramparts of moral theorizing about whose interests matter, environmental philosophers like Peter Singer gave serious thought to nonhuman animal suffering, and to whether it has analogues in sexist or racist oppression. Originating in "All Animals are Equal" (1974),[82] Singer argues that speciesism, the arbitrary privileging of one's own species, is, like racism and sexism: an incarnation of the quest to legitimate the rule of some human beings over others, human and nonhuman alike.[83] The closest that Wallace-Wells gets to considering whether "moral boundaries" are facts of nature as opposed to mere assertions of human (or at least male) superiority occurs in his discussion of bee colony collapse. But this discussion is instructive because, instead of taking an opportunity to engage with the question whether bee colony collapse can be usefully compared to the deterioration of human civilizations, or whether the concern for bee colony collapse implies a need for further reflection on moral boundaries, Wallace-Wells simply scolds those who'd dare to defend bee civilization as an analogue for human societies: "[i]t's not just bee rapture after all: we see visions of our own world being wiped out in the mysterious deaths brought about by Ebola, bird flu, and other pandemics . . . the more you read about colony collapse, the more you are filled with a kind of awe for just how much the internet is a divining rod by which we choose to intuit an end of days."[84] In other words, instead of showing his reader why the comparison of bee colonies to human civilizations is folly, Wallace-Wells introduces a red herring: he ridicules those who'd turn to the Internet to pursue these questions as if that was what was at issue. Such strategies may score a win for evasion, but they don't offer us any insight about how we might conceive moral boundaries by comparing bee colonies to human societies. The strategy is a distraction aimed at a dismissal.

Given his efforts at distraction, it's somewhat ironic that Wallace-Wells insists that the comparison of bee colony collapse to civilizational destruction is merely "millenarian," yet he then goes on to detail the causes of colony ruin in its clash with a "new breed of insecticide, neonicotinoids, which . . . effectively turned all bees into cigarette fiends." He has a ready-made opportunity to draw an analogy between bee "cigarette fiends," our heedless addiction to fossil fuels, and the disastrous consequences that follow from both. Are such comparisons limited? Sure; but are they no more than indulgent anthropomorphisms aimed at soliciting an emotional response? No; in this case, not only can they show us something about the potential consequences of addiction, as Wallace-Wells must think they can: he himself draws the analogy when he compares bees to cigarette fiends (bees don't smoke for fun). In short, Wallace-Wells wants to deploy comparisons to human behavior when it suits his descriptive objectives, but he wants to discourage anthropomorphizing that might raise questions about the moral status of nonhuman animals and the industries that depend on our willingness to turn a blind eye to their capacity to suffer. He offers his reader no criteria for this selective use of analogies, yet while their use to explain phenomena like bee colony collapse is an imperfect business,[85] "imperfect" does not mean "useless."

Anthropomorphisms are in fact vital to enterprises well beyond the "animation industry" to which Wallace-Wells consigns them (Wallace-Wells,. 152). Frans de Waal argues, for example, that to reject *in toto* their use in the behavioral sciences signals a form of "anthropodenialism," that is, a reactive commitment to human exceptionalism instead of the open mind necessary to doing good science.[86] Even setting aside the value of anthropomorphizing as an avenue for exploring the moral status of nonhuman animals, Wallace-Wells (as well as Epstein) seems to fit Waal's characterization, leaving us to wonder what his hardline "ignore the millenarians" strategy is really for. Fortunately, we needn't go far to discover the answer: in order to preserve the hardline boundary between the fossil fuel industry and animal agriculture, he needs to maintain a rigid, if fictional, moral boundary between human beings and nonhuman animals. His climate crisis solutions can make sense only in the context of one kind of addiction—fossil fuel consumption, not meat-eating. Wallace-Wells needs to cauterize avenues of comparison that might make his solutions to the climate crisis look less promising; he must keep our focus on what's filling our gas tanks, and not "what's for dinner." In short, anthropomorphizing threatens another variety of transgression that Wallace-Wells, like Epstein, cannot afford.

"Anthropodenialist"—an unflattering label and gawky word. Yet, understood in the context of denial^2, it's an apt description of pro-market environmentalists like Wallace-Wells and Mann. Consider, for example, Wallace-Wells' foray into the fraught free will versus determinism debate when, right or wrong, he insists "there's something strange" about the human desire to compare ourselves to critters:

> [i]t's natural, so to speak, to anthropomorphize animals—our whole animation industry is built on it, for starters. But there is something strange, even fatalistic, about such vain beings as ourselves identifying this strongly with creatures who operate so entirely without free will and individual autonomy that many experts in the field aren't sure whether we should think of the bee or the colony as the organism.[87]

That Wallace-Wells is willing to wade, seemingly nonchalantly, into the waters of what on all accounts is a thorny debate about whether there is such a thing as freedom of the will, who has it, how we know, and what it implies, signals just how far he's willing to go to preserve the moral boundary he needs to distinguish human beings and nonhuman animals. It's apparently not sufficient that we're at the "top of the food chain" or even that women and persons of color would be offended at the inclusion of nonhuman animals as rights-bearers. For Wallace-Wells "the capacity for "free will and individual autonomy" is emblematic of human exceptionalism, and thus fixes the moral boundary between those who can act of their own accord and those who, lacking free will, cannot; between those entitled to determine what counts as food, and those whose value lay in being food. Trouble is, the debate about whether there is any such thing as free will, even for human beings, is far from resolved, and the weight of the neurophysiological evidence is not necessarily on our side.[88]

Though there's much more to be said, the mere fact that brains are organs that, like hearts and lungs, are subject to the same laws of nature that ultimately dictate deterioration is cause for suspicion that, short of having an immaterial soul that can survive death, freedom of the will has any home in the human body. Whatever the case, these issues are far more complicated than Wallace-Wells acknowledges. So, we're left to wonder why he wades into such philosophically and neuro-physiologically deep waters other than as a pretext for making his moral boundaries seem obvious: of *course*, human beings have free will. Of *course*, nonhuman animals don't. That he's undeterred by the fact that claims like this are challenged from many quarters only clarifies the purpose of his foray: Wallace-Wells isn't looking to make a meaningful contribution to the debate about the possibility of self-determining action. He just needs "vain beings such as ourselves" to have something to be vain about, so he can legitimate his anthropodenialism.

Wallace-Wells wonders aloud why such "vain beings" would *ever* want to identify with creatures so lacking autonomy that there's no telling whether it's the animal or the collective that counts as the agent of an action. But this tone of insistence feels a bit "protest too much." We might wonder whether what motivates it is confidence that human beings really have free will and nonhuman animals don't, or anxiety borne of the effort to keep a clamoring genie in a bottle—a genie open to the possibility that bees might enjoy some level of sentience and thus some level of autonomy. If so, to then deny the possibility that other nonhuman animals might enjoy the same is anthropodenialism. We can see where this goes: if bees, then maybe cows, chickens, and pigs. The greatest threat to the anthropodenialist, however is this: we needn't resort to anthropomorphizing at all to show that bee-sentience is possible. According to leading neuroscientist Christof Koch:

> Evidence has showed that certainly they [bees] can recognize their beekeeper, so under normal conditions they would never sting their beekeeper because they recognize a combination of visual and olfactory cues . . . Their brain contains roughly a million neurons. By comparison, our brain contains roughly one hundred billion, so 100,000 times more. Yet the complexity of their brain is staggering. Per unit volume, their brain is obviously much less—I mean it's smaller than a piece of quinoa—but the complexity is staggering. It's ten times higher in terms of the density of our cortex. They have all the complicated components that we have in our brains, but in a smaller package. So there's no reason to presuppose there's something radically different about them.[89]

According to Koch, the situation is even scarier (if you're Wallace-Wells): what Koch is "talking about is the potential for sentience in individual bees," not merely the colony. For Wallace-Wells, the prospect of individually sentient bees implies something "fatalistic" in our speculations about bee consciousness. Yet, it only follows if the prospect of transgression—that bee consciousness can be compared to human consciousness *qua individual*—is a threat to human hegemony; and, of course, it is. After all, if nonhuman animal sentience became something, thanks to the sciences, to which we were compelled to pay morally relevant attention even at the level of bees, it could have the effect of drawing further attention to the suffering of nonhuman animals about whose sentience we have no doubt; if bees, what about cows, chickens, pigs, bats, pangolins? In short, capitalism depends on anthropodenialism, but just as the sciences relevant to climate change demonstrate its status as a crisis that we ignore in our fatal complacency, so too the sciences relevant to animal life—zoology, physiology, and so on—demonstrate the fact of our intimate evolutionary relationships with nonhuman beings, potentially even the lives of bees. But we must ignore this too because were sentience permitted to become an obstacle to commodification, the entire edifice of capital would fall.

The upshot for arguments like Wallace-Wells' and Epstein's is thus not especially flattering. Wallace-Wells' gambit to show that we can fix the moral boundary between human beings and nonhuman animals at the juncture of free will fails spectacularly on the science; if it fails at the level of insects, it assuredly fails at the level of mammals. Moreover, his reasoning is circular. Wallace-Wells argues that human beings have free will, that *only* human beings have free will, and therefore nonhuman animals *cannot* have free will. He defines what humans must have in virtue of its presumed absence in nonhuman animals, and then draws the conclusion that it's therefore "strange," even fatalistic," to compare ourselves to nature's effective machines. While there is much to debate concerning free will, the point here is not that Wallace-Wells is right or wrong about whether bee colony collapse can be compared to the demise of human civilization. The point is that the vanity Wallace-Wells ascribes to human beings is not innate disposition in light of facts, but rather anthropodenialism running interference against the disquiet created by the possibility that the commodification of nonhuman animal bodies is immoral. He claims that "[i]t's natural to anthropomorphize nonhuman animals" who "operate entirely without free will," yet he frets over how "strange and fatalistic" it is that we do so.

So too the pre-Civil War slave-holder who discounts the suffering of his human chattel by arguing that it's merely a negligible effect of an institution attuned to the benefit of the slave whose impulses need to be controlled, a duty left to the master who is also, conveniently, liberated to capitalize on the slave's capacity for labor. The slaver goes to great lengths, invoking the providence of God, the history of slavery among the Greeks and the Romans, and Biblical examples such as Abraham to justify the objectification of human beings.[90] Yet, as we might rightly conclude reading Nicole Hannah-Jones exquisite account of the history of slavery in her *1619 Project*, the key difference between the slaver and the anthropodenialist is that the "fatal complacency" that sustained American slavery for 400 years was finally disrupted by the Civil War and the *Emancipation Proclamation*.[91] In stark contrast, arguments for maintaining the commodity status of nonhuman animals are not only alive as ever, but play a key role as an absent referent in market-based solutions to the climate crisis like that offered by Wallace-Wells. In effect, arguments like Wallace-Wells' sustain institutions we know, *and know more every day*, to be cruel and unnecessary. The reason sentience is no obstacle to commodification on his account is because it has been preemptively consigned to the autonomic impulses of creatures absent free will, who can thus be denied to matter at all. If Francione is right, consignment to the morally irrelevant in the face of the obvious capacity for suffering is moral schizophrenia—yet somehow justified by "necessity." Maybe, but suffering hardly matters. As our capacity for that human, all too human form of denial, anthropodenialism, casts the die for an uninhabitable earth, the opportunity for suffering will become equal opportunity—just like the next incarnation of coronavirus, the war over potable water, or the attempt to escape the elements, themselves made monstrous by a climate that never cared about human life, but also no longer favors it.

NOTES

1. Gary L. Francione. "Animals—Property or Persons?" In *Animal Rights: Current Debates and New Directions*. Ed. Cass R. Sunstein, and Martha Nussbaum. (Oxford: Oxford UP, 2004), 108.

2. Francione, 108.

3. Andrew Freedman. "Tornado Outbreak Offers a Grim Climate Warning," *Axios*, 12.13.21. https://www.axios.com/tornado-disaster-kentucky-climate-change-warning-a4c2788c-46fd-4851-a55f-e373798814f9.html.

4. *People for the Ethical Treatment of Animals* (PETA). "What is Vivisection?" https://www.peta.org/features/what-is-vivisection/.

5. Francione, 111.

6. Francione, 113.

7. *National Humane Education Society*. "Government Regulation of Factory Farms." https://www.nhes.org/3372-2/.

8. *ASPCA*. "Oppose Right to Farm Legislation." https://www.aspca.org/improving-laws-animals/public-policy/oppose-right-farm-legislation.

9. Francione, 115.

10. Francione, 117.

11. Francione, 117–8.

12. Francione, 118.

13. Donna Haraway. "Speculative Fabulations for Technoculture's Generations: Taking Care of Unexpected Country." (*Australian Humanities Review*, May 2011), 4.

14. Kenny Torrella and Marina Bolotnikova. "Undercover Audio of a Tyson Employee Reveals 'Free-Range' Chicken is Meaningless." VOX, 8.2.23. https://www.vox.com/future-perfect/23724740/tyson-chicken-free-range-humanewashing-investigation-animal-cruelty.

15. Andreas Malm. *The Progress of this Storm: Nature and Society in a Warming World*. (Brooklyn, NY: Verso, 2020), 114.

16. Malm, 114.

17. Malm, 116.

18. Donna Haraway. "In the Heart of the Storm: An Interview with Donna Haraway; Part 1: Species Being in the Age of Climate Change, Coronavirus, and Capitalism." Science for the People, 23.3. https://magazine.scienceforthepeople.org/vol23-3-bio-politics/in-the-heart-of-the-storm-an-interview-with-donna-haraway/.

19. Maria Padrell, et al. "Invasive Research on Nonhuman Primates—Time to Turn the Page." *National Institutes of Health*, 10.11.21. https://www.ncbi.nlm.nih.gov/pmc/articles/PMC8532895/.

20. Padrell, et al.

21. Sarah Zhang. "America is Running Low on a Crucial Resource for Covid-19 Vaccines." *The Atlantic*, 8.31.20. https://www.theatlantic.com/science/archive/2020/08/america-facing-monkey-shortage/615799/.

22. Padrell, et al.

23. Haraway (2011), 5.

24. Nancy Fraser. Cannibal Capitalism. (Brooklyn, NY: Verso, 2022), 33.

25. Fraser, 11.

26. Maria Lugones. "Toward a Decolonial Feminism." *Hypatia*, 25.4 (Fall, 2010),. 742–759. http://www.iheal.univ-paris3.fr/sites/www.iheal.univ-paris3.fr/files/towards%20a%20decolonial%20feminism.pdf), 742

27. Lugones, 742.

28. Jackson Ryan. “CRISPR Gene-Editing Tool Used Inside Humans for the First Time.” *CNeT*, 3.4.20. https://www.cnet.com/news/crispr-gene-editing-tool-used-inside-humans-for-the-first-time/.

29. Alex Marson, et al. “CRISPR-Based Enhancers of DNA Vaccines for Covid-19.” Innovative Genomics Institute. https://innovativegenomics.org/projects/crispr-based-dna-vaccine-enhancer-covid-19/.

30. Lonnie Wong. “Researchers at UC Davis Use Rhesus Monkeys to Understand Long-Term Efficacy of Covid-19 Vaccines.” https://fox40.com/news/local-news/researchers-at-uc-davis-use-rhesus-monkeys-to-understand-long-term-efficacy-of-covid-19-vaccines/.

31. Emma Newburger. “A Major Antarctic Ice Shelf Could Shatter within Five Years, Scientists Warn.” CNBC, 12.13.21. https://www.cnbc.com/2021/12/13/a-major-antarctic-ice-shelf-could-shatter-within-five-years.html.

32. Wendy Lynne Lee. “Dewey and Climate Denial^{2}.” *Philosophy Now*, Issue 135, December 2019, 16–20. https://philosophynow.org/issues/135/Dewey_and_Climate_Denial_Squared, 16.

33. Nicole Fallert. “A Man Was Arrested for Allegedly Threatening to Kill Anthony Fauci and His Family.” Buzzfeed News, 7.27.21. https://www.buzzfeednews.com/article/nicolefallert/dr-fauci-death-threats.

34. Carolyn Fortuna. “The Deception Continues as Companies Hide Behind Fake Environmental Promises.” *CleanTechnica*, 11.23.21. https://cleantechnica.com/2021/11/23/the-deception-continues-as-companies-hide-behind-fake-environmental-promises/.

35. *Smithfield Farms*. “Helping Hungry Homes.” https://www.smithfieldfoods.com/Philanthropy.

36. Richard Epstein. “Animals as Objects, or Subjects, or Rights.” In *Animal Rights: Current Debates and New Directions*. Ed. Cass R. Sunstein, and Martha Nussbaum. (Oxford: Oxford UP, 2004), 148–9.

37. Epstein, 155.

38. Epstein, 144.

39. Epstein, 145–6.

40. Epstein, 148.

41. Epstein, 149.

42. Epstein, 150.

43. *Refugees International*. “Marking Two Years of Taliban Oppression: Statement from the U.S. Policy Advocates for Afghan Women and Girls,” 8.15.23. https://www.refugeesinternational.org/statements-and-news/marking-2-years-of-taliban-oppression-statement-from-the-u-s-policy-advocates-for-afghan-women-and-girls/.

44. *The Paisano, Editorial Board*. “Texas Fuels Patriarchy with New Abortion Law,” 9.7.21. https://paisano-online.com/26836/opinion/editorial/texas-fuels-patriarchy-with-new-abortion-law/.

45. *Stop the Traffik*. https://www.stopthetraffik.org/about-human-trafficking/the-scale-of-human-trafficking/.

46. Epstein, 150.

47. Epstein, 157.

48. David Wallace-Wells. *The Uninhabitable Earth*. (New York, NY: Tim Duggan Books, 2019), 226.

49. Wallace-Wells, 226.

50. Wallace-Wells, 226–7.

51. Epstein, 151.

52. Wallace-Wells, 224–5.

53. Wallace-Wells, 220.

54. David Wallace-Wells. "The Cautious Case for Climate Optimism." *The Intelligencer, New York Magazine*, 2.4.19. https://nymag.com/intelligencer/2019/02/book-excerpt-the-uninhabitable-earth-david-wallace-wells.html.

55. Wallace-Wells, 2019.

56. Wallace-Wells, 220.

57. Wallace-Wells, 220.

58. Wallace-Wells, 214.

59. Wallace-Wells, 227.

60. Wallace-Wells, 226–7.

61. Ashley Dawson. *Extinction: A Radical History*. (New York, NY: OR Books, 2016), 7.

62. Wallace-Wells, 6.

63. *Teach U.S. History.org*. "A Pro-Slavery Letter by S. Trott." http://www.teachushistory.org/second-great-awakening-age-reform/resources/pro-slavery-letter-s-trott.

64. Epstein, 151.

65. Carol Adams. *Neither Man nor Beast: Feminism and the Defense of Animals*. (Brooklyn, NY: Lantern Books, 2015), 74.

66. Fraser, 34.

67. Mark Stoll. *Profit: An Environmental History*. (Cambridge, UK: Polity Press, 2023), 68

68. Stoll, 68.

69. Wendy Lynne Lee. *Contemporary Feminist Theory and Activism: Six Global Issues*. (Peterborough, Canada: Broadview Press, 2010), 204.

70. Wendy Lynne Lee. *This is Environmental Ethics*. (Hoboken, NJ: Wiley Blackwell, 2023), 288.

71. Lee (2010), 204–5.

72. Jennifer Schuessler. "Bans on Critical Race Theory Threaten Free Speech." *New York Times*, 11.8.21. https://www.nytimes.com/2021/11/08/arts/critical-race-theory-bans.html.

73. Skyler Caruso. "Everything to Know About the Bud Light Controversy." *People Magazine*, 7.19.23. https://people.com/bud-light-controversy-everything-to-know-7547159.

74. Alex Woodward. "DeSantis Once Again Defends Slavery Curriculum: Enslaved People 'Showing Resourcefulness' Developed 'Skills.'" Independent, 8.7.23. https://www.the-independent.com/news/world/americas/us-politics/desantis-slavery-florida-response-b2388923.html.

75. Greg Graziosi. "Anheuser-Busch Criticized for Statement Appearing to Apologize for Dylan Mulvaney's Bud Light campaign." *Independent*, 4.15.23. https://www.independent.co.uk/news/world/americas/anheuser-busch-dylan-mulvaney-statement-criticised-b2320459.html.

76. Helen Reid. "Target Pride Backlash Exposes 'Rainbow Capitalism' Problem, Designer Says." *Reuters*, 5.31.23. https://www.reuters.com/business/retail-consumer/target-pride-backlash-exposes-rainbow-capitalism-problem-designer-says-2023-05-31/.

77. Malm, 221.

78. Epstein, 151.

79. Epstein, 151.

80. Wallace-Wells, 6–7.

81. Josephine Donovan. "Animal Rights and Feminist Theory," *Signs*, Vol. 15.2 (Winter, 1990). https://fewd.univie.ac.at/fileadmin/user_upload/inst_ethik_wiss_dialog/Donovan__J._1990._AR_and_Feminist_Theorie.pdf.

82. Peter Singer. "All Animals Are Equal." *Philosophic Exchange*, 5.1, Article 6. https://digitalcommons.brockport.edu/cgi/viewcontent.cgi?article=1179&context=phil_ex

83. George Yancy, and Peter Singer. "Peter Singer: On Racism, Animal Rights, and Human Rights," *Opinionator: New York Times*, 5.27.15. https://opinionator.blogs.nytimes.com/2015/05/27/peter-singer-on-speciesism-and-racism/.

84. Wallace-Wells, 152.

85. Julian Davies. "Anthropomorphism in Science." *National Library of Medicine, National Institutes of Health*, 10.11.2010. https://www.ncbi.nlm.nih.gov/pmc/articles/PMC2948194/.

86. Scott Sleek. "Why Anthropomorphism is Not a Scientific Sin." *Association for Psychological Science*, 4.30.19. https://www.psychologicalscience.org/observer/why-anthropomorphism-is-not-a-scientific-sin.

87. Wallace-Wells, 152.

88. Andrea Lavazza. "Free Will and Neuroscience: From Explaining Freedom Away to New Ways of Operationalizing and Measuring It." *Frontiers in Human Neuroscience*, 6.1.16. https://www.frontiersin.org/articles/10.3389/fnhum.2016.00262/full.

89. Cristoph Koch. "How Do We Wrap Our Minds Around Bee Consciousness?" *To the Best of Our Knowledge*, 7.28.18. https://www.ttbook.org/interview/how-do-we-wrap-our-minds-around-bee-consciousness.

90. U.S. History.org. "The Southern Argument for Slavery." https://www.ushistory.org/us/27f.asp.

91. Nikole Hannah-Jones. "The 1619 Project." *New York Times Magazine*, August, 2019. https://www.nytimes.com/interactive/2019/08/14/magazine/1619-america-slavery.html.

Chapter 6

"Webs of Life" and Death in the Kleptocene

"As Food," the "Four Cheaps," and Jason Moore's (Unwitting) Invitation to the Geo-Logic of the "Black Anthropocene"

"A STRIDENT CURRENT OF DISSOLUTIONISM"

Jason Moore gets so much right in his full-throttle critique of what he calls the *Capitalocene*, it's almost painful to discover that what he gets wrong results in an undermining distortion of his argument in *Capitalism in the Web of Life*. Nonetheless, by conflating *property* dualism with Descartes's *metaphysical* dualism in the critique of capitalism, by disregarding the pivotal role played by the commodification of sentience in the history of capital conquest, and by misinterpreting as an *era*, the Capitalocene, as opposed to a *stage* in the evolution of the Kleptocene, Moore misconstrues vital elements of the ontology of capital in capital*ism*. In short, Moore overlooks the intimately connected drivers of capital accumulation during its journey long *before* the "long sixteenth century." Mark Stoll sets the stage: "[c]apitalism has no single place or time of origin," but, Stoll continues, there are themes—extraction, communication, cooperation, competition, exploitation, commodification, invention—common to each kleptocratic turn-of-the-wheel toward the fully capitalized planet.[1] Moore does share a point of departure with Wallace-Wells and Mann: identifying capitalism as the primary, if not only, actor responsible for the devastation of the planet and its atmosphere. And Moore's work could have been revolutionary as opposed to merely reformist in virtue of his resistance to rehabilitative schemes that leave capital chastened (for a time) but intact. Moore's work seems a promising alternative to his contemporaries, and in some important ways this is true. What makes for disappointment, however, is that the historical breadth of his account of the ways in which "the manifold projects of capital, empire, and science are busy making Nature with a capital 'N'—external, controllable, reducible" assumes an undermining falsehood. While capital, empire, and science may "make Nature" in the sense that each offers different and often competing *concepts* of nature, nature itself, as Andreas Malm shows, is an independent entity and must be conceived as such for any critique of capitalism to make sense:

> Labour and nature possess an ineradicable *autonomy* from capital. Both are ontologically prior to it, antedate its appearance on earth, have a history as long as human history in the former case and geological history in the latter operating in accord to their own laws, and however hard ruling classes have subsequently sought to control them . . . that autonomy persists below the surface, even when the volcanoes seem dormant.[2]

In short, by treating nature as "Nature," that is, as the "manifold projects of capital, empire, and science," Moore conflates the concept of "nature" with its material reality, and thereby undermines the *ontological* conditions any critique of the Capitalocene requires to make sense of capitalism's impacts on the planet and its atmosphere, namely, the independence of nonhuman nature. He goes on to claim that, "the web of life is busy shuffling about the biological and geological conditions of capitalism's process."[3] But there would be no shuffling without the material conditions supplied by a nonhuman nature that predates and will post-date the resource theft that characterizes the Kleptocene. Profit ventures require a material reality to extract; resource theft is meaningless without resources to expropriate and extract. To argue that "Nature" is a creation of "capital, empire, and science" doesn't put the cart before the horse, *it vanquishes the horse*. It's hard to imagine a clearer example of the human chauvinism Moore rejects. After all, if "Nature" is determined by a conceptual creation made by and for human interests, what isn't? He might respond that he's referring not to nature, but to the "Nature" to which we have *epistemic* access. But this isn't much help since he provides no acknowledgement that the "Nature" we create for our capitalist projects is something other than nature, the autonomous material force that will outlast even the most crushing anthropogenic catastrophe.

Indeed, it's dispiriting to discover that Moore's radical aspirations falter on the shoals of what is essentially the same chauvinism as his fellows. But that is where we arrive once we see that the key organizing concepts of his historical analysis, especially, Society/Nature, "Human/Extra-human" and the "Four Cheaps," effectively re-inscribe what Malm calls a hybridist concept of "Nature" onto the reality of nature via the same logic of domination that Moore argues must be dismantled as a bulwark premise of capital's imaginary, the "web of life."[4] Put differently: Moore's historical account is undercut by a basic misunderstanding of the *relationship* between the pursuit of capital and nonhuman nature, a misbegotten narrative that originates in his appeal to René Descartes. Moore aims to dismantle Descartes' substance dualism, that is, the view that minds and bodies are two entirely different kinds of substances, that they occupy two metaphysically separate domains. But Moore also takes at face value that the way we conceive of the relationship between society and nature mirrors the Cartesian dualism that distinguishes minds from bodies. Hence, he argues that the use of the conjunction "and" can only misrepresent the relationship of society to nature, and therefore must be replaced by "society-in-nature" to correctly capture their mutually implicative "dynamic" as opposed to reinforcing the idea that society and nature are two distinct "substances." In short, if capital, empire, and science in fact *make* Nature, *but* if "society and nature" are conceived as two metaphysically distinct substances, Cartesian dualism must be abandoned as a faulty if not false representation of the nature/society relationship.

At first glance, Moore's argument against dualism feels compelling. After all, dualism does have a history that reaches back at least to the Ancient Greek's mind over body, men over women, citizen over slave, and human over nonhuman animals. But the problem is that not all forms of dualism are necessarily *substance* dualism. That two things are distinct in virtue of having different *properties* does not necessarily imply that they're different *kinds* of things or that they occupy different realities. If they did, there would be no basis for conflict or the struggle to *establish difference* because that difference would be given. But what the vast majority of dualistic thinking reflects *is* the struggle to justify mastery and subjugation in virtue of differing *properties*. Moore, however, anchors his critique of Nature and Society to substance dualism, the "famous argument about the separation of the mind and body," *and thus* "society and nature."[5] But whereas we rightly understand mind and body to occupy two mutually exclusive realities for Descartes, the same reasoning does not apply to nature and society since, while they may have differing properties, they do not occupy differing realities. Indeed, we can debate the merits of Descartes's substance dualism with respect to minds and bodies without any need to debate the relationship between society and nature; it's given that the latter pair have differing properties, but that conflicts arise *because* they occupy a single reality. Carolyn Merchant provides a clear picture of this distinction. As she spells out in her masterwork, *The Death of Nature*, even Descartes articulates a *concept* of nature whose properties are ready-made for the machinations of capital (Merchant, 0980). As Andreas Malm puts it:

> Carolyn Merchant traces the historical shift from a conception of nature as a mother to be revered and respected, an organic living being . . . to one of nature as a dead, inert object to be manipulated and controlled with maximum efficiency . . . *The Death of Nature* departs from the postulate that "natural and cultural subsystems" develop "in dynamic interaction." . . . Built into the emerging capitalist market economy was *an inexorably accelerating force of expansion and accumulation*, achieved, over the long term, *at the expense of the environment.*[6]

What Merchant shows is that the concept of nature to which capitalism gives rise is a radically different concept—a different set of properties—than that of more ancient peoples. Descartes's concept of the dead and inert makes nature vulnerable to the extraction and commodification that defines the ontology of capital as resource theft. In other words, while the material properties of nonhuman nature have been expropriated by a capitalist ontology whose aim is to convert whatever value we ascribe to them into exchange value, this does not imply that "Nature" is a creation of capital. Capitalism does not, for Merchant, instantiate "natural and cultural subsystems" in dynamic interaction, but rather establishes the conversion of all value into exchange value "at the expense of the environment." That the environment is a separate an independent entity does not imply a substance dualism that must be overcome in order to comprehend the relationship between the planet's material conditions and the exploits of capital. Rather, it simply implies a dualism where, regardless the way we conceive it (living or dead), nature is rightly understood as separate such that in the pursuit of profit we can do grave damage to its systems and capacity to support life. Such is not a "natural and cultural subsystem," but instead, as Nancy Fraser might put it, a capitalist culture that has effectively granted permission to the capitalist to conceive of nature as "dead," beyond harm, and suitable for the extraction of its wealth. For Merchant what is clear is that it only makes sense to talk about differing concepts of nature on the grounds that there is one set of material conditions, one reality whose destruction impacts its ecologies and the lives of its inhabitants.

What appears reasonable at first glance in Moore's foundational arguments with respect to the way we conceive the relationship between nature and society disintegrates once we see that the independence of nature does not require a metaphysics rooted in substance dualism that must be rejected in order to move forward. Moore argues "[t]he old language—Nature/Society—has become obsolete," and that "[r]eality has overwhelmed the binary's capacity to help us track the real changes unfolding, accelerating, amplifying before our eyes."[7] But it's not reality that has overwhelmed the Nature/Society binary; it's that the binary along with its countless layers of relationship has been hijacked by a capitalist ontology by which we're enculturated to believe that the properties of nonhuman nature exist to suffice our self-interest, are resources *for* us, that their supply is endless, and that their capacity for commodification needn't be jeopardized by any moral consideration of their status as alive or dead, organic or inorganic, sentient or inert. What Merchant shows (and Malm endorses) is the extent to which capitalism replaces our concept of material reality, and thus our enculturated experience of it, with one designed to support its ravenous need to grow or die. Nothing about this replacement is less material in nature (literally); it is simply chauvinistic and, in consequence, anthropogenic. Perhaps the "old" language of Nature/Society has become obsolete, but this isn't because it was rooted in substance dualism, but simply because in its confrontation with the real consequences of capitalist extractivism its myths have been shown to be false as well as destructive. What we know is that the reason the ontology of capital requires an enculturated denial of its destructive impacts for human and nonhuman nature is because capitalism is not an incarnation of Nature/Society, but rather a system of commodifying exploitation of a planet that will continue *as a planet* long after the capitalists are dead and gone. We know that the hierarchically ordered dualisms of which capital takes advantage may commit to subjugation one side of each binary pair, human over nonhuman, male over female, global North over global South, rich over poor, white over black, in virtue of properties whose assignment conforms to the logic of commodification. We know that the violence subjugation produces cannot be dissolved by claiming that, since substance dualism is false, the hybrids that replace it will be emancipatory.

Perhaps Moore could respond to this critique that the existential threat posed by the climate crisis is the reality that's bound to push the "old" language out of the way, making way for the reckoning of just how destructive Nature-in-Society has become. This would make sense if the "old" language reflected the Cartesian metaphysics Moore ascribes to it; that is, if Descartes's substance dualism really did govern our view of nature and therefore needed to be replaced by the hybrid, Nature-in-Society. But Cartesian substance dualism does not govern our view of nature; hence Moore's remedy is for the wrong disease. In fact, *Moore's remedy ignores the patient*. Nature-in-Society effectively *naturalizes* whatever human agents do, making anthropogenic climate change into as much a feature of nature as plate tectonics or photosynthesis. The reduction of "anthropogenic" to "Society-in-Nature" is, in other words, *deterministic*. There's nothing against which to do combat, nothing to mitigate: climate change just is the evolution of the Kleptocene, and the Kleptocene is no more than a reflection of the "Human-Society dynamic" that, naturalized as a Nature-in-Society that could have gone no other direction than ecological nihilism.

To be clear: Descartes *is* wrong; the world cannot be divided into two entirely separate substances, minds and bodies, that somehow interact. The planet is not dead and inert. *But capitalism is not committed to substance dualism, and this matters*. Moore could argue that the "new" vocabulary of mitigation, adaptation, and sustainability will supplant the "old" vocabulary by demonstrating the hybrid character of the Nature-in-Society relationship. But we have good reason to believe capitalism will continue to advantage itself via the dualisms that sustain it long after we bury Descartes. We have seen this "new" script in Wallace-Wells' and Mann's reformist proposals—sans substance dualism or its critique. That Moore conceives his own project as revolutionary as opposed to reformist doesn't save him from misconstruing what the "old" language is *for*: maintaining the social structures that benefit capitalist enterprise. The only "unfolding, accelerating, amplifying" that can matter to capitalism is either that which can be monetized to exploit a crisis or that which must be denied, if not otherwise defused, because it threatens to impede economic growth. Moore should not find it surprising that "a new language—one that comprehends the irreducibly dialectical relation between human and extra-human natures in the web of life—has yet to emerge." Why? *Because there is no "new" language*; or, better, there no compelling reason to retire the old language of an independent nature that can be impacted by the actions of human beings. While reality will eventually overwhelm the Nature/Society binary, it won't be because any "new language" will make the appraisal of this "reality" more possible than the "old" vocabulary of carbon trading or mitigation. Insofar as the premises of this "new language," "the irreducibly dialectical relation between human and extra-human natures in the web of life" themselves form a binary pair, their relation is destined to reproduce the same systemic erasure of sentience as a bar to commodification as does the old language. Why? First, because Moore reinscribes the binary pairs he rejects; second, as Malm shows, Moore "has fundamentally misunderstood the requirements for transcending the Cartesian legacy."[8]

Put differently: Malm argues that Moore's strategy for avoiding "the original sin of Cartesian dualism" ultimately results in both the rejection of the Nature/Society binary and its reinforcement. To see this, consider Moore's vocabulary strategy: "Moore wants the 'and' replaced with 'in.' It should be labour-in-nature, capital-in-nature, and so on—never *and*, the false bridge that betrays a worldview of nature/society as two hemispheres divided by a chasm . . . capitalism does not *have* an ecological regime, it *is* an ecological regime."[9] According to Moore, the result is a "world ecology" that offers a "superior dialectical framework" in part because it has defeated Cartesian dualism.[10] But, argues Malm, Moore's swap of the "old" for the "new" vocabulary is question-begging:

> Moore faults [John Belamy] Foster and colleagues for using the word "interaction" to describe the relation between nature and society, since this wrongly presupposes that the two can be separated to begin with—for two things to interact, they must first be apart—and proposes that we should instead ask how the two "*fit* together." But exactly the same critique can of course be levelled against that choice of words. For two pieces to fit together, they must first be two different pieces. Moore himself seems forced to employ the foul conjunction in phrases such as "human *and* extra-human nature, the soil *and* the worker," perhaps because a language of permanent in-hyphenation would be unreadable. It certainly would not solve any real conceptual problems.[11]

In short, use of the word "and" need not raise the ghost of Cartesian substance dualism; in fact, in the context of society and nature, its use merely recognizes the reality of an independent nature that can be affected by human action—the premise Moore requires to mount his critique of capitalism.

Malm argues that the reason Moore "fundamentally" misunderstands what is necessary to "transcend the Cartesian legacy" is that "there is nothing Cartesian about saying," for example, "labor and nature."[12] The only case where Descartes's malignant ghost would arise would be where what was claimed was that "labour and nature consisted of different substances or inhabited separate spheres, so that one could be analyzed without reference to the other."[13] But nothing in the critique of capitalism requires substance dualism; showing that the ontology of capital is kleptocratic—*ideologically dependent upon material resource theft*—and for that reason ecologically devastating with respect to human and nonhuman nature, undermines Moore's "hybridist" view. In short, there is no coherent critique of capitalism without reference to its independent material conditions. Moore is essentially arguing against a dualism that's irrelevant to that which advantages the capitalist, or as Malm puts it, Moore's approach "is comparable to denying that your heart is both an integral part of your body and a distinct organ with unique features and functions"; but, of course, your heart is both.[14] Moore's "superior dialectical framework" thus

> turns out to be a double collapse, such as in the following precis of his [hybridist] view: "Capitalism makes nature. Nature makes capitalism." Neither of these propositions is true. Capitalism emphatically does not make nature; nature most definitely does not make capitalism. It is the utter disharmony between the two that needs to be accounted for . . .[15]

In other words, if capitalism made nature and nature made capitalism—if nature and capitalism were really just mirror images of one another—the grounds for critique dissolve. Malm refers to hybridist arguments like

Moore's as "a strident current of dissolutionism":[16] "With no laws of society and no laws of nature—what is there left to study?"[17]

HUMAN/EXTRA-HUMAN

Among the binary pairs Moore introduces into his analysis of capitalism is "human/extra-human" whose role it is to replace Nature/Society on the premise that such a replacement advances, as Malm describes it, Moore's "hybridist" project. But, as we'll see, it's this binary, "human/extra-human," that lays bare a second distortion that discolors the argument in *Capitalism in the Web of Life*. In short, the way in which Moore articulates the relationship between the human and the "extra-human" precludes the pivotal role played by the sentient nonhuman in the logic of commodification. Indeed, by tacitly conceding to the capitalist the systemic omission of sentience as a barrier to commodification, Moore effectively authorizes the logic he seeks to undermine. Moore argues that:

> [v]alue-relations are a *systemic* phenomenon with a pivotal economic moment . . . [This] allows us to connect the production and accumulation of surplus value with its necessary conditions of reproduction. It recognizes, moreover, that these conditions extend beyond the circuit of capital: the accumulation of abstract social labor is possible through the appropriation of unpaid work (human and extra-human) . . . Importantly, capital's appropriation of unpaid work transcends the Cartesian divide, encompassing both human and extra-human work outside, but necessary to, the circuit of capital and the production of value.[18]

Leaving to one side, for now, Moore's faulty view of Cartesian dualism, what troubles his account of work is that while he's right that value-relations within capitalism are a "systemic phenomenon," to represent unpaid work as the province of the human *and the extra-human* requires the exclusion of the sentient nonhuman from the extra-human. Why? *It would be nonsense to depict sentient nonhuman animals as engaged in unpaid work.* "Unpaid" makes sense only where we can make sense of "paid"; while a chimpanzee may be rewarded for performing a complex task, being *paid* involves a wide set of concepts—currency, wage, time intervals, what distinguishes a "job" from "play" or leisure is, as far as we know, beyond the conceptual wherewithal of the chimp.

Whatever Moore intends by "extra-human," there's no other species of entity on earth besides human beings for whom the concept of "labor" or "unpaid labor" makes sense other than metaphorically, and that's not the sense in which Moore appears to intend it. Evidence suggests, for example, that bees may enjoy some level of consciousness, are sentient, and we sometimes describe honey making as "labor." But the bee is neither paid nor unpaid; nor do any of the attendant concepts such as "wages" or "overtime" apply other than figuratively to the bee, the bee hive, or bees as a species. These terms have no more literal application in this case than for maple trees producing syrup, or ants building hills. Anthropomorphizing is certainly an important explanatory tool both within and outside of the sciences, but this isn't because being part of the "circuit of capital" magically grants consciousness to rivers or mountains. Perhaps we could conceive nonhuman animals as extra-human in the sense that they're not homo Sapiens, but this does not capture what Moore appears to mean. While it's true that the exploitation of nonhuman animals is, like unpaid labor, "outside, but necessary to, the circuit of capital and the production of value," we'd hardly regard being prodded with a stun gun down a cattle kill-chute, being injected with bovine growth hormone, or being confined in a porcine birthing box as "labor," unpaid or paid. Such forms of coercion are not cruel because they're unpaid; they're cruel because they cause unnecessary suffering to sentient creatures. Kamran Nayeri makes this point starkly clear in his review of *Capitalism in the Web of Life* arguing that:

> If appropriated unpaid work is centrally important to capitalist accumulation and by appropriation we understand the dictionary definition ("The action of taking something for one's own use, typically without the owner's permission") then how can we view those who have been subjected to appropriation as "co-producers"? In 2011, more than 58 billion chickens, nearly 3 billion ducks, and some 1.38 billion pigs were slaughtered worldwide to be sold as food. Other farm animals slaughtered for food numbered in the hundreds of millions (turkeys, geese and guinea fowl, sheep, goats and cattle . . . It is clear that the meat industry quite consciously "worked through" nature by enslaving, torturing and mass murdering these billions of non-human animals. Should we call their victims "co-producers" of the capitalist meat industry? To what end?[19]

In short, Moore's concept of the extra-human requires him to take one of three untenable positions: (1) the systemic omission of the nonhuman sentient in favor of making everything a potential "co-producer"; (2) the lumping-all-into-one-category sentient and non-sentient in order to make everything a "co-producer"; or (3) the treating of everything sentient or non-sentient as an agent thus making everything a "co-producer." Obviously, these all come to the same: a reductionism to the catch-all "co-producer" made for Moore's "hybridist" view of Nature/Society, or as Nayeri puts it:

> Moore's methodology and theory that aim at combining social and natural categories by privileging contributions to capitalist accumulation from "unpaid

> work of human and extra-human nature" is incoherent. There is no way to reconcile the labor theory of value (or indeed any "theory of value") and appropriated flows of work/energy because the former is about the laws of motion of the capitalist mode of production and the latter obey the laws of physics.[20]

In other words, any theory aiming to explain "the laws of motion of the capitalist mode of production" that fails to recognize that such laws are ontologically distinct from the laws of physics that govern not work, but energy, is doomed to incoherence; *energy is not an agent*.

Put differently: factory farm workers may be harmed by poorly paid grueling labor, but they retain an agency that "farm animals slaughtered for food" numbering in "the hundreds of millions" do not and will not have. And we might go even further than Nayeri: Moore's conflation of work/energy actually contributes to the potential for cruelty. If both worker and farm animal are simply sites of exchange value—co-producers—in the generation of capital that is the factory farm, agency is entirely meaningless regardless to whom or what we attribute it. We could just as well attribute it to the stun gun or the butchering machinery. By authorizing an ontology whose governing premises require the omission of sentience as an obstacle to commodification, Moore effectively re-inscribes the logics of domination and commodification onto the "circuit" of capital, itself reductionist and deterministic insofar as it can make no place for agency or culpability. The human/extra-human binary *contributes* to the erasure of the value of sentience by conflating the sentient nonhuman and the non-sentient nonhuman. As Nayeri explains:

> [Moore] writes: "The concept of work/energy looms large in this argument [for the human/extra-human configuration of our relationship to nature]. . . . Work/energy helps us to rethink capitalism as a set of relations through which the 'capacity to do work'—by human and extra-human natures—is transformed into value, understood as socially necessary labor-time (abstract social labor)," (p. 14). However, this way of overcoming theoretical/analytical incongruency forces Moore to suggest that not only humans or other animals, but rivers, waterfalls, or forests also "work."[21]

As Malm puts it, these are the "new materialists." They make the "audacious claim" that "*inanimate matter* has as much agency as humans."[22] As Nayeri would likely agree, such a notion so thoroughly dilutes the concept of agency—and therefore culpability—that it makes a mockery of the critique of capitalism as a critique of the ways in which ecological crises like climate change are *anthropogenic*. If what "anthropogenic" means is not merely responsibility but *culpability*, it makes sense to say the fire is *responsible* for burning down the house referring to the physics of conflagration, but we'd not say (other than figuratively) that the fire was angry and vengeful. Similarly, we can say the stunned cow's body is responsible for spraying blood all over the slaughterhouse floor—but we'd be daft to blame the dying cow.

In short, the reality of the nonhuman sentient so undermines Moore's conception of paid and unpaid labor as to render the human/extra-human binary incoherent. The binary necessitates the reduction of extra-human to a conception of labor that hinges either on an "extra-human" cognitively equipped to perform labor or on the erasure of agency altogether. *But nonhuman sentient animals exist.* As such, their cries inevitably disrupt a "web of life" in which agency and even life are reduced to something that, insofar as agency is erased, looks more like Descartes's inert and infinitely pliable matter than a web of *life*. While Moore takes for granted the agency of human actors, he actually leaves no place among his binary pairs, paid/unpaid, human/extra-human, for agency to facilitate action. But human agency is not only a real thing, it's a necessary condition for the critique of capitalism as the product of culpable agency. As Malm puts it, "humans appear to have a special ability to think about their own thoughts and, crucially, about the thoughts of others" and only human beings "produce tools *for the production of other tools*."[23] Or, consider Nayeri who situates a similar observation even more directly in the critique of Moore: "[t]he problem here is not dualism but the recognition that to understand humanity we must understand humans not simply as biological beings but also as social beings who have unique powers to manipulate nature, including human nature, and to try to understand why in class societies, in particular industrial capitalism, these powers have come to debase life as we know it."[24]

Leaving no room for human agency and the class-based capitalist societies for which it is culpable, is, however, only one side of the Human/Extra-Human coin that spells trouble for Moore. By failing to include the nonhuman sentient in his analysis of labor, Moore misses one of the most crucial elements in the ontology of capital: the systemic elision of sentience as an obstacle *to the conversion of all value to exchange value*. The disarticulation of sentient nonhuman animal bodies materializes the disarticulation of value and thereby facilitates this conversion. It is the factory farm, the circus, the zoo, the lab that divorces nonhuman animals as objects of exchange from people understood as workers and consumers. As Cora Diamond shows, it's not suffering or its absence that supplies the reason we don't eat other human beings; it's because nonhuman animals, sentience notwithstanding, aren't people. While factory farm wage laborers may not be on the menu, their suffering counts for little more than the animals they're charged with "processing," and for the same reason: the logic of commodification nullifies the value of *suffering* even as it preserves an agency that it can put to the advance of capitalist interest. Agency, however, is also risky for the capitalist. Agents can resist commodification; they can demand higher wages and better working conditions. Such variables must be accommodated as potential costs within the kleptocratic calculus, creating even greater pressure to discount sentience as an additional expense. In short, what makes the subjugation of the working classes possible, thus emancipating the capitalist to advance the profit motive, isn't the conflation of agency with energy, but rather the systemic erasure of that which human beings and nonhuman animals have in common—the capacity to suffer.

Malm gets it right, but doesn't go quite far enough when he writes that "the history of capital is *the history of the successive attempts of the capitalist class to emancipate itself from the working class*,"[25] and further: "[t]he history of capital is thus also the history of successive attempts of the capitalist class to emancipate itself from nature."[26] Malm's right in both cases, but, somewhat like Moore, Malm implicitly conflates "nonhuman animal" with "nature" as if the sentience of the latter were of no import to the ontology of capital. Consider: capital seeks to achieve these emancipatory goals through the invention of machines that can replace and/or subdue labor and subdue and/or replace nature.[27] Mark Stoll provides a classic example of these dynamics in his discussion of James Watt and the steam-powered engine: "Steam engines let manufacturers conveniently locate factories near labor, transportation, and services, rather than where falling water or blowing wind provided power."[28] That is, the invention of the steam engine replaces falling water and blowing wind as a source of energy and, in so doing, subdues labor who will now, more than ever, be harnessed to the steam engine's superior capacity to drive production and to the location of the factory floor. The steam engine was hugely profitable for a time. Yet, like every other technology that depends upon labor and nature, argues Malm, the invention of such machines inevitably confronts capitalism as a "*self-contradictory, self-undermining enterprise*":

> [T]he only weapons capital can use for bringing down labour and nature are, of course, labour and nature. When it introduces a new technology for subsuming them, that force is predicated on the work of *other* workers and on the functionality of *other* substrata than those it serves to control, displace, absorb or process faster. Capital . . . seeks to emancipate itself from workers only to be drawn back into their inescapable net. The machine is the fulcrum of this impossible quest.[29]

Once again, Stoll provides a compelling historical example:

> The cotton textile industry had far-reaching consequences for the natural environment. Cotton mills operated at the end of a production process that began on American slave plantations . . . Suddenly very profitable, cotton plantations multiplied across the southern U.S. for half a century, often on land from which Cherokees, Creeks, and Choctaws had been removed or driven . . . In stifling

> heat and humidity, slaves cleared rich bottomlands of thick forests and undergrowth, then plowed, planted, thinned, weeded, wormed, and harvested cotton in an exhausting yearlong cycle . . . When emancipation in 1865 ended plantation gang labor and led to sharecropping and tenancy, the system collapsed . . . The South spiraled into poverty and soil into gullied exhaustion.[30]

It's hard to imagine a more "self-contradictory, self-undermining" enterprise than cotton production in the slave states toward the end and just after the American Civil War. Highly profitable for plantation owners, but dependent on the institution of slavery, the agency that ignited a civil war exposed the internal contradictions of a system ultimately unable to subdue or replace either the topsoil exhausted by over-planting or the labor emancipated by violent conflict over the agency of its enslaved "gang labor." But what makes institutions like slavery possible is the commodification of sentience; it is this defining feature of the ontology of capital that facilitates the treatment of human beings and families as chattel and machine, and it's this ontology that paves the way to the forced removal, starvation, and genocide of the indigenous peoples that had occupied these lands. Represented not as people but as an obstacle to establishing a plantation, the Cherokees, Creeks, and Choctaws are "cleared" as if no different than the forest that once cover the "rich bottomlands," the value of sentience having long been replaced by the profit promised by the cotton gin.

I suggest that a more illuminating and actionable account of the kleptocratic ontology of capitalism, one that captures its logic and history as a system of commodification for profit capable of destroying the planet's actual web of life, begins in two questions: how does the logic of domination fuel the logic of commodification? How does the concept "Nature" come to be *made* such that it can advantage the capitalist quest for endless profit and endless expansion? The answers begin and end—conceptually, historically, and for an overwhelmed reality—in a set of straightforward ontological precepts; capitalist enterprise must:

- Extract exchange value from nature regardless its particular material reality; sentient or non-sentient, organic/inorganic, living/nonliving, such distinctions are irrelevant other than in the agency of the capitalist whose authority is reinforced through the logic of domination.
- Recognize that there are no exceptions or exemptions to the logic of commodification.
- Conceive "Nature" as an inexhaustible treasure trove of extractible resources and a bottomless waste repository. It must also forget or systematically ignore the fact that the "Nature" "made" for capital is not nature. While extractible resources such as hydrocarbons, clean water,

and arable soil are exhaustible, nature itself will endure long after the capitalist "web of life" has rotted away.

- Naturalize the logic of domination *as* a logic of commodification. Insofar as advantage accrues to the capitalist via systemic structural inequality, sex, gender, race, and class, can be exploited as low-wage labor and/or unpaid labor. Insofar as sentience is no bar to commodification, species can be assigned the status of extractible resource.
- Normalize denial; enculturate the desire to consume as if it were a ubiquitous feature of human being; normalize the cognitive dissonance necessary to substitute "Nature" for nature, the mythical world of the capitalist's web of life for the reality of a finite planet and a limited atmosphere.

"Nature" must be cast as "external, controllable, reducible" and inexhaustible because it relieves us the moral responsibility for the environmental implications of resource theft; in the guise of the extra-human, "Nature" makes of nonhuman animals bodies another form of resource, for example, as food, and thus, as "external, controllable, and reducible" as male chicks tossed live into grinders. Moore's concept of "Nature" is thus as much party to the commodification of sentient creatures as is the capitalist's. But even more importantly, conceiving "Nature" not only as nonhuman but as fundamentally other-than or extra-human, authorizes the human chauvinism necessary to support denial cultivated through marketing, and to naturalize denial[2]—an ever-more difficult and thus necessary undertaking given the visceral evidence of ecological deterioration. Precluding the capacity for suffering as a bar to commodification is simply the first, though necessary, step on the way to realizing capital's kleptocratic character: nothing is off limits. In short, the "Nature" made by capital is by definition infinitely malleable and reproducible. It is *matter*, neither alive nor dead, but of value insofar as it can be materialized, manufactured, and monetized because exchange value is the primary if not the *only* value capital *can* recognize. "Life" for the capitalist's "web of life" refers not to "living" or "dead," but simply to its own metabolic processes, to its capacity to commodify without interruption, without end.

ERASE AND REPLACE: MOORE'S ABSENT REFERENT

To take an arial view: in *Capitalism in the Web of Life*, Jason Moore argues that "[j]ust as we have been learning to move beyond the dualisms of race, gender, sexuality, and Eurocentrism over the past four decades, it is now time to deal with the source of them all: the Nature/Society binary."[31] Yet, in failing to see that the Nature/Society binary is not "the source of them all," and that the ontology which informs capitalism belongs to a logic of commodification for which all value including that of sentience must be made reducible to exchange value, Moore dooms his analysis to the reincarnation of the structural inequalities he hopes to "move beyond." Like treating cancer with aspirin, Moore deals a glancing blow at the destructive effects of structural inequality but leaves the ontology that propels its reproduction century after century uninterrogated. He introduces us to a second binary, human/extra-human, arguing that it will act as a solvent to undo Nature/Society, but this additional binary offers no more than a temporary balm to our fatigue over the corrosive impacts of capitalism. It's thus no surprise that, like recognizing that aspirin treats only the symptoms of cancer, our relief at the chimeric dissolution of Nature/Society is bound to be disappointing and short-lived. As Malm and Nayeri show, Moore's unargued assumption that the source of all dualisms are variants of Descartes' ssubstance dualism subsidizes ecological catastrophe by erasing the critical distinction between agency and energy, human action and nature. In short, Moore's "hybridist" argument cannot hold human action accountable for environmental harm because it reduces human agency to naturally occurring phenomena.

We can, however, go further than either Malm's or Nayeri's critique: in its failure to probe the ontology of capital, Moore unwittingly signals the real culprit driving the logic of commodification, namely, the systemic erasure of the value of sentience. The capacity for sentience represents a value that can neither be constrained by the human/extra-human binary nor can the capitalist afford to recognize its significance as a bar to commodification. Expressions of empathy for suffering whether among human beings, extra-human creatures like Patricia Piccinini's imagined terran, or nonhuman animals discloses and indicts the ontology of capital. In short, the reality of suffering *leaks*; it transgresses borders, and in so doing, it exposes the kleptocratic—grow or die at all cost—*raison d'étre* of capital.

The transgressive to which Donna Haraway introduces us in her analysis of Piccinini's "fabulations" returns at this juncture to make its own plea for, as she puts it, a decolonizing ethic, in this case against Moore. The issue is not merely that Piccinini's terran critters violate the border imagined to exist between human/extra-human, but that such creatures remind us that some "borders" serve to naturalize fictions meant to fulfill specific human interests—including the chauvinistic belief that wrongs perpetrated against human beings exclusively lay at the root of all wrongs. Yet, because fictional creatures can remind us of very real ones, including those whose capacity for suffering is not unlike our own, the human/extra-human border is bound not merely for transgression but for the interrogation of its purpose, and for whom. Moore treats the border dividing Nature from Society as if it was *not* real, but rather a fiction created to serve the quest for capital at the cost of human society. Were such a dualism real, it would not be possible to dismantle it *as* the "source of all dualisms." But while "Nature" and "Society" function as crucial fictions for Moore's critique of capitalism, nature and society are in fact real independent things—*and they must be*. Otherwise, the subjugation of nature for the sake of its conversion to exchange value would not be necessary. It's thus hardly surprising that valuing the capacity for sentience must be preemptively purged from the pursuit of profit. Such values are inherently transgressive. They make a mockery of the human/extra-human binary just as they put the lie to Moore's account of paid versus unpaid labor. Hence, Moore's argument must itself fall in line with the ontology of capital. He cannot afford to acknowledge the pained gaze of the suffering extra-human/nonhuman and *at the same time* argue that the structural inequalities that define human institutions is *the* great moral wrong of capitalism. Like Wallace-Wells, Mann, and Francione, Moore's argument for the web of life created by capitalism turns out to sustain the human chauvinism that drives the profit motive. This is so despite Moore's revolutionary as opposed to merely reformist intentions.

We can go further. Although Moore's objective, namely, "learning to move beyond the dualisms of race, gender, sexuality" is certainly a noble one, it will be made impossible by his misidentification of its source. For insofar as the capacity for sentience *itself* transgresses the human/extra-human border, sentience exposes "border" as a contrivance of human interest designed to protect the presumptive superiority of human beings—as if sentience were the exclusively human trait of "Society." But this is false. While "Society" serves as the useful fiction of Moore's Nature/Society binary, it does not and cannot mirror natures or societies. For neither "nature" nor "society" divide neatly along the lines of the sentient/non-sentient. Some species of living nonhuman animals are distinguished from other species of living *and* nonliving things in virtue of the capacity for sentience; others are not. For some, for example chimpanzees, the attribution of "society" can be taken quite literally; for others, for instance, ants, the meaning of "society" is metaphorical—but nonetheless zoologically meaningful. "Extra-human" thus captures neither what signifies "human" uniquely, nor "nonhuman," it signifies neither "living," as distinguished from "non-living," nor "society" literally or figuratively. Moore's "extra-human" distinguishes sentient from non-sentient, but at the cost of reinforcing the very human chauvinism he seeks to dismantle. Put differently: insofar as Moore treats "extra-human" in the same essentially reductionist fashion as he treats Nature, as "not-a-living-human-being," he can provide no good reason to distinguish "extra-human" from mere exchange value.

Ultimately, Moore's dilemma is not only *that* sentient nonhuman animals exist but that his alternative binary constructions reinvent the logic of domination, and thus the structural inequalities that sustain the oppression and exploitation of sex, gender, and race *because* they implicitly reinforce the exploitation of species. One particularly salient example of this dilemma is provided by feminist theorist Carol Adams who spells out the connection between oppression with respect to race, gender, sexuality, and the erasure of nonhuman animal sentience in her analysis of the *absent referent*:

> In *The Sexual Politics of Meat*, I developed the concept of the absent referent to identify the process by which the animal used for corpse eating disappears both literally and figuratively. Animals in name and body are made absent as animals in order that flesh can exist. If animals are alive, they cannot be meat. . . . Animals are also made absent through language that renames dead bodies before consumers participate in eating them. The absent referent permits us to forget about the animal as an independent entity.[32]

Much like the sentient animal disappears into the "what's for dinner" of Cora Diamond's analysis of meat-eating, or becomes a "thing" whose misery can be discounted in Epstein's rejection of Francione's humane treatment principle, the experiential capacities of some among the extra-human are "made absent" by being appropriated into the binary opposition, Nature/Society. Here is where Moore is caught between the proverbial rock and a hard place: he needs the Nature/Society dualism *in order to dismantle it* as the source of all dualisms that sustain capitalism. But, insofar as the Nature/Society dualism authorizes absenting the nonhuman sentient referent, appeal to it as the source for all other dualisms is self-defeating. Why? Because it's not the source for all other dualisms: *nonhuman sentient/objectified*—the binary whose first half occupies the necessary status of *denied/erased*—is.

This brings us to another way in which the human/extra-human binary contributes to the maintenance of structural inequality: if the Nature/Society binary is to function as the "source" of all other dualisms, its opposing categories must stay put. And, insofar as they can be reinforced by the commodification of sentience and denial^2, they do stay put—reinforcing the advantage of the capitalist. The trouble, however, is that this "insofar" is threatened by analyses like Adams's whose analysis of the absent referent challenge Moore's human/extra-human construction as forcefully as it echoes Merchant's original critique of Cartesian dualism, or is transgressed by Piccinini's "fabulations." The prospect of some part of Nature leaking into Society through the intelligent gaze of a chimpanzee, the songs of whales, the expressive faces of "African meerkat-like beings," or the cries of cattle rammed down a slaughter chute, threaten to disrupt Moore's critique of capital by exposing a chauvinism at its core that cannot accommodate a sentient "extra-human." But, as Piccinini illustrates in the creation of the deliberately transgressive, sentience won't stay put and can't be constrained other than through the violence of that which secures the future for capitalism, namely, denial[2]. One especially stark way to put Moore's dilemma, then, is that not only does it implicitly sanction the exploitation of sentient nonhuman animals; in the interest of keeping the focus on the structural inequalities that plague human societies, it tacitly approves the denial of the violence to which the absent referent is routinely subjected.

The very fact of extra-human sentience and its ever-present threat of transgression undermines Moore's efforts to establish the dualism that he can dismantle, Nature/Society. Indeed, to dismantle it requires the denial of that which threatens to disrupt its constitution as the "root source," thereby revealing that it is not the root source. Acknowledging the extra-human sentient must then itself be subject to denial[2] returning us once more to Moore's tacit affirmation of the ontological conditions that sustain capitalism, namely, the denial that the capacity for sentience presents a moral obstacle to commodification. Whether the disruption is caused by Adams's insistence that we look into the faces of the nonhuman animals whose objectification *as* food derives from the commodification of sentience, or we recognize we're being looked at, even appraised, by Piccinini's "fabulations," human/extra-human can no more withstand scrutiny than the narrow human interests it favors, even if these interests are themselves molded by structural inequality, enculturated via the capitalist demand for consumption, and steeped in denial[2].

"Interests," however, do offer another avenue for thinking about the strategy Moore undertakes in his critique of capitalism. In its simplest formulation, because his analysis of Nature/Society precludes casting "extra-human" as anything other than "non-human," it also precludes the assignment of value to sentient nonhuman interests. But, as utilitarians like Gary Francione have argued, insofar as nonhuman animals can have interests and/or have things/actions which are *in* their interest without necessarily being able to conceive or articulate them, ignoring the relevance of "interests" as the concept applies to nonhuman animals is tantamount to destabilizing, diminishing, and potentially even erasing the moral relevance of "interests" *for anything*, including other human beings. For unless some morally relevant trait or capacity can be shown to definitively distinguish human beings as a species from all other species, can be shown to be fixed or permanent, the determination that human interests matter and "extra-human" interests do not is *arbitrary*. Moore might respond, of course, that he nowhere argues that extra-human interests, especially an interest in avoiding suffering, do not matter; and that would be true. But insofar as extra-human sentience poses a threat of disruption to Moore's argument that the Nature/Society dualism is at the root of all other dualisms that sustain capitalism, he can no more acknowledge the possibility that extra-human interests do matter than he can acknowledge the extra-human sentience that grounds them. Just as the effective denial of the value of nonhuman sentience preserves human/extra-human dualism, the denial of extra-human interests preserves its absent referent, and thus protects the arbitrary nature of its privileged human chauvinism. The trouble is that what is arbitrary cannot be made to stay in its place because its place is *arbitrary*. The arbitrary compromises the stability of the borders that Moore's critique of capitalism requires since its root source is itself a mythical hierarchy of value, in this case, one that preserves the hegemony of human interests and thus the logic that advantages the capitalist.

Upshot: good intentions notwithstanding, Moore's critique of capitalism reflects not a regime of capital that constitutes the web of life, not, in any case, the web of *all* life, but rather only that life which can be captured by the dualism Human/Extra-Human, Nature/Society. Such a critique is bound to be distorted by its absent referent. The terrified cow being stun-gunned down a slaughter chute is neither merely "Nature" nor a member of Society. Whether the cow can or can't formulate "stun gun" or "suffering" or "death" has no place in Moore's analysis of "ecology and the accumulation of capital" despite the very real violence to which the cow is subjected. Indeed, from the point of view of Moore's web of life, the reason Piccinini's "fabulations" solicit empathy from us is simply because we see human-like faces—instead of the package of "pink slime" to which the cow is consigned. Turning a blind eye to suffering, and hence to the commodification of sentience, reducing it to the generic catch-all extra-human Nature, "permits us to forget about the animal as an independent entity" thereby reinforcing a binary opposition more critical to capitalism than "Nature/Society": *Sentience/Objectification*. However, unacknowledged by Moore, this is the dualism that prohibits sentience from leaking into Nature not merely by recasting the capacity for sentience as absent, and thus in no need of moral consideration, but by delivering it to the machinations of capital as a consumable resource: meat.

Moore's failure to recognize that the source of all dualisms is not Nature/Society but rather Sentience/Objectification leads him to exclude nonhuman animals in his "dualisms of race, gender, sexuality, and Eurocentrism," undermining his analysis of *Capitalism in the Web of Life* as well as of suffering, transgression, and death. Indeed, once we concede that pigs are not poppies, dogs are not daisies, we're reminded of the denial demanded by Moore's claim that to dismantle the Nature/Society dualism is to strike a blow against capitalism itself. Yet so long as this tacit denial can be preserved nothing prevents capitalism from continuing to reinvent itself—no matter the cost to planetary ecologies or its many very real webs of life. And sentience is, in fact, no bar to commodification so long as it remains coded as *absent*, for absence permits us to deny that there is anything to deny: *denial*^{2}, pigs are poppies. Undermined too is that the suffering Moore associates with the wrongs of racism, sexism, and Eurocentrism have no moral relevance outside human being because "extra-human" sentient natures have no more *place* in that human future than factory farmed pigs have in the present other than as "what's for dinner." This becomes particularly clear when Moore effectively reinforces the absence of the sentient referent by making mention not, for example, of species we might still save from extinction, but of the "cyborgs, assemblages, networks, and hybrids" that "point the way forward."[33] Given, in other words, that the dualisms Moore theorizes track the logic of domination only as it impacts human beings, it seems the only nonhuman entities that could matter to some future web of life are the ones we create, the ones that can be *made to fit* the human/extra-human binary. Piccininni's "fabulations," after all, are only materialized fictions; cyborgs are real inventions of human imagination. The trouble, of course, is that once we take up the task of reclaiming the value of sentience outside of human chauvinism, we cannot help but see that Moore's "Nature" is not "natural," but rather the naturalized, yet otherwise fictional, half of a binary created to represent the history of a capitalism whose wrongs can be constrained to categories of evaluation whose focus is its impact on human beings—as opposed to a capitalism whose kleptocratic nature endangers the *totality* of the web of life.

The issue here is not that Moore's approach to the critique of capitalism is human-centered; he could reclaim a human-centeredness grounded in taking responsibility for the sentience/objectification dualism, the advantage capitalism takes of it, and then begin again, for example, in Adams's analysis of "corpse-eating," Diamond's discussion of "what's for dinner," or even Francione's rejection of nonhuman animals as "things." But Moore doesn't take that opportunity. Taking Nature/Society to be the source of all dualisms aligns Moore by default with Francione's necessity "justifications" for nonhuman animal suffering, and the human chauvinism of Wallace-Wells' fatal complacency, both of which reinforce the absent referent whose sole power lay in undermining the prospect that capitalism can be done in. Moore understands the environmental, economic, geographical, social, and political stakes for the planet and its human inhabitants when he remarks that the Nature/Society dualism "drips with blood and dirt, from its sixteenth century origins to capitalism in its twilight,"[34] but he misconstrues the Cartesian narrative when, as Malm shows, he conflates substance dualism with property dualism. Moore thus characterizes dualism *per se* as a narrative that "unfolds like this: capitalism . . . emerged *out of* Nature It drew wealth *from* Nature. It disrupted, degraded, defiled *Nature*. And now, or sometime very soon, Nature will exact revenge. Catastrophe is coming."[35] The conflation of the fictional "Nature" with nature could not be clearer: "Nature" "begins neither with 'humans' nor with 'nature' but with the relations that co-produce manifold configurations of humanity-in-nature."

It's easy to get lost here. After all, Moore refers to "organisms and environments, life and land, water and air." The problem is that mere reference to "organisms" cannot speak to the vital role sentience plays in crystalizing the ontological conditions of capital as capital*ism*. It is precisely because the capacity for sentience is discounted as morally significant, because its extra-human entities "dripping with blood and dirt" are consigned to exchange value, that the narrative can be made to seem plausible as a Nature/Society binary even as its referents remain absent behind the generic "organisms." Moore's human-like Cartesian "Nature" will enact revenge, but not for the reasons Moore stipulates, and at far greater cost than his analysis can accommodate. Humanity-in-nature is just one more way to preclude the possibility that underneath "dripping with blood and dirt" is a sentient creature suffering in injury; it is instead a form of tacit denial[2] whose effect is to *discount* that which deserves no more than reference. Although his reader may be convinced that his "double internality" of "humanity-in-nature/nature-in-humanity" defies reduction to the dualist narrative, its basic binary relation, Nature/Society, remains unchallenged: it is *structurally* unable to recognize any sentient nonhuman challenger to the narrative because their suffering cannot matter to its purpose, namely, the reclamation of *human* dignity against Cartesian dualisms of mind over body, white over black, male over female, humanity over nature. In other words, nonhuman sentience cannot be made to matter without imploding Moore's version of the web of life.

THE *OIKEIOS*: HOW THE "DIALECTIC OF LIFE-MAKING" REPRODUCES "MIGHT MAKES RIGHT"

Moore writes that he wants to "ask the reader to consider capitalism as a world-ecology, joining the accumulation of capital, the pursuit of power, and the co-production of nature in dialectical unity."[36] Thus far he's left "nature" largely undefined, but continues that:

> Far from asserting the unfettered primacy of capitalism's capacity to remake planetary natures, capitalism as world ecology opens up a way of understanding capitalism as already co-produced by manifold species, extending even to our planet's geo-biological shifts, relations, and cycles . . . [T]his perspective allows for the multiplication of questions that turn on the *oikeios*: the creative, generative, and multi-layered relation of species and environment.[37]

Defined as the *oikeios*, Moore's "Nature" endows not only human beings with agency as co-producers, but also "manifold species," "geobiological shifts," and the environment itself. Although he denies that capitalism has "unfettered primacy"—capital is not omnipotent—he nonetheless insists that as a co-producer with "Nature," capitalism is best understood as a vital and powerful player in the "creative, generative, and multi-layered relation of species and environment."

Yet, what we soon discover is that it's actually *human* agency that takes "primacy," and that what the *oikeios* is *about* is more consistent with human chauvinism than any life-making that includes nonhuman animals and their ecologies, agency or not. Moore effectively pays lip service to the planet and its "web of life," but quickly demotes it to a non-agential agent, that is, a placeholder agent in name only—a zombie whose "agency" can be solicited to fulfill objects of human self-interest and then returned to inactivity. Remote from the recognition of any distinction between sentient and non-sentient species, Moore sets the stage for the introduction of paid and un-paid work as well as Cheap Labor, but he also sets himself up for the hybridist self-defeat of his critique of capitalism:

> [t]he *oikeios* names the relation through which humans act—and are acted upon by the whole of nature—in our environment-making. Through the *oikeios*, premised on the dialectic of life-making, we may open new pathways for investigating how capitalism's historical geographies—past and present—are premised on specific configurations of humanity-in-nature.[38]

A charitable reading suggests that, insofar as Moore's is a critique of "capitalism's historical geographies," it makes sense that he'd privilege human beings as "environment making." Human chauvinism is at the root of capital, of value and its reduction to exchange; human agents are the creators and executors of the logic of domination and its capitalist incarnation as the logic of commodification. Unfortunately, such a reading can't make sense of Moore's selective attribution of agency to "Nature," agency he appears to insert at points throughout his argument as "dialectic life-making" only to swiftly return human agency to primacy. Nor, as Nayeri shows, can charity dissolve the "theoretical/analytical incongruenc[ies that] forces Moore to suggest that not only humans or other animals, but rivers, waterfalls, or forests also "work." Indeed, it seems ludicrous if not mercenary to treat members of endangered species like the Rufous Hummingbird as if they're candidates for agency. As Amy Chillag reports for CNN, September 2023:

> The Rufous hummingbird lost two-thirds of its population since 1970, according to the 2022 State of the Birds report. These tiny creatures are one of 70 bird species on the "Tipping Point" list that will lose another fifty percent of their populations in the same time frame if conservation doesn't improve. That list includes such flying beauties as the Golden-winged warbler with its stunning

> yellow cap and black mask. The reasons, scientists say, are multi-fold: habitat loss from climate change and human development, glass collisions, invasive species (domestic cats) and pesticides; many of the same reasons all wildlife globally have plummeted.[39]

No doubt Moore takes such tipping points seriously. But by what metric is he authorized to determine the conditions under which agency-attribution is warranted? Are Golden-winged warblers intentionally committing mass suicide? Do the Rufous hummingbirds want to recover their dwindling numbers? Of course such questions make no sense of the material causes of species and habitat loss; science should plainly be our guide here. *But nothing in Moore's hybridist "dialectic of life-making" precludes nonsensical queries like these*, or even worse—the attribution of a malevolent consciousness to "Nature" itself who might one day decide "she" has had enough of chauvinistic human folly and decides to release upon us a virus that makes Covid-19 seem like the common cold.

Fact is, hybridist distortion haunts the *oikeios*, undermining its value as an instrument of critique, and as such unwittingly offers far more charity to the capitalist than to the planet. There are several reasons for this blunder: first, insofar as Moore defends the Nature/Society binary, "environment-making" is fated to either preclude the actual environment or reduce everything, living and non-living, to the fundamentally social "dialectic of life-making." The Nature/Society binary can, in other words, provide no metric for distinguishing "Nature" from "Society," so it's possible that everything is "Nature" or nothing is, or that everything is "Society" or nothing is. Second, insofar as sentient nonhuman life forms are fundamental to any characterization of the environment *as* "environment" *for* a "manifold of species," their systemic absenting from Moore's Human/Extra-Human precludes the environment from the "dialectic of life-making." Just as everything or nothing is "Nature" and everything or nothing is "Society," so too either everything is "environment" leaving no room for sentient species—nonhuman or otherwise, or everything is sentient, leaving no room for non-sentient entities like "rivers, waterfalls, or forests." Moore appears to want to have his hybridist cake and eat it too.

Third, even if we accepted Moore's conflation of "Nature" with nature, "dialectic of life-making" can make no sense of species life, sentient or not. Whether we're referring to endangered species like the Rufous Hummingbird or plentiful mosquitoes, the "dialectic of life-making" provides no metric for characterizing or explaining the anthropogenic fates of particular sites within the dialectic since all are merely "life-making," until they're not, like the hummingbird. Lastly, insofar as Moore refers to the "environment" as "our environment," he exposes the underlying human chauvinism that bolsters the capitalist at the expense of human and nonhuman nature. He effectively exchanges the possibility of a real planet that, whatever damage has been done to its ecologies by human agency, will remain the planet long after we have done ourselves in for a counterfeit "dialectic of life-making" "planet" made to fit the capitalist "web of life."

Moore argues that his objective is to develop theoretical and analytical tools for "investigating how capitalism's historical geographies—past and present—are premised on specific configurations of *humanity-in-nature*." Moore seems to agree with philosophers like William Cronin who shows that among these geographies there's no such thing as untouched wild nature. "Wilderness," argues Cronin, is a myth created to fulfill the desires of mostly wealthy white industrialists looking to escape, conquer, exploit, or extract the American Western "frontier" of the late Nineteenth and early Twentieth centuries.[40] However, although Moore might agree with Cronin that "wilderness" is a myth, they differ in ways unfavorable to Moore with respect to how and why this is the case. Whereas for Cronin, the historical geographies of North America tell the story of the indigenous peoples for whom land was "home" for centuries before the white explorers' mythical "wilderness," for Moore there is no objective reality of "land" to be the *actual* home for some *or* the *fantasy* wilderness of others; each is just one more "configuration" of "humanity-in-nature." Given its association with the Nature/Society, Human/Extra-human binaries and the introduction of the "dialectic of life-making," what "humanity-in-nature" cannot mean is "outside human agency." For Cronin, that the land we call "America" existed prior to human habitation is a fact of nature disrupted by the emergence of indigenous human communities and much later by self-styled white conquerors of the "wilderness," men seeking property and adventure. But for Moore there could *never* have been actual wilderness because the "dialectic of life-making" cannot accommodate for any but a hybrid configuration of "human" and/in "nature." By the same token, what constitutes home for the America's indigenous peoples is, on Moore's account, merely an earlier configuration of "humanity-in-nature," having no more claim to objective reality than "wilderness."

In short, Moore's "dialectic of life-making" boils down to "might makes right." Neither "home" nor "wilderness" can have meaning beyond those whom a particular configuration of "humanity-in-nature" empowers with the authority to define it at any given time. What is "home" for some is "wilderness" for others, and because there's no fact of the matter to be discovered, there are no grounds upon which to argue that the white wealthy explorers are not equally entitled to determine the meaning of "home," "land," "wilderness," "savage," or any of the other terms used to justify expropriation, theft, removal, and cultural as well as material genocide. "Humanity-in-nature" can provide no grounds for the argument that the expropriation of lands inhabited by indigenous peoples is theft, and no argument that the Westward expansion exemplifies the kleptocratic nature of capitalism. Alternatively, we can characterize the Westward expansion as theft if we like, and we can call it "kleptocratic," but insofar as there's no metric for determining the truth, our games-with-words offer merely arbitrary place-holders instead of moral grounds for judgment. Moreover, if Moore's hybrid "humanity-in-nature" correctly describes "human" and "nature," there can never have been a time before the evolution of *homo sapiens* or after human beings are long gone: if humanity *is* "humanity-in-nature," there can never be a nature independent of humanity. But this is both absurd on its face and woefully undermines any critique of capitalism that depends for its credibility and force on the real damage to real ecologies, real species life, and real people done in the name of profit. As Malm shows, such a reality-deflating hybridism contradicts Moore's own implicit assumptions about the objective existence of nonhuman nature and thus undermines any claim Moore can make about capitalism's capacity for destruction, even to the human beings his human chauvinism clearly favors, not to mention to the nonhuman sentient life he largely ignores, and the planet he doubtless loves.

By reinforcing the human chauvinism signified by the use of "our" in reference to the environment, Moore's *oikeios* replaces the real webs of life of which we and countless other species are real members with an "environment-making" made for the removal of obstacles and the pursuit of capital. The notion that there's an "environment" to be "made" functions to obscure the reality of our material conditions as animals, thereby tacitly reinforcing the reduction of all value to exchange value. By treating "environment" as the generic conceptual material configured through various incarnations of "humanity-in-nature" as opposed to the interconnected specific ecologies through which homo Sapiens has evolved as a species of creature among others, Moore effectively strips "environment" of its moral status as a home endangered by human action. "Environment-making" discounts the material realities that limit, condition, and shape what is possible for human action in order to make way for an "environment" as an artifact of human making. Like the myths of endless and/or infinitely reproducible resources, "environment" functions as a useful tool for a particular incarnation of humanity-in-nature, namely, the *capitalist-in-nature* for whom "environment" is not an existential condition but rather a product tailored to the logic of commodification.

The implications of recognizing that "humanity-in-nature" is actually "capitalist-in-nature" are weighty: (1) it assumes what is manifestly false about the planet: even in the most ecologically apocalyptic "Road Warrior" scenario produced by a rapacious globalized kleptocracy, the "multi-layered relation of species and environment" will not be dissipated by capitalist environment-making. As recurring rounds of viral pandemic shows, planetary life will fight back. While few human beings are likely to survive a climate crisis that disrupts the atmosphere beyond our capacity to adapt, the planet will carry on, even recuperate, and the reason is that it is not "our" planet any more that the environment is "our" environment. Moore can counter that he doesn't intend "our environment-making" to be taken as totalizing or without remainder, but rather to signify the status of a Nature usurped and reorganized as resource within the capitalist web of life. But this won't work: (2) Capitalism is not "co-produced by manifold species, extending even to our planet's geo-biological shifts, relations, and cycles." Capitalism is a deeply enculturated form of human agency that advantages the capitalist at the expense of everyone and everything else. Its logics of domination and commodification have become naturalized to human consciousness and conscience, but "naturalized" does not mean by nature. Capitalism defines the relationship between people, their communities, their geographies and ecologies that, outfitted in line with the quest for profit, helps to "co-produce" the myth of a future that takes the quest for profit as its state-of-nature. Adding to the myth of endless resources the fiction that human beings are profit-driven by nature, capitalism imposes its own "web of life." *But myths are not descriptions*. Indeed, the capitalist web of life is *parasitic* on a reality whose webs of life are co-produced by the natural laws that govern the planet's geological, ecological, and evolutionary history. That it makes no morally relevant difference from the point of view of Moore's hybridism whether species extinctions are caused by Earth-smashing asteroids or the demand for whale oil collapses his critiques of capitalism into a natural disaster. Even war—a form of destruction whose impacts are rarely tallied in terms of ecologies destroyed—collapses into the determinism of "capitalism-in-nature."

Put differently: the idea that "capitalism's historical geographies" can be premised on "specific configurations of humanity-in-nature" solicits only one part of "our" story, and in a fashion distorted by what's made absent, namely, a "nature-in-humanity" preemptively erased through an "environment-making" cast as "acting" and "acted upon," but stripped of the materiality, specificity, and sentience necessary to address the environment as real. Instead, "capitalism-in-nature" authorizes *as* real and exhaustive a "web of life" made *for* the conceptual "co-productions" Moore needs for his critique of capitalism. Another name for "*as* real" is "fiction." Just as a fictional planet cannot support the greed of a real capitalism that treats its resources *as* endless, its sentient life *as* insensible to suffering, its ecologies *as* "co-productions," so too a critique whose appeal to the *oikeios* promises to survey the web of *life*, but concerns itself only with humanity-in-nature as "capitalism-in-nature" cannot articulate a "dialectic of life-making," for it has left out its own material conditions.

THE "FOUR CHEAPS": HOW TO KEEP CAPITAL IN THE CAPITALOCENE

The foregoing is intended as a critical conceptual excavation that deepens in specificity and force some of Malm's and Nayeri's claims against Moore's hybridist argument in *Capitalism in the Web of Life.* But perhaps Moore can counter with another argument against dualism, one that intersects with some very important themes at the intersection of capital and "class, gender, race, and nation":

> [d]ualism does not allow for greater specificity in our understanding of the "social" relations for a very good reason: it takes human differentiation as forming outside the *oikeios*. This comprises not only the accumulation of capital but also enduring patterns of class, gender, race, and nation. Are these not better understood as products and producers of the *oikeios*? From here we may ask, How do humans *fit* into the web of life, understood as a totality of distinctive and interpenetrating evolutionary trajectories . . . For me, the implications of privileging the differentiated unities of humanity-in nature/nature-in-humanity have made it impossible to go back to the dualist view.[41]

Moore is doubtless right that we cannot return to Cartesian *substance* dualism. The difficulty, however, is that because "dualism" need not refer to distinct substances, its alternative need not collapse humanity into nature. Indeed, as opposed to offering an explanation for the "enduring patterns of class, gender, race, and nation" of which the capitalist takes advantage, "humanity-in-nature" naturalizes such patterns and thereby insures their continuity. In other words, "human differentiation" need not form *outside* the "creative, generative, and multi-layered relation of species and environment" in order to defend human agency as an independent force culpable for the exploitation and subjugation of class, gender, race, nation, nonhuman species, and the environment.

Put more starkly: the reason it's impossible to "go back" to substance dualism is not because it's true *or* false. It's because it does not capture the ontology of capital in its material relations with the ecologies, patterns, and inhabitants of a real planet. However unwittingly, Moore's is a straw argument: although what is true for the logic of commodification is that *any* set of beliefs, concepts, ideologies, or assumptions—including substance dualism—is equal opportunity fodder for the conversion of value to exchange value, this does not imply that capitalism is committed to any set in particular; *it can't be*. The ontology of capital is mercenary and necessarily kleptocratic. If believing that "human differentiation [forms] outside the *oikeios*" can be put to the service of profit-seeking, we can expect the capitalist to exploit it to her advantage. Though beyond our scope here, it's easy to see how substance dualism might be deployed to expedite a marriage of convenience between the evangelical Christian notion of the soul and capitalist enterprise. Donald Trump's devoted evangelical base, for example, assumes a masculine over feminine, human over nonhuman nature, white over black/brown, global North over South that mirrors a substance dualism of mind over body—a myth that advantages the capitalist by differentiating agency from resource, producer over commodity. Such myths, religious or otherwise have, however, nothing to do with the truth or falsity of substance dualism, but rather everything to do with a logic of commodification for whom truth or falsity are merely potential sources of exchange value.

An instructive example of Moore's argument concerning how humans beings "fit" into the web of life is illumined by his account of "cheap food" and the "Long Green Revolution."[42] He begins by pointing out that the "Green Revolution emerged first in the United States in the 1930s,"[43] that it was facilitated by innovation in agricultural technology, and that it launched a "great leap forward in the provision of Cheap Food."[44] Moore argues that:

> The "magic" of this Green Revolution was found in an old script with a new twist. The new model reshaped world power, accumulation, and nature through a new configuration of capitalization and appropriation, taking shape in the 1930s with the introduction of hybrid corn and new, higher-yielding strains of wheat . . . Labor inputs fell by more than two thirds, and mechanization rose by 213 percent, between 1935–1970. Meanwhile, fertilizer and pesticide inputs increased by an extraordinary 1,338 percent. This was the "petrochemical-hybrid complex" systematically combining new plants, fertilizers, pesticides and irrigation schemes.[45]

The Green Revolution's impacts were, as Moore rightly notes, immense, including the rapid "extroversion" of American agriculture. Instead of being able to use seed stored from the previous season, farmers were compelled to "make an annual pilgrimage to seed stores" to buy "Frankenseeds" engineered by what quickly grew to be multinational corporations like Monsanto to produce single yield crops.[46] Competition for the most highly productive seeds harnessed to technological advance, particularly with respect to genetically modified, pest resistant, crop strains (GMOs) produced "the rapid shake-out of uncompetitive farmers," the rise of non-agricultural employment, and Cheap Food: "spending on food dropped from 24 percent to 14 percent of average household income."[47] "This rapid capitalization," Moore argues, "was made possible by an extraordinary alchemy: turning oil and natural gas into food . . . *petro-farming*."[48] "Two important transitions in capitalist agriculture followed. First, capitalist agriculture became massively inefficient in its energy use . . . The second . . . was toxification."[49] The first, highly wasteful energy use, was made possible by access to the "cheap energy" provided through advances in oil and gas extraction; the second the by-product of profligate use of herbicides and pesticides in order to maintain high crop yields able to counter the now radically degraded nutritive value of Cheap Food.[50]

Little in Moore's account thus far would seem to invite controversy. Indeed, it's the kind of story we'd expect from David Wallace-Wells or Michael Mann, Nancy Fraser or Mark Stoll, even Andreas Malm. Yet read through the lens of our current critique what we discover is that what Moore excludes from his account—*nonhuman sentient animal life reduced to resources such as Cheap Food*—exposes the limit beyond which he is apparently not willing to challenge the prevailing fictions that govern economic, geopolitical, and social life. Such an exclusion, moreover, is more damning in Moore's case than Wallace-Wells' or Mann's since Moore's is a *critique* of capitalism. His analysis is not aimed at reform through band-aid fixes like carbon trades; his critique does not, at least not intentionally, result in a defense of a salvation capitalism. If Moore had explicitly limited the scope of his critique to a demonstration of how the rapid capitalization of one sector of the globalizing economy—albeit a sector vital with respect to its impacts—was made possible via technological innovation, we might see little with which to quibble. The trouble is that Moore is talking about Cheap *Food* in a fashion that systemically conflates cows with corn, cheap energy with cheap chickens. He effectively treats one agent in the story of petro-farming, namely, the producers of cheap food intended for human consumption, as if "cheap food" were a category exhausted by corn, wheat, and other grains; as if the "extraordinary alchemy" of "turning oil and natural gas into food" was not also about turning hydrocarbons into nonhuman animal bodies; as if the only impacts with which we need concern ourselves are those for human beings. In short, Moore's interpretation of the history of the Green Revolution offers a clear illustration of his narrow focus on a humanity-in-nature that, while it follows from the conceptual framework that governs his approach to capital's historical geographies, also reveals why this framework fails to capture the material realities of "what's for dinner" *food.*

The story of petro-farming cannot be constrained, at least not without distortion, merely to the rise of GMOs and the use of chemical fertilizers, pesticides, and herbicides. This story is at least as much if not more about the rise of industrial-scale concentrated animal feeding operations (CAFOs), the petro-technologies that facilitate the rapid production, growth, slaughter, and disarticulation of animal bodies, the use of animal body waste as fertilizer, and the fact that the lion's share of grain is not produced for direct human consumption, but for factory farm subjugates. It will do no good, moreover, to add "animal agriculture" to Moore's original analysis of the Green Revolution: there's no natural place for the inclusion of "animal body" in his account of cheap food other than through the elision of the value of sentience—the reduction of animal bodies to commodities whose value can be assessed according to the same quantifiable metrics as grains. In short, the only "humanity-in-nature" that can "fit" Moore's "web of life" are white affluent Western(ized) men identified as the agents of capital. For insofar as the capacity for sentience is preemptively discounted as either a resource or an impediment only those whom the logic of domination has *already* empowered are exempt from the logic of commodification—*and only insofar as their agency can be successfully recruited to the pursuit of profit.* The ontology of capital that makes large-scale revolutions in agricultural production possible is the same as that which destines an increasing share of land-mass to grain production for "food" animals, subjects the working classes to poorly-paid wage labor, and builds its factories and waste processing facilities in communities of poor and/or minority populations.

Just as Wallace-Wells and Mann work to avoid any meaningful discussion of what counts as "food" in order to inflate the value of the solutions they propose to combat the climate crisis—solutions focused nearly entirely on fossil fuel extraction—so too Moore evades a discussion that would implode his consignment of nonhuman animal life to mere "extra-human nature" as if capitalism cannot be held accountable for its role in decisions about what we eat. Indeed, in a particularly telling passage concerned with the "evolution of herbicide resistant weeds," Moore remarks that

> At its core is the tension between capital's efforts to control and commensurate extra-human nature, and the latter's co-evolutionary capacity to elude and resist that control. This is the taming cycle: "the more [capital] tames natural processes, the more they spin out of control, provoking new and more aggressive taming measures with increasingly disastrous outcomes."[51]

Moore's doubtless right that organisms like super weeds will "elude and resist" herbicides like Round-Up Ready. He's right that the consequences of this struggle for control will be disastrous for the planet and its atmosphere. Nonetheless, the tacit reduction of all "extra-human" nature to this model of resistance so excludes the radically different forms presented by sentient creatures that it can only be read to reproduce the Nature/Society dualism Moore claims to dismantle. Industry does indeed deploy "more aggressive taming measures." But surely the response solicited by the use of a more potent herbicide isn't remotely comparable to the revulsion we experience finding out that male chicks who try to escape being ground up alive are "tamed" by being trampled on the factory farm floor; or that cattle who aren't killed by the stun gun are "tamed" by being gutted alive as they dangle upside down on a conveyor belt hook. Moore would doubtless be revolted by this suffering—but the problem is that his analysis of the geographies of capital can no more accommodate for the value of sentient nonhuman life than can Wallace-Wells or Mann, dooming it to the same critique of its implicit reinforcement of the logic of domination and the logic of commodification.

The failure of Moore's analysis is striking because, as he points out, "climate change is not simply one more 'environmental' issue to add to capitalism's cumulative woes. The nineteenth-century opening of the atmosphere as a planetary waste dump for capital's pollution has now reached a critical moment."[52] He's right. Yet even if we set aside the issue of nonhuman animal suffering under production regimes that discount it to focus solely, as Moore mostly does, on the impacts of the climate crisis for human populations, the story of capital cannot be told without taking account the commodification of sentience. That is, even if we're willing to conflate "taming measures" as otherwise different from each other as the production of a more toxic herbicide and the invention of larger baby chick grinders, ignoring animal agriculture's production of greenhouse gases is "not simply one more issue to add to capitalism's cumulative woes." As Alasdair Bland reports for *Smithsonian Magazine* as far back as 2012, we ignore the material infrastructure required for the mass manufacture of animal bodies *as* food at our environmental peril:

> In Brazil, forests are falling before the advance of soybean fields, cultivated largely as beef fodder. In New Zealand, the banks of wild streams are frequently found trampled and muddied by grazers . . . On parts of the Great Plains, cows, and the fields of grain they eat, have replaced pronghorn antelope and bison. Livestock ranchers worldwide have participated heavily in the extermination of wild predators. In California, overuse of river water for agricultural use, including a million acres of water-intensive alfalfa (the state's highest-acreage crop, used for feeding animals), has contributed to the long-term decline of wild salmon runs. Sixty percent of the state's alfalfa fields lie in the San Joaquin Valley, ground zero in the water wars between farmers and salmon fishermen. And the mighty, man-size totuava, a Mexican fish species that once spawned in huge swarms in the Colorado River delta, has just about vanished partly because the Colorado barely reaches the Sea of Cortez anymore . . . Much of the Colorado's flow is diverted to the Imperial Valley, a regional king of alfalfa hay production. Most California-grown alfalfa is fed to dairy cows—meaning, sadly, that the production of milk and of California's acclaimed cheeses may be as problematic as raising meat.[53]

In other words, even if we set aside issues concerning nonhuman animal suffering, the "new twist" on the "old script" of agricultural production cannot be written without the explicit recognition and integration of the role played by the commodification of nonhuman animals in industrialized animal agriculture.

Moore might respond that nothing in his account of petro-farming precludes, for example, acknowledging the land mass commandeered by grasslands or "finishing" feed lots needed to raise beef cattle—and that would be true. But the facts laid out in Bland's report cannot merely be tacked on to Moore's account of Cheap Food. Indeed, to do so would be tantamount to endorsing precisely the capitalism Moore seeks to undermine. Here's why: to ignore the critical role played by industrialized animal agriculture is to ignore the ontology of capital that makes Cheap Food *cheap*. What made the Green Revolution, and thus the reduction in the cost of grain production, possible was not *in the first place* either a "new configuration of power" or technological innovation *per se*; what made it possible was that the original kleptocratic configuration of power could be mechanized organizationally (multinational corporations) and technologically (assembly lines) to ever more globalized forms of mass production. But this configuration of primarily white male power is rooted in the commodification of sentience; it is instantiated in the web of life by what is necessary to the very possibility of *capital*: that nothing, living or nonliving, organic or inorganic, animate or inert, sentient or non-sentient can be exempted from the forces of commodification *unless it can be deployed to its execution.* Hence, when Moore argues that "[t]he imperative faced by capital to expand the zone of unpaid work faster than the capitalization of the *oikeios* is the historical basis through which capitalist power lumped together the epoch-making appropriation of 'women, nature, and colonies,'" he gets it exactly backwards. For although he's right that "[w]ithout women, nature, and colonies . . . accumulation falters," it's not because unpaid labor is necessary to accumulation *because* it goes unpaid; it goes unpaid because the logic that makes accumulation possible preemptively consigns "women, nature, and colonies" to resource; rendering "paid" as much a nonsense as "sentience" an obstacle. Neither Cheap Food nor Cheap Labor benefit from the maintenance of Human/Extra-Human except insofar as the binary helps to maintain the masculinist chauvinism that puts mostly white, affluent men at the helm of Big Agriculture, Big Animal Agriculture and Big Fossil Fuels and assigns women, nonhuman nature, nonwhite men, indigenous peoples, and nonhuman animals to the status of consumable, disposable, replaceable commodity.

In this same passage Moore insists that "[t]he appropriation of de-valued work must necessarily outweigh the capitalization of work, lest the costs of the Big Four inputs (labor-power, food, energy, raw materials) begin to rise, and opportunities for accumulation through commodity production and exchange . . . begin to decline."[54] But this too is backwards: capitalization has already appropriated and conditioned valuation *per se*. The Big Four count as "input" only insofar as they produce commodity value; de-valued/unpaid work only insofar as it does the same. Hence, when Moore argues just a bit later that "[t]he long Green Revolution owed its revolutionary achievements to plunder as much as productivity,"[55] he's certainly right. But he also discloses precisely what's missing in his understanding of the logic of commodification: plunder is no counterweight to productivity; *plunder is a necessary condition for productivity*. Plunder is simply another name for resource theft "liberated" by the elimination of the capacity for sentience as a bar to the creation of exchange value. The Capitalocene, in other words *is* the Kleptocene because *it has always been the Kleptocene*. The "new twist" is merely the old kleptocratic script veiled, as always, behind the myth of endless resources, technologically updated to maximize mass production.

THE ONTOLOGY OF RESOURCE THEFT

What makes Moore's "new twist" a boon for the capitalist *and* at the same time harbinger of an uninhabitable earth is that neither can be confronted without an understanding of what it is *in* the pursuit of capital that expedites resource *theft*; that a "new" twist on an old script devoted to accelerated and frantic plunder is not excess, but the predictable outcome of capital's governing ontology; that the relationship of capital to climate crisis is, however, perversely, mutually reinforcing in its nihilism. What makes it possible and profitable to conscript human beings as Cheap/Unpaid Labor is the die cast by a logic of commodification for which the value of sentient life has been preemptively discounted and is now a resource ready to be mechanized, consumed, discarded, substituted, and replaced—*ad infinitum*. In failing to recognize the fundamentally kleptocratic nature of capitalism, Moore's analyses of the "Cheaps" are fated to reproduce the conditions for this conscription. Concerning, for example, the conditions of mid-20th Century labor Moore argues that the "drive to reduce the turnover time of capital to zero is, in fact, a pivotal moment in the environmental history of capitalism."[56] Pivotal, yes—but predictable. Streamlined by the modern assembly line and outfitted with robotics, the quest for profit has not itself altered; it's simply accelerated via technological innovation to continue the realization of its kleptocratic objective.

In an especially telling example, Moore offers the factory farm as an instance of the shortened turnover time and expanded processing volume that mechanizing the production, slaughter, and processing of animal bodies makes possible. He refers to Concentrated Animal Feeding Operations (CAFOS) as the "factory as environment," that is, as an instance of the human-made environment in the production of food.[57] But Moore's choice of example is far more revealing than he likely realizes or would hope. First, that Moore could just as well have selected an example from industrial scale crop production (for instance, cereal manufacture) as opposed to the factory farm only reinforces a view of "extra-human" already stripped of its concern for sentience or suffering in nonhuman animals. He treats every example of "factory as environment" as if its conditions of labor were more or less the same, effectively nullifying differences that might solicit moral outrage concerning the suffering of nonhuman animals in exchange for a narrow focus on the conditions of human labor. In short, the very way Moore approaches "factory as environment" reinforces the human chauvinism capitalist enterprise requires to promote the conversion of animals bodies to exchange value as food.

Second, Moore's interest in the factory farm's particular incarnation of the web of life seems to go no further than the conditions that make "factory as environment" possible for labor *as* Cheap (human) Labor. The animal features merely as the necessary material, like wood pulp for paper manufacture or unrefined petroleum for making plastics, relevant to a particular form of mass production in the "environment." In other words, the environment *as ecology* is effectively replaced by a fictional "environment" in which nonhuman animal life (or any life other than human) has been systemically expunged in the interest of creating the "factory *as* environment." That the "factory as environment" serves the interests of capital is, of course, true. Yet precisely the same conception of "environment" also serves Moore's analysis of Cheap (human) Labor. The reduction of nonhuman animal bodies to raw material for processing into "meat" is as necessary a component of Moore's analysis of capitalism as it is of the logic of commodification. The sentient nonhuman animal isn't rendered material by the stun gun; its capacity for sentience has already been expunged and incorporated into the "factory as environment" structure of what makes "Cheap (human) labor" cheap by making *as food* cheap.

The "factory as environment" may operate on particular sorts of materials (grains, tobacco, cotton, water, nonhuman animal bodies), but it exists *for* a specific set of "Cheaps" whose producers, human beings, Moore positions as the exclusive locus of harm—Cheap Labor. But this labor can be so positioned *only* because the suffering of the "extra human" other has already been done away with, ontologically, morally, and literally. Cheap Labor preemptively consigns the object of its toil to the exchange value encapsulated by its turnover time, unaware that by acquiescing to a logic of commodification that discounts the sentience of its product, it discounts the value of its sentient Cheap (human) Labor. The structure of Cheap Labor thereby reaffirms the kleptocratic ontology that consigns its place in the capitalist web of life to the disposable and replaceable right along with the "extra human." In other words, human labor is made cheap first and foremost through a logic of commodification that erases the value of labor by the same mechanism it absents the value of sentience: the systemic removal of obstacles that threaten "grow or die." While Moore's alighting on the factory farm seems arbitrary, one more 1950s example of industrialization, the CAFO "factory as environment" in fact supplies the crucial model for all industrialization, including those which operate entirely robotically. That the products manufactured are disarticulated, depersonalized, *killed* animals may help Moore make his point about turnover time, but his claim that "[h]ere the factory *as* environment is on full display" is rendered false if not morally perverse by the denial necessary to make "full" convincing. What is on "full display" is not merely the oppressive conditions of Cheap Labor employed for Cheap Wages under cheap, and often dangerous, dehumanizing conditions; it's the wailing and screaming, the terror, blood, and guts of living "extra-human" beings beyond the massive volumes of soil, water, grains and labor necessary to produce a pound of "what's for dinner." Lastly, then, Moore writes (following Karl Marx's terminology from *Grundrisse*) that "[t]he annihilation of space by time transforms all life and space within the law of value's gravitational pull."[58] But this too is false. Once we acknowledge the many forms of resource theft, water, land, atmosphere, hydrocarbons, grains, rubber, life, labor, operationally necessary to the factory farm, the relationship between time and space is dramatically and *traumatically* altered. What Moore fails to see is that what is altered is the means-by-which capital pursues its kleptocratic course, not the course itself.

Appeals to transformations of space and time cannot capture the fact that the absent referents of the factory farm as environment, the cows, chickens, and pigs manufactured for human and other-than-human consumption, are not merely "transformed"; they're confined, mutilated, stun-gunned, gutted, slashed, slaughtered, and sold. "Killed" is transformative to be sure, but insofar as Moore's account of "time and space" relies on nonhuman animals to be present *as* absent, to be what defines a factory farm *as* a factory, "transformation" can only serve to camouflage the commodification of sentience, to disguise its kleptocratic character. Moore refers to "multi-layered relations of species and environment," but his consignment of factory farm animals to the "extra-human" is destined to ignore what we might call Cheap Sentience, burying it (literally and figuratively) under layers of human chauvinism that cannot fail to taint the "Cheaps" with the denial required to maintain the ontology of resource theft. In one sense, the capacity for sentience is stolen; it is of such weighty value as a bar to commodification, it must be "pinched" to prevent it from "infecting" unpaid labor with the demand for recognition, but preserved to maintain it as the special reserve of (some) human beings. But in another sense, sentience, like time and space, must be annihilated to make room for the factory as environment, the "space" of manufacture whose value preempts all other value. Moore's right that "[t]he genius of capitalism's Cheap Nature strategy was to represent time as linear, space as flat, and nature as external."[59] But the "catch" isn't that "capital-labor relations are not well equipped to map, code, survey, quantify, and otherwise identify and facilitate new sources of Cheap Nature."[60] The catch is that to demote the value of nature to "cheap," it has to be *de-animated*—stripped of any features or characteristics that might pose an obstacle to its commodification.

It's thus unsurprising that de-animation has already become naturalized in Moore's introduction of a critical moment in the spatial expansion of capitalist accumulation he calls the "commodity frontier":

> I wish to highlight two relational axes of these frontiers. First, commodity frontier movements were not merely about the expansion of commodity relations, although this was central. They were also, crucially, about the deployment of territorial power and geographical knowledges necessary for the commodity-oriented appropriation of unpaid work/energy. This unpaid work could be delivered by humans—women or slaves, for example—*or by extra-human natures, such as forests, soils or rivers*.[61]

The "deploying of territorial power" that defines the commodity frontier may be "about" the "expansion of commodity relations" through the "appropriation of unpaid work/energy." But it's underwritten by a human/extra human hybrid that dissolves the very agency responsible for any such deployment.[62] As Andreas Malm makes the point:

> For one genus of scholars, however, there can still be no higher pitch of ecstacy than the dissolution of binaries. The greatest pleasure and joy come the moment they can say: "those two categories you thought were two are one—I hereby claim them united! This is the intellectual concupiscence firing up Jason Moore" . . . [E]vents like Hurricane Katrina and Australian bushfires "simply blur the distinction between life and death." They do no such thing, of course. . . . Hybridism, then, can also be seen as a strident current of dissolutionism.[63]

Referring to the real frontiers of the extractivist industries, Kathyrn Yusoff argues for a "biopolitical" that, like Malm's, cannot be reduced to the mere division of matter into "nonlife and life."[64] Yusoff makes it abundantly clear in *A Billion Black Anthropocenes, or None* that there are responsible parties, that these parties are not merely "territorial powers" but specifically empowered patriarchs whose efforts to expand commodity relations is made possible by institutions like slavery by which indigenous/nonwhite human beings are reduced to the status of the extra-human—not because they're unpaid, but because "paid" and "unpaid" are relevant only for those identified as agents.

The meaning, in other words, of Malm's reference to the "intellectual concupiscence firing up Jason Moore" could not be made clearer than it is in Yusoff when she argues that

> The movement of energy between enslaved bodies in plantations, plants, long-dead fossilized plants, and industrialized labor is a geochemical equation of extraction in the conversion of surplus. But the racialized equation of energy is located in a larger field of production and semiotics of extraction. Slavery is not a byproduct of this process; rather, *slavery is driven by an indifferent extractive geo-logic that is motivated by the desire for inhuman properties*. Indigenous genocide and settler colonialism are also part of these extractive geo-logics. In this sense, slavery can be seen not as a confusion of subject-object in relation to inhuman categorization but as a total submission to the principle of extraction that was exacted through inhuman differentiation.[65]

Slavery is not a byproduct of capital conquest; it's "driven" by a logic of commodification, a *geo-logic*, that presupposes "submission to the principle of extraction" of what/whoever facilitates its profit-driven objective. "Submission," "genocide and settler colonialism" are part of this logic not because "the movement of energy" between "enslaved bodies" and "industrialized labor" is itself a hybrid of the human/extra human," but because "the desire for inhuman properties" is built into the geo-logic. Slavery is made possible, in other words, by a logic of commodification that is empowered to dissolve the value of sentient life in racialized human "others" precisely because that value has already been subsumed and erased in nonhuman "others." It's no wonder what is the driving force behind genocide. It's not a mythical course of nature stimulated by a human/extra human hybrid that ejaculates culpability into a void, Moore's "web of life"; it's the racialized intellectual concupiscence of those who'd defend the rights of human beings against their enslaving oppressors without undertaking any of the meticulous, if uncomfortable, reflection over the "desire for inhuman properties" it can colonize, overpower, and kill.

Put differently: the power of capital accumulation is not, at least originally, territorial; it is not geographical. It is kleptocratic and, as such "biopolitical," because it takes advantage of any and every vulnerability created by the structural inequalities that accrue to species, sex, race, species, and location regardless considerations of life or the capacity to suffer. "Geographical knowledge" may be knowledge of whatever can be deployed in the service of extractivist expansionism. But what comes to count as "knowledge" is determined by a set of presuppositions that define what counts as its (subject/subjugated) matter, empowering the capitalist to create a web of life that mirrors *him*. As Moore observes, "[c]apitalism has moved from peat and charcoal to coal and oil; from the breadbaskets of the Vistula, southern England, and the American Midwest; to labor frontiers in Europe and Africa, Latin America, and South and East Asia."[66] But territorial expansion does not determine the logic that drives this labor, paid and unpaid; it's a manifestation of the kleptocratic ontology of capital. Moore argues that "[t]hese are not repeatable events," and that is likely true, but it's not because "[s]ubstitutability does not unfold through infinite time and space."[67] Indeed, it does—at least in the ontology of resource theft. Yusoff offers a particularly telling example of the kleptocratic ontology of capital in the context of gold mining, one for which substitutability commands the starring role, and for which the ostensibly limitless potential for conversion to "nonbeing" is the catalyst crucial to the quest for profit:

> The division of matter into nonlife and life pertains not only to matter but to the racial organization of life as foundational to New World geographies. The biopolitical category of nonbeing is established through slaves being exchanged for and as gold. Slavery was a geologic axiom of the inhuman in which nonbeing was made, reproduced, and circulated as flesh. This *unmaking of subjects* constitutes a warp of dispossession in the progressive narrative of collective accumulation or geologic commons in which "we" all share.[68]

In the geo-logic of the extractivist industries, the "racial organization of life" is established through the slave that, so defined *as* "slave," can be exchanged for gold or horses or other slaves because all are conceived as endless resources. Infinitely substitutable in virtue of exchangeability, the "biopolitical category of nonbeing" in Yusoff's analysis of the "unmaking of subjects" functions to erase sentience as an obstacle to geographical expansionism by creating fully commodified, de-animated, extracted, disarticulated, exchangeable, Cheap Sentience into the materialities: slave, wife, meat. Contrary to writers like Moore, however, the "organization of life" that advantages the capitalist doesn't come that way; *it has to be made*—that is the function of the logic of commodification.

Slavery is not a "by-product" of capitalism. Rather, it's a necessary denominator in the extractivist "equation" of a mining operation. So too nonhuman animal bodies function as a necessary disarticulate in the "as food" calculus of "what's for dinner"; so too women's sexual reproductive capacities function as a necessary tool for the calculus of progeny, inheritance, land; so too "indigenous genocide and settler colonialism" function as a necessary binomial in the domination of geography and geology, the manifest destinies of righteous white conquerors, and the gold, silver, and uranium mines of their corporate successors. Yet, even though Yusoff's critique of extractivist capital as a racialized and racializing realization of the logic of commodification yields a clearer picture of the ontology of resource theft, especially with respect to advantage created for the capitalist through the dispossession codified as slavery, she does not quite capture the commodification of sentience as the archetypal moment in the creation of exchange value. No doubt, Yusoff escapes the resort to substance dualism that ensnares Moore's appeal to the human/extra-human. When she observes that "[t]he inhuman, as both geologic property and mode of subjective relation in chattel slavery, rendered a coercive interpenetration between human and inhuman categories,"[69] she hints at a subjectivity that cannot simply be reduced to exchange value, but must be coerced. Still, it remains unclear that Yusoff's probing analysis of "[t]he centrality of race to the production of humanity in the Anthropocene," even as she recognizes that any full understanding of this production "requires a reconfiguration of the subject at the center of white liberal ethical accounts,"[70] quite reaches the "geologic" that requires the annihilation of sentience as an ethical prohibition against commodification. Yet it is precisely the excision of sentience as a value that lubricates the interpenetration of human and nonhuman, making all forms of slavery and dispossession possible; and it is the deliberate reclamation of sentience that forms the first necessary component of any reconfiguration of the subject as an agent.

UPHILL CLIMBS/UNINTENDED CAPITULATIONS

While it seems an uphill climb at best to trace a course from the neo-liberal ethics of David Wallace-Wells, Michael Mann, and Gary Francione to Kathryn Yusoff's far more probing analysis of the racialized ontological conditions of extractivist capitalism, the comparison to Moore demands more nuance. For Moore is both less disappointing and yet more so in ways illuminating to the critique of capitalism as an inherently kleptocratic enterprise. On the side of "less," Moore is a philosophical fellow-traveler committed to an unflinching historical, economic, and sociological analysis of the conditions, as he puts it, of a web of life so permeated by capital that its demands come to define the very nature of reality itself. It's not hard to see the lure of hybridist ideas like humanity-in-nature. Our lives are so saturated by advertising and the naturalizing of mass consumption that it doubtless feels like capitalism *is* the web of life. Yet on the side of "more" disappointing, this same appeal to humanity-in-nature in the quest to tear down the Nature/Society dualism depends upon a straw boogie-man that neither reflects the true relationship between human chauvinism and nonhuman nature nor can make sense of the actual history of kleptocratic capitalism. Moore's critique of the substance dualism he presents as if it represented all forms of dualism makes way for his alternative, human/extra human. But in so doing he commits himself to a strategy for the critique of capitalism that omits the crucial role that the erasure of sentience and the capacity for suffering play in its governing logic of commodification. In short, by effectively aligning himself with the human chauvinism defended by Wallace-Wells, Mann, Francione, and even Richard Epstein, Moore forecloses on his own best intentions with respect to the critique of capitalism in a fashion, as Yusoff's analysis shows, that cannot be repaired merely by adding sentient nonhuman others.

Yusoff's careful conceptual excavation of the geo-logic of the extractivist industries illuminates not only the human chauvinism implicit in all five of these writers, but the forms of oppression and subjugation advantaging the profit-oriented agency of those preemptively privileged—white, wealthy, Western(ized) men. Along with the astute history provided by Mark Stoll and the robust defense of a nonhuman nature ultimately independent of human activities despite the anthropogenic impacts perpetrated by capitalism offered by Andreas Malm and Kamran Nayeri, it becomes clear that Moore's hybridism not only fails as a critique of capital, but as a view of reality. Yusoff makes a mockery of such hybridisms by showing how "black and brown death is the precondition of every Anthropocene origin story . . . the grammar and graphia of geology composes a regime for producing contemporary subjects and subtending settler colonialism."[71] What Yusoff shows, in others words, is how the appropriation of geology by profit-seeking mining operations is not merely enabled by prevailing bigotries to take advantage of the indigenous populations of countries like Bolivia and Peru, but is in fact anchored in a "Blackness" created as the crucial conduit, the "non-being" through which a capitalist regime is empowered to colonize, exploit, extract, export, and expel labor according to the logic of commodification. While Yusoff's "preconditions" fail to reach far enough into that heart of darkness that is the commodification of sentience itself, she nonetheless makes utterly clear that the dispossession and brutality at the core of capital accumulation intends from its very origins to subjugation, entitlement—the erasure of agency for all those whose suffering threatens "grow or die." No capitalism can reinvent itself as salvageable through savvy carbon trading schemes in Yusoff's account of extractivist regimes. There is no "web of life" not rooted in blood and death.

Moore might well agree with this latter observation. But the difference between the two critical theorists remains stark: "blood and death" "compose" an ontological condition in Yusoff's analysis of resource theft; in Moore, they remain a byproduct, an awful aftermath to be sure, but still mere consequence of capitalist excess. In Moore's Capitalocene there are earthquakes whose aftershocks are destructive, but their impacts are calculable according to ratios of cost to benefit; this is the Anthropocene. The Black Anthropocene, however, charts the seismology, the incessant deep-earth eruption of capital as resource theft mirrored in the "fungibility of Blackness and geologic resources,"[72] "organized around the grammar of the inhuman."[73] Moore's confusion of cause for consequence leaves his hybridist arguments in an untenable position: he cannot indict capitalism for its catastrophic impacts on the planet and its webs of lives because his analyses of the Cheaps can show only that the Capitalocene is guilty of excess. But there is no excess; there is merely the resource theft dictated by a logic whose only objectives are accumulation, investment, and profit-seeking. It's hard to imagine a more compelling demonstration of the logic of commodification than the Black Anthropocene whose the geo-logic derives its authority from the "grammar of the inhuman," that is, the syntax of commodification.

Moore might argue that regardless the concerns of historians and theorists like Yusoff, the Capitalocene versus Kleptocene debate is beside the point to the extent that what matters most is sounding the alarm concerning the urgency of avoiding environmental and economic catastrophe. Though this sentiment certainly has merit, what's also plainly true is that without the right analysis—or at least something closer to it—the likelihood of an effective response to crisis will remain elusive. What Yusoff's deeper probe of Blackness in the geo-logic of capitalism shows is that such crises are merely symptomatic of an underlying ontology of capital for whom "grow or die" will remain *the* driving force until the very roots of capital conquest are exposed and cauterized. Carbon trading schemes, market solutions, the "factory as environment's" reduction of nonhuman animals to the generic "extra-human," etc. leave the ontology of capital uninterrogated and thereby legitimate its continuation. The real crisis is thus not environmental or economic catastrophe; the real crisis lay in a system of exchange devoid of value other than what can be monetized, or as Yusoff makes the point: "[t]he Anthropocene is a project initiated and executed through anti-Blackness and inhuman subjective modes, from 1492 to the present, and it cannot have any resolution through individual liberal modes of subjectivity and subjugation. In short, that world must end for another relation to the earth to begin."[74] Moore fails to see that the Capitalocene's "web of life" will not come to an end other than in virtue of its nihilism because Moore fails to see that the Capitalocene *is* the Kleptocene. "Initiated and executed" via the commodification of sentience, his calls to action are bound to be stifled by the voices of the suffering subjugated, human and nonhuman. Yusoff "wants to challenge the racial blindness of the Anthropocene as a willful blindness that permeates its comfortable suppositions and its imaginaries of the planetary."[75] Yet, Moore's homogenizing appeal to the Human/Extra-Human can only confirm this blindness, thereby imagining a planetary whose web of life remains white, male, Western(ized). To be clear, Moore's blindness is not the result of any lack of sensitivity to critical matters of how racism and sexism advantage the capitalist. Rather, he fails to see how the capacity for sentience forms the elemental denominator linking race, sex, and species that, dispossessed, absorbed and digested by the logic of commodification, become transformed into the infinite exchange value required by the myth of endless resources. He thus gets it exactly backwards when he argues that: "[i]mportantly, capital's appropriation of unpaid work transcends the Cartesian divide, encompassing both human and extra-human work outside, but necessary to, the circuit of capital and the production of value.[76] What Yusoff shows concerning the geo-logic of Blackness is that capital does not appropriate unpaid work; *"unpaid" is built into the nonbeing of "Blackness."* There is no transcendence of the Cartesian divide because it is itself a tool, a weapon even, fashioned to the maintenance of "the circuit of capital and the production of value" for which there is no "outside." There is only what is commodifiable, and what is not; and the latter is an empty container.

In short, Moore cannot attach from the "outside" what is essential to capitalism *as* a kleptocratic regime; the commodification of sentience is not a detachable limb—it is the circulatory system of capital. To miss this critical aspect of the ontology of resource theft is to miss what is key to the explanation of subjugation, and thus to the analysis of labor, paid and unpaid, in the creation of the absent referent. As Yusoff argues:

> [a]s the Anthropocene proclaims that the language of species life—*anthropos*—through the universalist geologic commons, it neatly erases histories of racism that were incubated through the regulatory structures of geologic relations. The racial categorization of Blackness shares its natality with mining the New World.[77]

Blackness, in other words, is effectively created as a category of non-being for the purpose of being fitted to the regulatory structures, outfitted to the needs and hazards of mining. That such a creation is premised on the erasure not only of the history of racism, but of the people subjected to it constitutes an incarnation of denial[2]: denial first in the tacit maintenance of a universal *anthropos*—the universal "man" who haunts the work of Wallace-Wells, Mann, Francione, Epstein, and Moore, and second, the denial that there is anything problematic, much less racist, to deny. In effect, Moore, et al. permit both forms of erasure to stand; Yusoff invites their disruption, and thus allows for the possibility that even before Blackness may come the sentient Other whose "web of life" is equally annihilated by an extractivist regime, whose suffering goes equally, or more so, unrecognized. Or, more precisely: for Moore the erasures of Blackness, and its many analogues of ethnicity, geography, sexuality, and species, are permitted to stand despite his condemnations of racism and sexism; "extra-human," the one-size-fits-all "not-us," preemptively discounts the value of sentience no matter its material embodiment. Like his fellows, Moore has already crossed that Rubicon.

"Not going far enough" is not, however, "crossing the Rubicon." Yusoff does not quite see that the commodification of sentience itself underwrites the "natality" of Blackness (or "wife" or "worker"). Yet, "White geology," she argues, "makes legible a set of extractions, from particular subject positions, from black and brown bodies, and from the ecologies of place,"[78] that "gives rise to questions about agency and consent, around sentience and inhuman matter, and how material agency with and without subjectivity is thought outside the structures of cozy humanism and its languages of existence."[79] Yusoff's, in other words, is a "not going far enough" that provokes us to go further, whereas Moore's appeal to the human/extra-human dualism solicits the "cozy" humanism that invites us to stay put in the snug-and-smug myths of endless resources that subsidize human chauvinism. In short, Moore's "we" cleaves more closely to the familiar liberal territory of Wallace-Wells fatal complacency than Yusoff's deeply uncomfortable observation that:

> [i]f the imagination of planetary peril coerces and ideal of "we," it only does so when the entrappings of late liberalism become threatened. The "we" negates all responsibility for how the wealth of that geology was built off the subtending strata of indigenous genocide and erasure, slavery, and carceral labor, and evades what that accumulation of wealth still makes possible in the present—lest "we" forget that the economies of geology still largely regulate geopolitics and modes of naturalizing, formalizing, and operationalizing dispossession and ongoing settler colonialism.[80]

What Yusoff shows is that there is no "we" other than the mythical "we" created to authorize the "human" side of the "human/Other" divide, "naturalized, formalized, and operationalized" according to a logic of commodification that systematically dispossesses of value, of status as "we," whatever counts as "Other," as "extra-human," that is, *as* resource. "We" could just as readily superimpose other incarnations of sentience as a threat to late liberalism, namely, the "erasure, slavery, and carceral labor" of the "environment as factory farm." Its greenhouse gas emissions solicit images of planetary peril; the dispossession of its crowded "labor" images of inconsolable misery; its farrowing crates, baby chick grinders, and stun guns the piercing sounds of cruelty and anguish to which too many are numb. "We" can quibble over whether the systematic depersonalizing, slaughter, and disarticulation of nonhuman Others constitutes genocide. But it's that door that Yusoff leaves open—and Moore does not. Insofar as the extra-human adheres to the myth of endless resources as, for example, the cloned infinitely reproducible factory farm animal, the same door closed to a deeper probe of the commodification of sentience remains open to endless exploitation. And insofar as "extra-human" draws no distinction between clean water and the North Atlantic Right Whale, between drillable hydrocarbons and the Brazilian Merganser, it adheres to nothing less than the fiction that resources are endlessly reproducible and/or substitutable; in treating them all the same, it treats them all as equally inexhaustible. The trouble is that none are inexhaustible; the whales and the ducks are critically endangered; Scarce water and scarce gasoline will ignite war. There is, in fact, only one planet earth as far as anyone knows. It's not that Moore's "extra-human" cannot account for, say, the fact of the farrowing crate, it's that it cannot account for the "we" whose power and wealth authorizes the erasure of the *suffering* fact of the farrowing crate.

Another door that Yusoff leaves open to exploration is that which invites comparison between the "infinite reproducibility" of so-called food animals and the commodification of the reproductive sexuality of women. Both offer a window into the ontology of resource theft. What becomes "what's for dinner" in one narrative becomes "progeny" in the other; both signify property under the control of the "we" of what we might call White Agriculture. The exchange value of both is defined in the operational terms of insemination, cultivation, harvest, and future investment. Here too Moore seeks to situate the social and economic status of women within the fixed structures of unpaid labor, arguing that "one of the enduring legacies of Cartesian dualism," reproduced by some Marxists, and replayed in discussions between Marxists and socialist feminists concerns "the blindness of Marxists to the foundational contributions of another kind of invisible work: the daily intergenerational reproduction of human life . . . overwhelmingly performed by women."[81] He asks whether we can "ford this great divide." "I think we can," he continues, "[a]nd I think the way forward looks something like this":

> The substance of value *is* socially necessary labor-time. The drive to advance labor productivity is fundamental to competitive fitness. This means that the exploitation of commodified labor-power is central to capital accumulation, and to the survival of individual capitalists. But this cannot be the end of the story. For the relations necessary to accumulate abstract social labor are—necessarily—more expansive in scale, scope, speed, and intensity. Capital must not only ceaselessly accumulate and revolutionize commodity production: it must ceaselessly search for and find ways to produce Cheap Natures: a rising stream of low-cost food, labor-power, energy and raw materials to the factory gates . . . These are the Four Cheaps. The law of value in capitalism is a law of Cheap Nature.[82]

What is striking about this passage is that "the daily intergenerational reproduction of human life" is performed by *women* drops out, is rendered invisible, and is replaced with abstract references to "socially necessary labor time," "relations necessary to accumulate abstract social labor," and "the ceaseless search for ways to produce Cheap Natures." But it's not sufficient to leave unspoken that this unpaid labor is performed by women because the fact *that* it is women who are structurally positioned to perform it reflects a crucial feature of the ontology of resource theft. Indeed, a robust understanding of the role played by the structural inequalities advantaging the capitalist must include an analysis of the exploitation of women as unpaid labor.

Yet, while Moore treats women in effect as absent referents, Nancy Fraser commits her analysis of capitalism to an equally untenable position. She argues that capitalism has an "inside" and an "outside of the market:

> In capitalist societies much, though not all, of this activity ["birthing, socializing the young, building communities, producing and reproducing the shared meanings, affective dispositions, and horizons of value that underpin social cooperation"] goes on outside the market, in households, neighborhoods, and a host of public institutions, including schools and childcare centers; and much of it, though not all, does not take the form of wage labor.[83]

Moore is certainly right that unpaid labor is as much determined by the forces of capital as paid labor; *there is no "outside" to the market.* The "activity" Fraser wants to privilege particularly in light of its identity as "women's work"[84] is, in fact, crucial to the reproduction of labor and laborers, and thus forms a necessary condition for a functional logic of commodification. Nevertheless, Moore's position is also untenable, and for similar reasons: both Fraser and Moore miss elements that define the ontological conditions of capital conquest, namely, that in the conversion of all value to exchange value, labor—paid and unpaid—must be recruited to the pursuit of profit. Whether, following Yusoff, we call it geo-logic, reproduction-logic, *as* food-logic, erasure-logic, or simply the kleptocratic logic of resource theft, ignoring the deeply enculturated structures of subjugation from which the capitalist draws power and authority can only produce a highly distorted account of the fortunes and misfortunes of its march toward environmental catastrophe. Put differently: the idea that "birthing, socializing the young, building communities, producing and reproducing the shared meanings, affective dispositions, and horizons of value that underpin social cooperation" might escape the nihilism of the Kleptocene, or provide an alternative, or offer an avenue for post-capitalism reconstruction is as unlikely as the idea that there is an "outside" to the planet itself.

NOTES

1. Mark Stoll. *Profit: An Environmental History*. (Cambridge, UK: Polity Press, 2023), 6.
2. Andreas Malm. *The Progress of This Storm: Nature and Society in a Warming World*. (Brooklyn, NY: Verso, 2020), 197.
3. Jason Moore. *Capitalism in the Web* of Life. (Brooklyn, NY: Verso, 2015), 2–3.
4. Moore, 19.
5. Moore, 19 (my emphasis).
6. Malm, 184.
7. Moore, 5.
8. Malm, 180.
9. Malm, 179.
10. Malm, 179.
11. Malm, 170–80.
12. Malm, 180.
13. Malm, 180.
14. Malm, 180.
15. Malm, 182.
16. Malm, 186.
17. Malm, 182.
18. Moore, 54–5.
19. Kamran Nayeri. Kamran. "*Capitalism in the Web of Life*—A Critique." *Climate and Capitalism*, 7.19.16. https://climateandcapitalism.com/2016/07/19/capitalism-in-the-web-of-life-a-critique/#:~:text=Kamran%20Nayeri%20argues%20that%20Jason,impact%20on%20the%20natural%20world.
20. Nayeri.
21. Nayeri.
22. Malm, 87.
23. Malm, 164, 165.
24. Nayeri.
25. Malm, 200.
26. Malm, 201.
27. Malm, 201.
28. Stoll, 77.
29. Malm, 201.
30. Stoll, 83.
31. Moore, 4.
32. Carol Adams. *The Sexual Politics of Meat*. (New York: Bloomsbury Academic, 2015), 16–17.
33. Moore, 5.
34. Moore, 4.
35. Moore, 5.
36. Moore, 3.
37. Moore, 3–4.

38. Moore, 4.

39. Amy Chillag. "These Tiny Creatures are Losing Their Battle to Survive. Here's What We Can Do to Save Them." *CNN*, 9.3.23. https://www.cnn.com/2023/09/03/world/iyw-rufous-hummingbird-tipping-point-extinction/index.html.

40. William Cronin. "The Trouble with Wilderness." *Environmental History*, Vol 1.1 (Jan. 1996), 7–28. http://www.jstor.org/stable/3985059.

41. Moore, 12.

42. Moore, 249–55.

43. Moore, 249.

44. Moore, 249.

45. Moore, 250–1.

46. Chris Parker. "Frankencrops: Monsanto Seeks Control of America's Food Supply." *Phoenix New Times*, 7.25.13. https://www.phoenixnewtimes.com/restaurants/frankencrops-monsanto-seeks-control-of-americas-food-supply-6459304.

47. Moore, 251.

48. Moore, 251–2.

49. Moore, 252.

50. Moore, 252–3.

51. Moore, 273.

52. Moore, 275.

53. Alasdair Bland. "Is the Livestock Industry Destroying the Planet?" *Smithsonian Magazine*, 9.1.12. https://www.smithsonianmag.com/travel/is-the-livestock-industry-destroying-the-planet-11308007/.

54. Moore, 240.

55. Moore, 255.

56. Moore, 232.

57. Moore, 232.

58. Moore, 232.

59. Moore, 61.

60. Moore, 62.

61. Moore, 63 (my emphasis).

62. Malm, 178–83.

63. Malm, 186.

64. Kathryn Yusoff. *A Billion Black Anthropocenes or None*. (Minneapolis, MN: University of Minnesota Press, 2018), 5.

65. Yusoff, 16.

66. Moore, 66.

67. Moore, 66.

68. Yusoff, 5 (my emphasis).

69. Yusoff, 57.

70. Yusoff, 61.

71. Yusoff, 66.

72. Yusoff, 32.

73. Yusoff, 84.

74. Yusoff, 63.

75. Yusoff, xiii.
76. Moore, 55.
77. Yusoff, 2.
78. Yusoff, 4.
79. Yusoff, 9.
80. Yusoff, 106.
81. Moore, 52.
82. Moore, 53.
83. Nancy Fraser. *Cannibal Capitalism*. (Brooklyn, NY: Verso, 2022), 9.
84. Fraser, 10.

Conclusion

TERROR, URGENCY, EMPATHY

Ashley Dawson argues that "[c]apitalism is not necessarily more immoral than previous social systems with regard to cruelty to humans and the gratuitous destruction of nature. As a mode of production and a social system, however, capitalism requires people to be destructive of the environment." I think we can now see that Dawson misconstrues the moral question—slightly. The right question isn't whether capitalism is more or less immoral than whatever came before it. It's whether capitalism is survivable. It is not. Kathryn Yusoff argues that capitalism must end; Dawson shows that this is not for the sake of human beings alone. Indeed, Dawson answers his own question when he poses the rhetorical "[c]an capitalist society reform itself sufficiently to cope with the extinction crisis?" "This is not simply unlikely," he responds, "[i]t is impossible in the long run." While Dawson's focus is the loss of nonhuman animal species, David Wallace-Wells makes it clear that, given our fatal complacency, an earth made uninhabitable for human beings is not merely apocalyptic fantasy.

Yet Wallace-Wells, like Michael Mann and Gary Francione ultimately concede to the "Frankenstein" of capital accumulation, becoming effective apologists for reformist versions of an economic system whose premises resist reform. Theirs is a salvation capitalism promising in its fantasy of a regulatory utopia, dependent on denial, courting extinction. Jason Moore offers a verdant and meticulous picture of the Capitalocene's long, mottled, violent history lumbering and straining along the axes of the Cheaps, of unpaid labor, and of technological innovation. But Moore's account leaves capital open to a version of salvation blighted by extinction, the eruption of global pandemic, wars over access to water, and the Motherload of existential hazards, the climate crisis. Contrary to the reformers, the case for a desirable future is not going to be made on the premise that we have simply taken our love affair with products too far, and must therefore reign in the excess; it's that until we recognize that the fundamental governing predicate of capitalism is resource theft, that expunging the value of sentience from the logic of commodification guts it of even a glimmer of conscience, there will be no road to a future worth the struggle to achieve it. Reform is a pipe-dream. It makes capitalism unsalvageable, however much carbon trades and taxes, alternative energy sources, or new technologies promise us we can just keep on consuming and wasting and dumping. But my aims are not ultimately just criticism; mine is a call to revolution. The work before us requires revolutionary struggle to overcome not merely capitalism, but the ontology that supports the Kleptocene it has always been. At the center of the Kleptocene is Blackness, Heteropatriarchal instantiations of property and progeny, and at the core of every form of subjugation and commodification: the erasure of sentience as the most potent obstacle to the conversion of everything into a thing to be mass produced, sold, made rancid, and discarded. The basic drivers of capital accumulation are neither avarice nor greed, but rather predatory accretion borne of the absolute necessity to grow or die, outcompete or wither on the vine—using and using up everything on the earth to this end. There is no middle ground; there are no compromises left to make. There are instead a set of myths to overcome: myths about resources, about labor, about value, about life; fictions naturalized and normalized to feel like reality sustained by its carefully cultivated denial.

Capitalism doesn't give rise to the Kleptocene; the Capitalocene is the Kleptocene revealed bit by bit, catastrophe by catastrophe, throughout the history of resource theft. Indeed, the Black Anthropocene is the Capitalocene is the Kleptocene precisely because the commodification of sentience is authorized by what is essential to capital, namely, the reduction of value to its lowest common denominator: exchange that makes no allowance for the value we say we associate with suffering—or, contrary to Fraser, "birthing, socializing the young, building communities, producing and reproducing the shared meanings, affective dispositions, and horizons of value that underpin social cooperation." The myth of endless resources is itself dependent on denial[2]. We must not only deny that the planet is not an inexhaustible treasure trove of commodifiables, we must deny that there is anything to deny. Denial is, however, becoming harder and harder to sustain. Every time we turn on the news to witness billowing plumes of toxic smoke and ash choked upwards by the incinerated apartment buildings and houses and cafes and cars and people and grandmas and children and dogs and cats and cows and fields that, left in the blood-smeared wake of Russian armies, reminds us that the value we assign to life, decency, and beauty is easily discarded where there is fortune to be made, power to be seized, land to be annexed. The same logic of commodification that, vanquished of empathy, creates the conditions of dispossession, terror, hunger, environmental deterioration, and pandemic also produces the conditions of war. Though, I am reluctant to call the abject terror meted out against Ukraine war.

War involves conflict between two or more parties, however unequal in justification, armaments, and public support. The murderous violence raining down upon the people of Ukraine by the ultimate kleptocrat, Vladimir Putin, is not war; it's state-sponsored terrorism made possible by the geo-logic of the Black Anthropocene, the flattening dehumanization that is slavery, but also rape; that is unpaid labor, but also the casual back-of-the-head execution of bicyclists in Bucha. We have no excuse for surprise: the turn away from suffering toward the power made material as profit is a Rubicon crossed long ago, a walk we repeat every day when we turn away from the news to ask what's for dinner. But of course, this is entirely too simple. For as we've surveyed many times over, "we" divides along axes of power, privilege, advantage, but it also craters into the mass graves of genocidal massacres and factory farm waste lagoons. A people who can turn a blind eye to the suffering of their most vulnerable can blind themselves to anything. A civilization that can institutionalize such moral blindness as part of its worldview has foreclosed on the prospect of its own future. The Anthropocene is the Capitalocene is the Black Anthropocene is the Kleptocene because the logic of commodification dissipates the capacity for empathy, and because "we" have thus far not mustered the courage to reclaim it. And that, I suggest, is the meaning of nihilism.

Bibliography

116th Congress. H. Res. 10-9. *Green New Deal*. 2.7.19. https://www.congress.gov/116/bills/hres109/BILLS-116hres109ih.pdf.

Adams, Carol. *Neither Man nor Beast: Feminism and the Defense of Animals*. Brooklyn, NY: Lantern Books, 2015.

Adams, Carol. *The Sexual Politics of Meat*. Bloomsbury Academic, 2015.

Ag Daily. "Top Ten Most Popular Cattle Breeds in the United States." https://www.agdaily.com/livestock/top-10-cattle-breeds-united-states/.

Alexander, Michelle. *The New Jim Crow*. New York: New Press, 2020.

Allen, Karma. "Polar Bears May Be Extinct by 2100 if Arctic Ice Melts at Projected Rate, According to New Study." *ABC News*, 7.22.20. https://abcnews.go.com/US/polar-bears-extinct-2100-arctic-ice-melts-projected/story?id=71895289.

American Progress. "Act Now for Equal Pay." https://www.americanprogress.org/article/quick-facts-gender-wage-gap/.

American Society for the Prevention of Cruelty to Animals (ASPCA). "Oppose Right to Farm Legislation." https://www.aspca.org/improving-laws-animals/public-policy/oppose-right-farm-legislation.

Animal Equality News. "Investigation: Wet Markets in China Continue to Operate." https://animalequality.org/news/investigation-wet-markets-in-china-continue-to-operate/.

Animals Asia. https://www.animalsasia.org/us/our-work/cat-and-dog-welfare/.

ArcGIS. "The Sengwer." https://www.arcgis.com/apps/Cascade/index.html?appid=06640543a10b4a5ba3ebfa64224b5f2c.

ASPCA. "Oppose Right to Farm Legislation." https://www.aspca.org/improving-laws-animals/public-policy/oppose-right-farm-legislation.

Axon, Rachel, Kyle Bagenstose, and Sky Chadde. "Coronavirus Outbreaks Climb at U.S. Meatpacking Plants Despite Protections, Trump Order." https://www.usatoday.com/story/news/investigations/2020/06/06/meatpacking-plants-cant-shake-covid-19-cases-despite-trump-order/3137400001/.

Baker, Cayli. "The Trump Administration's Major Environmental Deregulations." *Brookings*, 12.15.20. https://www.brookings.edu/blog/up-front/2020/12/15/the-trump-administrations-major-environmental-deregulations/.

Banergee, Neela, et al. "Exxon: The Road Not Taken." *Inside Climate News*, 2015. https://insideclimatenews.org/book/exxon-the-road-not-taken/.

Bates, Mary. "Thinking Like a Pig." *Psychology Today*, 2.16.21. https://www.psychologytoday.com/us/blog/animal-minds/202102/thinking-pig.

Beef Magazine. "Here's Why China is Going to Boom." https://www.beefmagazine.com/livestock-management/here-s-why-china-is-going-to-boom.

Bender, Frederic *The Culture of Extinction*. Amherst, NY: Humanity Books, 2003.

Bison Timeline. *All About Bison*. https://allaboutbison.com/bison-in-history/bison-timeline/.

Bittman, Mark. "The Staggering Cost of Rising World Meat Production." *New York Times*, 1.28.08. https://www.nytimes.com/2008/01/27/business/worldbusiness/27iht-meat.1.9525251.html.

Bland, Alasdair. "Is the Livestock Industry Destroying the Planet?" *Smithsonian Magazine*, 9.1.12. https://www.smithsonianmag.com/travel/is-the-livestock-industry-destroying-the-planet-11308007/.

Bleiweis, Robin. "Quick Facts About the Gender Wage Gap." *Center for American Progress*, 3.24.20. https://www.americanprogress.org/issues/women/reports/2020/03/24/482141/quick-facts-gender-wage-gap/.

Bloom, Greg. "Here's Why China's Going to Boom." *Beef*, 11.20.20. https://www.beefmagazine.com/beef/heres-why-china-going-boom.

Bloomberg Green. "Wuhan is Returning to Life. So are its Wet Markets." *Bloomberg News*, 4.8.20. https://www.bloomberg.com/news/articles/2020-04-08/wuhan-is-returning-to-life-so-are-its-disputed-wet-markets.

Bold Nebraska. https://boldnebraska.org.

Bond, Cody. "Supreme Court to Decide the Fate of Franken-Seeds and Farming." *Generation Progress*, 2.24.13. https://genprogress.org/supreme-court-to-decide-the-fate-of-frankenseeds-and-farming/.

Bonneuil, Christophe, and Jean-Baptiste Fressoz. *The Shock of the Anthropocene*. Brooklyn, NY: Verso, 2017.

Breakthrough Institute. https://thebreakthrough.org.

Brickley, Peg. "J&J Opposes Former Talc Suppliers Bankruptcy Plan to resolve Cancer Claims." https://www.wsj.com/articles/j-j-opposes-former-talc-suppliers-bankruptcy-plan-to-resolve-cancer-claims-11610499939.

Broder, Jonathan. "BP Shortcuts Led to Gulf Oil Spill." *New York Times*, 9.15.11, https://www.nytimes.com/2011/09/15/science/earth/15spill.html.

Byington, Lillianna. "Smithfield Food Posts Q2 Loss After Spending 350 Million on Coronavirus." *Food Dive*, 8.12.20. https://www.fooddive.com/news/smithfield-foods-posts-q2-loss-after-spending-350m-on-coronavirus/583341/.

Cagle, Susie and Vivian Ho. "'Not Our Mission': Private Fire Crews Protect the Insured, Not the Public." *The Guardian*, 11.3.19. https://www.theguardian.com/us-news/2019/nov/03/not-our-mission-private-fire-crews-protect-the-insured-not-the-public.

Carrington, Damian. "Oil Firms' Climate Claims are Greenwashing, Study Concludes," *The Guardian*, 2.16.22. https://www.theguardian.com/environment/2022/feb/16/oil-firms-climate-claims-are-greenwashing-study-concludes.

Caruso, Skyler. "Everything to Know About the Bud Light Controversy." *People Magazine*, 7.19.23. https://people.com/bud-light-controversy-everything-to-know-7547159.

Center for Climate and Energy Solutions. "Australia's Carbon Pricing Mechanisms." https://www.c2es.org/document/australias-carbon-pricing-mechanism/.

Centers for Disease Control and Prevention (CDC). "Covid-19." https://www.cdc.gov/coronavirus/2019-ncov/index.html.

Centers for Disease Control and Prevention (CDC). "Janssen Covid-19 Vaccine (Johnson and Johnson)." https://www.cdc.gov/vaccines/covid-19/info-by-product/janssen/index.html.

Chapell, Bill. "Trump Administration Moves Closer to Allowing Oil Drilling in Arctic Refuge." *NPR*, 8.17.20. https://www.npr.org/2020/08/17/903239366/trump-administration-sets-plan-for-oil-drilling-in-arctic-refuge.

Chillag, Amy. "These Tiny Creatures are Losing Their Battle to Survive. Here's What We Can Do to Save Them." *CNN*, 9.3.23. https://www.cnn.com/2023/09/03/world/iyw-rufous-hummingbird-tipping-point-extinction/index.html.

Cleeland, Nancy. "OSHA Cite Meatpacking Plants for Coronavirus Failures." *SHRM*, 9.12.20.

Client Earth. "Greenwashing Files: ExxonMobil." https://www.clientearth.org/projects/the-greenwashing-files/exxonmobil/.

Collins, Patricia Hill. *Black Sexual Politics: African Americans, Gender, and the New Racism. New York:* Routledge, 2004.

Conley, Jason. "Sorry Meat-Eaters, Humans aren't the Top of the Food Chain." *Scientific Scribbles, University of Melbourne*, 10.20.18. https://blogs.unimelb.edu.au/sciencecommunication/2018/10/20/sorry-meat-eaters-humans-arent-at-the-top-of-the-food-chain/.

Cooper, Iman. "Commodification of the Black Body, Sexual Objectification and Social Hierarchies During Slavery." https://earlham.edu/media/2544034/commodification-of-black-bodies-iman-cooper-spring-2015.pdf.

Cronin, William. "The Trouble with Wilderness." Environmental History, Vol 1.1 (Jan. 1996), 7–28. http://www.jstor.org/stable/3985059.

Davies, Julian. "Anthropomorphism in Science." *National Library of Medicine, National Institutes of Health*, 10.11.2010. https://www.ncbi.nlm.nih.gov/pmc/articles/PMC2948194/.

Dawson, Ashley. *Extinction: A Radical History*. New York, NY: OR Books, 2016.

Deakin, Simon and Wolfgang Meng. "The Governance of Covid-19: Anthropogenic Risk, Evolutionary Learning, and the Future of the Social State." https://academic.oup.com/ilj/article/49/4/539/6020142.

Desmog Blog. "Michael Shellenberger." https://www.desmog.com/michael-shellenberger/.

Deveau, Scott, Saijel Kishan, and Joe Carroll. "ExxonMobil's Last Ditch Attempt to Stave Off a Climate Coup." *Bloomberg News*, 5.29.21. https://www.bloomberg.com/news/articles/2021-05-29/exxon-mobil-s-last-ditch-attempt-to-stave-off-a-climate-coup#xj4y7vzkg.

Diamond, Cora. “Eating Meat and Eating People.” In *Animal Rights: Current Debates and New Directions*. Ed. Cass Sunstein and Martha Nussbaum. Oxford: Oxford UP. 2004, 93–107.

Dlouhy, Jennifer. “Environmental Groups Warn Alaska Drillers not to Pursue ANWR Leases.” World Oil, 9.17.20. https://www.worldoil.com/news/2020/9/17/environmental-groups-warn-alaska-drillers-not-to-pursue-anwr-leases.

Dlouhy, Jennifer A., and Leslie Kaufman. “How the Oil Lobby Learned to Love Carbon Taxes.” Bloomberg Green, 3.4.21. https://www.bloomberg.com/news/articles/2021-03-04/how-the-oil-lobby-learned-to-love-carbon-taxes.

Donovan, Josephine, “Animal Rights and Feminist Theory,” *Signs*, Vol. 15.2 (Winter, 1990). https://fewd.univie.ac.at/fileadmin/user_upload/inst_ethik_wiss_dialog/Donovan__J._1990._AR_and_Feminist_Theorie.pdf.

Duncombe, Jenessa. “No Mask? You May Not Worry About Climate Change, Either.” *EOS*, 4.14.20. https://eos.org/articles/no-mask-you-may-not-worry-about-climate-change-either.

Durkee, Alison. “Texas Governor Vows to Sue Biden Over Climate Change Orders.” *Forbes*, 1.21.21. https://www.forbes.com/sites/alisondurkee/2021/01/28/texas-governor-abbott-vows-to-sue-biden-over-climate-change-orders/?sh=60ff86662db5.

Eavis, Peter, and Niraj Cockshi. “While the Pandemic Wrecked Some Businesses, Others did Fine. Even Great.” https://www.nytimes.com/2020/11/09/business/economy/companies-profits-losses-coronavirus.html.

Editorial Board, The Paisano. “Texas Fuels Patriarchy with New Abortion Law.” *The Paisano*, 9.7.21. https://paisano-online.com/26836/editorial/texas-fuels-patriarchy-with-new-abortion-law/.

Einhorn, Catrin, and Elena Shao. “How Hot is the Sea Off Florida Right Now? Think 90s Fahrenheit.” https://www.nytimes.com/2023/07/12/climate/florida-ocean-temperatures-reefs.html.

Engine No. 1. https://engine1.com.

Epstein, Richard. “Animals as Objects, or Subjects, or Rights.” In *Animal Rights: Current Debates and New Directions*. Ed. Cass R. Sunstein, and Martha Nussbaum. Oxford: Oxford UP, 2004, 143–61.

Esri. “The Sengwer.” https://www.arcgis.com/apps/Cascade/index.html?appid=06640543a10b4a5ba3ebfa64224b5f2c.

Euro News. “The Dark Side of Forest Conservation: The Sengwer Tribe and Embobut Forest.” https://www.euronews.com/living/2020/07/20/the-dark-side-of-forest-conservation-the-sengwer-tribe-and-embobut-forest.

ExxonMobil. “Growing the Gulf.” https://corporate.exxonmobil.com/Locations/United-States/Growing-the-Gulf.

ExxonMobil. “Sustainability at ExxonMobil.” https://corporate.exxonmobil.com/news/reporting-and-publications/sustainability-report.

Extinction Rebellion. https://rebellion.global.

Eyb, Lyn. “Scientists Say Australia’s Tony Abbott is Engineering an ‘Environmental Trainwreck.’” *Global Post*, 4.8.14. https://www.pri.org/stories/2014-04-08/scientists-say-australias-tony-abbott-engineering-environmental-train-wreck.

Fallert, Nicole. "A Man Was Arrested for Allegedly Threatening to Kill Anthony Fauci and His Family." Buzzfeed News, 7.27.21. https://www.buzzfeednews.com/article/nicolefallert/dr-fauci-death-threats.

Fassler, Joe. "ABC News Calls it 'Pink Slime.' Now USDA Says it Can Be Labelled 'Ground Beef.'" *The Counter*, 2.7.19. https://thecounter.org/bpi-pink-slime-ground-beef-usda-reclassifed/.

Feldstein, Stephanie. "Opinion: Biden Isn't Trying to Cut Meat Consumption. But He Should." *Washington Post*, 4.29.21. https://www.washingtonpost.com/opinions/2021/04/29/biden-isnt-trying-cut-meat-consumption-he-should/.

Fickling, David. "China's Giant Crop Takeover Has Failed. Time to Admit it." *Bloomberg News*, 12.10.20. https://www.bloomberg.com/opinion/articles/2020-12-10/chemchina-s-syngenta-takeover-is-a-failure-time-to-admit-it.

Food and Agriculture Organization of the United States. "Key Facts and Findings; By the Numbers: GHG Emissions by Livestock." http://www.fao.org/news/story/en/item/197623/icode/.

Fortuna, Carolyn. "The Deception Continues as Companies Hide Behind Fake Environmental Promises." *CleanTechnica*, 11.23.21. https://cleantechnica.com/2021/11/23/the-deception-continues-as-companies-hide-behind-fake-environmental-promises/.

Francione, Gary L. "Animals—Property or Persons?" In *Animal Rights: Current Debates and New Directions*. Ed. Cass R. Sunstein, and Martha Nussbaum. Oxford: Oxford UP, 2004, 108–42.

Frangoul, Anmar. "BP CEO Says Oil and Gas Giant is a 'Greening Company,' Refutes Greenwashing Accusations." CNBC, 2.15.22. https://www.cnbc.com/2022/02/15/bp-ceo-says-oil-and-gas-giant-is-a-greening-company.html.

Fraser, Nancy. *Cannibal Capitalism*. Brooklyn, NY: Verso, 2022.

Freedman, Andrew. "Tornado Outbreak Offers a Grim Climate Warning," *Axios*, 12.13.21. https://www.axios.com/tornado-disaster-kentucky-climate-change-warning-a4c2788c-46fd-4851-a55f-e373798814f9.html.

Gbagbo, Eileen. "The Dark Side of Forest Conservation: The Sengwer Tribe and Embobut Forest." https://www.euronews.com/green/2020/07/20/the-dark-side-of-forest-conservation-the-sengwer-tribe-and-embobut-forest.

Ghosh, Amitov. *The Great Derangement: Climate Change and the Unthinkable*. Chicago: University of Chicago Press, 2017.

Giddings, Paula. "The Origin of Lynching Culture in the United States." *Facing History and Ourselves*. https://www.facinghistory.org/resource-library/video/origins-lynching-culture-united-states.

Gillies, Rob. "Keystone XL Pipeline Halted as Biden Revokes Permit." Associated Press, 1.20.21. https://apnews.com/article/joe-biden-alberta-2fbcce48372f5c29c3ae6f6f93907a6d.

Goldhill, Olivia, and Nicholas St. Fleur. *STAT*, 12.3.20. https://www.statnews.com/2020/12/03/how-rich-and-privileged-can-skip-the-line-for-covid19-vaccines/.

Gosalvez, Emma. "How Habitat Destruction Enables the Spread of Covid-19." *North Carolina State University: College of Natural Resources News*, 4.22.21. https://cnr.ncsu.edu/news/2020/04/habitat-destruction-covid19/.

Grabell, Michael, and Bernice Yeung. "Meatpacking Companies Dismissed Years of Warnings but Now Say Nobody Could Have Prepared for Covid-19." *Propublica*, 8.20.20. https://www.propublica.org/article/meatpacking-companies-dismissed-years-of-warnings-but-now-say-nobody-could-have-prepared-for-covid-19.

Graziosi, Greg. "Anheuser-Busch Criticized for Statement Appearing to Apologize for Dylan Mulvaney's Bud Light Campaign." *Independent*, 4.15.23. https://www.independent.co.uk/news/world/americas/anheuser-busch-dylan-mulvaney-statement-criticised-b2320459.html.

Guardian Staff. "Woodside Petroleum Joins GHP and Rio Tinto to Call for Carbon Price." *The Guardian*, 11.13.18. https://www.theguardian.com/environment/2018/nov/14/woodside-petroleum-joins-bhp-and-rio-tinto-to-call-for-carbon-price.

Gustin, Georgina. "As the Livestock Industry Touts Manure-to-Energy Projects, Environmentalists Cry 'Greenwashing.'" *Inside Climate News*, 12.7.20. https://insideclimatenews.org/news/07122020/livestock-industry-manure-energy-natural-gas/.

Hall, Shannon. "Exxon Knew about Climate Change Almost 40 Years Ago." Scientific American, 10.26.15. https://www.scientificamerican.com/article/exxon-knew-about-climate-change-almost-40-years-ago/.

Haraway, Donna. "Speculative Fabulations for Technoculture's Generations: Taking care of Unexpected Country." *Australian Humanities Review*, May 2011, 1–18.

Haraway, Donna. "In the Heart of the Storm: An Interview with Donna Haraway; Part 1: Species Being in the Age of Climate Change, Coronavirus, and Capitalism." Science for the People, 23.3. https://magazine.scienceforthepeople.org/vol23-3-bio-politics/in-the-heart-of-the-storm-an-interview-with-donna-haraway/.

Harvey, David. *The New Imperialism*. Oxford: Oxford University Press, 2005.

Hermann, Christoph. *The Critique of Commodification*. New York, NY: Oxford University Press, 2021.

Holland, Alison. "Why Tony Abbott's Appointment as Indigenous Envoy Was a Diplomatic Blunder and a Policy Failure." https://theconversation.com/why-tony-abbotts-appointment-as-indigenous-envoy-was-a-diplomatic-blunder-and-policy-failure-106345.

Human Society of the United States. "HSUS Fact Sheet: Greenhouse Emissions from Animal Agriculture." https://www.humanesociety.org/sites/default/files/archive/assets/pdfs/farm/hsus-fact-sheet-greenhouse-gas-emissions-from-animal-agriculture.pdf.

Indigenous Peoples reject REDD. "REDD + Threatens the Survival of Indigenous Peoples." https://redd-monitor.org/2011/11/28/redd-threatens-the-survival-of-indigenous-peoples-new-statement-from-indigenous-peoples-rejects-redd/.

Innovative Genomics Institute. "CRISPR-Based Enhancers of DNA Vaccines for Covid-19." https://innovativegenomics.org/projects/crispr-based-dna-vaccine-enhancer-covid-19/.

Jacobs, Jennifer, and Drew Armstrong. "Trump's 'Warp Speed' Aims to Rush Coronavirus Vaccine." *Bloomberg News*, 4.29.20. https://www.bloomberg.com/news/articles/2020-04-29/trump-s-operation-warp-speed-aims-to-rush-coronavirus-vaccine.

Jacquet, Jennifer. "The Meat Industry is Doing Exactly What Big Oil Does to Fight Climate Action." *Washington Post*, 5.14.21. https://www.washingtonpost.com/outlook/the-meat-industry-is-doing-exactly-what-big-oil-does-to-fight-climate-action/2021/05/14/831e14be-b3fe-11eb-ab43-bebddc5a0f65_story.html.

Jones, Nikole Hannah. "The 1619 Project." *New York Times Magazine*, August, 2019. https://www.nytimes.com/interactive/2019/08/14/magazine/1619-america-slavery.html.

Kaur, Harmeet. "Only About 200 People Speak the Cherokee Language Fluently. The Tribe is Saving Some Vaccine Doses for Them." https://www.cnn.com/2021/01/12/us/cherokee-nation-language-speakers-vaccine-trnd/index.html.

Klein, Naomi. "Let Them Drown: The Violence of Othering on a Warming World." *London Review of Books*, 38.11, June 2016. http://www.lrb.co.uk/v38/n11/naomi-klein/let-them-drow.

Klein, Naomi. *This Changes Everything: Capitalism vs. the Climate*. Simon and Schuster, 2015.

Koch, Cristoph. "How Do We Wrap Our Minds Around Bee Consciousness?" *To the Best of Our Knowledge*, 7.28.18. https://www.ttbook.org/interview/how-do-we-wrap-our-minds-around-bee-consciousness.

Kolbert, Elizabeth. *The Sixth Extinction*. New York: Picador, Henry Holt and Company, 2014.

Krupp, Fred. "Exxon Investors Vote for Change in a Watershed Moment for the Climate." *Environmental Defense Fund*, 5.26.21. https://www.edf.org/media/exxon-investors-vote-change-watershed-moment-climate.

Lai, Rebecca K.K. "Abortion Bans: 9 States Have Passed Bills to Limit the Procedure This Year." *New York Times*, 5.29.19. https://www.nytimes.com/interactive/2019/us/abortion-laws-states.html.

Lancet, The. "Covid-19, Wet Markets, and Planetary Health." Vol. 4, June 2020. https://www.thelancet.com/pdfs/journals/lanplh/PIIS2542-5196(20)30122-4.pdf.

Latimore, Jack. "Abbott as Indigenous Affairs Envoy? Be Disturbed. Be Very Disturbed." *The Guardian*, 8.28.18. https://www.theguardian.com/commentisfree/2018/aug/29/abbott-as-indigenous-affairs-envoy-be-disturbed-be-very-disturbed.

Latour, Bruno. *Down to Earth: Politics in the New Climate Regime*. Paris: Polity Books, 2018.

Lavazza, Andrea. "Free Will and Neuroscience: From Explaining Freedom Away to New Ways of Operationalizing and Measuring It." *Frontiers in Human Neuroscience*, 6.1.16. https://www.frontiersin.org/articles/10.3389/fnhum.2016.00262/full.

Lavelle, Marianne. "Requiem for a Pipeline: Keystone XL Transformed the Environmental Movement and Shifted the Debate over Energy and Climate." *Inside Climate News*, 6.20.21. https://insideclimatenews.org/news/20062021/keystone-xl-pipeline-environmental-movement-energy-climate/.

Lee, Wendy, *This is Environmental Ethics*. Hoboken, NJ: Wiley Blackwell, 2023.

Lee, Wendy Lynne. "Dewey and Climate Denial^{2}." *Philosophy Now*, Issue 135, December 2019, 16–20. https://philosophynow.org/issues/135/Dewey_and_Climate_Denial_Squared.

Lee, Wendy Lynne. *Eco-Nihilism: The Philosophical Geopolitics of the Climate Change Apocalypse*. Lanham, MD: Lexington Books, 2016.

Lee, Wendy Lynne. *Contemporary Feminist Theory and Activism: Six Global Issues*. Peterborough, Canada: Broadview Press, 2010.

LeMenager, Stephanie. *Living Oil: Petroleum Culture in the American Century*. Oxford: Oxford University Press, 2014.

Leonardo DiCaprio Foundation. https://www.leonardodicaprio.org.

Levin, Bess. "Trump Declares Himself 'The No. 1 Environmental President.'" *Vanity Fair*, 9.8.20. https://www.vanityfair.com/news/2020/09/donald-trump-environment-roosevelt.

Lugones, Maria. "Toward a Decolonial Feminism." *Hypatia*, 25.4 (Fall, 2010), 742–59. http://www.iheal.univ-paris3.fr/sites/www.iheal.univ-paris3.fr/files/towards%20a%20decolonial%20feminism.pdf.

Lynteris, Christos, and Lyle Fearnley. "Why Shutting Down Chinese Wet Markets Could be a Terrible Mistake." *The Conversation*. https://theconversation.com/why-shutting-down-chinese-wet-markets-could-be-a-terrible-mistake-130625.

Malm, Andreas. *The Progress of this Storm: Nature and Society in a Warming World*. Brooklyn, NY: Verso, 2020.

Mann, Michael. *The New Climate War: The Fight to Take Back Our Climate*. Scribe, 2021.

Marson, Alex, et al. "CRISPR-Based Enhancers of DNA Vaccines for Covid-19." Innovative Genomics Institute. https://innovativegenomics.org/projects/crispr-based-dna-vaccine-enhancer-covid-19/.

Maudlin, Erin Stewart. *Unredeemed Land: An Environmental History of Civil War and Emancipation in the Cotton South*. Oxford: Oxford UP, 2018.

McCarthy, Bill. "Joe Biden Banning Burgers? FOX News, GOP Politicians Fuerl False Narrative." *Politifact*, 4.26.21. https://www.politifact.com/factchecks/2021/apr/26/fox-news-channel/joe-biden-banning-burgers-fox-news-gop-politicians/.

Mendoza, Naki. B. "Will Big Agriculture Mergers Impact Smallholder Farmers?" *DEVEX*, 9.29.16. https://www.devex.com/news/will-big-agriculture-mergers-impact-smallholder-farmers-88820.

Mongabay.com. "Three Pangolin Species Closer to Extinction: IUCN." 12.18.19. https://news.mongabay.com/2019/12/three-pangolin-species-closer-to-extinction-iucn/.

Montgomery, Sy. *The Soul of an Octopus*. New York, NY: Atria press, 2015.

Moore, Jason. *Capitalism in the Web of Life*. Brooklyn, NY: Verso, 2015.

Nathan, Debbie. "Black Men Disproportionately Represented on Sex Offender Registries." The Appeal, 11.15.18. https://theappeal.org/black-men-disproportionately-represented-on-sex-offender-registries/.

National Humane Education Society. "Government Regulation of Factory Farms." https://www.nhes.org/3372-2/.

National Pesticide Information Center. http://npic.orst.edu/ingred/petroleum-distillates.html.

Nayeri, Kamran. "*Capitalism in the Web of Life*—A Critique." Climate and Capitalism, 7.19.16. https://climateandcapitalism.com/2016/07/19/capitalism-in-the-web

-of-life-a-critique/#:~:text=Kamran%20Nayeri%20argues%20that%20Jason,impact%20on%20the%20natural%20world.

Newburger, Emma. “A Major Antarctic Ice Shelf Could Shatter within Five Years, Scientists Warn.” CNBC, 12.13.21. https://www.cnbc.com/2021/12/13/a-major-antarctic-ice-shelf-could-shatter-within-five-years.html.

Nickelsburg, Monica. “5 Modern Diseases Grown by Factory Farming.” The Week, 11.7.13. https://theweek.com/articles/457135/5-modern-diseases-grown-by-factory-farming.

Nielsen.com. “China’s Shifting Retail Landscape Signals the Permanence of Change Post Covid-19.” *Nielsen.com*, 12.16.20. https://www.nielsen.com/us/en/insights/article/2020/chinas-shifting-retail-landscape-signals-the-permanence-of-change-post-covid-19/.

Padrell, et al. “Invasive Research on Nonhuman Primates—Time to Turn the Page.” *National Institutes of Health*, 10.11.21. https://www.ncbi.nlm.nih.gov/pmc/articles/PMC8532895/.

Parenti, Christian. *Tropic of Chaos: Climate Change and the New Geography of Violence.* New York: Nation Books, 2011.

Parker, Chris. “Frankencrops: Monsanto Seeks Control of America’s Food Supply.” *Phoenix New Times*, 7.25.13. https://www.phoenixnewtimes.com/restaurants/frankencrops-monsanto-seeks-control-of-americas-food-supply-6459304.

Paul, Sonali. “Australia Explorers Step Up Hunt for Oil After Big Find.” *Reuters*, 10.1.19. https://www.reuters.com/article/us-australia-oil/australias-explorers-step-up-hunt-for-oil-after-big-find-idUSKBN1WG2ZM.

People for the Ethical Treatment of Animals (PETA). “What is Vivisection?” https://www.peta.org/features/what-is-vivisection/.

Porter, Robin. *From Mao to Market: China Reconfigured.* New York: Columbia University Press, 2011.

REDD. “Reducing Emissions from Deforestation and Forest Degradation.” UN. REDD Programme. https://www.un-redd.org.

Reid, Helen. “Target Pride Backlash Exposes ‘Rainbow Capitalism’ Problem, Designer Says.” *Reuters*, 5.31.23. https://www.reuters.com/business/retail-consumer/target-pride-backlash-exposes-rainbow-capitalism-problem-designer-says-2023-05-31/.

Refugees International. “Marking Two Years of Taliban Oppression: Statement From the U.S. Policy Advocates for Afghan Women and Girls,” 8.15.23. https://www.refugeesinternational.org/statements-and-news/marking-2-years-of-taliban-oppression-statement-from-the-u-s-policy-advocates-for-afghan-women-and-girls/.

Reklaitis, Victor. “Here are the Companies Poised to Profit from the Trump Border Wall.” *Market Watch*, 2.25.19.

Ridley, Matt. “The Bats Behind the Pandemic.” *The Wall Street Journal*, 4.9.20. https://www.wsj.com/articles/the-bats-behind-the-pandemic-11586440959.

Roberts, Jason. “15 Best Meat Chickens.” *Know Your Chickens*, 6.17.21.

Robins, Nicholas A. *Mercury, Mining, and Empire: The Human and Ecological Cost of Colonial Silver in the Andes.* Bloomington, IN: Indiana University Press, 2011.

Robins, Nicholas, and Nicole Hagen. "Mercury Production and Use in Colonial Andean Silver Production: Emissions and Health Implications." *NIH: National Library of Medicine*, May, 2012. https://www.ncbi.nlm.nih.gov/pmc/articles/PMC3346781/.

Romo, Vanessa. "Tyson Managers Suspended After Allegedly Betting If Workers Would Contract COVID." *National Public Radio,* 11.19.20. https://www.npr.org/2020/11/19/936905707/tyson-managers-suspended-after-allegedly-betting-if-workers-would-contract-covid.

RSPCA. "What are Farrowing Crates?" https://www.rspcaassured.org.uk/farm-animal-welfare/pigs/what-are-farrowing-crates/.

Ryan, Jackson. "CRISPR Gene-Editing Tool Used Inside Humans for the First Time." *CNeT*, 3.4.20. https://www.cnet.com/news/crispr-gene-editing-tool-used-inside-humans-for-the-first-time/.

Sangomla, Akshit. "US Elections 2020: A History of Trump's Climate Change Denial." Down to Earth, 11.3.20. https://www.downtoearth.org.in/news/climate-change/us-elections-2020-a-history-of-trump-s-climate-change-denial-74075.

Schiller, Ben. "The Gruesome Statistics Behind One of America's Most Dangerous Jobs." *Fast Company*, 3.1.16. https://www.fastcompany.com/3057169/the-gruesome-statistics-behind-one-of-americas-most-dangerous-jobs.

Schlosser, Eric. "The Prison-Industrial Complex." *The Atlantic*, December, 1998. https://www.theatlantic.com/magazine/archive/1998/12/the-prison-industrial-complex/304669/.

Schuessler, Jennifer. "Bans on Critical Race Theory Threaten Free Speech." *New York Times*, 11.8.21. https://www.nytimes.com/2021/11/08/arts/critical-race-theory-bans.html.

Schweller, Geoff. "Whistleblower Complaint Leads to SEC Investigation of Exxon." *Whistleblower Network News*, 1.20.21. https://whistleblowersblog.org/2021/01/articles/whistleblower-news/whistleblower-complaint-leads-to-sec-investigation-of-exxon/.

Scully, Matthew. "China's Wet Markets, America's Factory Farming." *National Review*, 4.9.20. https://www.nationalreview.com/2020/04/chinas-wet-markets-americas-factory-farming-both-violate-moral-common-sense/.

Seneviratne, Kalinga. "'Wet Markets' a Crucial Part of Asian Economy." *China Daily*, 4.29.20. https://www.chinadaily.com.cn/a/202004/29/WS5ea8d13ca310a8b2411527c7.html.

Sewell, Christina. "Removing the Meat Subsidy: Our Cognitive Dissonance Around Animal Agriculture." *Columbia University: Journal of International Affairs*, 2.11.20. https://jia.sipa.columbia.edu/removing-meat-subsidy-our-cognitive-dissonance-around-animal-agriculture.

Shields, Christopher. "In the Shadows of Dominion: Anthropocentrism and the Continuance of the Culture of Oppression." Doctoral Dissertation, East Tennessee State University, 2015. https://dc.etsu.edu/etd/2474/.

Singer, Peter. "All Animals are Equal." *Philosophic Exchange*, 5.1, Article 6. https://digitalcommons.brockport.edu/cgi/viewcontent.cgi?article=1179&context=phil_ex.

Sky News, Australia. "Tony Abbott: 10 Controversial Things Former Australian PM Has Said." https://news.sky.com/story/tony-abbott-ten-controversial-things-former-australian-pm-has-said-12063946.

Sleek, Scott. "Why Anthropomorphism is Not a Scientific Sin." *Association for Psychological Science*, 4.30.19. https://www.psychologicalscience.org/observer/why-anthropomorphism-is-not-a-scientific-sin.

Smallwood, Stephanie. "Turning African Slaves into Atlantic Commodities." *Saltwater Slavery: A Middle Passage from Africa to American Diaspora*. Cambridge, MA: Harvard UP, 2007.

Smith, Adam. "Wealth of Nations, Ch. 1." *Adam Smith Works*. https://www.adamsmithworks.org/documents/chapter-i-of-the-natural-progress-of-opulence.

Smithfield Farms. "Helping Hungry Homes." https://www.smithfieldfoods.com/Philanthropy.

Snow, Nick. "ExxonMobil to Pay 32.2 Million to Resolve Whistleblower's Suit." *Oil and Gas Journal*. 4.6.10. https://www.ogj.com/general-interest/article/17284815/exxonmobil-to-pay-322-million-to-resolve-whistleblowers-suit.

Stoll, Mark. *Profit: An Environmental History*. Cambridge, UK: Polity Press, 2023.

Stop the Traffik. https://www.stopthetraffik.org/about-human-trafficking/the-scale-of-human-trafficking/.

Stuart, Tessa. "Everything You Need to Know about Georgia's New Voting Law." *Rolling Stone*, 3.26.21. https://www.rollingstone.com/politics/politics-news/georgia-voting-bill-brian-kemp-voter-suppression-1147493/.

Suen, Thomas and Brenda Goh. "Wet Markets in China's Wuhan Struggle to Survive Coronavirus Bblow." Reuters, 4.12.20. https://www.reuters.com/article/us-health-coronavirus-china-wuhan-market/wet-markets-in-chinas-wuhan-struggle-to-survive-coronavirus-blow-idUSKCN21U03S.

Taub, Amanda. "Why the Taliban's Repression of Women May be More Tactical Than Ideological." *New York Times*, 10.4.21. https://www.nytimes.com/2021/10/04/world/asia/taliban-women-afghanistan.html.

Tavernise, Sabrina, and Richard A. Oppel, Jr. "Spit on, Yelled at, Attacked: Chinese Americans Fear for Their Safety." *New York Times*, 3.23.20. https://www.nytimes.com/2020/03/23/us/chinese-coronavirus-racist-attacks.html.

Teach U.S. History.org. "A Pro-Slavery Letter by S. Trott." http://www.teachushistory.org/second-great-awakening-age-reform/resources/pro-slavery-letter-s-trott.

The Conversation. "Why Tony Abbott's Appointment as Indigenous Envoy Was a Diplomatic Blunder and Policy Failure." 11.29.18. https://theconversation.com/why-tony-abbotts-appointment-as-indigenous-envoy-was-a-diplomatic-blunder-and-policy-failure-106345.

The Paisano, Editorial Board. "Texas Fuels Patriarchy with New Abortion Law," 9.7.21. https://paisano-online.com/26836/opinion/editorial/texas-fuels-patriarchy-with-new-abortion-law/.

The World. "Scientists Say Australia's Tony Abbott is Engineering an "Environmental Trainwreck.'" Global Post, 4.8.14. https://theworld.org/stories/2014-04-08/scientists-say-australias-tony-abbott-engineering-environmental-train-wreck.

Thompson, Andrea. "Death Valley Could Set a World Record Hot Temperature." *Scientific American*, 7.14.23. https://www.scientificamerican.com/article/death-valley-could-set-a-world-record-hot-temperature/.

Thomson, James. "Woodside Plays the Long Game from the 'Bathtub.'" Financial *Review*, 11.12.20. https://www.afr.com/chanticleer/woodside-plays-the-long-game-from-the-bathtub-20201112-p56e2b.

Torrella, Kenny, and Marina Bolotnikova. "Undercover Audio of a Tyson Employee Reveals 'Free-Range' Chicken is Meaningless." VOX, 8.2.23. https://www.vox.com/future-perfect/23724740/tyson-chicken-free-range-humanewashing-investigation-animal-cruelty.

United Nations Climate Action. "Water—At the Center of the Climate Crisis." https://www.un.org/en/climatechange/science/climate-issues/water.

*United Nations Climate Ch*ange (UNFCCC). "The Paris Agreement." https://unfccc.int/process-and-meetings/the-paris-agreement/the-paris-agreement.

Unpopular Science. "Why Fracking is Worse Than Coal." https://medium.com/@unpopularscience/why-fracking-is-worse-than-coal-578515a004f8.

U.S. Fish and Wildlife Service. "Timeline of the American Bison." https://www.fws.gov/bisonrange/timeline.htm.

U.S. History.org. "The Southern Argument for Slavery." https://www.ushistory.org/us/27f.asp.

Vorrath, Sophie. "Australia Dumps Carbon Price, as Repeal Passes Senate." *Renew Economy*, 7.17.14. https://reneweconomy.com.au/australia-dumps-carbon-price-as-repeal-passes-senate-22018/.

Wallace-Wells, David. "The Cautious Case for Climate Optimism." *The Intelligencer, New York Magazine*, 2.4.19. https://nymag.com/intelligencer/2019/02/book-excerpt-the-uninhabitable-earth-david-wallace-wells.html.

Wallace-Wells, David. *The Uninhabitable Earth*. New York, NY: Tim Duggan Books, 2019.

Warren, Karen. "The Power and the Promise of Ecological Feminism," *Environmental Ethics*, 12.2, Summer 1990, 125–46.

White, Alexander. "Why Does Australian PM Tony Abbott Support Fossil Fuel Subsidies?" *The Guardian*, 2.2.14. https://www.theguardian.com/environment/southern-crossroads/2014/feb/02/fossil-fuel-subsidies-tony-abbott-spc-ardmona-corporate-welfare#_=_.

White, Kyle Powys. "Indigenous Women, Climate Change Impacts, and Collective Action. *Hypatia*, 29.3, 2014, 559–616.

White, Natasha. "Bogus Carbon Credits are a "Pervasive 'Problem,' Scientists Warn." Bloomberg, 3.21.23. https://time.com/6264772/study-most-carbon-credits-are-bogus/.

Women's Sports Foundation. https://www.womenssportsfoundation.org/education/fight-equal-pay-womens-sports/.

Wong, Lonnie. "Researchers at UC Davis use Rhesus Monkeys to Understand Long-Term Efficacy of Covid-19 Vaccines." https://fox40.com/news/local-news/researchers-at-uc-davis-use-rhesus-monkeys-to-understand-long-term-efficacy-of-covid-19-vaccines/.

Woodside Petroleum, Ltd. "2019 Sustainable Development Report." https://files.woodside/docs/default-source/investor-documents/major-reports-(static-pdfs)/2019-sd-report/sustainable-development-report-2019.pdf?sfvrsn=73cea616_14.

Woodward. Alex. "DeSantis Once Again Defends Slavery Curriculum: Enslaved People 'Showing Resourcefulness' Developed 'Skills.'" Independent, 8.7.23. https://www.the-independent.com/news/world/americas/us-politics/desantis-slavery-florida-response-b2388923.html.

World Meteorological Association. "United in Science Report: Climate Change Has Not Stopped for Covid-19." 9.9.20. https://public.wmo.int/en/media/press-release/united-science-report-climate-change-has-not-stopped-covid19.

World Vision. "Hurricane Harvey: Facts, FAQs, and How to Help." https://www.worldvision.org/disaster-relief-news-stories/2017-hurricane-harvey-facts.

World Wildlife Federation. "Beef." https://wwf.panda.org/discover/our_focus/food_practice/sustainable_production/beef/.

Yancy, George, and Peter Singer. "Peter Singer: On Racism, Animal Rights, and Human Rights." *Opinionator: New York Times*, 5.27.15. https://opinionator.blogs.nytimes.com/2015/05/27/peter-singer-on-speciesism-and-racism/.

Yusoff, Kathryn. *A Billion Black Anthropocenes or None*. Minneapolis, MN: University of Minnesota Press, 2018.

Zhang, Sarah. "America is Running Low on a Crucial Resource for Covid-19 Vaccines." *The Atlantic*, 8.31.20. https://www.theatlantic.com/science/archive/2020/08/america-facing-monkey-shortage/615799/.

Zhang, Xiaobo. "Chinese Livestock Farms Struggle Under Covid Restrictions." *International Food Policy Research Institute*, 3.26.20. https://www.ifpri.org/blog/chinese-livestock-farms-struggle-under-covid-19-restrictions.

Index

the 1619 Project, 205, 209. *See also* Jones, Nikole Hannah

Abbott, Greg, 24, 44n16
Abbott, Tony, 141, 143, 145–47, 148, 150, 158nn75, 159nn81–83
abortion, 74, 77n60, 184, 198, 207n44
absent referent, 27, 205, 224, 227–31, 245, 252, 255
Adams, Carol, 27, 45n25, 193, 199, 208n65, 227–28, 230, 256n32
advertising, 18, 22–23, 39, 57, 60, 63, 70, 81, 93, 117, 124, 143, 149, 153–55, 164–65, 167, 169, 181, 197, 249
"affective labor," 9, 11–12, 255
African Americans, 68, 77n48, 193
agency, 3–7, 9–10, 12, 17, 26, 56, 85, 87–92, 101, 105, 125, 131–32, 146, 166, 183, 220–21, 222–23, 225, 231–34, 236–38, 240, 246, 250, 253
Alexander, Michelle, 68–69, 77n45, 77nn49–51
American Petroleum Institute, 149
American Society for the Prevention of Cruelty to Animals (ASPCA), 206n8
animal agriculture (concentrated animal feeding operations), 8, 19, 25–27, 41, 55, 103, 119–21, 124, 136–40, 155, 157nn57–58, 164–65, 169, 187, 190, 199, 202, 240, 242
animal bodies, 19, 21, 25, 32, 38, 42–43, 53, 56, 64, 66–71, 79, 90, 104–5, 110, 118, 137, 161, 164, 169, 175, 189, 191, 194–95, 205, 213, 221, 224, 227, 239–41, 244, 248
animal rights, 18, 28, 64–65, 68, 73, 75, 77n55, 89, 101–2, 105, 118, 156n11, 161, 163, 175, 183–84, 187, 194, 196–200, 203, 205n1, 207n36, 209nn81–3
Anthropocene, 19–21, 44n5, 141–42, 249–50, 251–52, 261
anthropodenialist, 202–3, 205
anthropomorphism, 201–2, 209nn85–86
Arctic National Wildlife Reserve, (ANWR), 23–25, 32, 43, 44n11
authoritarian, 81, 172.

Bolsonaro, Jair, 171
bees, 201–4, 219
bigness, 100–1, 109
Big Greens, 25–27, 101, 129
bison, 20, 95–96, 112n34, 154, 241
Black Anthropocene, 246, 250–52, 257n64, 260–61
Bonneuil, Christophe, and Jean-Baptiste Fressoz, 20–21, 44nn5–6

Breakthrough Institute, 4, 15n23
British Petroleum (BP), 4, 14, 15n20, 92, 105, 112n27

Capitalocene, 5, 7, 108, 211, 212, 243, 250–51, 260–61
capitalization, 238–39, 242
carbon trade, 62, 125, 132, 134, 139–40, 189–90, 239
carbon tax, 134, 138–40, 145, 149–51, 159n93, 186–87, 189–90
Carson, Rachel, 116–17, 139.
Cartesian dualism, 213, 215–18, 227, 230–31, 237, 254. *See also* substance dualism
"Chaotic World System," 11–12, 14, 22, 35, 52, 96, 109
Cheap Food, 117, 120, 238, 239–40, 242, 244, 248, 254–55
Cheap Nature, 246, 254–55
chickens, 35, 101, 113n15, 164, 166–67, 180, 203–4, 219, 245
China, 28, 32–33, 36, 38–40, 47nn54–55, 45n28, 45n32, 45n36, 46n41, 46nn48–52, 47nn54–55, 53–54, 76n14, 82, 85, 89–91, 102, 140
Civil War, 68, 71–72, 77n54, 154–55, 205, 223
climate crisis, v, 3, 4, 8, 9, 11, 14, 23, 24, 35, 38, 42, 49, 50–52, 55, 57–60, 62–63, 66, 74, 75n7, 79–82, 85, 87–88, 91, 98–99, 101–3, 105, 108, 110, 115–19, 121–27, 129, 132–34, 136, 138–40, 143, 146–48, 167, 170, 180, 186–89, 190–91, 197, 199–202, 204–5, 215, 236, 240–41, 243, 259
coal mining, 1, 4, 137, 140, 143, 145, 248
cognitive dissonance, 3, 85, 102, 111, 137–38, 140, 152, 154, 157n57, 163, 175, 224
Coll, Steve, 23
Collins, Patricia Hill, 69, 77n48
colonialism/neocolonialism, 24, 147, 247–48, 250, 253
commodification of sentience, 3, 6, 9–10, 18–20, 27, 32, 34–35, 37–38, 42–43, 58, 60, 64–67, 69–70, 72, 84–85, 88–89, 90, 94, 97, 101–2, 105, 107–8, 116, 137, 148, 154, 164–66, 175, 177, 179, 182, 185–88, 191, 198–200, 204–5, 211, 216, 218, 220, 223–25, 228–29, 240–45, 248–54, 260
commodity frontier, 246
consumption, v, 3, 19, 24, 27, 31, 36–37, 39, 41–43, 51–52, 84, 90, 102–3, 108–9, 113n56, 116–21, 123, 136–38, 152–53, 155, 169, 176, 180, 202, 228, 239, 245, 249
Cooper, Iman, 66–67, 76n38, 76n40
coral bleaching, 60–61
Covid-19, 10, 26, 28–30, 35–36, 38–39, 42, 44n8, 45n22, 46n39, 46n42, 46n46, 46n49, 71, 89, 92, 97, 100–1, 103–6, 110, 113n48, 112nn28–29, 133, 171, 173–75, 179–80, 206n21, 207nn29–30, 233
cow, 9–10, 19, 21, 26–27, 30, 36, 53, 61, 64, 73, 90, 105, 118, 137, 164, 192, 203–4, 221, 229, 239, 241, 245
CRISPR gene editing, 180, 207nn28–29
critical race theory, 196, 208
Cronin, William, 153–55, 159nn100–105, 234, 257n40
cruelty, 11, 21, 28–30, 36, 44n3, 93–4, 137, 162, 165–66, 175, 191, 206n14, 220, 259
"crying Indian," 126–27, 130–31,

Dawson, Ashley, 11–12, 14, 16n47, 16n49, 17, 19–22, 35, 37, 44n1, 46n43, 46n45, 76n26, 95–96, 106–8, 114n67, 112n33, 112n35, 191, 208n61, 259
Deep Water Horizon, 93
deforestation, 1, 29, 50, 111, 132, 135, 138, 146, 182, 194
democracy, 123

denial, 2–3, 8, 22, 24, 30–31, 36, 43, 57, 81, 84, 86, 91–92, 102, 105, 108–10, 112n24, 116, 123, 125, 135, 152, 172, 175, 180–82, 185, 189, 196, 198–99, 201–5, 207n32, 215, 224, 227–29, 231, 245, 252, 259, 260
denial², 181–82, 185, 189, 196, 198–99, 202, 207n32, 224, 227–29, 231, 252, 260
DeSantis, Ron, 196, 208n74
Descartes, Rene. *See* substance dualism
desertification, 37
desirable future, 181, 259
Dewey, John, 181, 207n32
"dialectic of life-making," 231–34, 236
Diamond, Cora, 72–73, 57n55–8, 118, 156n11, 162–63, 165, 198, 200, 221, 227, 230
DiCaprio, Leonardo, 122–25, 131–32, 156nn19–20
disarticulation of value, 32, 42, 141, 149, 161, 221, 239, 253
disaster capitalism, 62–63, 96–97, 149, 152, 179
Donovan, Josephine, 199, 209n81
drought, v, 21, 54, 82, 93, 135
dualism, 211, 213–18, 221, 224–31, 237–38, 240, 249, 253–54

elephant, 123, 191–92
Engine No. 1, 130–32, 135, 157nn43–46
Environmental Defense Fund (EDF), 129–31, 157n41, 265. *See also* Krupp, Fred
Environmental Progress, 4
"environment-making," 232–33, 235–36
epistemic opacity, 142–44, 149
Epstein, Richard, 182–88, 190, 192–93, 196–99, 201–2, 204, 207nn37–42, 207n46, 208n47, 208n51, 208n64, 209nn78–79, 227, 250, 252
exchange value, v, 2–3, 5, 9–10, 12, 17–22, 25, 27, 29, 31, 35–37, 42, 61, 64, 67, 85, 88, 93–94, 97–98, 101–2, 107, 116, 126, 142, 149, 163, 168, 174–75, 177, 179, 193, 195, 200, 214, 220–21, 223–26, 231–32, 235, 237–38, 242–44, 249, 251–52, 254–55
extinction, 1–2, 7, 11, 14, 16nn47–48, 17, 19–21, 23, 25–26, 35, 37–38, 44, 46n40, 55, 59–60, 62, 76n26, 95–96, 106–7, 112n33, 124, 127, 146, 148, 171, 175–76, 182, 191, 194, 208n61, 230, 236, 257n39, 259
extra-human, 212, 216–21, 224–31, 233–4, 240, 242, 244–46, 249, 251–54
extractivism, 1, 3, 37, 55, 134, 167, 171, 189, 215, 246–50, 252
extreme weather, 21, 37, 43, 54, 82, 99, 127, 134
ExxonMobil, 4, 22–26, 32, 43–45, 56, 60, 83, 85, 88, 92, 112n21, 115, 118, 120–21, 126, 129–31, 135–36, 141, 144, 149, 157nn41–42, 157nn52–53, 158nn78–79, 167, 189

factory farms, 18–19, 28–29, 35, 46n46, 90, 92, 118, 128, 163, 168–69, 175, 182, 206n7, 266. *See also* animal agriculture
fatal complacency, 70–72, 74, 82, 90–91, 105–6, 111, 116, 135, 138, 155, 180–82, 192, 204–5, 230, 253, 259
Feldstein, Stephanie, 102–3, 113n56, 113n59
Feminism, 45n25, 75, 77n59, 200, 206, 208n65
firenado, 62, 97, 108–9, 11, 173, 182,
food security/insecurity, 34, 36–42, 50, 55, 82, 94, 96, 134
fossil fuels, 2, 56, 61–63, 70, 87, 118, 121, 135, 137, 139–41, 143, 150–51, 177, 201, 242. *See also* hydrocarbons
fracking (slickwater hydraulic fracturing), 140, 159n92
Francione, Gary, 5, 7–8, 161–67, 169, 172–76, 178, 180, 182–85, 188, 192,

197, 201, 205, 206n2, 206nn5–6, 206nn9–12, 226–28, 230, 249–50, 259
Frankenseeds, 238
Frankenstein, 59, 75, 85, 98–99, 109, 116, 139, 175, 259
Fraser, Nancy, 9, 11–13, 16n46, 16nn52–54, 15nn33–35, 15n39, 26–27, 29–30, 35, 45n24, 25nn30–31, 62–63, 76nn35–36, 81, 153, 159n101, 176, 194, 200, 206nn24–25, 208n66, 214, 239, 255, 258nn83–84, 260
free-range, 44n3, 44n7, 44n9, 92, 164–65, 167, 174,
free will, 199, 202–3, 204–5, 209n88

gender, 23, 74, 77n48, 77n63, 177–79, 196, 224, 226–27, 229, 237
genetically modified organisms (GMO), 39–40, 238–39
geopolitics, 15n30, 35
Ghosh, Amitov, 3, 15
God, 146, 154, 162, 192–93, 195–96, 205
Gore, Al, 115–17, 126, 133, 139
Gosalvez, Emma, 46
Green Revolution, 238–40, 242–43
greenhouse gas emissions, 4, 6, 25–27, 41–43, 58, 70, 83–84, 87, 91, 101, 103, 106, 110, 118–21, 130, 133, 136–39, 141, 146, 149–50, 167, 188, 190–91, 199, 253
green washing, 4–5, 15nn20–22, 46, 57, 70, 112n21, 115, 164–65
"grow or die," v, 3, 13, 18, 196, 225, 250–51, 260

Haraway, Donna, 167–72, 175–78, 180, 200, 206n13, 206n18, 206n23, 225
Harvey, David, 4, 15, 24
Heartland Institute, 116
Heteropatriarchy, 65, 74, 75
hippies, 57–58, 62, 64
hierarchical inequality, 74. *See also* structural inequality
"horizons of value," 9, 255, 260
human chauvinism, 3, 6, 31, 61, 75, 85, 87, 91, 94, 98, 123–24, 138, 151, 161, 166, 172, 174, 179, 182, 185–86, 190, 195, 212, 224, 226, 229–30, 232–33, 235, 242, 244–45, 249–50, 253
humanity-in-nature, 230–32, 234–37, 239–40, 249,
hybridism, 85–87, 235–36, 246, 250
hydrocarbons, 1, 23, 38, 87, 119–20, 134, 137, 223, 239, 245, 254. *See also* fossil fuels

illegal wildlife trade, 34, 36–38
imperialism, 23, 28, 32, 35, 41–42, 50, 90, 92, 95,
indigenous, 8, 17, 20, 25–26, 51, 56, 70, 74, 77n64, 79, 84, 87, 95–96, 104, 132, 146–47, 153–54, 159nn83, 171–72, 194, 198, 200, 223, 234–35, 242, 246–48, 250, 253

Johnson and Johnson, 11, 92–93, 112n29, 261
Jones, Nikole Hannah, 205, 209, 265. *See also* the 1619 Project

Keystone XL Pipeline, 140, 158nn65–66
Klein, Naomi, 93, 98, 122n32, 136, 138
Kleptocene, 4, 7, 19, 26, 35, 44, 88, 108, 169, 179, 191, 212
Kleptocracy, 21, 199, 235
Koch, Christoph, 203–4, 209n89
Kolbert, Elizabeth, 11, 16, 35
Krupp, Fred, 129–30, 157n41. *See also Environmental Defense Fund* (EDF)

labor, 1, 8–13, 19, 33, 42, 49, 56, 69–70, 72, 88–9, 94, 104, 107–9, 120, 126, 134, 175, 183, 193–95, 205, 217–24, 226, 232, 238, 240, 242–48, 250, 252–55, 259–61

Lancet, 36–39, 41–43, 46n42
"larger system," 11, 116–17, 121–22, 125–28, 131, 134, 139
Latour, Bruno, 80–83, 85–87, 89, 111nn4–9, 168, 188
Lee, Wendy Lynne, v, 15n30, 45, 67, 75, 76n33, 77n42, 77n44, 157n40, 157n47, 157n56, 181, 188, 195, 200, 207n32, 208nn69–71
"Left" and "Right," 79, 81–84, 94–95, 97, 98–99, 111
LeMenager, Stephanie, 150–52, 155, 159nn94–95, 159n97, 159n99, 163, 170
LGBTQ, 197
logic of commodification, 2–6, 9–10, 12, 14, 17–20, 22, 24–27, 30–33, 35–38, 41–43, 53, 56, 58–60, 62, 64, 66–68, 70, 74, 82, 85–90, 94–95, 97, 100–1, 104–5, 107–11, 116–17, 123, 126, 132, 134, 137, 139, 142, 145, 150, 166, 169, 177–78, 186–89, 192–94, 199, 215, 218, 220–21, 223–25, 232, 235, 237–38, 240–41, 243–45, 247, 250–53, 273–75
logic of domination, 67, 74–75, 86, 195, 213, 220, 223–24, 232, 236, 260–61
lynching, 67, 76n41
Lugones, Maria, 177–80, 206n26, 207n27
Lynteris, Christos and Lyle Fearnley, 32–34, 41, 45nn34–35, 46nn37–38

Malm, Andreas, v, 2–3, 5–12, 14nn10–14 15nn15–18, 16nn50–51, 23, 26, 32, 44n12, 45n23, 67, 76n39, 83, 85–89, 111nn11–17, 112n18–19, 119, 123–25, 132, 143, 149, 151, 156n13 156n21, 156nn23–27, 168–72, 174, 176, 197, 206nn15–17, 209n77, 212–18, 220–22, 225, 230, 235, 237, 239, 246–47, 250, 256n2, 256n6, 256nn8–17, 256nn22–23, 256n25–27, 256n29, 257nn62–63. *See also Progress of this Storm*
Mann, Michael, 5, 7–8, 115–17, 119–49, 151, 155, 156nn1–5, 156n14, 156nn17–18, 156n22, 1565nn29–30, 157nn31–39, 157n44, 157nn48–49, 157n51, 157nn54–55, 158nn60–64, 158n67, 158n69, 159nn84–90, 165, 167, 182, 187, 192, 197, 201–2, 211, 216, 226, 239–41, 249–50, 252, 259
McKibbon, Bill, 115
meat, 9, 19, 21, 27–29, 36–37, 41–43, 53, 71–73, 77n54, 79, 91–92, 100–2, 103–5, 112n28, 113n48, 113n53, 113n56, 113n62, 116–21, 122–25, 32, 136–39, 156n7, 156n11, 156n16, 157n57, 164–65, 267–69, 175, 188, 202, 219, 227, 229, 241, 244, 248–49, 251, 256n32
Merchant, Carolyn, 213–15, 227
militant opposition, 2–3, 5–7, 11, 14, 32, 89, 102, 151, 153, 167, 177, 179
Moore, Jason, 5, 7–8, 211, 212–22, 224–41, 243–55, 256nn3–5, 256n7, 256n18, 256n31, 256nn33–37, 257n38, 257nn41–45, 257nn47–52, 257nn54–61, 257nn66–67, 258n76, 258nn81–82, 259
moral boundary, 64–72, 74, 176, 195–96, 199, 202–4
myth of endless resources, 43, 55, 58, 95, 104, 108, 116, 138, 152, 182, 185, 215, 235–36, 243, 252–53, 260

Nader, Ralph, 127, 129
Native American, 95, 127
Nature/Society, 86, 213–16, 218–19, 224–31, 233–34, 240, 249
Nayeri, Kamran, 219–21, 225, 232, 237, 250, 256nn19–21, 256n24
necessity exception, 172, 175, 185, 188, 192
Neoliberalism, 1, 5, 7, 62
"New Climactic Regime," 80–82
nihilism, 21, 85–86, 166, 181, 215, 243, 251, 255, 261

No REDD in Africa Network (NRAN), 51–52, 55, 84

Oikeios, 231–3, 235–7, 242
ontology of capital, 2–4, 7, 11, 13, 17, 82, 85, 87, 89, 102, 149, 164, 166, 169, 194, 198, 200, 211, 214–15, 217, 220–23, 225–26, 237, 240, 242–45, 248–49, 251–52, 254–55
Oppel, Richard A, Jr., 90, 112

pangolin, 29, 30–32, 35–36, 38, 46, 76n18, 90, 174, 180, 204
Parenti, Christian, 89, 93, 112
People for the Ethical Treatment of Animals (PETA), 102, 206n4
Piccinini, Patricia. 167–70, 172–73, 174–80, 182, 225, 227–29
pigs, 19, 29–30, 35, 41, 101, 164, 166–67, 169, 177, 203–4, 219, 229–30, 245
plantation capitalism, 10, 9, 222–23, 194
Porter, Robin, 40, 45, 54, 76nn14–17
preemptive omission, 27, 106
prison industrial complex, 4, 68, 77n46, 200
property, vi, 2–3, 52, 54, 67–68, 132, 161, 165–66, 183, 184–85, 193–95, 205n1, 211, 230, 234, 249, 254, 260
Progress of this Storm, 2, 14n9, 44n12, 206n15, 256n2
Public Interest Research Group (PIRG), 127, 129, 131–32

race, 4–5, 59, 66–67, 69, 72, 81, 87, 101, 110, 131, 177–79, 188–89, 191, 196, 209n72, 224, 226–27, 229, 237, 247, 249, 252
racism, 13, 69–70, 75, 77n48, 79, 90, 93–94, 96, 104, 147, 201, 209n83, 230, 251–52
refugee, 127, 198, 200, 207n43
reproduction, 12, 26, 153, 218, 225, 254–55
reproductive labor/sexuality, 9, 13, 195, 248, 254
resource theft, v, 4–5, 13,17, 21,7 32, 43, 55, 66, 97, 107–8, 153, 188, 194, 212, 214, 217, 224, 235, 243, 245, 248–52, 254–55, 259–60
Reducing Emissions from Deforestation and Forest Degradation (REDD), 50–52, 55–57, 63, 83–84, 87, 111n10, 132, 134, 140, 190
renewables, 80, 91, 96, 132, 144–45, 147, 150, 187
rights, 18, 28, 52, 64–65, 68, 73, 75, 77n55, 89, 101–2, 104–5, 118, 125, 128, 148, 156n11, 161, 166, 184, 187, 194, 196, 198–200, 203, 209n81, 209n83, 247
Robins, Nicholas, 114n63
rule of capital, 8, 24–26, 30, 32, 34, 37, 43, 54–55, 58–60, 62, 64–67, 69–70, 85, 98–102, 104, 107–9

salvation capitalism, 8, 59, 115, 125–26, 128, 136, 140, 239, 259
Schlosser, Eric, 68, 77n46
Scully, Matthew, 28–31, 33, 45n28, 46n41
Sengwer, 51–57, 65, 76n11, 76n13, 77nn9–10, 132–34, 139
sentience, 3, 6–7, 9–10, 18–21, 27–28, 32, 34–35, 37–38, 42, 57–58, 60, 64–65, 67, 69–70, 72, 83–85, 88–91, 94, 97–98, 101–3, 105–8, 111, 116, 137, 148, 154, 163–66, 174–75, 177, 179, 182–88, 190–95, 198–200, 203–5, 211, 216, 220–31, 236, 240–46, 248–54, 259–60
sexism/heterosexism, 13, 70, 79, 201, 230, 251–52
sexuality, 69, 72, 178–79, 195, 224, 226–27, 229, 252, 254
Shellenberger, Michael, 4–5, 14, 15n24
Shields, Christopher, 44n4
Silent Spring, 116
silver mining, 248

Singer, Peter, 64, 73, 201, 209n82–83
slavery, 1–2, 53, 65–72, 76, 103–5, 183, 193–96, 198–99, 205, 208–9, 223, 246–49, 253, 261
Smallwood, Stephanie, 67
Smithfield Farms, 41, 60, 85, 100–1, 103–4, 109–10, 119n54, 120, 182, 207n35. *See also* Sullivan, Kenneth
"speculative fabulation," 167–70, 174, 206n13
starvation, 53–54, 84, 223
Stoll, Mark, 1–2, 7–8, 10–11, 13, 14nn1–8, 15n27, 15n32, 15n36–38, 15nn40–41, 15n45, 16nn55–56, 37, 46n44, 68, 77, 117, 151–52, 156n9, 159n96, 170, 194, 208nn67–68, 211, 222, 239, 250, 256n1, 245n28, 256n30
structural inequality, 52, 74, 99, 147–48, 197, 200, 224–25, 227–28. *See* also hierarchical inequality
suffering, 1, 6–9, 14, 17–21, 25, 27, 29, 35, 42, 53, 57, 65–67, 71–74, 89–90, 92, 94, 97, 100–1, 111, 134, 137–38, 148, 163–66, 168, 172, 175, 183, 187–88, 190–91, 198, 200–1, 204–5, 219, 221, 224–26, 228–31, 236, 241, 244, 250–52, 254, 260–61
Sullivan, Kenneth, 100–5, 109. *See also* Smithfield Farms
substance dualism, 213–17, 225, 230, 237–38, 249, 213–17, 225, 230, 237–38, 249
sustainable, 6, 27, 36, 38–39, 43, 45n26, 49–50, 52, 55, 62–63, 96, 102, 158n76, 191
survivable, 8–9, 259
Syngenta, 40, 46

Tavernise, Sabrina, 90, 112
techno-utopia, 59, 62, 107, 111
Texas, 24, 44n16, 118, 144, 151, 184, 207n44
"top of the food chain," 64–66, 90, 102–3, 186, 188, 190–91, 203
transgressive, 175, 177, 179–80, 186–87, 225–27
Trump, Donald, 44n13, 82–83, 90–91, 98, 102, 106, 112nn23–24, 112n28, 113n38, 135, 140, 157n50, 173, 238
Tyson, 18, 21–22, 42, 44n3, 44n7, 44n9, 106, 114n65, 118, 120, 206n14

United Nations, 44nn14–15, 50, 55–56, 75nn6–7, 84, 121, 132, 156n12, 200
United States, 24, 40, 45n17, 45n22, 61, 75n6, 82, 99, 113n52, 138, 144, 156n12, 157n58, 238, 259, 76n41
unpaid labor, 218–19, 221, 224, 226, 242–43, 245–46, 248, 252, 254–55, 273, 275

vegan, 31, 64, 66, 70–71, 100, 105, 110, 119–21, 122–5, 136, 138, 182, 185, 192
vegetarian, 73, 118
violence, 11, 35, 54, 112n20, 112n32, 151–52, 155, 176–77, 191, 194, 200, 215, 228–29, 261

Wallace-Wells, David, 5, 7–8, 15nn28–29, 15n31, 24, 45n18, 49–51, 53–72, 74–75, 76n12, 76nn19–25, 76nn27–30, 76n32, 76n34, 76n37, 77n52, 79–87, 89–90, 94, 98–100, 102–3, 105–10, 113nn39–47, 114nn68–75, 114nn77–78, 116, 119, 134, 136, 152, 159n98, 165, 167, 180–82, 184, 186–92, 197, 199–205, 208nn48–50, 208nn48–60, 208n62, 209n80, 209n87, 211, 216, 226, 230, 239–41, 249–50, 252
war, v, 2, 11–12, 35, 42–43, 68, 72, 77n54, 89, 95, 115, 122, 126, 132–35, 139, 141, 154–55, 156n1, 175, 205, 223, 236, 241, 254, 260–61
warming condition, 2–3, 11, 87, 89, 125, 169, 171, 173–74, 197
Warren, Karen, 74–75, 77n59, 79, 81, 136, 200

weapons, 52, 125, 191, 222
"web of life," 211–13, 216, 218, 221, 223–24, 226, 229–32, 234–40, 242, 244, 247, 249–52, 256n2, 256n19
wet markets, 27–30, 32–41, 42–43, 45n28, 45n32, 45nn34–35, 46nn37–38, 47n55, 51, 53–54, 62, 89, 92, 94, 101, 112n30
whales, 20, 37–38, 59–60, 62, 96, 227, 236, 254
wilderness, 152–55, 159n100, 234, 257n40
World Wildlife Federation, 4, 26, 45n26

xenotransplantation, 180
Xi, President, 40

Yusoff, Kathryn, 198, 246–49, 250–53, 254–55, 257nn64–65, 257nn68–74, 258n75, 258nn77–80, 259

Zhang, Sarah, 206n21
Zhang, Xiaobo, 46n46
zombie, 167, 169, 177
zoo/zoonotic, 19, 22, 28–30, 32, 34–36, 38, 41, 101, 127, 175, 180, 185, 221, 226

About the Author

Wendy Lynne Lee is Professor of Philosophy at Commonwealth University of Pennsylvania, Bloomsburg where she has taught for thirty-one years. Her areas of expertise include environmental philosophy, feminist theory, philosophy of mind/brain, ecological aesthetics, Critical Theory, and Marxist thought. Her most recent books include *This is Environmental Ethics* (20221) and *Eco-Nihilism: The Philosophical Geopolitics of the Climate Change Apocalypse* (Lexington Books, 2017). She has published a number of scholarly essays including recent work in animal rights, food security, and violence institutionalized in, for example, slavery, the prison system, and Native American Reservations. She is a mother, sister, daughter, grandmother, a long distance runner, an amateur photographer, and companion to her dog, Bohden, two cats, a parrot, and a ferret.

www.ingramcontent.com/pod-product-compliance
Lightning Source LLC
LaVergne TN
LVHW091526200926
848483LV00002B/316
* 9 7 8 1 7 9 3 6 0 7 9 6 6 *